Computers for Business
A Managerial Emphasis

Computers for Business
A Managerial Emphasis

HUGH J. WATSON
Associate Professor of Management

and

ARCHIE B. CARROLL
Associate Professor of Management

Both of the University of Georgia

 1976

BUSINESS PUBLICATIONS, INC. Dallas, Texas 75231
Irwin-Dorsey International   Arundel, Sussex   BN18 9AB
Irwin-Dorsey Limited   Georgetown, Ontario   L7G 4B3

First Printing, January 1976

ISBN 0-256-01611-9
Library of Congress Catalog Card No. 75–22679

Printed in the United States of America

Preface

U ntil fairly recently, the books available for the first course in computers stressed computer hardware and programming languages —often to the exclusion of other important topics. Over the past couple of years this orientation has started to change as instructors and authors have begun to devote more attention to information systems, computer applications, and the managerial aspects of the computer. This trend is continued in this book. It is written for the vast majority of students in the introductory course who will be *managers* and computer *users* rather than computer *specialists*. The implications of this approach result in the following characteristics of the book:

1. A minimal amount of material is included on computer hardware.
2. Only those programming languages that are frequently taught in business schools are covered.
3. Solid coverage of information systems is presented.
4. Material on both routine data processing and computer assisted decision making applications are included.
5. An examination is made of how to plan for, select, and implement a computer system.
6. The numerous impacts of the computer on management and the organization are considered.
7. Material on the computer's historical development and its current and future effects on society is introduced.

The net effect of this approach is that the student should gain a *broad* managerial understanding of the computer and its functioning, applications, and implications for business and society as well as a capability for and an appreciation of computer programming.

The book is written for the first course in computers in a business school and hence assumes no previous exposure to the computer.

v

Unless a heavy emphasis is placed on programming proficiency, no supplementary texts are required.

The intended audience for this book is the first undergraduate business course in computing. Most business schools now require such a course for all students. Not only is such a course usually deemed necessary to prepare students to enter the contemporary business world, but it is normally used to satisfy the AACSB accreditation requirement for "a basic understanding of the concepts and applications of . . . information systems."

A growing number of business schools also require graduate students to include a computer course in their program of study. While this book was not written specifically for the graduate market, its managerial emphasis makes it well suited for such courses.

If supplemented with outside readings, the book can also be used in a second course in computing. In some schools the first course in computers deals primarily with computer hardware and programming languages. A later course then focuses upon information systems, applications, and managerial topics. This book is appropriate for such courses.

We feel that an extremely important function of the Preface is to provide an overview of the sequence and content of the chapters which comprise the book. It therefore seems appropriate to preview each chapter, discussing how it might best be used.

Chapter 1, "An Overview of the Computer," is designed to provide a broad introductory perspective on computerized data processing. Not only does this chapter describe the overall nature and purpose of data processing, it also illustrates and explains what flowcharts and computer programs look like. Also discussed are the components of a typical computer system and how they process a program. Since most students have had little or no previous exposure to computers, this chapter provides a "big picture" which is enhanced and expanded upon in subsequent chapters of the book.

Chapter 2, "Business Applications of the Computer," which is largely descriptive, examines how the computer is used in various functional areas and by different industries. It can be read, understood, and appreciated by most students with little additional help from the instructor. To the instructor who wishes to provide a more "managerial flavor" to the course, however, this early look at management applications in business can provide an ideal springboard for further discussion.

Chapter 3, "The Historical Evolution of Computers," is another largely descriptive chapter that can be easily understood by the student with little instructor assistance. It is an important chapter, however, and provides the student with a historical sense of how the computer field has experienced an exponentially increasing rate of technological change over the years since its initial development. One topic that might demand further amplification by the instructor is the treatment of the various computer generations.

Perhaps the most difficult chapter in the book is Chapter 4, "The Computer's Hardware and Its Operating System." This is the one chapter that really gets down to the "bits and bytes" of the computer. When a highly managerial approach is taken to the course, this chapter can be omitted without losing continuity in later chapters.

Chapter 5, "Systems and Program Flowcharting," introduces the student to flowcharting. The program flowcharting discussions and illustrations are integrated with the programming languages of Chapters 6 and 7, and they should be studied together. An attempt has been made throughout the book to integrate the materials on flowcharting, programming, and applications.

Chapter 6, "The BASIC Programming Language," examines BASIC, the most popular time-sharing language. It is the second most frequently taught language in colleges of business administration. FORTRAN, which is covered in Chapter 7, "The FORTRAN Programming Language," is the most often taught. In both chapters an attempt has been made to provide sufficient detail and illustrations so that a supplementary language text is not necessary. The authors have been successful in teaching the introductory course with only the materials contained in this book. This approach is different from that of books that cover many languages but none in sufficient detail that they can stand alone as a language source.

Chapter 8, "Routine Data Processing Applications," covers those computerized routine data processing tasks that are necessary to keep most large organizations from being drowned in a sea of paper work. Though these applications are normally developed by computer specialists, it is useful for management to know what the most likely applications of the computer are and what is involved in developing them. The assignments at the end of this chapter provide an opportunity for practicing the flowcharting and programming skills previously learned.

Chapter 9, "Computer Assisted Decision Making," considers an increasingly important type of computer application—the integration of management science techniques and models with the computer. The instructor will have to exercise caution in making assignments from this chapter so that the student's quantitative background is not exceeded. Probably only one topic in the chapter should be assigned at a time. When properly used, this is one of the most exciting chapters in the book. It also provides the opportunity for further developing flowcharting and programming proficiency.

Chapter 10, "Information Systems and Management," discusses the multifaceted aspects of information systems. This chapter and the three that follow delve into the managerial considerations associated with having a computer in an organization.

Chapter 11, "Planning for, Selection, and Implementation of Computer Systems," considers the implementation of computer systems, starting with the feasibility study and continuing through to the review of the effectiveness of the system that has been installed.

Chapter 12, "The Impact of the Computer on Management," considers the impact the computer has upon the management group in such areas as the managerial environment, the nature of decision making, the number of managers, and other important topics such as these.

Chapter 13, "The Impact of the Computer on the Organization," investigates the effects that the computer has upon organization structure. This chapter covers topics such as the placement of the computer in the organization, the organization of the data processing department, and the effect the computer has on other departments.

The authors understand that many instructors do not feel as comfortable with the managerial aspects of the computer as they do with computer hardware and programming languages. Consequently, the case entitled "St. Joseph's Hospital" has been included as an appendix. This case provides an excellent vehicle for discussing the managerial aspects of the computer and should be used in conjunction with Chapters 10–13.

Chapter 14, "Computers and Society," discusses a number of the nonbusiness applications of the computer and the effect that computers are having upon automation, privacy, human values, and individualism. These extremely timely topics provide a nontechnical close to the introductory course in computers. This chapter considers ramifications of the computer that are seldom covered but which are essential in our modern times.

The first few class meetings of the introductory computer course are the most frustrating to teach because of the large number of topics that must be quickly introduced. For example, it is important at an early point to provide an overview of how the computer functions, discuss some of the computer's major uses, and have the students begin programming so that they appreciate the type of effort that will have to be put forward in the course. We have found the following sequencing of chapters to be effective:

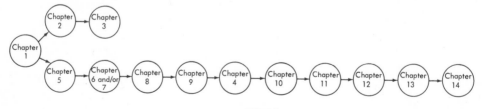

The course starts with Chapter 1 which provides an overview of the computer. While the instructor is discussing Chapter 1 and beginning the flowcharting and programming materials in Chapters 5, 6, and 7, the students can be studying on their own Chapters 2 and 3 about business applications and the historical evolution of computers. After a basic programming proficiency has been mastered, the two applications chapters, 8 and 9, can be studied in order to develop a working knowledge of computer applications and also to extend and enhance flowcharting and programming skills. We then turn to Chapter 4, "The Computer's Hardware and Its Operating System." We prefer teaching this chapter later in the course because, hopefully, by this time student fears about computers and the course have been alleviated and student curiosity about how the computer processes programs has emerged. After this technical chapter has been covered, the student has a solid grasp of computer applications, computer hardware, and mastery of a programming language and is ready to move into the four managerial chapters, Chapters 10–13. The St. Joseph's Hospital case in Appendix D fits in nicely with the teaching of these chapters. The course closes on a nontechnical note with Chapter 14 on computers and society.

A book is usually the result of the efforts and contributions of many people. Such is the case with this one. Students at the University of Georgia and the University of Hawaii are to be thanked for their "debugging" contributions. The book was field tested for a year at each of these schools. The students helped detect errors and point out areas where the materials were not clearly presented. A number of colleagues and reviewers made valuable suggestions for improving the book as it moved through revisions. These people include Ralph Sprague, Mark Simkin, and Bill Long at the University of Hawaii, K. Roscoe Davis at the University of Georgia, Charles Gallagher at Florida Technological University, and Bill Shrode at the Florida State University. Many people have helped type the various drafts of the book and special thanks go out to them. They include Nancy Parks, Jackie Ogletree, Gail Masaki, Masyo Matsukawa, and Lourdes Bostock. And finally, but not least, thanks to our graduate assistant, Vince Howe, who tenaciously tracked down needed materials for the book.

Athens, Georgia
December 1975

HUGH J. WATSON
ARCHIE B. CARROLL

Contents

1 An Overview of the Computer   3

The Computer: A Brief Description: *Advantages of the Computer. Disadvantages of the Computer. Types of Computers.* Introductory Definitions and Concepts. Software Preparation: *Systems Flowcharting. Program Flowcharting. Programming. Documentation.* Computer Hardware: *Input Unit. Primary Storage Unit. Arithmetic/Logic Unit. Control Unit. Output Unit. Secondary Storage.* Program Execution.

2 Business Applications of the Computer   27

The Scope of Computer Applications. Applications in Accounting and Finance. Banking and Credit Applications: *Banks with On-Site Computers. Revolutionary Changes in Banking Credit. Electronic Funds Transfer Systems. Reducing Credit Fraud.* Manufacturing Applications: *Computer-Controlled Production Processes. Enter the Minicomputer. Hierarchical Factory Computer Systems.* Marketing Applications: *Sales Forecasting. Advertising Applications. Sales Analysis.* Other Business Applications: *Airlines Industry. Travel Bureaus. Stock Brokerage. Hospital Administration. Hotel-Motel Industry. Heat Generation.*

3 The Historical Evolution of Computers   51

The Abacus. Early Mechanical Calculators: *Pascal's Calculating Device. The Leibnitz Calculating Machine.* The Jacquard Loom. Babbage's Difference and Analytical Engines. Hollerith's Punched Card Machine. The MARK I Computer. The ENIAC Computer. Von Neumann's Contributions. Commercially Available Computers: *The UNIVAC I. The ILLIAC IV.* Other Computer Developments. Computer Generations. Concluding Remarks.

4 The Computer's Hardware and Its Operating System   75

Storage Facilities: *An Overview of the Storage Function. The Binary Digit. Character Representation. Addresses. Storing Instructions. Arithmetic/Logic and Control Unit Registers.* Circuitry for Computations in the Arithmetic/Logic Unit. Secondary Storage Facilities: *Punched Cards. Magnetic Tape.*

Paper Tape. Magnetic Disks. Magnetic Drums. Data Cells. A Comparison of Storage Media. Operating Systems: *The Controlling Function. The Facilitating Function.* Future Trends.

5   Systems and Program Flowcharting   **107**

Systems Analysis and Design. Systems Flowcharting: *Illustrations of Systems Flowcharts.* Program Flowcharting: *Single-Pass Execution. A Branching Decision. Loops.* Subscripted Variables in Program Flowcharting.

6   The BASIC Programming Language   **131**

The Role Played by Terminals. Communicating from a Terminal. The BASIC Language: *Programming Statements. Line Numbers. Characters. Computations. Substitution Activities. LET Statement. Input. Output. END Statement. STOP Statement. REM Statement. RUN,BASIC. An Illustration. Branching. Looping. Systems Commands.* Advanced Concepts in BASIC: *Subscripted Variables. Strings. Functions and Subroutines.*

7   The FORTRAN Programming Language   **159**

Deck Makeup. Positioning the Code. A Sample Program. FORTRAN Statements: *Characters. Arithmetic Assignment Statement. Input/Output Statements. STOP and END Statements. An Illustration. Branching. Looping.* Advanced Concepts in FORTRAN: *Subscripted Variables. Input/Output with the A Format. Subprograms.*

8   Routine Data Processing Applications   **195**

Common Business Applications: *Sales Order Processing. Inventory Control. Customer Billing. Accounts Receivable. Accounts Payable. Other Applications.* Routine Data Processing Programs: *The Edit Program. The Update Program. The Register Program. The Action-Document Program. The Summary Program.* The Payroll Application: *Payroll Master File. Payroll Master File Update. Inputs to the Payroll Application. The Payroll Edit Program. The Payroll Register Program. The Payroll Check Program. The Payroll Journal Program. Periodic Reports.* Concluding Remarks. Commonly Required Algorithms: *Sorting. Sequence Checking. Table Lookup. Subtotals.* Summary.

9   Computer-Assisted Decision Making   **225**

Modeling: *Systems Thinking. Characteristics of Mathematical Models.* Packaged Programs. Classical and Modern Aids to Decision Making: *Classical Method. Modern Method.* Computer Search for Optimality. Simulating Managerial Thought.

10   Information Systems and Management   **255**

Informal Information Systems. Formal Information Systems: *The Computer's Role. Data. Data Sources. Data Hierarchy.* Progress in Information Systems.

Management Information Systems: *An Integrated Data Base. A Hierarchical Information Structure. A Decision-Support Orientation.* Decision-Support Systems. Information System Evolution: *Management's Information System Responsibilities.*

11 Planning for, Selection, and Implementation of Computer Systems   277

General Thoughts on Planning. Management Planning for Computers: *Gaining Management Support. Planning for the Total Effort.* Conducting the Feasibility Study: *Need for a Study. Nature of Feasibility Studies. Steps in the Feasibility Study.* Computer System Selection: *Rent, Lease, or Purchase. Other Approaches.* Preparing Organizational Resources for Change: *Personnel. Physical Arrangements.* Systems Design and Programming. Installing Equipment. Appraisal, Follow-up, and Review. Concluding Remarks.

12 The Impact of the Computer on Management   303

Computer Impact on the Managerial Environment. The Computer and Managerial Functions. The Computer's Impact on Lower Management. The Computer's Impact on Middle Management: *Results of Some Studies.* The Computer's Impact on Top Management: *A Disparaging View. The Manager's Planning Horizon.* Concluding Remarks.

13 The Impact of the Computer on the Organization   323

Organizational Structure and Technology. Organizational Location of the Computer: *Location 1: Accounting or Payroll Department. Location 2: Specific Operating Department. Location 3: An Independent Department.* Organization of the Data Processing Function. Span of Control and Levels of Management. Departmental Impacts and Alterations: *Creation of New Departments. Elimination of Old Departments. Modification of Existing Departments.* Line versus Staff Authority of the Computer Department. The Centralization—Decentralization Issue: *Bases for Examining the Issue. Determining the Extent of Centralization.* Preparing for Organizational Change.

14 Computers and Society   347

Computers in the Nonbusiness World: *Applications in Education. Health and Medical Applications. Applications in Government. Other Societal Applications.* Computers and the Individual: *Effects of Automation of Work Processes. The Issue of Privacy. Human Values and Individualism.* Concluding Remarks.

Appendix A. Glossary   **377**

Appendix B. The Binary Number System   **385**

Appendix C. The Punched Card and the Keypunch Machine **389**

Appendix D. St. Joseph's Hospital   **394**

Index   **405**

Computers for Business
A Managerial Emphasis

The Computer: A Brief Description

Advantages of the Computer, Disadvantages of the Computer, Types of Computers

Introductory Definitions and Concepts
Software Preparation

Systems Flowcharting, Program Flowcharting, Programming, Documentation

Computer Hardware

Input Unit, Primary Storage Unit, Arithmetic/Logic Unit, Control Unit, Output Unit, Secondary Storage

Program Execution

Assignments

References

This is probably the first course you have taken that deals specifically with computers. This chapter has been written to provide you with a valuable "big picture" viewpoint of computers in business. It introduces terminology, illustrates how you will use the computer, and discusses how the computer functions. Throughout the book this overview will be supported with increased detail, further illustrations, and other important topics.

1

An Overview of the Computer

It would be an understatement to say that computers have influenced modern science, engineering, medicine, education, and business. In fact, many of the technological developments we take for granted today would not be in existence without the powerful capabilities of the computer and its ancillary equipment. With its speed, versatility, and capacity, the modern-day computer has indeed generated what could properly be termed a computer revolution.

Nowhere has the computer had a greater impact than on business. Just within the past 20 years, it has made business more of a science and has overturned long-established modes of managing organizations. Some experts estimate that nearly half of all computers in existence today are used for business applications. Only a few examples can demonstrate the profound influence computers have had on business and the managing of organizations: automated payroll accounting, inventory control systems, fully computerized industrial plants, automatic customer billing, sophisticated computer forecasting, and comprehensive management information systems.

The influence of the computer on business has become so important, in fact, that increasingly the subject is being added to the curriculum as a mandatory course of study for students of business administration. Moreover, there is hardly a field of scholarship in which the computer has not already been recognized as assuming a significant role. Not only has the computer become an integral part of the physical sciences and business, but it also figures in technological developments in the liberal arts, the humanities, law, anthropology, linguistics, and even music.

Why are these developments occurring? What exactly is a computer, and what gives it such versatile capabilities? How does a computer process data? To what uses can a computer be put? How has the computer evolved? What is the potential of this machine that is revo-

3

lutionizing not only business but life in general? This book attempts to answer these and other important questions for students of business administration.

THE COMPUTER: A BRIEF DESCRIPTION

A *computer* is a high-speed machine which receives data and instructions, processes the data into information, and then furnishes the results in a form which is readable either by a person or another machine.

Advantages of the Computer

The major advantages of the computer as a data processing instrument are its speed, its accuracy, its capacity for storing vast amounts of data, and its versatile analysis capabilities. The speed of the modern computer is almost too great to comprehend. It can add 20-digit numbers in only a few millionths of a second, and it has printers that can generate output at the rate of 1,000 or more lines per minute. In fact, the computer is so fast that in seconds it can perform work that would ordinarily take several men many years.

The computer's capacity for handling an extremely large quantity of work, and its capacity for storage and high-speed retrieval, make it indispensable for most modern businesses. Computers are especially productive in handling jobs which are repetitive, tedious, and time-consuming. In addition, with their ability to store large masses of data and to retrieve needed data quickly, computers provide a means for coping with the increasing complexity of business.

Disadvantages of the Computer

The disadvantages the computer is charged with are somewhat misleading. It is usually not the disadvantages of the computer that are at issue but rather faults emanating from the people associated with it. For example, most customer billing errors are not due to the computer's computational errors but result either from data inputs that were incorrectly specified or deficiencies in the computer's operating instructions—and both of these are human mistakes. Yet it is not uncommon to hear the charge that the computer make a mistake. For most people it is much more convenient to blame a machine which lacks human feelings (the fictional HAL in Stanley Kubrick's *2001: A Space Odyssey* excepted) than it is to single out the true source.

However, the computer is a *vehicle* for many of the horror stories that are popularized by the media. Computer costs can go out of sight with few tangible returns, some computer systems never live up to

"This is rich, Harry. Account number 345-26-4155
wishes correspondence with a human being."

© *Datamation*

their vendor's presale claims, the computer's output is not always
appropriate for management's needs, the data stored in large computer systems can be grossly misused. But these are unfavorable
developments that can be eliminated or minimized by effective
managerial action. And that is what this book is about.

Types of Computers

There are basically two types of computers: analog and digital.
The purpose of an *analog computer* is to provide an easily manipulated and measured analog, or likeness, of a system. An analog computer uses electrical circuits to simulate the behavior of other types
of physical systems; for example, a mechanical system involving
forces and masses can be simulated by an electrical circuit with
voltage sources, resistors, capacitors and inductors. Since analog com-

puters are used almost exclusively for engineering rather than business applications, this book is confined to an examination of digital computers.

As the name implies, the *digital computer* computes with digits — that is, with discrete numbers. It performs typical numerical operations such as adding, subtracting, multiplying, and dividing, just as a conventional desk calculator does. However, the digital computer's speed, storage capacity, and versatility make comparison with a calculator unfair. The digital computer's mode of operation has been likened to that of a turnstile in that both utilize discrete units, or numbers; as people pass through a turnstile, they are counted in a digital fashion. Because of the large number of business applications which require a counting or arithmetic facility, the digital computer has found extensive applications in business and management.

INTRODUCTORY DEFINITIONS AND CONCEPTS

The terminology used in this book is designed to eliminate, as much as possible, the barriers to understanding that are often erected for the business student. Definition of a few terms here should help keep the student from becoming lost in the "jargon jungle."[1]

A major term used in this book is *electronic data processing*, often more simply called *data processing*. The modifier "electronic" refers to the use of electronic equipment to process the data. This equipment includes the digital computer and its peripheral equipment. *Data* are defined as facts or concepts that are known or assumed, usually stated in numerical form.[2] *Processing* refers to operations performed on the data — for example, arithmetic calculations, classifying, sorting, summarizing, and so on.

A useful distinction can be made between data and information. *Information,* for our purposes, will refer to data that have been processed in a prespecified manner so as to be more meaningful to the potential user. As an illustration of this distinction, assume a *computer program* (a set of instructions which directs the computer's operations) is written to help a professor handle the paper work involved in his 200-member class in Introduction to Computers for Business. This program is designed to input student test and homework scores, weight tests and homework according to a specified weighting scheme, and calculate final grades according to some predetermined classification system (e.g., 90–100 = A, 80–89 = B). In this case the data include such inputs as test and homework scores, and

---

[1] Appendix A provides a glossary of terms that are frequently encountered in working with computer specialists.

[2] The singular form of data is "datum," which sounds strange to most of us.

FIGURE 1–1
Data Conversion to Information

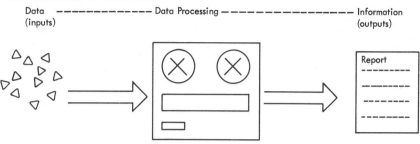

the information generated includes such output items as each student's weighted score, final grade, and so on. Data are converted into information useful to the professor by processing the input data according to prespecified arithmetical and logical operations. Figure 1–1 depicts this typical conversion process.

Some discussion of Figure 1–1 is necessary, especially in regards to what happens to data once they are converted into information. Basically, two things can happen to information: it can go directly to management and be used, or it can itself become data for further processing. Thus information which has been processed from data can become data inputs to some higher level of processing. In the case of the professor's grades, as term grades (information) are generated from test scores and homework scores (data), a basic data processing activity occurs. As far as the students are concerned, however, the processing of data is not complete at this point. The professor's grades are then sent to the registrar's office, where they are combined with other professor's grades and are then processed in order to obtain term grade reports and overall grade point averages for the students. In other words, the information that is generated by the professor's data become data inputs for additional processing by another computer program.

Introducing some further terminology, a useful distinction can be made between computer hardware and software. *Hardware* refers to the computer itself and all of its support equipment. It is essentially the "nuts and bolts" of the computer, the hardware you might want to kick if you are frustrated in using the machine. *Software* includes computer programs and supporting material for their use. Relating these important terms to the example above, it could be said that the computer program the professor writes to process the students' test and homework scores is software, while the equipment (e.g., card reader, central processing unit, printer) used to run the program is hardware. Figure 1–2 should help point out the differences.

FIGURE 1–2
Computer Hardware and Software

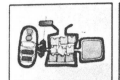

the devices themselves, the electronics and mechanics are referred to as hardware, but...

the directions that make the hardware perform operations are known as

SOFTWARE

A computer's programs, plus the procedure for their use.

(**PROGRAM**)
A set of instructions for performing
computer operations.

Courtesy of IBM

SOFTWARE PREPARATION

Before the computer can be used the software must be prepared. Software preparation commonly includes systems flowcharting, program flowcharting, programming, keypunching the program and data (in a card-oriented system), and documenting. The systems flowcharting, program flowcharting, programming, and keypunching occur before the keypunched program and data are input to the computer. Once the computer program is running successfully, the manager has his information. The work is then documented so that the program can easily be used by all personnel.

As a vehicle for discussing software preparation, and later the functioning of the hardware, we will refer again to the professor who wants to use the computer to assist him in processing students' grades. All of the steps he follows in preparing to use the computer and the manner in which the computer processes his inputs (e.g., program and data) will be described.

Systems Flowcharting

As a first step in preparing the software, the professor might develop what is known as a systems flowchart. A *systems flowchart* provides a graphical presentation of the interactions of data, personnel, and equipment in carrying out a particular data processing task. Figure 1–3 shows such a flowchart which is simple because the task itself is not complicated. The professor might not even bother drawing a systems flowchart for such an elementary situation. With data processing problems that are more complex, however, a systems flowchart is quite helpful in designing the system and improving understanding and communication of it.

Even though systems flowcharting is not taken up in detail until Chapter 5, "Systems and Program Flowcharting," the interpretation of Fig. 1–3 is almost self-evident. The initial inputs to the data processing system are paper documents (indicated by the shape of the flowcharting symbol) that contain the students' grade records. In our example, the paper documents are the pages from the professor's grade book which contain each student's entries. There is a record of each student's performance on each unit of homework and test. The *record* for each student contains the data that have been entered into the grade book during the term. Each homework mark and test score is said to be a *data element* of some student's record, and each record is composed of data elements. The total collection of related records is commonly referred to as a *file*. In our example, the professor has a file (collection of student records) on student performance in his Introduction to Computers for Business class.

The systems flowchart shows that the professor's program and the students' records are keypunched on cards (this also is revealed by the shape of the flowcharting symbol). Figure 1–4 illustrates how a student's record might appear on a punched card which records the student's name and homework and test scores.

FIGURE 1–3
Systems Flowchart for the Processing of Students' Grades

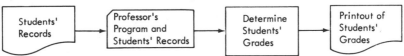

FIGURE 1–4
Keypunched Student Record

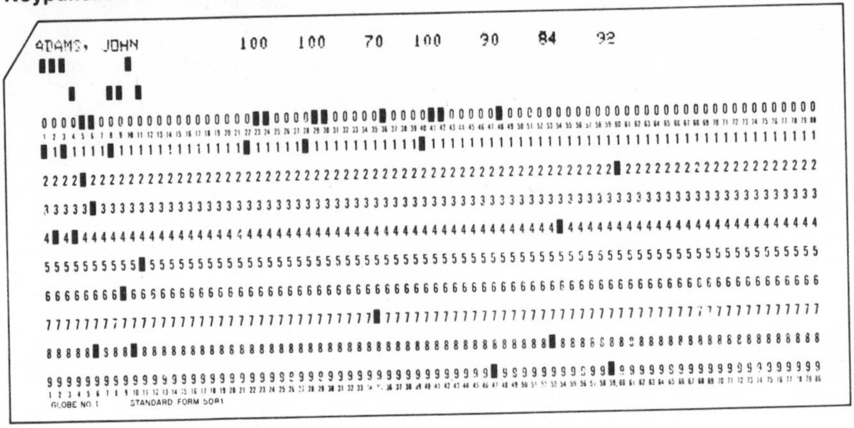

The professor's program and students' records are then input to the computer, and processing takes place. The computer's hardware performs the operations as directed by the professor's program. Homework and test scores are weighted appropriately and final grades are determined, based upon the programmed criteria.

The end product from this data processing system is a printout which includes the students' final grades. Figure 1–5 shows how such a printout might appear.

Program Flowcharting

Before the computer can process data into information, it must be given specific instructions as to what operations are to be performed on the data. These instructions are specified by writing a computer program, but before this is done a common preparatory step is the development of a program flowchart. A *program flowchart* graphically specifies the sequential operations that the computer is to perform,

FIGURE 1–5
Printout of Students' Grades

NAME	POINTS	GRADE
ADAMS, JOHN	90.00	A
ALMOND, LEIGH	84.25	B
ARP, ROSALIND	88.00	B
BAKER, SAM	68.25	D
BATES, JESS	94.00	A
BELOVUSS, JANE	75.75	C
BIXBY, MARK	72.00	C

FIGURE 1-6
Program Flowchart for Determining Students' Grades

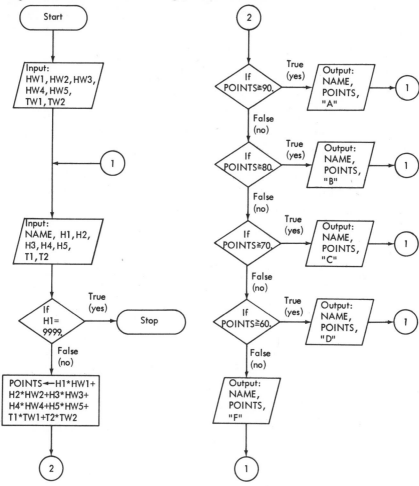

and thus it provides the basis on which the computer program is written. The program flowchart details the actual processing of data that is frequently characterized by just a single block in the systems flowchart. In our example, the program flowchart spells out how the computer is to determine the students' grades, an activity which is a single block in the systems flowchart. An example of a program flowchart is given in Figure 1-6.

Discussing in detail the professor's program flowchart would be getting ahead of ourselves, since the topic is considered in depth in Chapter 5. However, a few general observations can be made at this point. The flowchart shows that the weights to be applied to the homework and test scores are one set of data inputs. Reflecting the fact that the professor has five homework and two test scores for each student, the *variable names* HW1, HW2, HW3, HW4, HW5, TW1, and TW2 are used to identify the various *weights*. Another set of data inputs is comprised of the students' records, whose placement on punched cards has already been seen (Figure 1–4). The variable names NAME, H1, H2, H3, H4, H5, T1, and T2 are used with the student's name and homework and test *scores*. A student's weighted average is computed by summing the products of the weights times the scores, and it is then associated with the variable named POINTS. A series of tests is then made to determine whether the student's weighted average (POINTS) "earns" a grade of A, B, C, D, or F. The final output includes the student's name, weighted average, and final grade in the course.

Programming

A program flowchart indicates all of the computer operations necessary to generate the desired information. The next step in software preparation involves *coding* (writing) a computer program from the program flowchart. It is worth mentioning that a well-thought-out program flowchart provides the basis for writing a computer program in any one of several programming languages. While the specific details of programming the computer are not taken up until later, an overview of some of the more important programming concepts and languages is within the scope of this chapter.

The computer actually "understands" only *machine language,* the language computer programmers had to use when computers were first introduced. Unfortunately for the first programmers, machine language was, and is, very difficult to use, since all instructions have to be coded in binary form—all 0s and 1s. The reason for this condition will become clearer later when we consider what takes place inside the computer. Imagine, however, the difficulty of having to write or look at strings of nothing but binary digits. While some programs are still written in machine language, virtually all business applications are now programmed in higher level languages.

Because of the difficulty associated with remembering operation codes and storage locations coded in binary (for example, "addition" might be 0001 1010), *symbolic programming languages* were developed. This advancement permits the use of symbols such as ADD, for the addition of numbers, and X, for a variable named X.

Why are symbolic and other programming languages possible if the computer understands only machine language? Before this question can be answered, the role of the language-translator com-

FIGURE 1-7
The Role of Language Translators

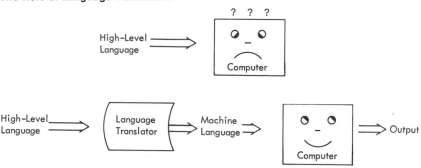

ponent in data processing must be discussed.[3] A *language translator* is a computer program, usually supplied by the computer manufacturer, which translates the high-level language into machine language (see Figure 1–7). The *source program* (the high-level language program that has been written) is translated into an *object program* (a machine language program) by the language translator. Without language translators, using the computer would be very difficult, and many of the modern data processing accomplishments would not have been possible.

While the development of symbolic languages made programming far easier, there still had to be a one-to-one correspondence between a programming statement and a machine operation. The next advancement in programming languages utilized the concept of *macro instructions*. This development permits the programmer to write a single programming statement which, when translated, generates several machine language instructions. Almost all of the popular modern-day programming languages, such as BASIC and FORTRAN, employ the macro instruction concept.

If languages such as BASIC and FORTRAN (frequently called *procedure-oriented languages*) are far easier to use then machine or symbolic languages, why are not all programs written in these languages? The answer lies in the cost tradeoff between programming and computer running time. The language translator has to translate the high-level language into machine language. In general, the machine language program generated by the language translator is not as efficient as a machine language program written by a skilled programmer because it has a longer running time. So while programming time is reduced when high-level languages are used, computer running time is usually increased. On the other hand, machine

---

[3] Language-translator programs are sometimes referred to as *processors*. Specific types of translators are commonly referred to as *compilers, assemblers,* or *generators*.

FIGURE 1-8
Cost Tradeoffs with Various Programming Languages

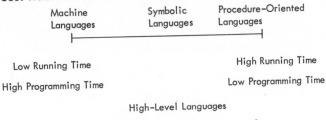

language programs run more efficiently but take greater skill and time to write. Ideally, therefore, the language selected should minimize the sum of the programming and running-time costs (see Figure 1-8).

Since this book is written for future managers rather than computer specialists, only high-level languages are discussed. Those tasks that might be best programmed in a low-level language, such as a payroll application, should be turned over to professional programmers with advanced training. Managers do not have the time, interest, or background for such an assignment.

It should be mentioned that fewer and fewer programs are being written in machine or symbolic languages. This situation is evolving as language translators are developed that can generate machine language programs which are as efficient as those prepared by humans, or more so.

Even with attention limited to high-level languages, a large number still might be considered. Two languages—BASIC and FORTRAN—have been selected for detailed description in this book. The choice of these particular languages was based upon considerations such as application, general availability, ease of learning, and future usefulness to management.

An increasingly important way managers interface with the computer involves sitting at a terminal and providing instructions or data inputs to the computer and receiving output back via the terminal. While the manager is normally sharing the computer's time with other users, because of the computer's speed he is seldom aware that he does not have the computer all to himself. In this situation the manager is said to be operating in a *time-sharing* environment. One of the most important time-sharing languages is BASIC (an acronym for *B*eginners *A*ll-purpose *S*ymbolic *I*nstruction *C*ode). In addition to being quite useful, it is an easy first language to learn.

Probably the most widely used high-level language is FORTRAN (an acronym for *FOR*mula *TRAN*slator). Developed in the late 1950s, FORTRAN is frequently used for applications requiring extensive mathematical and statistical computations. It is particularly well suited for large computer-assisted decision-making applications (e.g., simulation studies). It is more difficult to learn than BASIC, but it provides more flexibility.

In the professor's processing of students' grades, he is able to write an appropriate computer program from the program flowchart (Figure 1–6). Since all of the students' records have been entered on punched cards, a batch-processing language such as FORTRAN would probably be used. *Batch processing* refers to collecting data over a period of time and then processing the data all in one batch. In our example, the batch of data refers to the students' homework and test scores. Figure 1–9 shows a FORTRAN program for determining students' grades that was written from the program flowchart.

While the *programming statements* may be somewhat confusing at this point, by comparing the FORTRAN program with the program flowchart it is possible to gain a general understanding of what a computer program looks like and how it functions. In later chapters on the BASIC and FORTRAN programming languages (Chapters 6

FIGURE 1–9
A FORTRAN Program for Determining Students' Grades

```
C       THIS PROGRAM DETERMINES STUDENTS' GRADES
        WRITE(6,50)
    50  FORMAT('1','NAME',20X,'POINTS',4X,'GRADE')
        READ(5,100)  HW1,HW2,HW3,HW4,HW5,TW1,TW2
   100  FORMAT(7(F4.2,1X))
   200  READ(5,300)  N1,N2,N3,N4,N5,H1,H2,H3,H4,H5,T1,T2
   300  FORMAT(5A4,7(F4.0,2X))
        IF(H1.EQ.9999.) GO TO 900
        POINTS=H1*HW1+H2*HW2+H3*HW3+H4*HW4+H5*HW5+T1*TW1+T2*TW2
        IF(POINTS.GE.90.) GO TO 400
        IF(POINTS.GE.80.) GO TO 410
        IF(POINTS.GE.70.) GO TO 420
        IF(POINTS.GE.60.) GO TO 430
        WRITE(6,350) N1,N2,N3,N4,N5,POINTS
   350  FORMAT('0',5A4,4X,F6.2,7X,'F')
        GO TO 200
   400  WRITE(6,405) N1,N2,N3,N4,N5,POINTS
   405  FORMAT('0',5A4,4X,F6.2,7X,'A')
        GO TO 200
   410  WRITE(6,415) N1,N2,N3,N4,N5,POINTS
   415  FORMAT('0',5A4,4X,F6.2,7X,'B')
        GO TO 200
   420  WRITE(6,425) N1,N2,N3,N4,N5,POINTS
   425  FORMAT('0',5A4,4X,F6.2,7X,'C')
        GO TO 200
   430  WRITE(6,435) N1,N2,N3,N4,N5,POINTS
   435  FORMAT('0',5A4,4X,F6.2,7X,'D')
        GO TO 200
   900  STOP
        END
```

and 7) a more gradual and systematic approach to programming will be used. All that is intended here is to provide an overview.

Even experienced programmers do not generate computer programs that are error-free the first time around. The process of removing errors from a computer program is known as *debugging* the program. In general, two types of errors are made—programming errors and logic errors.

A *programming error* (also referred to as a *clerical* or *syntax error*) occurs when a programming statement does not follow the rules of the language, as when a variable name is too long. Unless the error is a very minor one, the computer's processing of the program stops when a programming error is encountered. The language translator then directs the printing of what is known as a diagnostic message. The *diagnostic* indicates which statements are in error and need to be corrected before the program is run again.

Logic errors occur when the series of computer operations that have been designed and programmed to process the data do not produce the desired results. The program can be completely free of programming errors but still not generate the desired output. Unfortunately, logic errors can be extremely difficult to detect, since the computer does not have the capability to locate them. The erroneous output also can sometimes look correct at first glance, and mistakes may not be found until much later.

There are two related procedures for checking a program for logic errors. The first involves "playing computer"—going through the programming statements just as the computer does. This method is especially good for locating careless logic errors. A second method is to run test data for which the correct output is known. If the program's output is the same as that expected, this is a good indication, but no guarantee, that the program's logic is correct.

The FORTRAN program shown in Figure 1–9 contains neither programming nor logic errors. This lack of errors does not mean that the professor did everything right the first time around. Rather, it probably indicates that he had the tenacity to continue working on the program until it was finally correct. Such perseverance is commonly required in working with the computer.

Documentation

The last and least exciting (but nevertheless important) part of software preparation is *documentation*—providing a permanent record and reference for the work that has been done. Because this activity is not particularly creative, there is a tendency to slight it.

Unfortunately, poor documentation can be quite costly to an organization. The documentation frequently provides the only reasonable starting point for finding newly uncovered program problem areas, making required modifications to the program, or perhaps even knowing the use of a particular program that has not been run in some time. Anyone who has ever picked up an undocumented program quickly appreciates how difficult or impossible it is to use.

There is no standard form for program documentation. However, the following items should provide sufficient documentation in most cases:

1. Statement of the program's objectives.
2. Program flowchart.
3. Symbol table.
4. Computer program.
5. Sample data input.
6. Sample data output.
7. Comments.

It seems appropriate to begin the documentation with a statement of the program's objectives. The program flowchart reveals the logic of the program used to generate the information. The symbol table is valuable in that it defines the variables used in the program. When the computer program is supplied with the sample data, it should generate the sample data output. The comments section can be used for a wide variety of items, including the analyst's or programmer's name, when the program was written, appropriate references, and other related information. When the documentation is completed, the user has gone through all of the steps associated with software preparation.

COMPUTER HARDWARE

After a computer program and the data have been prepared, they are input to the computer. In order to understand what then happens to the program and data it is necessary to consider the computer's logical structure. Although many different kinds of computers have been developed—varying in size, cost, capability, and speed—nearly all have essentially the same basic components. The schematic diagram in Figure 1–10 illustrates the typical computer system. Each component of the configuration will be briefly examined. Figure 1–11 is presented to help you better relate actual pieces of hardware to the basic components. It illustrates a popular modern computer system.

FIGURE 1–10
Components of a Typical Computer System

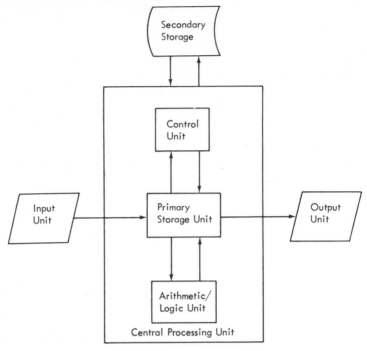

Input Unit

The input to a computer is the "raw material" of the calculating process, consisting of the user's program and data. The component of the system that enters these inputs into the computer system is the input unit.

Before being input to the computer, the program and data must be converted into a form which is *machine-readable*—capable of being read by a machine. Many different *storage media* can be used for inputting to a computer—punched cards, paper tape, and magnetic tape, to mention just a few. Each of these storage media has advantages and characteristics which make it more desirable than others under a given set of circumstances. The media are input to the computer through *input devices* such as card readers, paper tape readers, magnetic tape drives, and keyboard consoles. The more common and more important storage media and input devices are shown in Fig. 1–12.

Primary Storage Unit

The central processing unit (commonly called the CPU) of the computer is composed of an arithmetic/logic unit, a control unit, and

FIGURE 1–11
An NCR Century 200

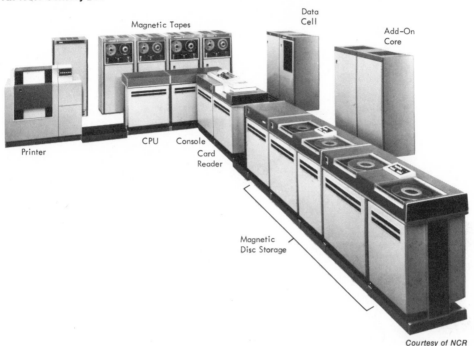

Courtesy of NCR

a storage unit. It is the primary storage unit that serves as the computer's main memory.[4] Some of the functions performed by the primary storage unit include: (1) storing data until needed for processing, (2) storing the final results of processing until released as output, (3) storing intermediate results while other operations are being performed, and (4) storing program instructions while the data processing is being performed. In some ways the role of the computer's storage unit can be viewed as being somewhat analogous to the retention function of the human brain.

Arithmetic/Logic Unit

The arithmetic/logic unit of the central processing unit performs mathematical and logical operations such as addition, subtraction, and comparison. In a sense it is the real "computing" component of the computer, since it is in the arithmetic/logic unit that the actual ma-

---

[4] In working with the computer you will notice a tendency to refer to the computer in humanlike terms. As has just been seen, the computer's storage facility is frequently referred to as "memory."

FIGURE 1–12
Storage Media and Input Devices

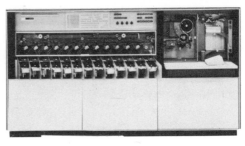

Courtesy of IBM

nipulation of data takes place. Specially designed electrical circuitry within the arithmetic/logic unit performs the mathematical and logical operations that are within the computer's designed range of capabilities.

Control Unit

The function of the control unit of the central processing unit is to direct operations within the computer system. The control unit operates according to instructions set forth in the user's stored program. It serves such purposes as directing where data should be stored and what operations should be performed upon the data.

Output Unit

After the computer's operations have been completed, it is necessary to make the output of the operations available to potential users. The output of a computer can be made available in a number of different forms, basically either be in a form which is immediately available in man-readable form or in one which is conducive to further operations or storage. A form which would be immediately usable is a computer printout, and one which would be conducive to further operations or storage is data output on punched cards, paper tape, or magnetic tape. The desired form of the output will be dictated by the use that the computer user plans to make of the output. Figure 1–13 shows some of the more common and useful output storage media and output devices.

Secondary Storage

A computer system cannot function without the five basic components just described — input, storage, arithmetic/logic, control, and output units. However, almost all medium to large systems have another feature that is vital in providing many of the applications required by business organizations. This feature is *secondary storage* — storage that is secondary and external to that provided by the primary storage unit of the central processing unit. Secondary storage is made available through storage media such as magnetic disks and drums and data cells that have the capacity for storing millions of pieces of data. Data and programs can be quickly retrieved by the computer from these secondary storage media.

PROGRAM EXECUTION

As a conclusion to this chapter we will consider how the computer processes the professor's program in the example given above. This

FIGURE 1–13
Storage Media and Output Devices

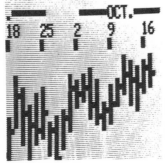

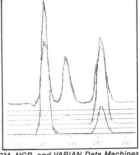

Courtesy of IBM, NCR, and VARIAN Data Machines

discussion should help make clear the roles played by the various components of a computer system.[5] However, the computer can be meaningfully used with only minimal (if any) understanding of how its hardware functions. Only computer specialists really need to have a detailed knowledge of what goes on inside a computer system.

In the discussion of the professor's program the point has been reached where an appropriate computer program has been written and keypunched, along with the students' records. The professor then reads the cards into the computer via a card reader (as illustrated in Figure 1–12), which is one component of the computer's input unit. The program then is translated into machine language by an appropriate language translator; in our example, this would be one for translating a FORTRAN program. Most computers have several language translators, at least one for every programming language that can be used on the system. The language translators are part of the computer's *operating system*, which is a set of computer programs that are permanently stored within the computer and help run and monitor the system, facilitate computer usage, keep records, and so on. Much more will be said later about operating systems.

After a machine language program has been produced by the language translator, the resulting object program is retained in the computer's storage unit. Just before a particular programming statement is *executed* (performed by the computer), the instruction is read into the control unit, and the data that are to be operated upon by the instruction are moved into the arithmetic/logic unit. The stage is then set for the actual manipulation of the data, because the instruction is in the control unit and the data in the arithmetic/logic unit. When the programming statement is executed, the data are operated upon by electronic circuits that are associated with the arithmetic/logic unit and have the capability for performing functions such as addition, subtraction, comparison, and so on. Once the statement is executed the next instruction is read into the control unit, the results from the previous operations are either left in the arithmetic/ logic unit for further processing or are read back into the storage unit, and new data are read into the arithmetic/logic unit.[6] The process then repeats itself.

Once the processing of data is complete, the results are available to be output from the output unit. With the example that we have been describing, the output device used would be a printer such as that

---

[5] To some extent the discussion involves a few simplifications in comparison to what actually takes place in a large computer system. Later, in Chapter 4, "The Computer's Hardware and Its Operating System," more complete descriptions will be given on certain aspects of computer operations.

[6] Actually all of this activity does not take place simultaneously, but the net effect is as described.

shown in Figure 1–13. The actual output would be as illustrated in Figure 1–5. The professor now would have the information needed to enter grades onto the grade roll.

ASSIGNMENTS

1-1. What is a computer? What differentiates it from a calculator?

1-2. What is meant by electronic data processing? Give an example from your own experience.

1-3. Discuss the relationship between data and information.

1-4. Differentiate between computer hardware and software.

1-5. What is the purpose of a systems flowchart?

1-6. What does a program flowchart show?

1-7. Describe the role played by a language translator. Why is it important?

1-8. What is meant by program documentation?

1-9. What are the basic components of a computer? Describe the functions they serve.

1-10. Discuss what takes place when a computer program is executed.

REFERENCES

Books

Burch, John G. and Felix R. Strater *Information Systems: Theory and Practice.* Santa Barbara, Calif.: Hamilton Publishing Co., 1974.

Dock, V. Thomas and Edward Essick *Principles of Business Data Processing.* Chicago: Science Research Associates, 1974.

Fink, Stuart S. and Barbara J. Burian *Business Data Processing.* New York: Appleton-Century-Crofts, 1974.

Mader, Chris and Robert Hagin *Information Systems: Technology, Economics, Applications.* Chicago: Science Research Associates, 1974.

Silver, Gerald A. and John B. Silver *Data Processing for Business.* New York: Harcourt Brace Jovanovich, 1973.

Spencer, Donald D. *Introduction to Information Processing.* Columbus, Ohio: Charles E. Merrill Publishing Co., 1974.

Vazsonyi, Andrew *Introduction to Electronic Data Processing.* Homewood, Ill.: Richard D. Irwin, 1973.

The Scope of Computer Applications

Applications in Accounting and Finance

Banking and Credit Applications

Banks with On-Site Computers, Revolutionary Changes in Banking Credit, Electronic Funds Transfer Systems, Reducing Credit Fraud

Manufacturing Applications

Computer Controlled Production Processes, Enter the Minicomputer, Hierarchical Factory Computer Systems

Marketing Applications

Sales Forecasting, Advertising Applications, Sales Analysis

Other Business Applications

Airlines Industry, Travel Bureaus, Stock Brokerage, Hospital Administration, Hotel-Motel Industry, Heat Generation

Assignments

References

Whereas the first chapter examined important terminology and concepts in the computer field, the present chapter provides an overview of how the computer has been used in a wide range of business applications. You should gain a sense of appreciation of the computer's pervasiveness in the business world by examining these applications.

2

Business Applications
of the Computer

The primary reason computers have experienced such tremendous growth can be summed up in one word—applications. If it were not possible to make so many applications in the business world, computers would hardly have gained such widespread acceptance. And, if these applications did not prove to be economically justifiable and feasible, continued development would have been curtailed. Managers are pragmatic people, and this characteristic has led them to initiate an apparently unbounded growth cycle for computers. New applications of the computer are being discovered at such a rapid pace that it would be impossible for all but the most sophisticated information system to monitor and catalog progress (which, of itself, would be a monumental data processing task).

There are a number of reasons why computerized data processing has become necessary and attractive to many business organizations. Perhaps the most fundamental one is related to the sheer size or volume of paperwork to be processed. As business organizations experience rapid rates of growth, there are concomitant increases in the number of personnel needed to handle the resultant paperwork. Thus the volume of paperwork which must be processed, and the related increasing numbers of personnel necessary to perform this work, drive costs to the point where managers have an attractive incentive for developing less costly ways of handling these tasks.

Computers, with their large storage capacities, make it possible to store vast quantities of organizational data. This data can be *accessed* (i.e., retrieved from the storage medium) with a speed that far exceeds that of manual systems. Most large business firms could not effectively compete without systems for the speedy retrieval of data.

A major advantage of computerized data processing is accuracy. After computer applications have been carefully developed and tested, few errors of computer origin ever occur. Most "computer mistakes" can be traced back to human origins.

Computers can not only perform old tasks better than alternative methods can, they also permit management and the organization to do things that were formerly not possible. These new possibilities can result in increased organizational effectiveness and profitability. For example, computer-based planning models allow management to evaluate alternative plans for action better. Such planning efforts are usually more limited in noncomputerized environments.

THE SCOPE OF COMPUTER APPLICATIONS

The *scope of computer applications* refers to the computer's feasible range of applications. When computers first appeared on the business scene, they were used primarily for routine data processing applications such as recordkeeping and payroll preparation. In other words, the computer assumed the elementary role of performing clerical operations. More extensive applications evolved as technology improved and managers and computer specialists learned more of what could be done with the computer.

Part of the larger sphere of application can be attributed to an increase in the sophistication and usefulness of management science techniques (quantitative approaches to solving management problems). The developments in the management sciences came about because of the need to make decision making a more rational, information-using process. Many management science techniques require the availability of a computer, and it is not surprising that computers and the management sciences have matured hand in hand. It has been the application of management science techniques that has led to the emergence of decision-support-oriented uses of the computer.

Figure 2–1 illustrates the approximate evolution of computer usage from the 1950s to the present and into the 1980s. The precise mix of routine data processing and decision-support-oriented applications is an estimate, and the figure is designed to depict only the general trend. The left side of the figure indicates that the computer was used

FIGURE 2–1
The Evolution of Computer Applications

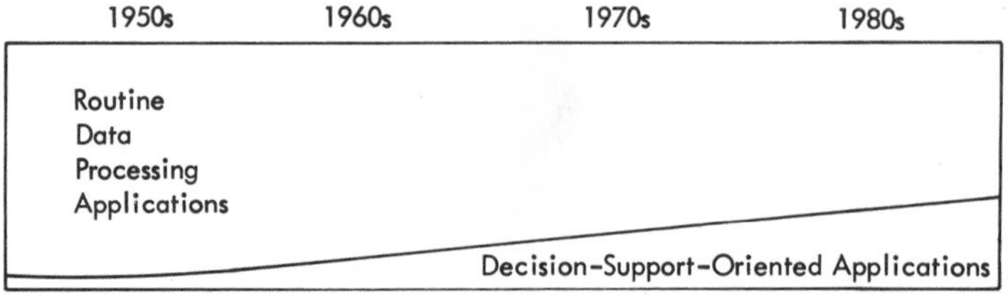

almost exclusively for routine clerical applications when it was introduced in the 1950s. Now it is increasingly being used by managers to generate information that supports decision making, as indicated at the right.

It should be noted that the computer is still used primarily for routine data processing applications, and will be into the foreseeable future. However, the relative mix of applications is changing. As we consider some of the many functional areas of business (e.g., accounting and finance, production) in which managers have found the computer useful, we will examine this range of applicability to illustrate how this trend has developed in these areas.

APPLICATIONS IN ACCOUNTING AND FINANCE

It is fitting to first discuss computer applications in accounting and finance, for that is where it was initially utilized in most business organizations. The accounting department usually stored most of the data for the business firm. In fact, the accounting department (originally known as the bookkeeping department) was often the reservoir of most of the organization's operating data, even including such items as inventory data and sales records. Because the accounting department is the keeper of data and is required to perform tasks heavily oriented to data processing, such as payroll preparation and general ledger accounting, it is not surprising that the computer was often first located in that department and programmed for the routine applications performed there. To this day accounting applications remain the bread-and-butter work of most computer systems.

There are several areas in which the computer has proven to be extremely useful in the accounting function. These pertain primarily to routine applications such as sales accounting, payroll preparation, accounts receivable, and customer billing. In general, these are bookkeeping or recordkeeping functions that involve considerable amounts of data but only simple arithmetic calculations. In each of these areas, the computer provides the advantages of speed, storage capacity, and accuracy, along with decreased clerical expenses.

Computer applications in accounting and finance, however, have become increasingly sophisticated in recent years. For example, computers are being employed to simulate an organization's future financial status. This type of simulation involves the construction of a mathematical model of the firm's financial picture (e.g., revenue, costs, cash flow, income), which is then manipulated in order to analyze possible outcomes under varying sets of conditions. Information of this type is useful to support decision making.

As an illustration of a financial simulation, consider a large manufacturing firm that is attempting to estimate what its budget and cash position will look like for the next five years. A simulation model can be built which will reveal the effect on income, costs, profits, and other variables of possible conditions that might occur. For example, what will be the impact on the firm's cash position if the collections from the West Coast are delayed three weeks or if catalog sales are down an unexpected 15 percent during the first calendar quarter? Financial simulation, thus, is a method of analysis which utilizes the computer to aid management in planning and in the prediction of critical financial variables.

In addition to simulation, the importance of the computer in the finance and accounting function has been enhanced by its provision of reports which immensely aid management in its performance of its planning and controlling functions. The vast capabilities of the computer make it easier for management to have access to data and reports which during precomputer days could not be economically and accurately assembled. In fact, the ease with which the computer can generate reports has the potential for creating a paperwork jungle which, if left uncontrolled, could swamp managers with data and information. Consequently, control mechanisms must be developed to aid management to determine the need and justification for existing and projected reports.

The accounting and finance areas have been made more sophisticated by the availability of the computer, but these advancements have not been made without problems. For example, complex computer accounting systems raise serious questions about possible fraud. In recent years, the origin of numerous cases of fraud, theft, and embezzlement have been found in computer-aided complicity.

The most notable case of computer fraud occurred in the 1973 Equity Funding Life Insurance scandal, in which the computer aided a large number of Equity Funding employees in a $60 million fraud scheme.[1] Though most data processing professionals at the time scoffed at the idea of a "criminal computer," the computer field in general was indicted for not having appropriate controls and safeguards to assure against such occurrences. What makes this case especially intriguing, however, is the fact that Equity Funding's vice president for management information systems insisted that the Equity data processing division had the same basic controls as 90 percent of the computer installations in the country. Thus, apparently, the computer was employed within the constraints set up to safeguard against such abuses.

It thus appears that present safeguards and control mechanisms

---

[1] "On the Coast-to-Coast Trail of Equity Funding," *Business Week*, April 21, 1973, pp. 68–72.

that are built into accounting systems do not control 100 percent against abuses. The audit function in accounting has therefore necessarily taken on a new dimension—checking for computer-assisted theft.[2] Hence, with the many benefits of the computer have come potential problems which must be dealt with by management. It is certain that as a response to these newly discovered problems more CPA auditors will be signing up for computer science courses.

BANKING AND CREDIT APPLICATIONS

Applications of the computer in the banking and credit fields illustrate the dynamic effects the computer can have on entire industries. Banking institutions were one of the first types of business organizations to experience large financial gains through computer automation. Banks proved to be ideal customers for computer manufacturers during the early 1960s, when most large banks computerized their accounting and bookkeeping operations. Once they were able to automate their check processing operations, banks opened the door for new potentially profitable areas of banking services.

Today banking employs the computer in a wide variety of ways. Over 2,000 automated teller systems, for example, have been installed in the United States. Some of these systems involve cash-dispensing machines such as that employed by Citizens and Southern National Bank in the Southeast, activated by coded credit cards and a memorized numerical combination that the customer simply punches into a keyborad device. More expensive systems permit the transference of funds from savings accounts to checking accounts, accept payments of bills, and provide full bank statements on request.[3] Carrying this concept further, the City National Bank of Columbus, Ohio, has announced plans to install automatic tellers in local stores and in popular retail centers in Cleveland.[4]

Not all banks have computerized their operations, however; some have insufficient volume to justify computerization. Most banks that have been able to justify the purchase or rental of a computer economically are actively seeking new and different areas of banking services that can be provided by the computer. Some large banks, for example, have moved in the direction of full-service financial institutions, offering such bank computer services as payroll handling, account reconciliation, accounts receivable servicing, professional

---

[2] R. A. McLaughlin, "Equity Funding: Everyone is Pointing at the Computer," *Datamation*, June 1973, pp. 88–91.

[3] "Computers Rush into Your Daily Life," U.S. *News and World Report*, November 5, 1973, pp. 45–46.

[4] Ibid., p. 46.

billing, mortgage servicing, utility billing, and a wide variety of other computerized services for their clients.[5] Organizational economics dictate that banks that have invested in computers diversify into areas which provide opportunities to gain new sources of revenue. This is especially true for banks with their own on-site computers.

Banks with On-Site Computers

Banks with on-site computers must be concerned with finding additional applications for idle computer time.[6] Thus the computer has had a revolutionary effect on the banking industry, giving it a great incentive to seek out new areas of application. Once check processing was electronically automated, bank managers sought other banking functions with large-volume characteristics which suggested possible gains from computerization — for example, in handling time deposits (savings accounts), installment loans, business loans, real estate loans, and other banking services. In addition, bank managers are using the computer in conjunction with management science techniques such as the model for processing bad checks which is illustrated in Chapter 9, "Computer-Assisted Decision Making."

In addition to banking-related applications, large banks are increasingly offering their data processing services to small businessmen. This is possible because in most cases the banks' computers are "paid for" by the banks' regular data processing requirements, but excess computer time is normally available. Therefore low-cost data processing services can be offered which small businesses can take advantage of. Bank of America in California is one bank that offers data processing services on a wide scale. It is estimated that this bank does 69 percent of all the computer service business in Southern California; for example, it processes about 1,000 payrolls in that area. Though banks do not typically advertise these services on a public level, many do have aggressive marketing efforts that get the message across.[7] Data processing services by banks appear certain to grow.

Revolutionary Changes in Banking Credit

An examination of modern banking practices indicates that some revolutionary changes are appearing over the horizon. Though banks

---

[5] J. A. O'Brien, "Bank Computer Services: The State of the Art," *The Banker's Magazine*, Summer 1971, pp. 51–56.

[6] For a good discussion of this see W. A. Longbrake, "Computers and the Cost of Producing Banking Services," *Journal of Bank Research*, Autumn 1973, pp. 194–99.

[7] E. D. Myers, "Banks as Service Bureaus," *Datamation*, June 1973, pp. 72–73.

FIGURE 2–2
On-Line Video Display Terminal Used in a Savings and Loan Association

Courtesy of IBM

first employed computers to mechanize the straightforward tasks of bookkeeping and check processing, they are currently moving into areas such as *on-line* data processing. As it pertains to banking, the on-line concept basically refers to a process for "capturing" data as close to the point of transaction as possible, for example, at the teller's window or during the sorting of checks. The idea is to store the data electronically (e.g., on magnetic tape or magnetic disk) for later retrieval without need for all of the conventional interim paper work.

Figure 2–2 illustrates the operation of an on-line system in a savings and loan association. This computer-based system employs a video display terminal to handle a wide variety of services for customers.

Illustrations of what financial institutions are doing today as a direct consequence of the computer's capabilities suggest what the future may have in store for the consumer. Progress such as the following is representative:

1. Customers of Seattle First National Bank are now able to dial the bank's computer (with the aid of a plastic device) and pay bills, keep track of their household budgets, and even encode certain in-

formation that they may later need for income tax returns (such as interest payments and medical expenses). A $6.50 a month charge is made for this service.

2. City National Bank and Trust Company of Columbus, Ohio, is moving ahead with plans to install terminals in major stores and supermarkets which will permit customers to use credit cards to make "paperless" payments.

3. In Atlanta and San Francisco, automated clearinghouses are permitting the electronic distribution of payrolls and automatic crediting of employees' bank accounts. In addition, banks are encouraging customers to make use of single multipayment checks to pay many bills at one time.

4. In Delaware, Wilmington Savings Fund Society has issued plastic "money cards" which authorize the immediate transfer of funds from the bank to the account of the merchant with whom the customer has done business. Customers get a 2 percent discount if they use their cards at participating merchants.

5. Seven financial institutions in Pittsfield, Massachusetts, including a savings bank, a federal credit union, and commercial banks, are cooperating in an effort to establish a citywide electronic payment system. If their plans go through, this city could become a model for small-town electronic payment systems.[8]

Each of these examples illustrates the quickened pace of computerized banking. Banks are closely related to the possibility of cashless, checkless business transactions which are aided by the characteristics of evolving electronic fund transfer systems.

Electronic Funds Transfer Systems

Electronic Funds Transfer Systems (EFTS) are intricate networks of fund transfers by computers which could bring about a cashless, checkless transaction system. As some of the examples presented above illustrate, transactions could take place without the exchange of cash or the writing of checks. Funds would simply be exchanged from the accounts of the parties involved in the transaction. However, implementation of the concept suggests a wide range of problems, such as the setting up of computer terminals, communications links, and the expenditure of billions of dollars.

The scale on which EFTS is currently being experimented with can best be seen in Atlanta and San Francisco, which were mentioned earlier. In these cities automated clearing houses are distributing company payrolls electronically and automatically crediting employees' bank accounts. The Atlanta Payments Project has future

[8] For a discussion of these five applications, see "The Quickened Pace of Electronic Banking," *Business Week*, September 15, 1973, p. 116.

FIGURE 2–3
Ten-year Timetable for Electronic Funds Transfer System Introduction

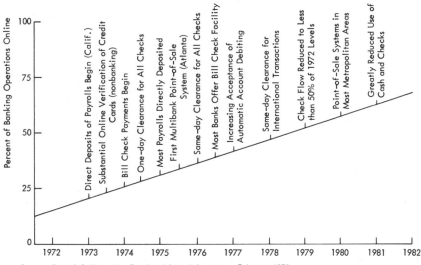

Source: Frost & Sullivan, Inc. Reprinted from *Infosystems*, February 1973.

plans to establish a regional electronic payments system that will extend electronic, cashless, checkless transactions to the retail sales level. Both the Atlanta and the San Francisco developments are under the leadership of COPE (Committee on Paperless Entries).[9]

EFTS, of course, would be a giant step for banking—and for retail establishments and citizens as well. A key element of such a system would be a point-of-sale terminal located in retail establishments. This terminal would electronically transfer funds through a vast information network connected with bank computer centers, verification centers, and other communication links. The basic technology for such computer applications is already available.

The trend in retail sales applications which will eventually lead to EFTS is exemplified in the recent installation by Sears, Roebuck and Company, the nation's largest retailer, of an estimated 40,000 electronic point-of-sale registers and nearly 700 central computers from Singer Company, Inc. This trend is being followed by most large retail firms.[10]

Widespread usage of EFTS is just a matter of time, and rapid progress is being made on its implementation. Figure 2–3 gives a ten-year timetable for the introduction of EFTS and documents or projects estimates for introduction of its various components through 1982.

---

[9] Ibid, pp. 116–21.
[10] *U.S. News and World Report*, November 5, 1973, p. 46.

Reducing Credit Fraud

Although the point where ETFS is fully operational has not yet been reached, the computer has assumed an important role in the credit field in the reduction of fraud. This may seem somewhat paradoxical, since (as we have already suggested) the computer is also employed in perpetrating fraud. Like most technology, however, the computer has the potential for both social benefits and detriments.

By employing computers extensively, credit card companies have been able to reduce monetary losses sharply. Computers now make it possible to shorten the amount of time necessary to notify retail businesses of stolen cards from several weeks to several minutes. As a consequence, fraudulent use of credit cards has been greatly reduced, and companies that were losing in excess of $10 million several years ago now report yearly losses in the range of $1.5 million. Some spokesmen in the multibillion-dollar credit card industry anticipate that within several years they will be able to institute computerized systems capable of monitoring even the hourly spending patterns of cardholders.

The computer has created a quickened pace in banking and credit. However, the evolution of systems such as ETFS will create problems and challenges that are many times more complicated than those faced by bankers and credit companies today. The challenges posed for young businessmen by the advent of widespread computer usage in the banking and credit fields promise to be exciting and demanding.

MANUFACTURING APPLICATIONS

It has only been in recent years that the computer has become an integral component of many manufacturing operations. We have described how naturally the computer fit into such areas as accounting, finance, and banking. Figure 2–4 illustrates the changing mix of computer applications, in which manufacturing is capturing an increasing share.

In industrial production, computers have been found to be useful and advantageous in such areas as running production lines, monitoring product quality control, gathering information from multiple sources, controlling production (e.g., coordinating orders, machine loads, inventories), automatically guiding machines by numerical control, and managing inventory systems. Several of these uses are of such importance that they merit closer examination.

Computer-Controlled Production Processes

Numerous manufacturing concerns now employ computers to operate and control manufacturing processes. Some plants have

FIGURE 2–4
The Changing Mix of Computer Applications

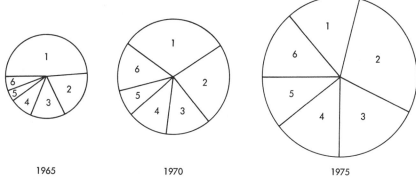

1. Financial and Administrative
2. Manufacturing
3. Marketing
4. Distribution
5. Research, Development and Engineering
6. Other

Source: *Automatic Data Processing Newsletter,* vol. 16, no. 7 (April 3, 1972), p. 3.

become so automated, in fact, that they practically run themselves. For example, computers are used in large chemical processing facilities to conduct an ongoing, continuous analysis of processes, making changes in inputs or processes where needed and monitoring output quality. With its capability for gathering and assimilating data from numerous points, the computer can control operations almost instantaneously.

Other illustrations of how computers aid manufacturing processes include the following:

1. Under the control and direction of a computer at Polaroid, a roll of color film is sped through a large machine to be coated with a layer of dye no more than a few 10,000ths of an inch thick.

2. In a huge Phillip Morris warehouse, a computer directs an operatorless stacker-crane down an aisle to unload Marlboro cigarettes into an appropriate section. Before entering the warehouse, the computer accurately identifies the brand coming off the production line and decides the specific location to store it.

3. New carburetors designed for the 1975 General Motors automobiles were administered a battery of tests by a computer and automatically adjusted for performance against auto emission standards by computer-driven wrenches and screwdrivers.[11]

When the computer is tied to or linked with an ongoing production

---

[11] "Minicomputers That Run the Factory," *Business Week*, December 8, 1973, p. 68.

process such as those described above, the arrangement is said to be *on-line*, a term which refers to any arrangement or complex of equipment which is directly connected to the computer. Another characteristic of such systems is the *real-time* concept, which is associated with the length of time necessary for the computer to respond to an input. A real-time capability means that the computer can respond quickly enough to inputs so that human or machine actions will be affected. Such features are necessary in linking the computer into the operation and control of ongoing production processes. With these on-line, real-time features, the computer can play a significant role in coordinating manufacturing processes.

Until relatively recently, the computer has been used in controlling production operations only in areas such as chemical production and oil refining which entail large-volume processing. In these industries instruments are used to record data which are then input to a computer, which subsequently modifies or adjusts processes where necessary — as by controlling switches, valves, and so on.

A major reason why the computer has not been used until recently in other industries has been the cost factor. Just ten years ago it was difficult to find a computer system selling for less than $100,000. Only in extremely large-volume industries such as chemicals and oils could the computer's cost be justified.

As for the control of machinery on the factory floor, it was not until the 1960s that the concept of *direct numerical control* caught hold in manufacturing. Numerical control is a system which employs punched tape or some other automatic control mechanism to direct the operation of machines or machine systems. Most frequently, manufacturing machines that are computer controlled are lathes, boring machines, riveting machines, looms, and so on. It is clear how economies could be gained by having computers direct the operations of such machines.

Enter the Minicomputer

It is predicted by many that the minicomputer, contrasted with the large, expensive computers of the past, will bring another revolution in computer sales and usage. The minicomputer is thought to be the technological advance that will accelerate the introduction of computer applications in manufacturing environments.

Minicomputers — those small, low-cost, highly reliable, several-thousand-dollar machines — can handle tasks on the factory floor that were heretofore not thought of as computer applications. The economical minicomputer has various capabilities: (1) controlling other, larger machines, (2) directing the testing of products at intermediate production stages, (3) guiding the movement of materials and products through the factory, and (4) controlling conveyer belts that transfer raw materials and finished products to and from the production line.

Hierarchical Factory Computer Systems

The minicomputer, coupled with a new concept of employing it called the hierarchical concept, promises to alter the manufacturing function significantly. The *hierarchical concept* employs minicomputers that are programmed for simple tasks such as controlling a particular machine on the factory floor. This concept involves numer-

FIGURE 2–5
Hierarchy of Minicomputers at Work in a Factory

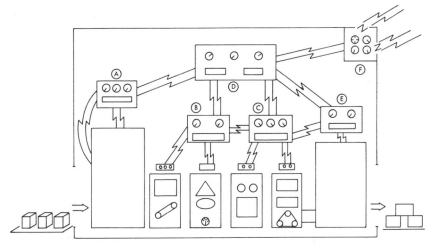

ous "minis," each controlling various other machines and simultaneously communicating critical operating data to higher level supervisory computers.[12] This is where the name "hierarchical" comes from — the minicomputer controls other machines, gathers data, and passes these data up to a higher level computer in the factory, and this computer in turn transfers the data to central factory computers which can then calculate production costs, store inventory data, perform production scheduling, and so on. In a hierarchical fashion, then, data move from the factory floor via minicomputers to a central location which may very possibly be linked to an organization's central financial data processing system.[13] This evolutionary building-block notion is the precursor of complete factory automation. Figure 2–5 illustrates how

---

[12] This hierarchical concept and an elaboration on the minicomputer can be found in "Minicomputers That Run the Factory," *Business Week*, December 8, 1973, pp. 68–78.

[13] Ibid., p. 70.

a hierarchy of minicomputers would control flows into the factory, processes inside the factory, and output flows from the factory.

A brief description of this process follows. A storage minicomputer (A) directs the movement of raw materials into the plant, checks for quality of raw materials, and moves them into the production process. The supervisory minicomputer (B) gets instructions (e.g., production schedules) from the central factory computer (D), which instructs mini B to carry out production in a certain way (e.g., production specifications). Another minicomputer (C) assumes a quality control function to assure that products are meeting quality standards. If so, products move on. If not, mini C instructs mini B and central computer D on adjustments necessary in the process. The warehouse minicomputers (E) supervises boxing, shipping, and so on. Central factory computer D sends assembled data to the main computer (F) at organizational headquarters, where data and information are used for managerial reporting and decision-making purposes.

The trend in the manufacturing environment is toward more computer applications. With developments such as the minicomputer and direct numerical control, opportunities for productivity and quality improvements seem to be not just a dream but a likely reality. Between the years 1972 and 1973, sales of minicomputers were up over 50 percent, and many of these went directly into manufacturing applications. IBM has predicted, for example, that manufacturers will spend in excess of $6.5 billion annually for plant automation equipment by the mid-1970s, as contrasted with expenditures of $1.6 billion in 1965—an increase of over 400 percent.[14] Minicomputer applications are one of the most significant developments since factory automation itself.

MARKETING APPLICATIONS

As managers have come to acknowledge that effective marketing is equated with profitable business, the computer has found its way into an increasing number of marketing applications. At one time marketing was narrowly conceived as the business function of selling. Today, however, marketing has expanded into a sophisticated body of knowledge which can be labeled *marketing management*, and this expansion is due in no small part to the advent of the computer and the attendant information technology.

As Figure 2–4 above showed, marketing applications have not grown at the pace of others such as manufacturing. Like manufacturing, and accounting, marketing applications began as rather routine mechanizations of paper work and other highly structured activities.

[14] Ibid., p. 69.

Early marketing uses of the computer were in such areas as customer order processing, inventory recordkeeping for finished goods, sales data compilation and reporting, and other such straightforward data processing tasks. The computer, therefore, was viewed as simply a glorified high-speed calculator and not as a powerful instrument for analysis and support of decision making.

The marketing function in business became more pervasive as the economy developed, with the result that typical marketing functions now include such specialized responsibilities as sales forecasting, advertising, sales analysis, test marketing, distribution, mail marketing, and marketing information systems. A brief examination of several of these areas reveals some of the opportunities for computer applications in marketing.

Sales Forecasting

Over the years numerous surveys and polls on computer applications have revealed that forecasting sales is a frequent computer use. In developing an overall marketing strategy, the manager needs reasonably accurate answers to such questions as: "What will sales for my respective products be over the next five years? Will they increase or decline? By what amounts?" Accurate and reliable forecasts of sales are necessary to underpin any efforts to plan for the future in the complex, dynamic environment of the 1970s and beyond.

It is from sales forecasts that most business decisions are derived: total company budget in dollars, funds available for advertisement, research and development prospects, production policies, capital equipment expenditures, plant expansion, personnel decisions, and so on. Since so many managerial decisions are contingent upon sales forecasts, the necessity for these forecasts, or estimates of future sales, to be accurate and up to date is obvious.

Before the computer, sales forecasting had been of necessity reduced to a rather elementary process. Managers did not have the capability (or the time) to sit down with their relatively slow-speed desk calculators and "grind out" information. Furthermore, their forecasting models had to be kept relatively simple. Sales forecasts were in aggregate form, yielding total sales but not necessarily sales on a product-by-product basis. They were also aggregate in terms of territory, not being broken down into specific sales territories. Indeed, it was possible for total forecasts to be accurate but figures for specific territories and specific products to be way off. This was not very comforting for a divisional manager in Houston who had on inventory a stockroom full of products, while the divisional manager in Nashville lost sales because he could not keep enough goods in stock to meet demand.

Though the computer did not solve all of management's problems in regards to sales forecasting, it went a long way toward improving accuracy in forecasting efforts. With its tremendous speed and prodigious capacity to digest millions of pieces of data and to systematically detect and analyze relationships between variables, the computer could provide greatly improved and more sophisticated sales forecasting. For example, with the computer it is now easy to employ statistical techniques such as time series analysis, exponential smoothing, correlation analysis, and regression analysis.

With the aid of powerful statistical tools such as these and the computer's capability to perform the requisite calculations, sales forecasting has become immeasurably more sophisticated. It is now possible to generate numerous detailed economic forecasts as elements of management plans for future organizational growth. Highly detailed, individual forecasts for hundreds of products, broken down into sales regions, now permit a kind of comprehensive planning which was not feasible prior to the computer.

Advertising Applications

Many marketers formerly believed that advertising is one of those "creative" areas that could not be affected by the computer. Experience has indicated that this is not so. Not only has the computer had an effect on the advertising function, but there is a potential for future payoffs.

One important area of application is in *media planning*, which refers to the determination of which advertising media to use to effect the optimal "bringing together" of advertisement and potential consumer. Appropriately designed computer-based information systems can make information such as media rates and availability more easily obtainable. This is one way the computer makes it possible to apply the scientific method to advertising decision making. Recent years have seen efforts to develop media selection models through techniques such as simulation and linear programming.[15]

Sales Analysis

Computers have been used extensively in recent years in *sales analysis*, the careful, systematic examination of a company's sales experience in a multitude of dimensions. Analyzing sales by such diverse characteristics as product line, salesmen, territories, cus-

---

[15]T. C. Taylor, *The Computer in Marketing* (chapters from *Sales Management Magazine*, 1970), p. 73. See also "A Status Report on Computers in Marketing," *ADP Newsletter*, April 1, 1974.

tomers, and time periods permits the marketing manager to exercise close control over operations. Real-time data make it possible for managers to keep track of how current sales performance figures compare with previous experience and stated goals, and thus their ability to respond to problems quickly is improved.

The computer's computational speed makes it possible in many instances for the decision maker to be given daily performance reports with data on the previous day's sales. Such timely updating of sales performance aids managers at various levels. Top management, for example, uses computer-generated information as the basis for decisions on deployment of resources. These strategic decisions determine such factors as the firm's product mix or what products ought to be emphasized. The sales analysis application has become extremely important in the past year or two as managers have had to scrutinize their product lines in relation to raw material shortages and the energy crunch.[16] Middle managers use sales analysis data for control purposes, as in identifying gaps between plans and operations, and lower level managers use it to improve service to selective customers or areas and to keep track of sales trends by product, area covered, salesman, and so on.

It has been suggested that the day will soon come when retail sales analysis will take place on an on-line, real-time basis.[17] For example, the proper coding of products and a tie-in between the cash register and a computerized data base will make it possible for marketers to receive instantaneous sales data indicating what product was sold, its price, its size (as in the case of a garment), where it was sold, and so on. Sales analysis at this sophisticated level will provide marketing managers with immediate knowledge of sales and inventories which will aid immeasurably in the planning and control of both the production function and the sales function.

One of the most innovative current applications of computers in marketing involves the use of portable computer terminals. Portable terminals, which are about the size of a typewriter and range in price from $2,600 to $3,800, permit the user to telephone a computer which may be miles away and gain instant access to its data. Salesmen for Hoffman-LaRoche, Inc., a pharmaceutical firm, carry terminals with them on sales calls to answer doctor's questions about new drugs. Batten, Barton, Durstine & Osborn, Inc. uses remote terminals to test new ad campaigns and marketing strategies as part of a computer modeling program. Other terminal users include firms such as General Motors, AT&T, and Kentucky Fried Chicken.[18]

---

[16] "The Squeeze on Product Mix," *Business Week*, January 5, 1974, pp. 50–55.

[17] Taylor, *Computer in Marketing*, p. 98.

[18] "Portable Computer Terminals," *Business Week*, August 31, 1974, p. 79.

OTHER BUSINESS APPLICATIONS

Though it would not be possible to enumerate and discuss all the business activities that are supported by the computer, we will briefly examine how a few industries have been revolutionized by its use.

Airlines Industry

Critical tasks in the airlines industry involve the planning and monitoring of flights. These functions have become highly complex with increases in the number of flights, the number of routes, and the speed of aircraft. Numerous factors affect each flight decision: wind, temperature, cloud cover, passenger loads, fuel availability, fuel consumption, and so on. In addition, these factors are subject to rapid, last-minute changes, all of which may ultimately have some bearing on the safety of passengers.

With computers, it is now possible to provide pilots and flight dispatchers with the up-to-the-minute information necessary to plan flights and monitor flight progress. Using real-time, on-line systems, it is possible to communicate flight plans to many different geographical regions so that the latest information can be displayed on

"THIS GENTLEMAN SAYS THAT HIS SEAT IS ALREADY TAKEN"

© Datamation

visual displays or teletypewriters. Plans can be changed without any significant delay in communicating information to those who need timely status reports.

Computers also have the capability of monitoring and controlling the actual progress of flights by comparing progress against planned flight programs and reporting discrepancies existing at several check-points. If notable variations exist, the computer can calculate a new flight plan which takes into consideration such variables as wind, fuel consumption rate, and so on, and the new flight plan can be simultaneously communicated to all points that need it. Computers also play a vital coordinating role in complex airlines reservation systems. Thus the computer has become an indispensable element in the airlines industry.

Travel Bureaus

Travel bureaus provide another interesting illustration of modern computer applications. The travel bureau's function of making vacation and travel arrangements entails numerous scheduling details — hotel accommodations, travel plans, rental car reservations, and so on. Reservations must be made, confirmations sent to customers, and billing done, often on one of many different price and payment plans. The innumerable details that must be handled in order to ensure customer satisfaction make the computer a natural in this area.

Stock Brokerage

The computer also has an indispensable role in the stock brokerage field today. The need for instantaneous transfer of information between the broker's main office, branch office, and stock exchanges is one illustration of why the computer is so vital in this area. Consider the following example of how brokers execute stock purchase orders. A stockbroker receives an order to buy 100 shares of XYZ Industries. If this order took place at a branch office, the order is then relayed to the brokerage's central communications headquarters, where it is checked for proper content and format and then stored. The order to buy is also relayed to the stock exchange floor, with a transmittal time of just a few seconds. After the order is executed, this information is communicated back to the computer center, where the purchase is compared with the original order. A confirmation order is then automatically sent back to the branch office where the order originated.

Hospital Administration

Two problems which concern hospital administrators in both public and private hospitals today include rising administrative costs

FIGURE 2–6
Monitoring a Doctor's Service Report in a Hospital Setting

Courtesy of Ampex

and improvement in the efficiency of personnel and facilities. Computerized systems have been developed to facilitate hospital administrative cost control. These systems are designed to provide more efficient methods of accounting, billing, processing medical reports, reducing admission time, and generally improving the efficiency of administrative operations. Figure 2–6 illustrates the monitoring of a doctor's service report via the computer.

Hotel-Motel Industry

Until recently, the vast hotel-motel industry for the most part has resisted the intrusion of the computer into its operations. The computer manufacturers, however, can offer the world market of over 80,000 hotels help with their characteristic problems of confused reservation lists, inaccurate charges, congested reservation lines, and checkout bottlenecks.[19]

An increasing number of hotel and motel firms (such as Holiday Inns, Howard Johnson's, Sheraton) are adopting contemporary data processing systems to deal with these typical industry problems. One computer manufacturer, Motorola, has teamed up with Holiday Inns to design a minicomputer developed specifically for the hotel industry, with special terminals and programs for the four major hotel management functions: reservations, guest accounting, room control, and housekeeping scheduling. The system costs about $100,000 per hotel.

One of the interesting features of this computer system (called Inn-Scan) is a housekeeping subsystem. With this subsystem, each cleaning maid carries a small black box (called Maidaid) which is used in conjunction with the room telephone. When the computer's phone number is dialed, the box transmits a signal to the computer to identify which room the maid is in, and after the room has been cleaned it signals the computer that the room is ready for occupancy. Thus the hotel is able to keep up-to-the-minute records on room availability. The computerized system also facilitates the room check-in and check-out procedure, ordinarily a time-consuming, cumbersome procedure.

Other experiments are taking place with hotel computerization. A small company, four-year-old Mobydata, has a $40,000–$50,000 system in a Howard Johnson's motel and five systems going into Sheraton Hotels in the East. Electronic Engineering Company of California is designing systems in the $200,000 range for larger hotels such as the Sheraton Waikiki in Hawaii and a 2,100-room hotel in Las Vegas. It is not necessary, however, to have an in-house system installed. NCR has a new system called HOST which provides remote computer services to hotels for approximately 26 cents per room per day.[20] Electronic advancements such as these have the potential for revolutionizing the hotel-motel market in the United States and abroad.

Heat Generation

A unique use of the computer which illustrates the serendipity that characterizes modern business activity was discovered recently. The discovery involved putting the heat that the computer emits to use in heating a building. In Hartford, Connecticut, Hartford Insurance Group designed its new building to utilize the computer's heat-

---

[19] "Doing the Chores for Hotels," *Business Week*, September 15, 1973, p. 212.
[20] Ibid., p. 212.

generating characteristic in this way.[21] Though the computer is not usually thought of as a furnace, the owners of this building capitalized on otherwise wasted energy and installed a heat recovery system that is designed to heat the building with a savings equivalent to about 81,000 gallons of oil during its first year of operation in 1975.

Though computers today generate far less heat than they did in the days of vacuum tubes, the larger computers do emit a considerable number of BTUs. The system is basically simple. Hot air generated by the computer's operation will heat water which in turn will pass through a system of pipes and coils, where fans will blow the heated air through the building. It should be pointed out, of course, that in order to make heating of this kind practical, a data processing center must occupy a sizable portion of the building space (e.g., 10 percent), and the computers must operate around the clock. Experiments such as these will be watched closely by other major users of computers, especially in the energy-short conditions of today.

ASSIGNMENTS

2-1. Discuss the reasons underlying the rapid growth in the use of computers in business organizations.

2-2. Discuss the relationship between the increased use of the computer and the increased usefulness of the management sciences.

2-3. What is meant by computer simulation? How can simulations of the accounting and finance functions be useful to management?

2-4. Discuss the risks and opportunities for fraud in a computerized accounting system. What safeguards or controls can be employed to control these occurrences?

2-5. Suggest some advantages and disadvantages of EFTS.

2-6. Discuss the major advantages and disadvantages of the minicomputer. Speculate as to possible uses of the minicomputer in the future.

2-7. Explain the "hierarchical concept" as it relates to computer systems.

2-8. How has the computer aided the marketing function? Do some research on your own to learn of some possible applications not mentioned in the book.

2-9. How have the airlines utilized computer systems? What are some of the serious risks inherent in their applications?

---

[21] "Where Computers Supply the Heat," *Business Week*, January 5, 1974, pp. 23–24.

2-10. Contact a local organization that has a computer facility and discuss with the data processing manager the applications for which its system is being used. Prepare a report based upon your conversation.

REFERENCES

Books

Avery, L., Ron Coverson, John Humphries, and Brian Meek (eds.) *Computers and the Year 2000*. Manchester: NCC Publications, 1972.

Brikle, John and Ronald Yearsley (eds.) *Computer Applications in Management*. Princeton, N.J.: Brandon/Systems Press, 1970.

Rothman, Stanley and Charles Mosmann *Computers and Society*. Chicago: Science Research Associates, 1972.

Smith, Samuel V., R. H. Brien, and J. E. Stafford (eds.) *Readings in Marketing Information Systems*. Boston: Houghton Mifflin Co., 1968.

Stehlin, Kurt R. *Computers and You*. New York: World Publishing Co., 1972.

Sturt, Humphrey and Ronald Yearsley (eds.) *Computers for Management*. New York: American Elsevier Publishing Co., 1969.

Taylor, Thayer C. *The Computer in Marketing*. Sales Management, Inc., 1970.

Articles

Automatic Data Processing Newsletter, vol. 16, No. 7 (April 3, 1972), p. 3.

"Doing the Chores for Hotels," *Business Week*, September 15, 1973, p. 212.

Gibson, C. F. and R. L. Nolan "Managing the Four Stages of EDP Growth." *Harvard Business Review*, January–February 1974, pp. 76–88.

Longbrake, W. A. "Computers and the Cost of Producing Banking Services." *Journal of Bank Research*, Autumn 1973, pp. 194–99.

"Minicomputers That Run the Factory." *Business Week*, December 8, 1973, pp. 68–78.

O'Brien, J. A. "Bank Computer Services: The State of the Art." *The Banker's Magazine*, Summer 1971, pp. 51–56.

"The Quickened Pace of Electronic Banking." *Business Week*, September 15, 1973, p. 116.

Reistad, D. L. "Beyond the Credit Card." *The Banker's Magazine*, Spring 1971, pp. 96–100.

Taylor, T. C. "The Computer in Marketing." *Sales Management Magazine*, 1970, p. 73.

"Where Computers Supply the Heat." *Business Week*, January 5, 1974, pp. 23–24.

The Abacus

Early Mechanical Calculators
Pascal's Calculating Device, The Leibnitz Calculating
Machine

The Jacquard Loom

Babbage's Difference and Analytical Engines

Hollerith's Punched Card Machine

The MARK I Computer

The ENIAC Computer

Von Neumann's Contributions

Commercially Available Computers
The UNIVAC I, The ILLIAC IV

Other Computer Developments

Computer Generations

Concluding Remarks

Assignments

References

Chapter 3 suggests the historical aspects of development of the computer. The intention is to characterize the evolving nature of the computer and to give due credit to pioneers whose contributions served as underpinnings to the concept of computers as we know it today.

3

The Historical Evolution of Computers

Although the computer as we know it today is largely a mid-20th-century phenomenon, a comprehensive history of the computer and computing devices must go back several centuries. Counting and computing aids arose as the need to count and to quantify became more sophisticated. A chronology of computer development could easily be considered part of a comprehensive history of counting, an activity in which man has been engaged and fascinated with for thousands of years. However, our discussion of the computer's development will be limited to what might be termed landmark accomplishments which directly contributed to, or played a major role in, the development of modern computing devices. While the possibility exists that we may not mention certain people or accomplishments that others might, we expect this chapter to give you a realistic appreciation of how the computer got where it is today.

The beginnings of computer development were slow, but the pace has quickened in modern times. This chapter will review evolutionary stages in the computer's emergence and then examine the various generations of computers as they have been developed. Figure 3–1 is presented to aid in the conceptualization of the developments to be discussed. This figure, "Landmarks in the History of Computer Development," relates the developments to a time continuum ranging from the abacus, which dates back to before Christ, to the ILLIAC IV of the 1970s.

THE ABACUS

One of the earliest counting devices was the abacus. Evidence exists that this device was developed independently by both the Chinese and the Greeks sometime between 1000 and 300 B.C. The

51

FIGURE 3–1
Landmarks in the History of Computer Development

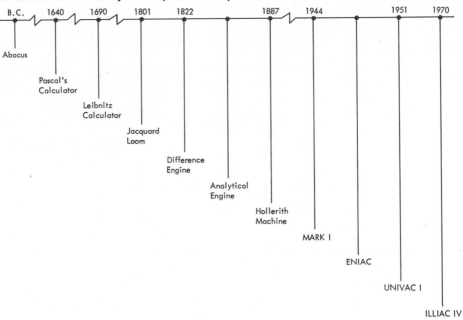

FIGURE 3–2
The Abacus

Courtesy of IBM

abacus is basically a configuration of beads strung on rods set parallel in a frame. In counting with an abacus, the beads in the upper portion of the frame count as five each and those in the bottom portion as one each. To register a number, beads are moved towards the center horizontal counting bar.

Although the abacus has not been widely used in the United States, some Chinese merchants still use it today for counting purposes. The abacus has been an important computational aid in Oriental countries for thousands of years, and a talented abacus operator can perform many computations at speeds comparable to those attained by skillful calculating machine operators. Figure 3–2 illustrates the ancient abacus.

EARLY MECHANICAL CALCULATORS

Pascal's Calculating Device

It was not until the 17th century that significant development in calculating aids took place. Around 1640–42, Blaise Pascal, a young French mathematician, developed a simple adding machine to aid him in the computational work he did for his father, who operated a tax office.

Pascal's device, which is illustrated in Figure 3–3, had a series of toothed wheels. On each of the wheels there were teeth representing the digits from 0 through 9. When a wheel was rotated past 9, a small projection on the wheel caused the next wheel to rotate automatically. Thus, as one wheel turned past 9, it exchanged its ten teeth for one

FIGURE 3–3
Pascal's Calculator

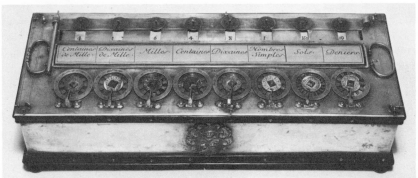

Courtesy of IBM

tooth on the next wheel. It was this "tens carrying" feature that made the Pascal machine so unique for its time.

The Leibnitz Calculating Machine

Around 1690, the German mathematician and philosopher Gottfried Leibnitz invented a machine which was patterned after and improved upon Pascal's calculating device. Its distinguishing characteristic was that it could perform multiplication and division as well as addition. Like Pascal's machine, however, the Leibnitz calculator was not completely reliable.

Many improvements were made over the years on the landmark inventions of Pascal and Leibnitz. In 1870, for example, Frank Baldwin developed a calculating machine aimed at improving the reliability of the earlier devices. In almost all cases, however, these early computing machines were not practical. Manufacture of a mechanical instrument with moving parts created many problems with which the crude processes of the time could not cope. Nevertheless, these machines formed the foundations for the development of more advanced calculating devices.

The efforts of Pascal and Leibnitz were necessary formulations in the development of the modern keyboard adding machine. Although the modern computer owes something to these developments, other lines of advancement were emerging which were different from the mechanics of the early calculating devices. Specifically, the contributions of Joseph Jacquard and Charles Babbage were providing developments which would eventually play a significant role in the coming computer revolution.

THE JACQUARD LOOM

An accurate history of the digital computer must include mention of other developments that had a great impact on its eventual appearance. Such a development was the Jacquard loom (see Figure 3–4). Joseph Jacquard was a Frenchman who by 1801 had developed and patented an automatic weaving loom with an operating characteristic that would prove to be extremely valuable to computers. This characteristic was the utilization of punched card instructions to control the patterns which were woven into cloth.

The weaving of patterns by hand had been an exceedingly slow and tedious process which involved the efforts of at least two men and usually required several weeks just to set up the operation. The weaving process is basically a task of intermixing cross threads with lengthwise threads in a prescribed fashion so that the output is a specific pattern or design on the cloth.

FIGURE 3–4
Jacquard's Loom

Courtesy of IBM

Jacquard's loom automated the production of cloth designs through the use of punched card instructions. By storing the instructions for a particular pattern on a set of cards, the loom was able to duplicate the pattern exactly at any time. In the operation of the loom punched card instructions were inserted; if a hole appeared on the card the loom was instructed to lift a thread, and if no hole appeared the loom would depress the thread, thus creating the desired weave pattern on the cloth. Jacquard's major contribution was the notion of inscribing instructions on cards through the use of punched holes. It might be said that the Jacquard concept preceded by over 100 years the zero-one, yes-no, off-on, binary system of the modern digital computer.

BABBAGE'S DIFFERENCE AND ANALYTICAL ENGINES

The contributions of the English mathematician Charles Babbage are significant in the evolution of thought and technology which culminated in the modern computer. Babbage's accomplishments and scientific output were phenomenal, and he was recognized as a genius by his contemporaries. His contributions to computer development were first his difference engine and later his analytical engine.

Babbage developed and around 1822 demonstrated the use of the difference engine, a mechanical calculating device constructed for the purpose of creating numerical tables. Today students of business and science take such mathematical tables for granted, but during Babbage's day this was not the case. Many countries went to great expense to commission mathematicians to create voluminous mathematical tables for publication.

The difference engine (shown in Figure 3–5) was a highly specialized machine designed solely for the automatic computation of mathematical tables. While developing this engine, however, Babbage saw visions of a machine with an even greater calculating capability. He had in mind more of a general-purpose calculating machine, one whose capacity, diversity, and capability would far surpass his basic difference engine.

After much effort Babbage designed the analytical engine, a com-

FIGURE 3–5
Babbage's Difference Engine

Courtesy of IBM

FIGURE 3-6
Babbage's Analytical Engine

Courtesy of IBM

puting machine with many of the same fundamental features as today's modern computers. Babbage's computer had a store or memory device, a mill or arithmetic device, a punched card input system (fashioned after the Jacquard loom punched card idea), and an external memory store. Although Babbage may have borrowed Jacquard's idea regarding punched card instructions, he adapted the punched cards to the storage of data as well as guidance of the engine's operations.

Like the difference engine, however, the analytical engine was never produced commercially. Not only did it have reliability problems, but the embryonic machine manufacturing industry of the 1820s did not yet have the capability of producing the precise, complex mechanical parts that were necessary for the engine's construction and reproduction. A portion of Babbage's analytical engine is illustrated in Figure 3–6.

Babbage's contributions were significant, but they did not induce further development of mechanical computing devices until quite a few years later. Babbage died in 1871,[1] approximately 40 years after he first conceived his analytical engine. It would not be until well into the 20th century that further significant developments would be made in automatic computing devices. The gap between his efforts and the later emergence of the Harvard MARK I computer in the 1930s gives some indication of the anachronistic genius of Charles Babbage.

HOLLERITH'S PUNCHED CARD MACHINE

Herman Hollerith, the inventor of the earliest practical punched card tabulating machine, had possibly read of the efforts of Babbage and the developments of Jacquard. Although it was Jacquard who first demonstrated the potential of punched cards for instructing

FIGURE 3–7
Hollerith Electrical Tabulator

Courtesy of IBM

---

[1] Daniel A. Wren, *The Evolution of Management Thought* (New York: Ronald Press, 1972), pp. 68–69.

FIGURE 3-8
Hollerith's Fame in 1890

Courtesy of IBM

machines, Hollerith must be given credit for utilizing a punched card approach for large-scale counting purposes.

Hollerith was hired by the U.S. Census Bureau for a special project aimed at developing a more sophisticated technique for census taking. His machine-readable card approach and a series of related equipment which employed machine-readable cards were developed around 1887. Hollerith's equipment is shown in Figure 3–7 on page 58.

The counting procedure essentially involved the use of encoding data onto cards through the use of punched holes. After the data had been entered onto the cards, it could be stored and used again at a later time. This in itself was an advance over previous census-taking methods. With the Hollerith approach, the tabulating time was only a fraction of that required previously, and the 1890 census was completed in roughly two and one-half years, less than one third the time previously required. Figure 3–8 on page 59 shows how Hollerith was honored by *Scientific American* in 1890.

It was in 1886 that Hollerith founded the Tabulating Machine Company for purposes of commercially manufacturing and distributing his invention. Years later his company would merge with others to become what is known today as the International Business Machines Corporation (IBM).

Hollerith's punched card system has evolved into punched card approaches to data processing which have widespread usage in business, education, and government. Though his punched card invention had little to do directly with computers and calculating machines, the approach created an effective input in the development of computing machines. It is for this significant contribution that Hollerith holds a place in the history of computer development.

THE MARK I COMPUTER

The first digital computer, the MARK I (Figure 3–9), was designed and built under the direction of Harvard professor Howard Aiken, working closely with IBM engineers. They began work in 1937, and it is interesting to note that the MARK I was almost completed before Aiken learned of the earlier work of Charles Babbage. Such an information and communications breakdown surely inhibited the emergence of computing devices during the early developmental days.

The MARK I, completed in 1944, is considered to be the first digital computer. The internal operations of the machine were controlled automatically with electromagnetic relays, and the counters were mechanical devices. Consequently, the MARK I could not be considered an *electronic* computer but rather an *electromechanical* one. Nevertheless, the computer handled automatic computations

FIGURE 3–9
MARK I Computer

Courtesy of IBM

after the program had been set up and the input data had been supplied. The MARK I is significant because it was the first automatic sequence-controlled calculating machine that could perform an extended series of arithmetic and logic operations without human intervention, beyond the initial starting of the machine.

Something was lacking, however. Greater speed was needed, and the MARK I could not supply this capability. The need would not remain unfulfilled, however, because several years later J. Presper Eckert, Jr., and John W. Mauchly, along with several colleagues, would form a computer company (later to be a division of Sperry Rand Corporation) which would build a completely electronic digital computer, the ENIAC.

THE ENIAC COMPUTER

The decade from the early 1940s to the early 1950s was a revolutionary and dynamic period for computer progress and advancement in the United States. This dynamism must be attributed in part to the pressing demands of World War II and in part to the initiative and drive of the computer's developers. The ENIAC (*Electronic Numerical Integrator And Calculator*) was originally conceived as a machine whose purpose would be the computation and compilation of ballistics tables for the military, and hence it was supported by funds provided by the U.S. Army. Because it was designed for the specific purpose of creating tables, the ENIAC did not have general-purpose capabilities.

Through its use of electronic pulses, the ENIAC improved upon the MARK I computer considerably. Compared with any previous electromechanical machine, the ENIAC could process data in minutes rather than the hours required by earlier machines. The ENIAC

FIGURE 3–10
The ENIAC

Courtesy of Sperry Rand Corporation

(Figure 3–10) was an extremely large, space-consuming computer, but nevertheless it added the speed that was to be expected from a device its size. The dominant feature of the ENIAC was its electronic nature, a characteristic which gave it a primary place in the history of computers. With the ENIAC, the computer revolution was well underway.

While the ENIAC's role in the evolution of computers is established, a 1974 court case threw conventional wisdom about its development and origin into disrepute. Eckert and Mauchly built the machine, but a Federal District Court judge has ruled that "Eckert and Mauchly did not themselves *first invent* the automatic electronic digital computer, but instead derived that subject matter from one Dr. John Vincent Atanasoff" (emphasis added). This finding is significant because up to this time Eckert and Mauchly were, as *Datamation* magazine put it, "the high priests of electronic digital computer invention."[2]

---

[2] "Will the Inventor of the First Digital Computer Please Stand Up?" *Datamation*, February 1974, pp. 84, 88–90.

Atanasoff was a professor at Iowa State College in Ames, Iowa, from 1930 to 1942, during which time he did most of his significant work on the digital computer. The court case revealed that Eckert and Mauchly's development of the ENIAC was based upon concepts that had been originated by Atanasoff. None of the credit might have come to Atanasoff if it were not for the patent suit filed by Sperry Rand against Honeywell, Inc., charging that Honeywell had infringed upon Eckert and Mauchly's patent for the ENIAC. It is somewhat ironic that the suit backfired, resulting in the ruling that Sperry Rand's ENIAC patent was invalid.

VON NEUMANN'S CONTRIBUTIONS

A noted mathematician, John von Neumann, became familiar with the work of Eckert and Mauchly during a stay at the University of Pennsylvania. After becoming interested in the computer work in progress and its potential for numerical analysis, Von Neumann did some writing which described the computer logic being developed at that time.

In a 1946 paper written in collaboration with two others, Von Neumann suggested that *binary numbering systems* be used in computers and that *instructions* for computers, in addition to data, could be stored internally by coding them in numerical form. Though these concepts could not be worked into the ENIAC because of their late development, they were incorporated into the EDVAC (*Elec*tronic *Discrete Variable Automatic Computer*), which was being worked on during the same time. The EDVAC was not completed until 1952, but it became the prototype of the stored-program computer (i.e., with operation instructions internally stored) in the United States.

COMMERCIALLY AVAILABLE COMPUTERS

The UNIVAC I

In the middle to late 1940s, electronic computers of various sizes, types, and capabilities began to appear. The computers and devices we have discussed thus far were for the most part one-of-a-kind ventures which were designed for specific purposes and funded by various private and governmental agencies. From the commercial standpoint, however, no efforts at manufacturing and sale of computing devices had been apparent.

The first commercially available electronic computer is generally considered to be the UNIVAC I (*UNIV*ersal *A*utomatic *C*omputer). It was developed also by Eckert and Mauchly and put into use in

FIGURE 3–11
UNIVAC I

Courtesy of Sperry Rand Corporation

1951 at the Census Bureau. The Eckert-Mauchly company later became a part of Remington Rand, constituting the Remington Rand Univac Division of the Sperry Rand Corporation.

The UNIVAC I (Figure 3–11) had several differentiating characteristics. One of its most distinctive and practical features was its capability for processing alphabetic as well as numeric data. The programs for the UNIVAC were also designed to utilize records stored on magnetic tape rather than the usual punched Hollerith-type cards.

The ILLIAC IV

Of the numerous commercial computers that have appeared since the UNIVAC, one of the most notable is the ILLIAC IV, the $30 million supercomputer which is largely the brainchild of Professor Daniel L. Slotnick of the University of Illinois. Designed in the late 1960s and built by Burroughs Corporation, the ILLIAC IV is believed to be the most powerful computer in existence. It is essentially 64 individual computers wired into a gridlike array and is capable of executing 150 million instructions per second.[3]

The ILLIAC IV is so huge and powerful that it requires a separate large-scale computer to direct its input and output. Eventually, it is

---

[3] "Illiac IV Is the Fastest Ever," *Business Week*, September 8, 1973, p. 74 ff.

estimated, it will be operating 21 hours per day and will keep 200–300 programmers busy three shifts a day. To demonstrate that supercomputers like the ILLIAC know no bounds in terms of size, Slotnick's original design for the computer called for 256 individual central processors, a computational facility about equal to the combined capacity of all the computers in the world at that time. High costs plus criticism from other computer makers cut the project's size down to 64 parallel processors.[4]

OTHER COMPUTER DEVELOPMENTS

In contrast to supercomputers such as the ILLIAC IV, one of the more recent computer developments has been the emergence of small, low-priced computers, which have been dubbed "minicomputers" (see Figure 3–12). Fast-changing technology in the computer field, coupled with the desire to apply computer power to numerous new applications, has created a trend to minicomputers which is gaining momentum in the 1970s.

FIGURE 3–12
PDP–8/E Minicomputer

Courtesy of Digital Equipment

---

[4] Ibid., p. 78.

Because minicomputers are small and low in cost, they can be utilized economically in areas that were previously ruled out because of size or cost. Minicomputers first appeared in the 1960s and have been rapidly accepted since. The $2,000 minicomputer of today is thought to be more reliable, powerful, and easier to use than the $100,000 machines of a decade ago. In addition, minicomputers can be applied to single tasks and can operate without the direction of large, centrally controlled machines.[5]

The main technological advance which has permitted the economical development of minis is the development of semiconductor integrated circuitry. It is estimated that more than $700 million worth of minicomputers were shipped in 1973, up 50 percent from 1972, and the nation's top 500 manufacturers disclosed in a survey that they anticipate doubling their use of minicomputers over the next several years. Some experts are suggesting that the minicomputer is the most powerful single tool for productivity improvement in the next decade.[6] And sales growth projections anticipate an increase exceeding 20 percent per year through 1977, as compared to 7 to 10 percent per year growth in general-purpose computer sales for the same period.[7] Chapter 2 discussed some of the special applications of the minicomputer which have emerged in recent years.

Before the dust has settled on the minicomputer's emergence, microcomputers have also been developed. The appearance of microcomputers in 1972 illustrates the computer industry's characterization of rapid product growth and technological change, a trend which seems to exhibit no signs of slowing down. In the microcomputer, a single, tiny semiconductor chip contains all the necessary arithmetic/logic unit circuitry.[8]

Most minicomputer manufacturers first scoffed at the idea of the microprocessor chip, but it was rapidly accepted by a number of users and the appearance of a number of more sophisticated, later generation versions has brought much attention to the industry. Thus in the period of over a decade and a half since the first transistorized models were developed, computers have been rapidly getting less expensive and smaller. The products that have benefited from microcomputer technology are just appearing on the market, but it is anticipated that hundreds of applications beyond those handled by regular computers will be possible.

---

[5] "Minicomputers That Run the Factory," *Business Week*, December 8, 1973, p. 69.

[6] Ibid., p. 69.

[7] "Minicomputer Sales Turning Skyward," *Computer Digest*, vol. 8, no. 10 (October 1973), p. 3.

[8] "Microcomputers Throw the Industry Off Balance," *Business Week*, March 16, 1974, p. 56.

The "computer on a chip" makes available computing power of a capacity heretofore unanticipated. Applications range from communications terminals, to scientific instruments, to pinball machines. Though the low-cost technology is still developing, already companies are using it in such applications as automobile wheel alignment devices, check processors, blood analyzers, electronic cash register terminals, and other areas that previously could not be handled by larger, more costly computing equipment.[9] The intriguing potential of minicomputers and microcomputers, and advances to come, make the computer industry an exciting one to watch in the years ahead.

'WE'VE LOST THE MAIN PROCESSING UNIT'

© *Datamation* ®

COMPUTER GENERATIONS

Significant progress has been made in the technological advancement of computers from their late 1940 and early 1950 beginnings to the ILLIAC IV and the minicomputers. In terms of technological change, the computer evolved through three distinguishable phases or generations. The *first generation* of computers, which included

---

[9] "Microcomputers Aim at a Huge Market," *Business Week*, May 12, 1973, pp. 180–81.

the early machines such as the ENIAC and the IBM 650, was characterized by the use of *vacuum tubes* for internal operations. These tubes generated considerable heat, making it necessary to place them in air-conditioned rooms, and they required massive space availability. The computers themselves were of mammoth size; the ENIAC, for example, weighed approximately 30 tons. The size of first-generation computers and their air-conditioning requirements created many problems in the areas of maintenance and repair.

Though these first-generation machines were superior to their earlier electromechanical counterparts, they did not compare with the capabilities of later computers. They possessed limited main storage capacity, were punched card oriented, even for files, and had slow input/output (I/O) time. The input time refers to the length of time it takes for data and programs to be read into the machine before processing takes place, and the output time refers to the length of time it takes to receive output from the machine once processing is completed. These machines mostly used symbolic language programming and had little or no applications software.

The *second generation* of computers evolved in the late 1950s. The most significant improvement of these second-generation machines was the substitution of *solid-state components* for the awkward, space-consuming vacuum tubes used in earlier computers. Tiny transistors and diodes used in the second-generation computers greatly reduced the size and space requirements of the computer hardware. As a result of the introduction of these smaller parts, less power was required to operate the machines, and greater reliability could be introduced into the system. Consequently, these second-generation computers were more compact in size, generated

FIGURE 3–13
A Second-Generation Computer

Courtesy of Sperry Rand Corporation

less heat, and had simplified maintenance and repair requirements. (See Figure 3–13.)

Second-generation computers possessed increased computational speeds, increased main storage capacity, and faster I/O. In addition, they made it possible to use tape files (rather than punched cards) and procedure-oriented programming languages (FORTRAN, COBOL), and they were accompanied by the beginnings of utility software (sort/merge, tape-print).

Most computers in use today are members of a *third-generation* computer technology. Third-generation computers have substituted microelectronic or *integrated circuits* for the transistors of second-generation equipment. Microscopic-sized integrated circuits have the capabilities of transistors which are hundreds of times larger in size. In addition, a miniature integrated circuit can do the same work as the first-generation tubes, which are thousands of times larger. Each of the circuits contains over 150 electronic components, and yet they are many times smaller than an ordinary paper clip.

The principal advantages of the miniature integrated circuit are small size, increased speed, and improved performance. Modern computers are hundreds of times faster than their early 1950 counterparts. Whereas computer speed was initially measured in *milliseconds* (thousandths of a second), second-generation computer speed was measured in *microseconds* (millionths of a second), and current third-generation speed can sometimes be expressed in *nanoseconds* (billionths of a second).

In addition to more computational speed and greater storage capacity, third-generation machines have faster and more versatile I/O. They also employ the use of disk and drum files. The third generation is characterized by advanced utility software (early database management systems), packaged applications software, and the beginnings of time-sharing. Figure 3–14 illustrates a third-generation computer system.

A *fourth generation* in the computer industry is still evolving, and there is evidence that it will gain maturity during the 1970s. Indications are that the fourth generation will evolve gradually rather than appearing at a discrete point in time as characterized, for example, by the transition from first- to second-generation computers. Though IBM does not call its IBM System/370 series a fourth-generation computer (see Figure 3–15), many do consider it at least a third-and-a-half-generation computer because of its advanced characteristics.

There is some debate as to the characteristics of this forthcoming generation, but some of its distinguishing features have been suggested. For example, new computer systems are likely to employ large-scale integrated circuitry, nanosecond execution speeds, and

FIGURE 3–14
Third-Generation Computer System

Courtesy of IBM

billion-bit memories. In addition, future generations of systems will probably stress more optimal communication capabilities designed to facilitate user-machine interfaces.

The fourth generation of computers will be easier to use by the average businessman, with individual video display units becoming commonplace. The new generation, therefore, will stress facility of use and application. English language and applications-oriented programs will increasingly become available for widespread use as the generation matures. In addition, since breakdowns will be very costly, redundant system features which will be capable of continuing processing after a partial failure will become available. Table 3–1 summarizes some of the dominant aspects of the evolution of computer generations.

FIGURE 3–15
The IBM System/370

Courtesy of IBM

TABLE 3–1
The Computer Generations

Generation	Approximate Dates	Principal Characteristics
First generation	Early 1950s to late 1950s	Use of vacuum tubes for internal operations Heat and size problems Large maintenance requirements Limited main storage capacity Punched card oriented (even for files) Slow I/O Mostly symbolic language programming Little or no applications software Example: IBM 650
Second generation	Late 1950s to Mid 1960s	Use of solid-state components (transistors and diodes) Greatly reduced size Increased speed Greater reliability Less heat Increased main storage capacity Faster I/O Use of tape files Procedure-oriented programming languages (FORTRAN, COBOL, etc.) Beginnings of utility software Example: IBM 1401
Third generation	1964 to Present	Use of integrated circuitry Smaller size Greater speed, reliability, performance, versatility Faster and more versatile I/O Use of disk and drum files Packaged applications software and advanced software Beginnings of time-sharing Example: IBM 360
Evolving fourth generation	Early 1970s to present	Use of large-scale circuitry Increased speed, storage capacity Ease of use through user interface Faster file devices More applications software Increased use of time-sharing Widespread use of minicomputers and microcomputers

CONCLUDING REMARKS

It is far easier to look back at the historical development of computing devices prior to the 20th century than to depict accurately what has happened since the 1940s and 1950s. Indeed it is far easier to examine the forties and fifties than it is the sixties and seventies.

The exponential pace of technological advancement in computing equipment is staggering.

The computer revolution has been so pervasive that it is difficult to find an area of life that has been left untouched by these machines. The pace of change is so rapid that it is not possible to remain up-to-date merely by reading books, which can become outdated soon after they are published. The accelerating advancement of recent years can only be monitored by daily attention to current events. However, it is hoped that the outline of the development of the computer in this chapter has given you an appreciation of the advances in knowledge and equipment that have occurred. You will doubtless be faced with others as you take on a position in business, government, education, or some other field.

ASSIGNMENTS

3-1. What is the significance of Pascal's calculator in the evolution of computers? The Leibnitz calculating machine? The Jacquard loom?

3-2. Differentiate between Babbage's difference engine and his analytical engine.

3-3. How significant are the contributions of Herman Hollerith to the evolution of the modern computer?

3-4. Distinguish between the MARK I computer and the ENIAC computer. Between the ENIAC and the UNIVAC I.

3-5. What were the major contributions of Von Neumann to the development of computers?

3-6. Do research on the contributions of John V. Atanasoff. Why is it only recently that he is receiving credit for the work he did on computers during the 1930s?

3-7. Outline the generations of computers and their distinguishing characteristics.

3-8. Characterize the differences between minicomputers and microcomputers. What applications can you anticipate that will be possible with mini and micro technological advances?

REFERENCES

Books

Bernstein, Jeremy   *The Analytical Engine: Computers—Past, Present and Future.* New York: Random House, 1963.

Bowden, B. V.   *Faster than Thought.* New York: Pitman Publishing Corp., 1953.

Eckert, W. J. and Rebecca Jones   *Faster, Faster: a Simple Description of a Giant Electronic Calculator and the Problems It Solves.* New York: McGraw-Hill Book Co., 1955.

Goldstine, H. H.   *The Computer from Pascal to von Neumann.* Princeton, N.J.: Princeton University Press, 1972.

Gruenberger, Fred (ed.)   *Expanding Use of Computers in the 70s: Markets, Needs, Technology.* Englewood Cliffs, N.J.: Prentice-Hall, 1971.

Hartman, Alvin J.   *The International Computer Industry: Innovation and Comparative Advantage.* Cambridge, Mass.: Harvard University Press, 1971.

Martin, James T. and A. R. D. Norman   *The Computerized Society: An Appraisal of the Impact of Computers on Society over the Next Fifteen Years.* Englewood Cliffs, N.J.: Prentice-Hall, 1970.

Montagu, Ashley and Samuel S. Snyder   *Man and the Computer.* Philadelphia: Auerback Publishers, 1972.

Mosely, Maboth   *Irascible Genius.* London: Hutchinson of London, 1964.

Nikolaieff, George A. (ed.)   *Computers and Society.* New York: H. W. Wilson Co., 1970.

Rosenberg, J. M.   *The Computer Prophets.* New York: Macmillan Co., 1969.

Thomas, Shirley   *Computers: Their History, Present Applications and Future.* New York: Holt, Rinehart, & Winston, 1965.

Articles

Burke, A. W., H. H. Goldstine, and John von Neumann   "Preliminary Discussion of the Design of an Electronic Computer." *Datamation*, September 1962, pp. 24–31 and October 1962, pp. 36–41.

"Illiac IV Is the Fastest Ever." *Business Week*, September 8, 1973, pp. 74, 78.

"Making Management Sense Out of Minicomputers." *Automatic Data Processing Newsletter*, vol. 16, No. 9 (May 1, 1972).

Rhea, J.   "Industry Moving into Fourth Generation." *Computer Digest*, October 1968.

Smith, W. D.   "Fourth Generation Crowds Adolescent Third." *Computer Digest*, December 1968.

"Will the Inventor of the First Digital Computer Please Stand Up?" *Datamation*, February 1974, pp. 84, 88–90.

Withington, F. G.   "Five Generations of Computers." *Harvard Business Review*, July–August 1974, pp. 99–108.

Storage Facilities

An Overview of the Storage Functions, The Binary Digit, Character Representation, Addresses, Storing Instructions, Arithmetic/Logic and Control Unit Registers

Circuitry for Computations in the Arithmetic/Logic Unit
Secondary Storage Facilities

Punched Cards, Magnetic Tape, Paper Tape, Magnetic Disks, Magnetic Drums, Data Cells, A Comparison of Storage Media

Operating Systems

The Controlling Function, The Facilitating Function

Future Trends

Assignments

References

This is the one chapter that gets down to the "bits and bytes" level of the computer. It is a tough chapter, one that cannot be covered adequately in a single sitting. But by the time you have mastered this material, you should have a greater appreciation of the nature of the computer's hardware, how it functions, and the role played by the computer's operating system.

4

The Computer's Hardware and Its Operating System

Describing in simple terms what goes on inside a computer system is not an easy task. Considerable technical detail is involved, and the wide variety of computers on the market compounds the description problem. A narrow line has to be drawn between unnecessary detail and the misrepresentation that could result from oversimplification.

As this chapter was being written, the authors kept in mind that its audience would be composed of current and future managers rather than computer specialists. Managers need to know only enough about the computer's internal structure and operations to permit them to talk intelligently with computer specialists. If managers do find themselves in decision-making situations concerning computers where highly technical knowledge and skills are required, computer specialists should be brought in for consultation.

In this single chapter a large number of technical topics are discussed. A broad overview of a computer system's storage capabilities is followed by a more micro discussion of storage at the smallest unit—the binary digit. With this information it becomes possible to discuss how data and instructions are stored inside the computer. Then we will discuss and illustrate the actual processing of the data by the arithmetic/logic unit circuitry under the direction of the control unit, and describe the devices and media utilized in secondary storage, which plays a vital mass storage role in a computer system. The final component to be discussed is the operating system, which controls the computer's operations and facilitates computer usage. The chapter closes with a look at what the future holds in terms of possible advances in computer hardware and software. While this is a long chapter, mastery of it should facilitate communication with computer specialists.

STORAGE FACILITIES

Chapter 1 noted that the computer's central processing unit is composed of an arithmetic/logic unit, a control unit, and a storage unit. The storage unit serves as the computer's main memory. It will be seen in this chapter that the arithmetic/logic and control units also have storage capabilities, even though the storage there is very limited in amount and specialized in its use.

Computer storage facilities can be distinguished as being internal or external. *Internal storage* is memory contained within the central processing unit; it is also called main, primary, core, or fast memory. *External storage* is memory outside of the central processing unit, frequently referred to as auxiliary, secondary, or slow memory. External storage provides computer systems with the storage capacity necessary for many business applications, such as storing the records of thousands of charge card customers.

Computer storage is also classified as either *on-line* or *off-line*; the distinction being whether or not the central processing unit has complete, direct control over the storage medium. For example, data stored on punched cards represent off-line storage, since the computer cannot completely control their use in processing (i.e., the user must input the cards before the data stored on them can be used in processing). Media such as data cells, magnetic disks, and magnetic drums are on-line, since the central processing unit can directly access (retrieve) and use any data or program stored on them.

An Overview of the Storage Function

Figure 4–1 illustrates the storage terms and relationships referred to in this section. Any off-line, external storage of data and instructions must be input to the central processing unit through an appropriate input device before processing can take place. These inputs are then usually stored temporarily in on-line, external storage to await processing and are moved to primary storage when their turn arrives.[1] Arithmetic/logic and control unit storage are utilized during program execution. The instruction being processed is stored in the control unit, and data and computational results are temporarily stored in the arithmetic/logic unit. Once processing is completed, the results are stored in on-line, secondary storage or primary storage until an appropriate output device is activated. The output then becomes off-line, external storage for any further processing.

---

[1] This is one of several places in this chapter where the concepts presented in Chapter 1 are enhanced and expanded upon.

FIGURE 4-1
An Overview of Computer Storage

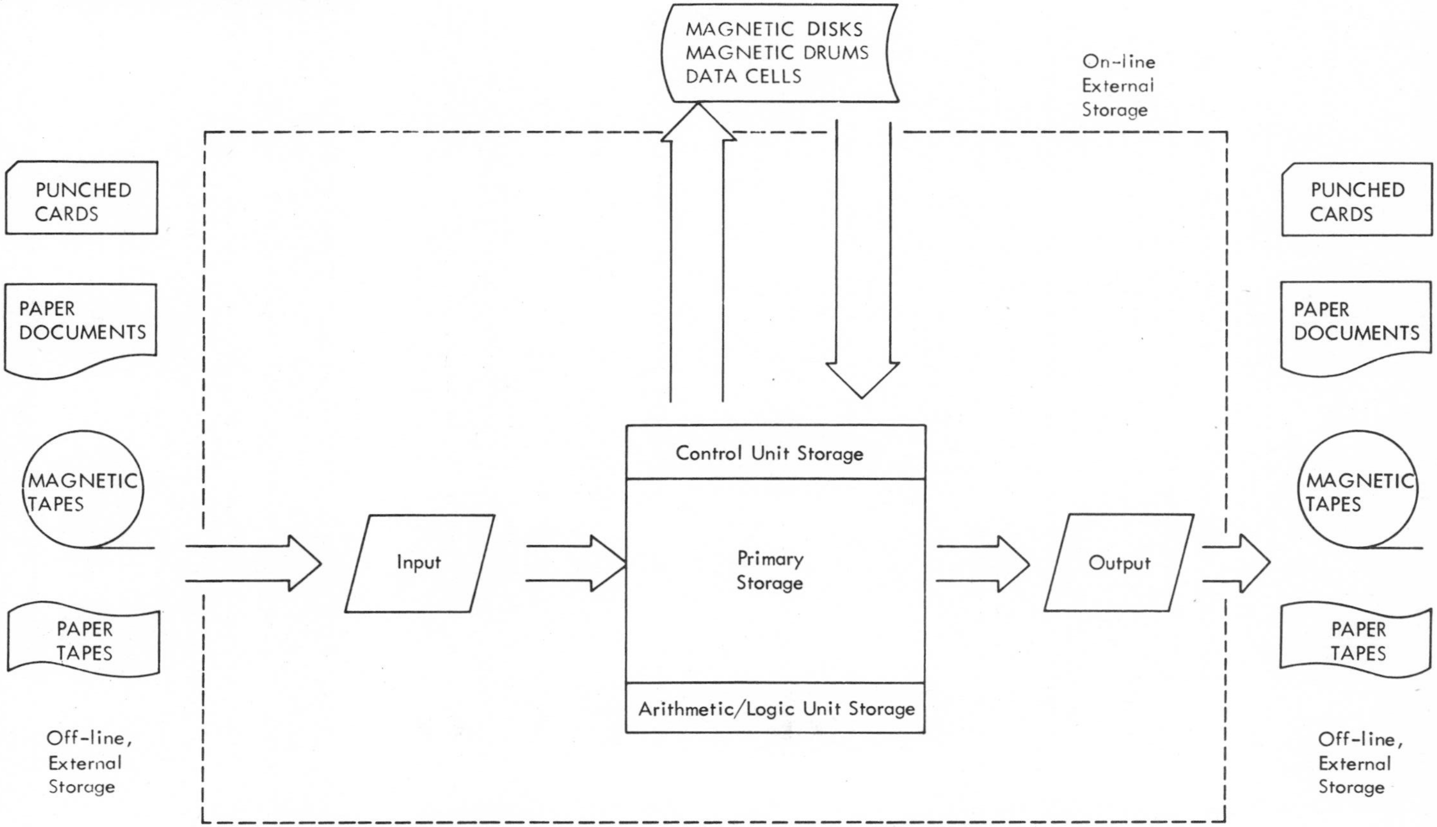

The Binary Digit

We will now turn from the broad perspective to examine primary computer storage at the micro level. Historically, a number of media have been used for primary storage, such as vacuum tubes and magnetic drums. Today, ferrite cores are the most commonly used storage medium in computers. A *ferrite core* is a doughnut-shaped ring, as small as a few thousandths of an inch in diameter, which can be quickly and easily magnetized in either of two directions. Figure 4–2 is a simplified illustration of how a single core appears in storage; keep in mind, however, that its actual size is less than that of a pin-head.

When an electrical current is passed through the *current wire*, the core is magnetized (polarized). The direction of magnetism fol-

FIGURE 4–2
Simplified Illustration of a Core

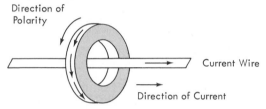

lows the familiar right-hand rule of physics. Since the electrical current can flow in either of two directions, the core is polarized either clockwise or counter-clockwise. These two *states* can be used to store 1–0, off-on, true-false, yes-no (i.e., binary) conditions.

Although Figure 4–2 shows only a single core on the current wire, actually there are many such cores. In order to avoid magnetizing all of the cores on the wire, each one has two current wires passing through it, and each wire carries half of the current necessary to magnetize the core (see Figure 4–3). Thus only the desired core is magnetized.

Having the core magnetized in one direction or the other (off-on, yes-no, 1–0) is of little value unless its direction can be sensed. Consequently, each core usually has two additional wires—a *sense wire* and an *inhibit wire* (see Figure 4–4).

In order to test the direction of magnetism, the computer sends a voltage pulse through the two current wires. The direction of the current is such as to magnetize the core in a direction interpreted to be 0 (counterclockwise in most computers). If the core is already magnetized in the 0 direction, no change results. However, if the core is in the 1 direction, flipping the direction of magnetism induces a current

FIGURE 4–3
Core with Two Current Wires

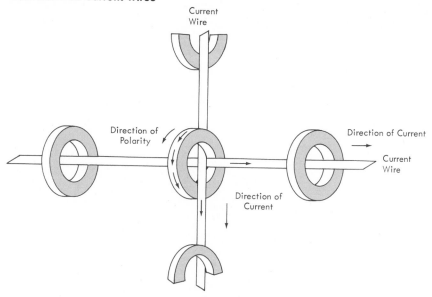

in the sense wire. The effect is that a current is induced in the sense wire if the core is in the 1 direction, and no current appears if the core is in the 0 direction. Consequently, the computer is able to read the state of any core.

FIGURE 4–4
Full Illustration of a Core

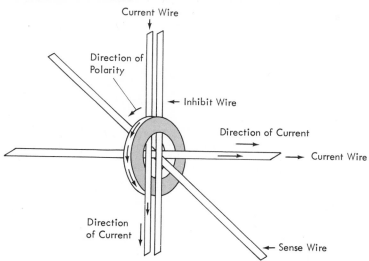

The next (and final) step is to change any 1 that was changed to a 0 back to its original state. This objective is accomplished by attempting to magnetize the core in a 1 direction. If no current appeared in the sense wire during the testing phase (equivalent to a 0 condition), the computer transmits a voltage pulse along the inhibit wire which negates the attempt to magnetize the core in the 1 direction. However, if a current was induced in the sense wire (equivalent to a 1 condition), the computer suppresses any voltage pulse in the inhibit

FIGURE 4–5
Plane of Ferrite Cores

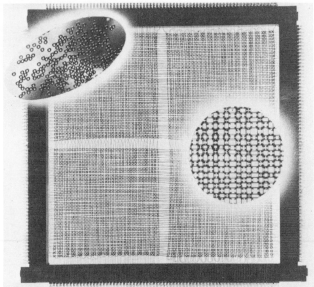

Courtesy of IBM

wire. This act permits the core to be magnetized in the 1 direction, its original state.

You should now be able to understand how the computer stores and tests for a 0 or 1 condition. The magnetized core is referred to as a *binary digit* or *bit*. It represents the smallest unit of storage within the computer. Ferrite cores placed in planes (as illustrated in Figure 4–5) provide most computers with their primary storage capacity.[2]

---

[2] The popular IBM System/370 series uses semiconductor rather than core storage. Many other storage media are in the experimental stage and have excellent long-run potential.

Character Representation

A single binary digit is obviously not sufficient for representing all of the characters that are used in programming. A single bit can stand for only a 1 or a 0. But by using groups of bits in an appropriate coding scheme, it is possible to store letters, numerals, and special characters. Many different codes are available and in use, but third-generation computers generally employ what is known as eight-bit binary coded decimal. Eight bits are used in representing a single character. These bits making up a character are commonly referred to as a *byte*.

TABLE 4–1
Character Representation in EBCDIC (numerals and letters)

Character	EBCDIC	Character	EBCDIC
0	1111 0000	I	1100 1001
1	1111 0001	J	1101 0001
2	1111 0010	K	1101 0010
3	1111 0011	L	1101 0011
4	1111 0100	M	1101 0100
5	1111 0101	N	1101 0101
6	1111 0110	O	1101 0110
7	1111 0111	P	1101 0111
8	1111 1000	Q	1101 1000
9	1111 1001	R	1101 1001
A	1100 0001	S	1110 0010
B	1100 0010	T	1110 0011
C	1100 0011	U	1110 0100
D	1100 0100	V	1110 0101
E	1100 0101	W	1110 0110
F	1100 0110	X	1110 0111
G	1100 0111	Y	1110 1000
H	1100 1000	Z	1110 1001

One of the most popular eight-bit codes, *Extended Binary Coded Decimal Interchange Code* (EBCDIC), is partially shown in Table 4–1. A close look at the table shows that for each character there are eight bits divided into two groups of four each. The first group of four is known as zone bits and the second of four as numeric bits (see Figure 4–6). It can also be seen that there is a pattern to EBCDIC. In particular, the numeric bits carry the binary number system equivalents of the base-ten number system.[3]

How is a byte related to the planes of ferrite cores? In many computers a vertical slice of cores represents a byte. Figure 4–7 shows the EBCDIC representation of the number 5. The darkened cores indicate a 1 direction of magnetism.

---

[3] Appendix B provides an introduction to the binary number system.

FIGURE 4-6
Zone and Numeric Bits
in the EBCDIC Coding of
the Number 1

Zone Bits				Numeric Bits			
1	1	1	1	0	0	0	1

FIGURE 4-7
EBCDIC Representation of the Number 5
in Storage

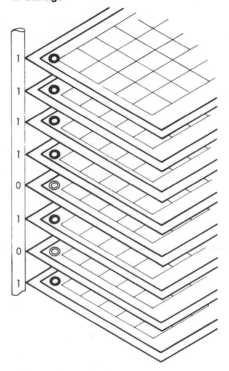

Addresses

Data and instructions are logically grouped series of characters, and we have shown how a character is stored in the computer's memory. In order to be used, data and instructions must be placed in computer storage in such a way that they can be referenced when needed. This objective is accomplished by associating an *address* with the computer's storage locations. For example, the address of the storage location for the variable X might be 3,620. Whenever the value of X changes, location 3,620 is used to store the new value.

An analogy is frequently made between the addresses in computer

FIGURE 4-8
The Analogy between Computer Storage and a Mailbox

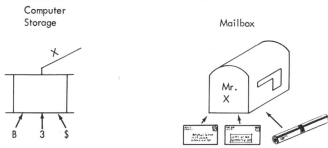

storage and mailboxes in a post office. Just as Mr. X might rent box No. 3,620 one month and the next month Mr. Y might rent it, for one program, address 3,620 might be assigned to the variable X and for the next program, the address could be given to the variable Y. Another aspect of the analogy is the contents of a storage address and a mailbox. Into each address a wide variety of characters can be placed, and many different types of mail can go into one box (see Figure 4-8).

Once the basic concept of an address is understood, the next question that must be answered is, How many bits comprise a storage location? or stating it differently, How big is the mailbox? The number of bits of storage associated with a particular address depends upon the manufacturer and make of the computer. At one extreme are *character-addressable* machines. In computers of this type each address stores only a single character. When more than one character is needed to represent data or an instruction, a string of addressed locations is used. These locations form a variable-length *word*. Computers of this type are said to have *variable-word-length storage*.

On the other extreme are computers that assign a fixed number of bits to a word—typically 24, 30, 32, 36, 48, or 60 bits. Each address is then associated with a word consisting of a specific number of bits. Computers of this type are *word-addressable* and have *fixed-word-length storage*.

Many modern computers permit the use of both fixed- and variable-length words. A common approach is to structure primarily for fixed-word-length storage but provide the user with instructions which modify the number of bits associated with a word.

It would be of little interest how words are structured within the computer if this did not have a considerable bearing upon the computer's operating characteristics. Variable-word-length computers store data and instructions most efficiently because there are no unused bits. In routine data processing applications, this characteristic is frequently very important because of the large amount of data that must be stored. However, the arithmetic/logic unit circuitry for fixed-word-length computers is more efficient than its variable-word-length counterpart. This is so because arithmetic in variable-word-length computers is performed *serially* on one character at a time, while fixed-word-length computers perform computations in *parallel*, all characters in a word being processed at once. If numerous, complex computations must be made, as in many computer-assisted decision-making applications, fixed-word-length computers offer an advantage. Many third-generation computers permit both variable- and fixed-length storage and computations.

Storing Instructions

Instructions for directing the computer's operations, such as the statement GO TO 300, which causes an unconditional transfer of control to the programming statement numbered 300, are discussed in Chapters 6 and 7. Here, however, it is appropriate to investigate how instructions such as the GO TO statement appear when placed in storage.

The programming languages included in this book are all procedure-oriented languages. A language translator is used to translate the high-level language into machine language. It is the machine language instructions, appearing as strings of 1s and 0s, that are retained in storage and direct the computer's operations.

Any machine language instruction contains an operation code and up to three addresses (the number depends upon the computer). The *operation code* specifies the action that the computer is to take (e.g., add two numbers, branch to a specified point). The *address(es)* indicate where data can be found, the location of the next instruction to be processed, or where the result of the processing is to be placed. The exact form of the machine language instruction varies with the computer, but an operation code and at least one address are always included.

The examples that follow assume that the computer has *an operation code* and *two addresses* associated with each machine language instruction.[4] Consider the programming statement,

$$X=X+Y$$

This statement causes the value of Y to be added to the value of X and the result retained in the storage location for X. When translated by the language translator, an instruction like this results in several machine language instructions being generated. The most interesting

---

[4] This book has been written to be largely machine independent; this is to say that it does not base discussions and examples on a single computer system. However, when a point is illustrated, a specific type of machine must be selected for discussion purposes.

FIGURE 4–9
Illustration of a Machine Language
Instruction

0001 1010	0001	0011
Operation Code	Location of X	Location of Y

of these instructions might appear as shown in Figure 4–9. A previous machine language instruction has placed the values of X and Y in addresses 1 and 3, respectively. The operation code directs the computer to add the contents of 0011 (address 3, the location of Y) to 0001 (address 1, the location of X).

Arithmetic/Logic and Control Unit Registers

The addresses specified for X and Y are not primary storage locations, but rather are registers in the arithmetic/logic unit. *Registers* provide the storage capability for the arithmetic/logic and control units.

The role of registers in processing data and instructions is best understood by considering what happens to a program upon input. As has been discussed previously, the program normally is temporarily stored in secondary, on-line storage prior to processing and is transferred to primary storage when its processing turn arrives. When program execution begins, the *sequence register* (also referred to as a program counter) in the control unit keeps track of the primary storage address of the next instruction to be processed. Initially, the sequence register holds the address of the first statement in the program. The instruction designated by the sequence register is then split into two parts and read into control unit registers. The operation code is stored in the *instruction register*, while the *address register*(s) stores the address(es) associated with the operation code.

Several different arithmetic/logic unit registers are used in processing a program. The *storage register* retains data coming from or going to main storage. An *accumulator register* accumulates the result of data being added. A *multiplier-divider register* holds the multiplier for multiplication and the divisor for division. *General-purpose registers* are, as their name implies, capable of serving several different purposes, such as that of an accumulator.

Understanding of the role of these registers can be improved by considering a specific example, the machine language instruction for adding the value of Y to X and storing the result in the memory location for X; such as was introduced in Figure 4–9 above. If this programming statement were in address 8 in primary storage, the sequence register just prior to processing would appear as shown in

FIGURE 4–10
The Sequence Register

Sequence Register

Figure 4–10. The instruction in primary storage address 8 is then split into two parts, with the operation code being read into the instruction register and the addresses into address registers (see Figure 4–11). The machine language statement is the same one we have been discussing.

Previous machine language instructions already have caused the values of X and Y to be stored in arithmetic/logic unit registers. Specifically, the value of Y (assume it to be 2) is located in address 3, a storage register. The value of X (assume it to be 4) is stored in address 1, an accumulator register (see Figure 4–12). It must be remembered that the value of Y is to be added to the value of X. Upon execution of the machine language instruction, the value of Y (which is 2) is added to the value of X (which is 4), and the result (6) is stored in the accumulator register, the temporary location of the value for X.[5]

FIGURE 4–11
The Instruction and Address Registers

Instruction Register

0001   1010

Operation Code

Address Registers

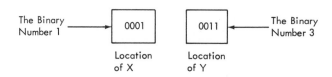

Location   Location
of X   of Y

[5] In our example we have been discussing a computer which uses two addresses and, hence, two address registers in processing each instruction. In this situation one of the numbers to be added has to be stored initially in an accumulator register. Computers that have three addresses associated with each instruction function differently. For example, if two numbers are to be added, the two numbers are first placed in storage registers and then added in a separate accumulator register. The sum is then transferred out of the accumulator register by another machine language instruction.

FIGURE 4-12
The Storage and Accumulator Registers

Thus is can be seen that the registers in the control unit are responsible for storing the instruction that is to be processed and keeping track of the next instruction to be executed. The registers in the arithmetic/logic unit store the data that are currently being manipulated. How computations and comparisons are carried out by the computer is considered next.

CIRCUITRY FOR COMPUTATIONS IN THE ARITHMETIC/LOGIC UNIT

The manipulation of data by a computer's arithmetic/logic unit circuitry is best explained through Boolean algebra, a type developed by the 19th-century English philosopher-mathematician George Boole, who died before the importance of his work was ever realized. In Boolean algebra *all data inputs are in binary* and all arithmetical and logical functions are broken down into AND ($\cap$), OR ($\cup$) or NOT ($\sim$) operations. With these basic operators, all arithmetical and logical operations can be performed.[6] The Boolean operators are illustrated in Table 4-2.

The intersection ($\cap$) operation is associated with the word "and." It resembles the mathematical operation of multiplication, and a centered dot ($\cdot$) is sometimes used in place of the symbol $\cap$. In other words, A$\cap$B, A$\cdot$B and A AND B can be employed somewhat inter-

TABLE 4-2
Boolean Operators

A	B	A$\cap$B	A$\cup$B	$\sim$A	$\sim$B
1	0	0	1	0	1
1	1	1	1	0	0
0	0	0	0	1	1
0	1	0	1	1	0

---

[6] It is easy to see why Boole's work was not appreciated during his lifetime, since it was not until the advent of the computer that an algebra system based on the binary number system was of any practical value.

FIGURE 4–13
An AND Circuit

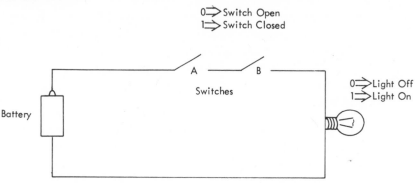

changeably. In a similar vein, A∪B, A+B and A OR B are used to mean the same thing. NOT B can be used in place of ~B.

The electronic circuits which carry out the arithmetic and logical data processing requirements simulate Boolean algebraic operations. In other words, the electronic circuits are electrical analogs of the paper and pencil manipulation of data by Boolean operators. To understand this point, consider the AND circuit shown in Figure 4–13. Only when switches A and B are closed (in a 1 position) is current able to flow and light the bulb (the equivalent of a 1 condition). If either switch A or B is open (in a 0 position), no current is able to flow and light the bulb, since no closed path exists.

An OR operation can be performed by wiring the switches in parallel rather than in series. The OR circuit is shown in Figure 4–14. Current is able to flow and light the bulb (a 1 condition) whenever switch A or B is in a closed position (a 1 state).

Actual arithmetic/logic unit circuitry does not employ moving

FIGURE 4–14
An OR Circuit

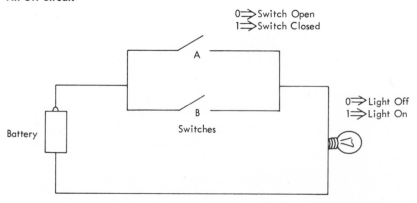

parts like the switches shown. Instead, semiconductors such as transistors and diodes are used to perform the same functions. The logic of the circuits is the same, however. The circuitry that performs the required mathematical and logical operations such as adding and comparing is simply appropriate combinations of the basic circuits that have been just described.

SECONDARY STORAGE FACILITIES

Considerable attention has been devoted to storage within the central processing unit. Also important to many business applications, however, is the capability for storing massive files of data. In many instances these applications require more memory than is available in the main storage unit. This section examines the major secondary storage media and devices demanded by many business applications.

A large number of storage media are classified as secondary storage (see Figure 4–1). Included in this category are off-line media such as punched cards, magnetic tape, and punched tape. Off-line storage media serve three important purposes—input, output, and permanent storage. On-line secondary storage media, such as magnetic disks, magnetic drums, and data cells, are also important. On-line, secondary storage is used to enhance a computer system's total storage capacity.

Punched Cards

The oldest and most familiar secondary storage medium is the punched card. A keypunch machine is used to punch characters onto the card.[7] Figure 4–15 shows a *card reader* (an input device), *card punch* (a keypunch machine) and a *Hollerith punched card* with perforation patterns. The Hollerith punched card holds up to 80 columns of data and/or instructions. A single numeral, letter, or special character can be punched into each column. The character punched is identified by a coded series of punched holes.

Punched cards are a convenient storage medium for several reasons. All of the data stored are both man- and machine-readable. Any card can be easily replaced by another card when changes are desired, and the cards provide permanent, reliable storage.

Punched cards do have disadvantages, however. They are read by card readers, which are relatively slow input devices—even very fast card readers can only read several thousand cards per minute. In addition, because not much data can be stored on a single card,

---

[7] Instructions on how to use a keypunch machine are provided in Appendix C. The official name for a keypunch machine is a *card punch*, but it is seldom referred to by this name.

FIGURE 4–15
Card Reader (left), Card Punch (right), and Hollerith Punched Card (bottom)

Courtesy of IBM

they are a bulky storage medium. The contents of 20 cards could be stored on just one inch of magnetic tape. From a cost point of view, cards are relatively expensive; while a single card is not particularly costly, it takes many of them to store even a moderate amount of data.

Magnetic Tape

The primary medium for off-line storage of large quantities of data is magnetic tape. A magnetic tape can be encoded in several different ways; the *magnetic tape encoder* shown in Figure 4–16 places characters on the tape through typing operations at a keyboard. A *tape drive* (also shown in Figure 4–16) inputs the contents of a

FIGURE 4–16
Magnetic Tape (top), Tape Encoder (bottom right), and Tape Drive (bottom left)

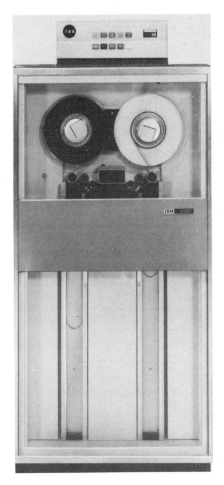

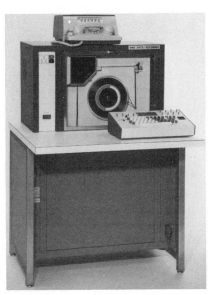

Courtesy of Mohawk Data Sciences, Inc. and IBM

magnetic tape to the computer and can also encode the tape as part
of an output operation.

Magnetic tape is coated with a thin layer of a ferromagnetic material that is easily magnetized. The width of the tape is divided into

a number of *tracks* (also referred to as channels) that store data. A cross section of tracks, which is called a *frame*, records a single character. The number of tracks to a frame depends upon the coding scheme employed; most commonly, magnetic tape has either six or eight tracks. Figure 4–16 shows a magnetic tape with several characters encoded. The darkened spots represent a 1 condition of magnetism, while no spot indicates a 0 condition.

Magnetic tape offers several advantages. It can store a large quantity of data at a relatively low cost. A reel of magnetic tape 2,400 feet long costs around $20 and can store up to 1,600 characters per inch of tape. In addition, the tape drive which reads the tape is a relatively fast input device, capable of inputting the equivalent of 25,000 cards per minute.

The major disadvantages of tapes are matters of convenience. The contents of a tape cannot be visually read like a punched card. In order to change a tape, it must be mounted on a tape drive, the desired location on the tape found, and the change made. In most computer centers a magnetic tape must be given to a computer operator for mounting, and frequently there are forms that must be filled out. Thus, when the amount of data involved is small, using magnetic tape can be inconvenient.

Paper Tape

Another popular off-line storage medium is paper tape. Like punched cards and magnetic tape, paper tape can be read, can be the result of an output operation, or can simply store data.

A paper tape can be prepared in several different ways. A *tape punch* can be used to punch character-coded holes. A paper tape can also be generated as a by-product of other business machine operations, such as an adding machine or cash register operations. Also, most terminals used for time-sharing have the capability for punching a paper tape.

Characters are encoded on paper tape much as on magnetic tape. The major difference is that punched holes are used rather than magnetized spots. The number of tracks to a tape depends upon the coding scheme employed, but five-, seven-, and eight-track tapes are common (see Figure 4–17).

There are several advantages to using paper tape. Data collected on paper tape from other business machine operations requires little additional preparation prior to input to the computer. Paper tape is quite useful in a time-sharing environment, because data or instructions can be prepared off-line and then input to the computer from a terminal. It also serves as a convenient permanent storage medium for storing a program or data until needed. Paper tape is a relatively

FIGURE 4–17
Paper Tape (top), Tape Reader (bottom left), and Tape Punch (bottom right)

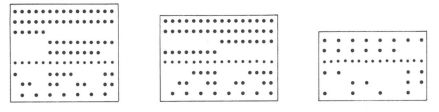

8-CHANNEL   7-CHANNEL   5- CHANNEL

Courtesy of IBM and NCR

inexpensive storage medium, less costly than punched cards, for example. Paper tape input/output devices also are relatively inexpensive and easy to maintain.

One disadvantage of this medium is that coding on paper tape is difficult to read or verify. Making corrections requires either repunching the tape or splicing in changes. Input/output devices for paper tape, as for punched cards, are relatively slow. For example, a *paper tape punch* (see Figure 4–17) can punch only about 300 characters per second, while a *paper tape reader* can process only about 2,000 characters per second. These are relatively slow speeds.

Magnetic Disks

Magnetic disks are the most popular form of on-line, external storage. Each disk is coated with a ferromagnetic material that can be magnetized with binary coding. The disk's surface is divided into a number of concentric circles known as tracks, each of which is used to store data.

A number of disks are usually combined in order to form a *disk pack* (see Figure 4–18). A disk pack, or a set of disks, is placed in a disk drive in order to allow the contents of the disk to be input to the computer or to encode output from the computer on the disk. Disk packs are usually semipermanently placed in a disk drive, but they can be removed and hence do provide off-line storage possibilities.

Magnetic Drums

At one time magnetic drums were used for primary storage. Today drums store data and programs that are used frequently during processing, such as mathematical tables and functions and certain operating system programs.

A *magnetic drum* is a cylinder with a thin layer of a ferromagnetic material coating the surface. Drums have 200 major *tracks*, each made up of four *subtracks*. Each track stores data and/or instructions. A magnetic drum is mounted on a drum storage drive which rotates the drum past fixed read/write heads. Figure 4–19 shows magnetic drum storage.

Data Cells

Data cells provide the largest secondary storage capacity. A *data cell* is made up of a large number of cards or strips coated with a ferromagnetic material. Each card or strip contains tracks which store data. Ten cards or strips comprise a *subcell*, twenty subcells make up a *cell* and ten cells are placed in a *cell drive*. Each card or strip is extracted by a mechanical device when needed and are read or encoded by read/write heads. Figure 4–20 shows a data cell.

A Comparison of Storage Media

Off-line storage media (punched cards, magnetic tape, paper tape) are limited to *sequential access*. With sequential access the stored

FIGURE 4–18
Magnetic Disk Pack (top), Closeup of a Disk Pack (center), and Disk Drive (bottom)

Courtesy of IBM

FIGURE 4–19
Magnetic Drum Storage

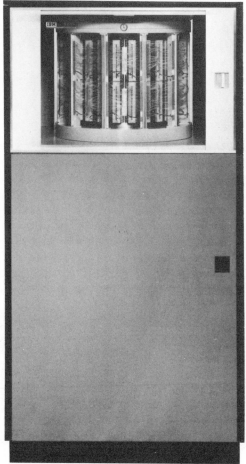

Courtesy of IBM

data items are searched sequentially until the desired item is found. It is much like going through a reel of a movie film from the beginning in search of a particular frame.

On-line storage media (magnetic disks, magnetic drums, data cells) offer sequential, direct, and indexed-sequential access. With *direct* (random) *access*, the desired data item is found directly on the storage medium without searching through all of the stored items. It is similar to being able to pick up a phonograph arm and move it directly to a desired song. *Indexed-sequential access* is a mix of sequential and direct access. When a stored data item is desired, an index is consulted which directs the search effort to a subset of the

FIGURE 4-20
Data Cell

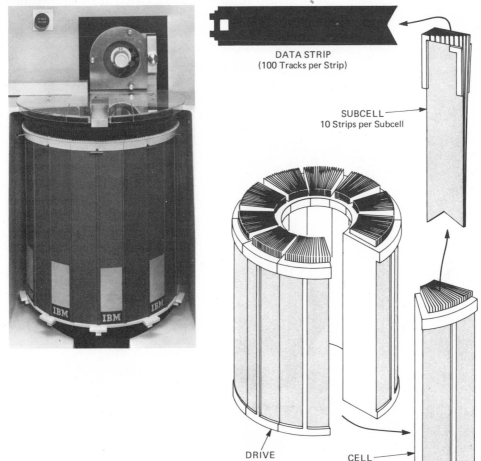

DATA STRIP
(100 Tracks per Strip)

SUBCELL
10 Strips per Subcell

DRIVE
10 Cells per Drive

CELL
20 Subcells per Cell

Courtesy of IBM

entire storage medium. This subset is them searched sequentially until the data item is located. It is analogous to an eight-track tape player which allows immediate access to a desired track and then plays all of the songs on that track.

On-line storage media can store millions of bytes of data and access the data in milliseconds. The fastest *access times* (the time required to retrieve a desired piece of data) are provided by magnetic drums, but they store the smallest amount of data. The largest storage capacity is provided by data cells, but they have the longest access times.

Magnetic disks fall between these two media in terms of both storage capacity and access times. Magnetic drums provide more costly storage than magnetic disks, which in turn are more expensive than data cells. Stated differently, the faster the access time, the more costly the storage medium.

OPERATING SYSTEMS

To this point, our consideration of what goes on inside a computer system has dealt with the computer's hardware — the input, primary storage, control, arithmetic/logic and output units, plus secondary storage media and their input/output devices. Any thorough treatment of a computer system's operations, however, must include discussion of one important piece of software — the computer's operating system. These systems essentially provide the means whereby computers are able to function effectively.

An *operating system* is a set of computer programs which serve two primary functions: to help control the computer's operations, and to facilitate and expedite use of the computer. We will examine

FIGURE 4–21
Activities Performed by an Operating System

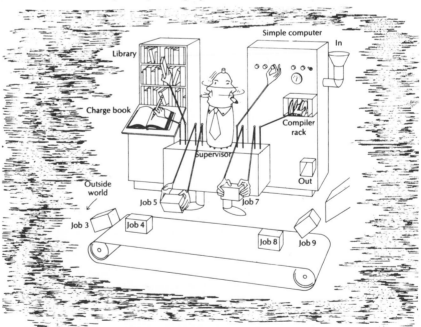

Source: From *Introduction to Computer Science: Problems, Algorithms, Languages, Information and Computers*, by John K. Rice and John R. Rice. Copyright © 1969 by Holt, Rinehart and Winston, Publishers.

some of the activities performed by a typical operating system (see Figure 4–21).

The Controlling Function

Computers have not always had operating systems. In the "old days" the computer operator assumed many of the tasks now commonly performed by an operating system. The operator had responsibilities for controlling the activities of input and output units, scheduling the running of programs, starting and stopping program execution, recordkeeping, and so on. But this system did not provide for efficient operations in the use of either the operator's time or, more importantly, the computer's resources. Operating systems evolved when it was recognized that most of these tasks could be performed by appropriately written computer programs. Today, operating systems are integral to most computer operations.

Operating systems vary considerably in their capabilities. In general, the more complex the computer system, the more sophisticated the operating system. Consider some of the controlling activities and responsibilities of a typical operating system in a large third-generation computer.

An operating system interfaces with the input and output units. Before much can be said about this interface, more must be explained about these units, whose activities are actually governed by their own control unit. Sometimes there is a separate control unit for each input/output (I/O) device, but frequently a single control unit governs several devices. The I/O units also have storage capabilities. The storage may be external to the central processing unit (such as on a data cell, magnetic disk, or magnetic drum), or it may actually be internal to the central processing unit (i.e., a "slice" of primary storage). With this storage capability, data and instructions can be *buffered* between the I/O devices and the central processing unit, or in other words, temporarily stored between the two.

The ability to buffer data and instructions considerably enhances the computer's capabilities. The input unit can accept programs and data from several input devices and store them until the operating system calls for their transfer to primary storage for processing. When processing is completed, the operating system can transfer the results back to the output unit, where they are stored until an appropriate output device is free. In both cases the result is that processing and I/O activities become largely independent, a factor which helps make it possible to utilize the computer's resources more efficiently. I/O devices are exceptionally slow in comparison to the speed with which processing takes place within the computer, and letting the central processing unit (CPU) sit idle while these devices are operating would be quite wasteful. If the computer allows for I/O with buffers, the CPU is free to operate independently of the I/O devices.

However, overlapping I/O activities with computations does not usually utilize the CPU fully. Even though programs and data can be quickly transferred from buffers to main storage, it is still costly to have the CPU remain idle while waiting for its next task. In order to increase the efficiency of computer systems, *multiprogramming* has come into existence. With multiprogramming, more than one program resides in primary storage at the same time. The computer works upon one program for a while, and then periodically, under the direction of the operating system, switches to the processing of one of the other programs available in main storage. In this way the CPU is utilized with maximum efficiency.

Another procedure which has the same objective as multiprogramming—increased system efficiency—but accomplishes it in a different manner is *multiprocessing.* This refers to a computer system which has several separate control and arithmetic/logic units but shares a common storage unit. The input and output units are also shared. With this configuration more than one program can actually be processed at a time. The operating system plays a vital role in controlling the activities in a multiprocessing system.

The operating system also performs *job scheduling*, deciding what jobs are to be run and when. For example, programs that require long running times usually are held until the system is relatively free, whereas short programs have a fast *turnaround* (the length of time between when the program is input and when the output is received). The operating system tries to schedule jobs in a way that utilizes the computer's resources best.

Another responsibility of an operating system is *recordkeeping.* The operating system keeps track of such things as the user's name, the program's name, the account number to be charged, and how much to charge for the run.

The Facilitating Function

The programs of an operating system that serve a facilitating function are designed to make the computer easier to use. Whereas the programs in the operating system that perform a controlling function are supplied by the computer manufacturer, many of the programs in the facilitating realm are written by in-house programmers and are added to the operating system. One group of programs that usually fall in this category is *applications programs.* These are programs that perform frequently required computer-assisted decision making or routine data processing applications. A customer billing program is a good example of an applications program.

The language translators that convert the user's programming code into machine language are also part of the operating system. Without language translators the user would have to program his applications in machine language. Most language translators are obtained from the computer manufacturer.

An operating system contains a number of programs that serve to make the programmer's life easier. Because data processing applications frequently involve the manipulation of large files of data, an operating system includes *sort/merge* programs which can be called upon to merge, update, and sort data files. Some routines for processing data (such as finding the absolute value of a number) are needed by many different programs. Therefore the operating system includes a number of preprogrammed routines that are available to the user and can save considerable programming time. For the user who wants to store semipermanently in secondary storage a program he or she has written, there is an operating system program which controls the storing and retrieving of user's programs. Without this program, the computer operator would have to devote substantial amounts of paper work and time to these activities. These examples of the capabilities of a typical operating system are far from exhaustive, but they do serve to illustrate some of the more interesting and important capabilities of an operating system.

The programs that make up an operating system are stored either in main storage or on-line secondary storage. In general, the programs that perform a controlling function reside all the time (or nearly all) in main storage. The programs that facilitate the use of the computer are primarily stored in secondary storage and are called into primary storage only as they are needed.

FUTURE TRENDS

The digital computer has only been commercially available for about 20 years. That is an amazingly short period of time, considering the developments that have taken place. And the advancements are still coming, and at an increasing rate! Much of the technology that exists today, especially in regards to hardware, will be obsolete within a few years. While it is probably only the computer specialists who will be able to keep up with all of the advancements, it is important for managers to be aware of emerging trends.

Changes are taking place in I/O media and equipment. Currently, most input is via punched cards. While this medium for input will continue to predominate, its importance will decrease over time. Magnetic tape will be increasingly used, especially as the result of keyboard-to-tape typing. Magnetic tape storage density will also increase, thus reducing its cost as a storage medium.

Time-sharing from terminals will become more important. It is even possible to envision the day when many professional people will be able to do most of their work at home, using a terminal to obtain required data and information, to perform required calculations and analyses, and to interface with other employees. Such a development is consistent with emerging technology, movement toward the flexible work hours concept, and concern over environmental problems (more workers at home means fewer cars on the road).

"Let me show you our new economy model . . . ."

Increasingly, data will be recorded in machine-readable form. Rather than designing systems that require data to be transformed from original source documents to an appropriate input medium, the original source will be amenable to input. In some instances the data will be input at the point of transaction (e.g., an accounts receivable record will be updated when a sale is rung up). In other instances an optical character recognition (OCR) machine will be used to read the contents of a source document.

High-speed printers will probably continue to be the primary output device. However, output from terminals, perhaps equipped with a cathode ray tube (CRT) for visual display, will become more common.

Changes in the central processing unit are also taking place. Technology is providing circuits which perform calculations more quickly and reliably than ever before; for example, computation time has decreased by about a factor of 5 between 1970 and 1975. The result is lower cost per unit of computation. This is not to say, however, that *total* computing costs will decrease. Most organizations are using the computer and peripheral equipment more, and in ways not thought of only a few short years ago.

Ferrite cores are currently used for primary storage in most computers. Other storage media do exist, however, and will probably ultimately replace cores as the most popular form of main storage. Some of these possibilities include thin film, plated wire, and semiconductor storage. Semiconductors are particularly promising because of the speed with which they permit data to be stored and accessed. Many other possibilities are also being investigated.

Secondary, on-line storage is also being improved. Greater storage densities are being realized with conventional media such as magnetic disks and magnetic drums. New media are being developed that promise the possibility of trillions of bits of storage.

An interesting new development is *firmware*, which is hardware that performs functions usually performed by software. For example, language translators have been presented in this book as computer programs (software) which translate a high-level language into machine language. A piece of hardware that performs this same function would be classified as firmware. The benefits of firmware include greatly enhanced speed and reliability.

It is normally software rather than hardware that impedes computer usage, but the trend is toward extending, standardizing, and simplifying existing programming languages. In addition, new, more powerful languages are being developed. More efficient language translators are being designed, with the result that high-level languages will be increasingly used and machine and symbolic language programming will be reduced substantially. Operating systems are being developed that will utilize the computer's resources more efficiently, as well as making the computer easier to use. In particular, applications programs, either supplied by the manufacturer or purchased from outside vendors, will eliminate the need for much routine programming.

All future trends indicate that the computer will be more versatile, faster, more reliable, more efficient, and easier to use. As a result, it will become an increasingly integral component of organizational operations.

ASSIGNMENTS

4-1. Classify the following storage media as either internal or external:

    a. punched card   *c.* data cell
    b. ferrite cores   *d.* magnetic tape

4-2. Distinguish between on-line and off-line storage.

4-3. Discuss how the current, sense, and inhibit wires function.

4-4. What is the relationship between bits, bytes, characters, and words?

4-5. Using EBCDIC, show how the following characters and words would be stored in memory:

    a. 8   *c.* 63
    b. C   *d.* BIG

4-6. Discuss the difference in the way words are formed in fixed- and variable-word-length computers.

4-7. What functions do the following registers perform?

    a. sequence   *d.* accumulator
    b. instruction   *e.* address
    c. general-purpose

4-8. Using Boolean algebra, complete the following table:

A	B	$(A \cap B) \cup A$	$(\sim A \cup B) \cap (A \cup B)$
1	0	1	—
1	1	—	—
0	0	—	0
0	1	—	—

4-9. Compare the speed of input/output devices for punched cards, magnetic tape, and punched tape. What are the relative storage capacities and costs of these off-line secondary storage media?

4-10. Compare the access times, storage capacities, and costs of magnetic disks, magnetic drums, and data cells.

4-11. Discuss the activities and responsibilities assumed by an operating system.

4-12. Describe the processing of a computer program from input to output (where does it go, what happens to it at each step, and so on).

4-13. Talk with a local computer manufacturer's sales representative about his company's forthcoming technological advances. Prepare a report based upon your conversation.

REFERENCES

Books

Bohl, Marilyn   *Information Processing.* Chicago: Science Research Associates, 1971.

Davis, Gordon B.   *Introduction to Electronic Computers.* New York: McGraw-Hill Book Co., 1971.

Dock, V. Thomas, and Edward Essick   *Principles of Business Data Processing.* Chicago: Science Research Associates, 1974.

Gupta, R.   *Electronic Information Processing.* New York: Macmillan Co., 1971.

Mader, Chris, and Robert Hagin   *Information Systems: Technology, Economics, Applications.* Chicago: Science Research Associates, 1974.

Sanders, Donald H.   *Computers in Business.* New York: McGraw-Hill Book Co., 1974.

Silver, Gerald A. and Joan B. Silver   *Data Processing for Business.* New York: Harcourt Brace Jovanovich, 1973.

Vazsonyi, Andrew   *Introduction to Electronic Data Processing.* Homewood, Ill.: Richard D. Irwin, 1973.

Wegner, P.   *Programming Languages, Information Structures and Machine Organization.* New York: McGraw-Hill, 1968.

Systems Analysis and Design
Systems Flowcharting
  Illustrations of Systems Flowcharts
Program Flowcharting
  Single-Pass Execution, A Branching Decision, Loops
Assignments (Basic Flowcharting Concepts)
  Subscripted Variables in Program Flowcharting
Assignments (Advanced Flowcharting Concepts)
References

Systems and program flowcharting are examined in detail in this chapter. These topics are extremely important in working with information systems and in developing computer programs. You will have to study this material carefully and practice it intensively in order to fully master it. These efforts will be rewarded, however, when you study the programming and applications chapters.

5

Systems and Program Flowcharting

$\mathbf{W}$hen Chapter 1, which presented an overview of the computer, discussed what is involved in using the computer, one of the steps illustrated was the development of systems and program flowcharts. It was pointed out that the *systems flowchart* graphically represents the interactions of personnel, data, and equipment in satisfying a data processing objective, and the *program flowchart* visually depicts the sequential operations the computer must perform in order to generate the desired information. A computer program can be written by coding the program flowchart into an appropriate programming language. The program flowcharts presented in this chapter provide a vehicle for illustrating the BASIC and FORTRAN programming languages which are presented in the next two chapters. Consequently this chapter and next two are best studied concurrently.

The primary focus of this chapter is on systems and program flowcharting. Both the rationale for these flowcharts and the specific techniques involved in preparing them will be explored. First, however, the topic of systems analysis and design will be introduced, since systems and program flowcharting are frequently viewed as subsets of systems analysis and design.

SYSTEMS ANALYSIS AND DESIGN

A common suggestion whenever a managerial information need is encountered is "Let's get the information from the computer." Certain reports may be required for the performance of the managerial functions—planning, organizing, staffing, directing, and controlling. Perhaps the computer will be used for the recording and processing of massive files of data, or a "sticky" managerial problem will be at least partially analyzed on it. Whatever the underlying purpose, a systems analysis and design must be conducted before the computer can be put to use.

The systems analysis and design is commonly performed by systems analysts working in conjunction with management and other computer specialists. The magnitude of the task varies considerably. In some instances all that is required is the writing of a few programs to be run on existing equipment. At the other extreme is the development of complex information systems, which are expensive and time-consuming to plan, create, and implement. They can cause considerable organizational change and affect the organization's functioning and performance for a long time.

It is not possible to explore in this book all that a major systems analysis and design entails. Months, even years, can be devoted to analyzing and designing information systems. Entire books and courses are devoted to this important topic. All that will be attempted here is a brief introduction, plus an indication of some of the factors and problems that can be encountered. Chapter 10, "Information Systems and Management," and Chapter 11, "Planning for, Selection, and Implementation of Computer Systems," also touch upon this topic as they consider the manager's role in developing information systems and in planning to install computer systems.

A *systems analysis and design* considers the interactions of personnel, data, and equipment in providing desired information. Many factors influence the nature, magnitude, and difficulty of the task. These factors include:

1. The type of information needed, its format and distribution.
2. The availability, form, and location of the data.
3. The willingness of those involved to supply the needed data, and the cooperation provided in developing the system.
4. The funds allocated to the development of the system.
5. The available manpower—clerks, operators, programmers, and analysts.
6. Available equipment.

A systems analysis and design must consider both the logic that will underly the system and the hardware that will be required in implementing the logic. Obviously, sound logic must be the basis of the system if it is to fully and efficiently meet the needs of the end user (i.e., the recipient of the information). The hardware selected supports and helps carry out the logic of the system.

The systems analysis and design must always begin with a close examination of the output specifications for the system. Unless the system satisfies the needs of the end user, it will be of no value. Consequently, it is good practice to state the output specifications carefully and in great detail.

Once the output specifications have been established, the next step is to determine how to generate the output. This involves consideration of such data processing factors as the computer programs that will have to be written, the data files that will be needed, procedures for updating the files, and so on.

The next step involves the determination of the system's input specifications. Only after the output and processing specifications have been established is it possible to state what inputs will be necessary. The input specifications include considerations such as data content, data sources, data format, and input media.

After the output-processing-input specification sequence has been completed (in this order), forms for the collection of data are obtained, equipment is selected, and the required computer programs are written. Other necessary tasks are also performed once the initial specifications have been determined.

A number of problems might be encountered during the systems analysis and design. It is not uncommon to discover that the end user has not thoroughly considered his information requirements. Simply stating a need for inventory data, for example, is not nearly specific enough. The manager must specify exactly what information concerning inventories is needed (e.g., what items, cost figures, levels).

Existing computer and peripheral equipment are not always adequate for an application management may have in mind. Systems design must always be kept within the capability of existing equipment, unless the purchase or rental of additional hardware can be considered. This option must then be evaluated in terms of the benefits to be derived from having the new equipment versus the costs of purchasing (or renting) and maintaining it.

In order for the system to meet the output specifications, appropriate input data must be provided. Consequently, the systems analysis and design must consider the sources and forms in which the data inputs will be needed. It is entirely likely that the required data are not currently available, which can lead to the problems associated with securing data from other departments, forms design, data reliability, and so on.

All information systems involve individuals at one or more points. The role they play in the success or failure of any system cannot be stressed enough. Basically poor systems can function satisfactorily, given good human support, while systems that appear excellent on paper can fail dismally when faced with human resistance. Initial resistance to change is a common human characteristic that needs to be considered when developing any system that involves people.

Systems flowcharting is normally initiated early during a systems analysis and design in order to record the emerging form of the proposed system. As mentioned previously, systems flowcharting can be viewed as a subset of systems analysis and design. Because it is the systems flowchart that managers most often encounter in their dealings with computer specialists, it is given special consideration here.

SYSTEMS FLOWCHARTING

A systems flowchart depicts the entire flow of data through a data processing system. It indicates the sources of data, the medium through which the data are input to the computer, the operations performed, the medium through which the output is received, and the nature of the output. Thus the systems flowchart provides a visual representation of the interactions of personnel, data, and equipment. While this type of flowchart does not usually conform to a rigid structure, certain symbols are commonly used. The most important symbols employed in systems flowcharting are as follows:

Systems Flowcharting Symbol	Description
	Processing A processing of data by the computer
	General Input/Output A general symbol for the input/output of data
	Punched Card Input/Output The input/output of data by punched card
	Magnetic Tape Input/Output The input/output of data by magnetic tape
	Communications Link The transmission of data from one location to another via communication lines

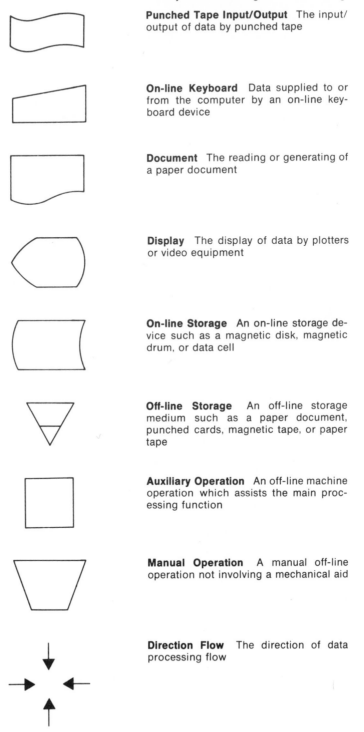

Punched Tape Input/Output The input/ output of data by punched tape

On-line Keyboard Data supplied to or from the computer by an on-line key- board device

Document The reading or generating of a paper document

Display The display of data by plotters or video equipment

On-line Storage An on-line storage de- vice such as a magnetic disk, magnetic drum, or data cell

Off-line Storage An off-line storage medium such as a paper document, punched cards, magnetic tape, or paper tape

Auxiliary Operation An off-line machine operation which assists the main proc- essing function

Manual Operation A manual off-line operation not involving a mechanical aid

Direction Flow The direction of data processing flow

Templates and flowcharting worksheets are commercially available to facilitate the preparation of neat flowcharts.

Illustrations of Systems Flowcharts

To illustrate the use of systems flowcharting symbols, consider a simple inventory recordkeeping system in which the current inventory levels are kept on a magnetic tape master file. At the close of operations each week a list of transactions affecting inventory levels is read in from punched cards. The computer processes the data in such a way that the master file is updated to reflect the week's transactions and an inventory status report is printed out. This series of operations is depicted in the systems flowchart of Figure 5–1. Note that no details of how the computer actually satisfies the data processing objectives are included; this detail is presented in a program flowchart.

A systems flowchart can be used to illustrate a regional sales manager interfacing via a computer terminal with the company's sales forecasting model. Consider a situation in which last month's sales summaries have recently become available, and the sales manager wants to use these data to develop his region's sales forecasts for the next two quarters. Sitting at a terminal, he establishes remote communications with the computer located at company headquarters and instructs the program for the sales forecasting model to be called

FIGURE 5–1
Systems Flowchart for a Simple Inventory System

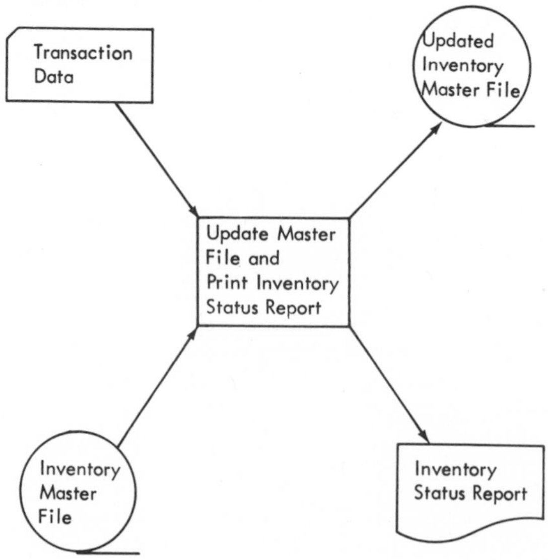

FIGURE 5–2
Systems Flowchart for Remote Sales Forecasting

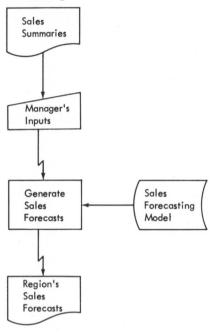

from on-line storage. After the program has been *loaded* (i.e., placed) in primary storage, the manager types in the requisite data inputs. The computer processes the data through the preprogrammed forecasting model, and the next two quarters' forecasts are printed out at the manager's terminal. The output is then used by the sales manager to assist in planning, organizing, and controlling future activities in his region. Figure 5–2 presents a flowchart for this system.

PROGRAM FLOWCHARTING

A program flowchart is a detailed presentation of the logic the computer follows in satisfying management's information requirements. All of the details included in a program flowchart can be covered by a single item in a systems flowchart. For example, in the sales forecasting illustration (Figure 5–2), the generation of the sales forecast is a single block in the systems flowchart. A program flowchart would describe in detail the logic underlying the sales forecasting model.

The program flowchart also provides a useful vehicle for the initial formulation of an *algorithm*. The algorithm is the series of operations that the computer is to follow in order to generate the desired information. Standard flowcharting symbols define the computer's range of capabilities and hence the limits upon an appropriate algorithm. If a proposed algorithm cannot be expressed in a flowchart, the analysis procedure has not been defined well enough to be translated into a computer program.

Experienced programmers often do not need to develop carefully detailed flowcharts because they are accustomed to thinking in terms of algorithms. However, this ability is not a common one, and the preparation of program flowcharts forces algorithmic thinking and helps develop facility in conceptualizing algorithms. Over time it may be possible to rely less and less upon the formal structure of flowcharts, but they are always useful for keeping track of evolving logic.

A carefully prepared program flowchart can be turned over to a skilled programmer for coding into a computer program. All of the required computations, tests, comparisons, and so on are indicated by the flowchart. Ideally, the flowchart can be translated into any one of a large number of programming languages.

Since a flowchart graphically presents the logic of a computer program, it provides a convenient reference for finding logic errors. It is much more difficult to find logic errors in a computer program than in its flowchart.

Because computer programmers generally have considerable job mobility, a company frequently finds itself using programs that were written by personnel who are no longer with the organization. If modifications to any of these programs are required, a flowchart is an invaluable aid to understanding the original programmer's logic. This factor is so important that considerable progress has been made in programming the computer to draw flowcharts from programs. Anytime a program is changed, it can be rerun in order to generate an up-to-date flowchart.

Certain symbols are commonly used in developing program flow-

Program Flowcharting Symbol	Description
	Processing A processing of data by the computer
	Input/Output Input/output of data by the computer

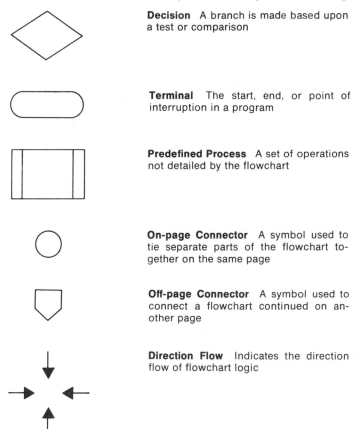

Decision A branch is made based upon a test or comparison

Terminal The start, end, or point of interruption in a program

Predefined Process A set of operations not detailed by the flowchart

On-page Connector A symbol used to tie separate parts of the flowchart together on the same page

Off-page Connector A symbol used to connect a flowchart continued on another page

Direction Flow Indicates the direction flow of flowchart logic

charts, as with systems flowcharts. The above symbols are used with program flowcharts.

One of the easiest ways to learn flowcharting is by studying examples, a generalization which is especially true in regard to program flowcharting. By considering a number of examples, it is possible to gain an understanding of the proper use of program flowcharting symbols. In addition, examples provide insights into how the computer's basic capabilities can be turned into useful algorithms.

Single-Pass Execution

The first flowchart illustrates what is known as *single-pass execution*[1] (see Figure 5–3). It is so called because a single data set is in-

---

[1] The approach to program flowcharting presented in this book is highly structured and is very close to that used in actually writing a computer program. The authors prefer this approach because it requires you to think hard about a problem before trying to write a program for it. A less structured approach does exist, and is favored

FIGURE 5–3
Program Flowchart with
Single-Pass Execution

put, processing takes place, and an output is generated. The flowchart presents an algorithm for computing an hourly worker's gross salary. Inputs include the employee's identification number, hours worked, and hourly wage rate, with the *variable names* ID, HOURS and RATE used to store the values that are input. Storage provisions are also made for SALARY, the variable name for the worker's gross salary, which is the product of the values for HOURS and RATE. Output is comprised of the values stored in ID, HOURS, RATE, and SALARY.

Computer Storage

by some instructors. For example, in Figure 5–3 descriptions such as "Input Employee Record," "Compute Salary," and "Output Employee Record" might be used. With this approach the actual details of how to perform each operation are left for the programming stage.

Note that in the computation of SALARY an asterisk (*) is used in place of the usual multiplication symbol (×). This is a carryover into flowcharting from programming languages, in which the asterisk is used to specify a multiplication operation. Also note that an arrow symbol (←) is used to indicate a *substitution activity*. In this case the product of the values for HOURS and RATE is substituted into the computer's storage location for SALARY.

A Branching Decision

A slightly more complex version of the above flowcharting illustration occurs when time and a half is paid for all hours worked over 40.

FIGURE 5–4
Program Flowchart with
a Branching Decision

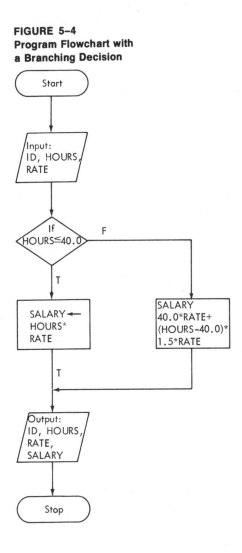

This situation requires the use of the computer's *branching* capability (see Figure 5–4). Branching occurs when the next operation performed is determined on the basis of a test or comparison. The difference between the flowcharts in Figures 5–3 and 5–4 is the inclusion of a test to see whether or not the employee has worked only 40 or fewer hours. If so, SALARY is determined by the TRUE (T) branch of the flowchart. If not, the FALSE (F) branch computes SALARY on ' the basis of time and a half for all hours worked over 40.[2] This flowchart also illustrates single-pass execution, since only a single employee's record is input, processed, and output.

Loops

Another important capability of a computer is *looping* — branching back and repeating a series of steps. Indeed, it is this looping capability that accounts for the computer's great computational strength.

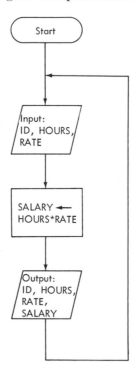

FIGURE 5–5
Program Flowchart with a Loop

---

[2] Some people prefer to construct their branches in terms of YES and NO options rather than TRUE and FALSE. This approach is perfectly satisfactory. The authors prefer the TRUE and FALSE approach because it is more in keeping with how programming languages are structured.

A loop is illustrated in Figure 5–5, which is identical to Figure 5–3 except that a loop has been added. With this flowchart, the computer will continue processing employee records until all records have been analyzed. This is not an illustration of single-pass execution, since multiple inputs, processing, and output are involved.

A Loop with a Counter.   In Figure 5–5, looping terminates when the data inputs are exhausted. However, this method for stopping a loop is not usually desirable because it does not lead to a natural program termination. Instead, the operating system must intervene and terminate program execution, with the consequence that an error message is printed. In general, it is better to include in the flowchart logic a procedure for deciding when control should pass out of the loop. One method that is extremely useful involves the inclusion of a *counter* (see Figure 5–6). A *counter variable* is used to record the

FIGURE 5–6
Program Flowchart with a Loop and a Counter

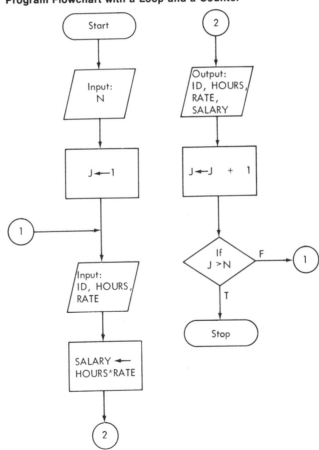

number of times a step, or series of steps, has been performed. When used for controlling an input loop, a counter variable keeps track of the number of records that have been input.

The first operation in Figure 5–6 shows the input of what is referred to in a punched card environment as a *header card.* The number of records, N, to be processed is placed on the header card, the first card in the data deck. Following the input of the header card is a step called *initializing a variable,* in this case storing the value 1 in the computer's storage location for the counter variable J. The actual counting of the number of records is accomplished with the substitution activity, J←J+1. The first time through the loop J takes on the value 2, J←1+1. It is important to note that J←J+1 is a substitution activity and not an algebraic equation. The loop is repeated until J, the counter which is *incremented* by 1 each time a record is processed, is greater than N, the number of records.[3]

All of the flowcharts preceding Figure 5–6 contained a small enough number of operations that a single top-to-bottom logic flow was all that was needed. In Figure 5–6, however, two columns are required to present the algorithm, and an on-page connector symbol is used. The first and second columns of the flowchart are tied together by the on-page connector symbols numbered 2. These connector symbols indicate that the bottom of column one of the flowchart picks up again at the top of column two.

Off of the FALSE (F) branch of the test of whether J>N is an on-page connector symbol numbered 1. This connector symbol indicates that the algorithm's logic calls for a branch to another connector symbol numbered 1, in this case, back to the input of values for ID, HOURS, and RATE. The purpose of an on-page connector symbol is to reduce the number of lines on a flowchart and thus make it easier to read.

A Loop with a Last-Record Check.   An alternative and more widely used method for terminating the reading of input data is to use a *last-record check.* With this approach a special record is placed at the end of the data. A test is then included after the input of each record to see whether or not the input is the special record that marks the end of the data. In a punched card environment this special last record is placed at the bottom of the data deck and is referred to as a *trailer card* or *end-of-file card.* The reason this approach is more popular than using a counter is that it does not require a knowledge of the number of records to be processed. An example of a last record check is pro-

---

[3] You might wonder at this point why, for example, that J is not initialized with a value of 0, and then control would pass out of the loop when J is equal to N. This logic can be used, but because of the way many programming languages are structured it is frequently more convenient to use the illustrated approach.

FIGURE 5–7
Program Flowchart with a Last-Record Check

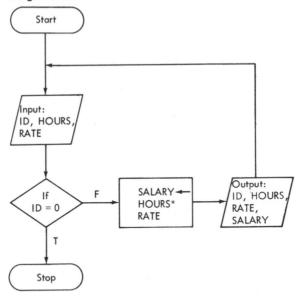

vided by the flowchart shown in Figure 5–7. It assumes that the end-of-file record has a value of 0 for the employee identification number (there is no worker with this identification number). When this ID of 0 is read, control passes out of the input loop (see Figure 5–7).

A Loop with an Accumulator. From the examples given it might appear that loops are used primarily for the input of data. Actually, the applications of loops are much broader. For example, assume that management wants to determine the *total* gross earnings for *all* hourly workers. In order to provide this information it is necessary to loop all of the values for SALARY through an *accumulator*. This procedure is illustrated in Figure 5–8.

Outside of the loop, TOTSAL, the *accumulator variable* in this illustration, is initialized with a value of zero. The first time through the loop TOTSAL takes on a value equal to the gross earnings (SALARY) computed for the first worker. Each subsequent pass through the loop causes the most recently computed value for SALARY to be added to the previous total. After all of the inputs have been processed, the value for TOTSAL, the total of gross earnings, is output.

Compact Loop Representation. Three different methods for terminating an input loop have been presented: (1) running out of data (not recommended); (2) passing out of the loop when a counter variable exceeds a specified value, and (3) a last-record check. The second

FIGURE 5–8
Program Flowchart with an Accumulator

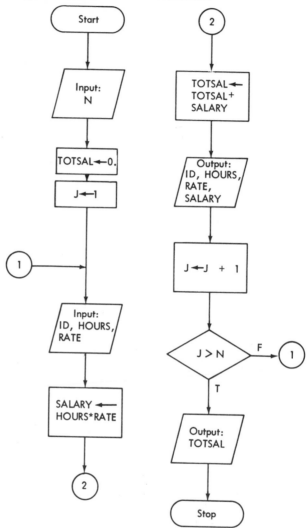

of the three, a loop with a counter, is the most general of the three since it can be used not only with input loops but with any type of loop. Since it is so widely used, compact flowcharting representation of this type of loop has been developed. As you develop increasingly sophisticated program flowcharts, the advantages of having a compact loop representation will become apparent. The predefined process symbol, ⬚, is employed to represent the setting of the counter

FIGURE 5-9
Program Flowchart with Compact Loop
Representation

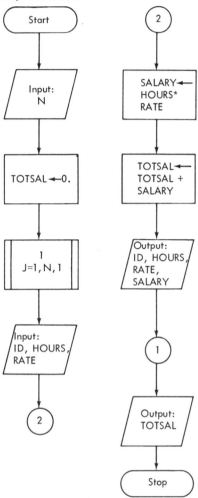

variable to some initial value, incrementing the counter variable at the bottom of the loop, and testing to see whether or not the counter variable exceeds a specified value and control should pass out of the loop. With this simplified representation, an on-page connector symbol is used to mark the bottom of the loop.

Figure 5-9 shows how Figure 5-8 would have looked had the predefined process symbol been used for the loop. The top value in the predefined process symbol provides the number of the on-page connector symbol that marks the bottom of the loop. The bottom portion identifies the loop variable, its lower limit, its upper limit, and the increment. In order to enhance the readability of the flowchart, a dotted line can be included to show the operations encompassed by the loop.

This introduction to program flowcharting has shown how, given just a few basic operations, surprisingly sophisticated algorithms can be developed. You should now try to develop appropriate flowcharts for the assignments that immediately follow this section. After developing a reasonable facility for drawing program flowcharts and coding simple programs, the next step is to study the section on subscripted variables which follows in this chapter. While this material is not particularly difficult, it is at a higher level of abstraction than that presented above, and it is best studied after the basic skills have been mastered.

ASSIGNMENTS (BASIC FLOWCHARTING CONCEPTS)

5-1.   Every charge and payment to a customer's account is recorded on a punched card. These cards are batch processed in order to update existing records. The old account balances are stored on magnetic tape. The objective of the data processing is to update the magnetic tape of account balances and to print out the customer account numbers and new balances. Prepare a systems flowchart for the charge account system described above.

5-2.   A proposed point-of-sale credit card checking system would have the sales clerk type on a keyboard the credit card number and the amount of the sale. This information would then be communicated to a remote computer. Stored on-line at the computer facility would be a listing of all valid credit card numbers and the maximum allowable per-unit charge for each charge account. Based upon this checking, approval or disapproval of the credit sale would be communicated back to the sales clerk. Prepare a systems flowchart of the credit card checking system.

5-3.   When the purchasing department places an order, a record of the order is stored in the computer's memory. When the invoice (bill) from the vendor arrives, it is also stored. Another important document is the receiving report, which indicates that the ordered item has arrived. With the on-line system described here, the order, invoice, and receiving report are all placed in computer storage from a terminal. Once all of these inputs have been received, recorded, and checked, a voucher is printed out and sent to the accounts payable department. The voucher results in a payment check being sent to the vendor. Prepare a systems flowchart for this system.

5-4. On a daily basis banks have to update customer's checking account balances for all new withdrawals and deposits. Prepare a program flowchart that updates the old balance (BAL) by adding the precalculated sum of the deposits (DEP) and subtracting the precalculated sum of the withdrawals (WITH). Include in your input operation the customer's account number (NUMBER). Prepare a flowchart that is appropriate for processing just one record and another that accommodates multiple records.

5-5. At the end of each quarter, certain data are recorded on punched cards for all graduating seniors. Specifically, the cards include the student's name (NAME), graduation grade point average (GPA), and a code number for his degree (DEGREE), as shown below:

College	Code Number
Arts and Sciences	1
Business	2
Education	3
Engineering	4

    a. Prepare a program flowchart that prints out the name and graduation grade point average of all students who finished with a 3.5 or better. Use a header card to control the input loop.

    b. Prepare a program flowchart that outputs the names of all graduates of the College of Business. Employ a last-record check on the input loop.

5-6. The water company charges a fixed fee of $3.50 for anywhere between 0 and 175 gallons consumed. From 175 to 500 gallons, a price of $.02/gallon is charged, while all gallons above 500 are billed at a rate of $.01/gallon.

    a. Prepare a program flowchart which inputs a single customer's identification number (ID) and the number of gallons consumed (GAL). Output should be the customer's identification number, the number of gallons used, and the amount of the bill (BILL).

    b. Repeat part *a*, but allow for multiple customer records. Employ a last-record check on the input loop.

5-7. The formula for simple compounding is $A = P(1+i)^N$, where
    A = Amount after N compounding periods
    P = Principal
    i = Interest rate per period
    N = Number of compounding periods

Prepare a program flowchart that inputs P, i and N. The objective of the flowchart is to compute and output the amount accumulated, A, after *each* of the N compounding periods.

5-8.   A total of N students have taken a test. Their tests scores (TSCORE) and identification numbers (ID) are punched on cards and input. Prepare a program flowchart that determines and outputs:

    a.   The mean test score

    b.   The identification number and test score of the student with the highest score. (There is only one student with the highest test score.)

*Subscripted Variables in Program Flowcharting[4]

Up to this point only simple variables have been encountered. A *simple variable* is one that has a single storage location in the computer's memory. For example, the simple variable HOURS has only one location reserved for it:

Computer Storage

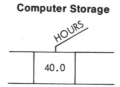

When the next value for HOURS is input, the previous value is erased from memory and is thus lost forever.

Sometimes it is important to be able to store a whole series of values for a variable. In order to accomplish this objective, it is necessary to designate a string of storage locations. Data stored in this manner is referred to as an *array*. A variable that has a string of locations reserved for its use is referred to as a *subscripted variable*. Each position in the string is identified by a subscript. The general form for a subscripted variable is:

Variable Name(Subscript)

An example is:

HOURS(3)

If all of the employee identification numbers, hours worked, and wage rates are input into storage as subscripted variables, the stored values would appear as shown on the next page.

---

[4] All sections and assignments in this book involving subscripted variables are indicated by an asterisk.

Computer Storage

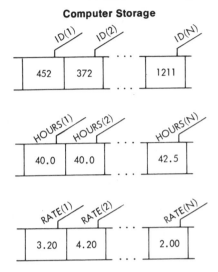

Stored in ID(1), HOURS(1), and RATE(1) are the employee identification number, hours worked, and wage rate for the first hourly worker. In ID(2), HOURS(2), and RATE(2) are the data for the second employee—and so on through the total of N workers.

In order to illustrate the use of subscripted variables, assume that management wants as output the identification number and salary of the worker whose gross earnings is the largest (for simplicity at this point, assume there is only one such employee). The program flowchart in Figure 5–10 accomplishes this objective. A loop is used to input the values for the subscripted variables. As J varies from 1 to N, the values for ID(J), HOURS(J), and RATE(J) are input. For example, when J=2, the values for ID(2), HOURS(2), and RATE(2) are placed into storage. The variable TOPSAL is then initialized with a value of 0. TOPSAL in this algorithm stores the top salary figure that has been found at any point in time. In the next loop, gross earnings (SALARY (K)) is computed for the employee whose subscript corresponds to the current value of K. For example, when K=4, the gross earnings of the fourth employee is computed, SALARY(4) ← HOURS(4) + RATE(4). A test is made within the loop to determine whether the current value of SALARY(K) is greater than TOPSAL, the top value for SALARY(K) found previously. If this test proves true, TOPSAL is assigned the value of SALARY(K) and the identification number associated with ID(K) is stored in IDTOP. If the test proves false, K is incremented by 1 and another pass through the loop is made—unless the last record has been processed. When the looping is completed the identification number and salary of the employee

FIGURE 5–10
Program Flowchart with Subscripted Variables

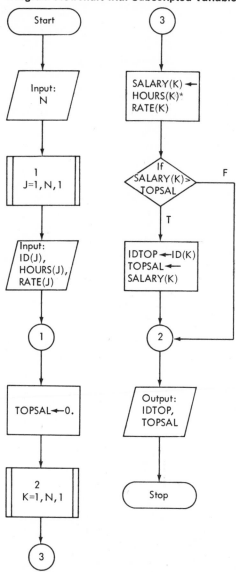

with the largest gross earnings are output. Processing is then complete.

In addition to singly subscripted variables, double and higher subscripted variables are possible with most computers and programming languages. Their general form is:

Variable Name (Subscript 1, Subscript 2, . . . Subscript N)

An example is:

MATRIX(4,3 . . . 8)

The applications at an introductory level of these higher order subscripted variables are limited and therefore are not discussed here.

ASSIGNMENTS (ADVANCED FLOWCHARTING CONCEPTS)

°5-9. The program flowchart of Figure 5-8 uses simple variables in accumulating the salary total. Prepare a program flowchart which accomplishes the same data processing objectives as Figure 5-8 but which employs subscripted variables for the worker's identification number, hours worked, and wage rate.

°5-10. Input on data cards are the employee's identification number (ID), departmental code number (CODE), and gross earnings for the current pay period (GROSS). Prepare a program flowchart that inputs the employee records (use subscripted variables) and then totals the gross earnings in each department. Output the departmental code numbers and the gross earning totals for each department. There are three departments, with code numbers 1, 2, and 3.

°5-11. Referring to assignment 5-10, modify the program flowchart so that any three departmental code numbers can be used. In other words, make the departmental code numbers data inputs (once again use subscripted variables).

REFERENCES

Books

Bohl, Marilyn *Flowcharting Techniques.* Palo Alto, Calif.: Science Research Associates, 1971.

Chapin, Ned *Flowcharts.* Princeton, N.J.: Auerback, 1971.

Farina, Mario V. *Flowcharting.* Englewood Cliffs, N.J.: Prentice-Hall, 1970.

Schriber, Thomas J. *Fundamentals of Flowcharting.* New York: John Wiley & Sons, 1969.

Silver, Gerald A. and Joan B. Silver. *Data Processing for Business.* New York: Harcourt Brace Jovanovich, 1973.

The Role Played by Terminals

Communicating from a Terminal

The BASIC Language

Programming Statements, Line Numbers, Characters, Computations, Substitution Activities, LET Statement, Input, Output, END Statement, STOP Statement, REM Statement, RUN, BASIC, An Illustration, Branching, Looping, Systems Commands

Assignments (Basic Concepts)

Advanced Concepts in BASIC

Subscripted Variables, Strings, Functions and Subroutines

Assignments (Advanced Concepts)

References

This and the next chapter cover the programming languages selected for inclusion in this book. BASIC, presented in this chapter, is the most popular time-sharing language. Programming languages cannot be mastered simply through reading; they must be practiced. The assignments included here and in the applications chapters provide you with practice opportunities.

6

The BASIC Programming Language

Until recently, managers who wanted to use the computer had to either work through an intermediary or become fairly knowledgeable in regards to computer programming, operating systems, and hardware. Now it is easier for managers in many organizations to employ the computer, largely due to the increasing availability of simplified programming languages and computer terminals. Computer terminals such as the one shown in Figure 6–1 allow the user to enter data or instructions to the computer without having to go to the organization's computer center. As many users have discovered, these terminals are relatively easy to operate. In addition, to support and facilitate terminal usage, simplified programming languages have been developed. As a consequence of these developments, a manager can operate from a terminal with less knowledge about hardware, operating systems, and computer programming than was formerly required for computer usage.

This chapter briefly examines the use of terminals and, in general, remote communications with the computer. The major focus, however, is on the BASIC programming language. Because of its simplicity, BASIC is currently the most widely used terminal-oriented language, but other programming languages can also be used from a terminal, depending upon the computer system.

THE ROLE PLAYED BY TERMINALS

Figure 6–2 depicts the method which we suggest will be increasingly used by managers to interface with the computer. Data or instructions are typed in from a remote terminal. These inputs are carried via communication lines to the central computer facility, processing takes place, and output is returned to the user. Some of the

131

FIGURE 6–1
Modern Computer Terminal

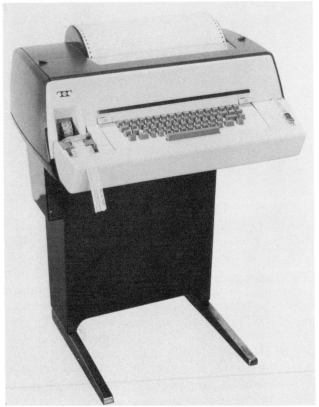

Courtesy of the TELETYPE Corporation

application areas include sales forecasting, budgeting, evaluation of sales promotion plans, and production scheduling.

Terminals are not always the best way to use the computer. Some jobs can be done much better by *batch processing,* a method whereby the data are accumulated over a period of time and then processed in one batch. While this approach is very efficient, it often does not provide a *real-time capability*—by which data output is received in time to influence decision making. However, not all applications must be real-time. For example, preparing a monthly payroll is a natural batch-processing application. Another consideration that influences whether an application is to be batch processed or run on a terminal is the amount of data involved. With a terminal all of the data are normally entered manually. If there is a considerable amount of data to be processed, using a terminal may not be feasible because of the time

FIGURE 6-2
Managers Interfacing with the Computer from a Terminal Equipped with a Video Display

Courtesy of WANG Laboratories, Inc.

required to input the data. This point should not be overemphasized, however. Considerable progress is being made toward establishing data bases that can be "tapped" by time-sharing terminals. Still, terminal operations are usually more expensive than batch processing and should not be relied upon unless there are good reasons for doing so.

The primary uses of the computer are for *computer-assisted decision making* and *routine data processing.* The former is concerned with computerized problem solving and analysis, while the latter involves the electronic processing of large files of data. (These applications are considered in detail in Chapters 8 and 9.) Many computer-assisted decision-making applications are performed from terminals, while most routine data processing applications are batch processed.

COMMUNICATING FROM A TERMINAL

The user of a terminal wants to process data in order to obtain needed information. The data may be processed by a program that has been written by someone else and is stored within the computer, or the user may enter his own program. Programs that have been previously written and stored are known as *packaged* or *canned* programs (see Chapter 9). User-written programs must be expressed in a programming language that is compatible with the capabilities of the available computer system.

With both packaged and original programs, it is first necessary to establish communications with the computer. The exact manner in which communications are established depends upon the computer system being used. A common arrangement is where a terminal such as is the one shown in Figure 6–1 is linked to the computer through a telephone line.[1] A device known as an *acoustic coupler* serves as an intermediary between the terminal and the computer by encoding and decoding the data transmitted over the telephone line. In order to use the terminal, the user turns it on, presses an appropriate button on the acoustic coupler (for example, the TALK button), picks up the telephone, and dials a number designated by the computer center. When communications have been established, a high-pitched tone is heard over the telephone. The user then presses another appropriate button (for example, the DATA button), places the telephone back into the acoustic coupler, and types in an appropriate identification and password (i.e., a code word). This last procedure ensures that only authorized users have access to the computer. When these inputs generate a response from the computer, the user can call a packaged program or enter his own. After the user obtains his data analysis, he signs off from the system.

THE BASIC LANGUAGE

The BASIC programming language was originally developed at Dartmouth College in order to facilitate student use of the computer. Today it is the most widely used time-sharing language. *Time-sharing* refers to a situation in which multiple users concurrently share the computer. In a terminal environment this means that many terminals can be actively connected to the computer at the same time.

In most ways BASIC is similar to FORTRAN, which we will discuss in Chapter 7. The structure of both languages makes them well suited for performing mathematical and statistical computations. However, BASIC is much easier to learn and use than FORTRAN, especially in regard to the input and output of data. While BASIC does not have all of the capabilities of FORTRAN, for the casual computer user (most managers), the limitations are minor.

Because there is no standard form for BASIC, slight differences in the language exist from system to system, and some systems have

---

[1] In some instances there is a cable that directly links the terminal to the computer.

features not available on others. Transferring from one system to another is not usually difficult, though, since most versions of BASIC are very similar. The version of BASIC presented in this chapter is patterned after that for the Control Data Corporation 6000 Computer Systems.

BASIC instructions and data are usually typed in by a user sitting at a terminal, but many terminals have the capability for the input and output of BASIC programs and data from paper tape. When paper tape is used as an input medium, programs and data can be prepared off-line and then quickly and efficiently input to the computer. BASIC is not exclusively a terminal language but can also be used for batch-processing applications. This use is relatively infrequent, however, because of the language's limited capabilities.

Programming Statements

Two types of programming statements are input to the computer — executable and nonexecutable. The *executable statements* cause some action within the program, such as making a computation. *Nonexecutable statements* simply provide information to the computer

FIGURE 6–3
A BASIC Program for Figure 5–3

```
UGA 6400 INTERCOM 3.0 PSR 344    ⎫
DATE 07/15/75                    ⎪
TIME 11.59.01.                   ⎪
LOGIN                            ⎪
ENTER USER NAME-UGABUS02         ⎪
ENTER PASSWORD-                  ⎬       LOGIN procedures
XXXXXXX                          ⎪
07/15/75 LOGGED IN AT 11.59.58.  ⎪
        WITH USER-ID HX          ⎪
        EQUIP/PORT 14/05          ⎭
COMMAND- EDITOR                  ⎫       Systems commands
..FORMAT,BASIC                   ⎭
..10 REM COMPUTES WORKERS' GROSS SALARY ⎫
20 READ I,H,R                    ⎪
30 DATA 0420,40,2.60             ⎪
40 S=H*R                         ⎬       User's program
50 PRINT "ID","HOURS","RATE","SALARY"    ⎪
60 PRINT I,H,R,S                 ⎪
70 END                           ⎭
RUN,BASIC                        ⎬       Systems command

ID        HOURS      RATE      SALARY ⎫
420        40         2.6       104.  ⎭   Data output

  BYE,BYE              ⎫ Systems           ⎫
COMMAND - LOGOUT       ⎭ commands          ⎪
CP TIME 1.071                             ⎬  LOGOUT procedures
PP TIME 15.929                            ⎪
CONNECT  TIME     0HRS       3MIN.        ⎪
07/15/75        LOGGED OUT AT 12.02.59    ⎭
```

system, such as defining the number of subscripts for a subscripted variable. A program usually contains both executable and nonexecutable statements.

Figure 6–3 shows a complete BASIC program that has been coded from the flowchart of Figure 5–3. Items typed in by the user are shown in boldface; everything else is response from the computer.[2]

Line Numbers

In BASIC, every programming statement must be assigned a unique line number. With most computer systems the number of digits in each line number is limited to four or five. In general, it is good practice to skip numbers between consecutive statements; this facilitates the later addition of statements, since the computer executes statements according to increasing line number rather than by the order in which they are entered. Only one statement can be entered on a line, and it can be no longer than one print line. If a line number is repeated, the new statement takes the place of the old. This procedure offers a relatively simple way of changing programming statements.

Assigning Line Numbers

Examples	*Comments*
10– 20– 30– 40– 50–	Permits the easy insertion of additional programming statements.
10– 30– 20– 40– 50–	The programming statements are executed in the order 10, 20, 30, 40, 50.
10– 20– 30– 40– 50– 20–	The programming statement associated with the first reference to line 20 is destroyed.

Characters

In writing BASIC statements the following characters can be used:

Numeric......................0 through 9
Alphabetic..................A through Z
Special ....blank . , + − * / ( ) = < > " ;

---

[2] On your computer system, the interactions between the user and the computer will probably be somewhat different.

Every programming statement is made up of combinations of these characters. Additional characters included on most terminal keyboards can be used in literal statements, which are discussed later.

Computations

In most analyses, certain computations must be made, such as computing an hourly worker's gross salary. These computations are performed in accordance with arithmetic expressions made up of constants, variables, and operators.

Constants are numbers that do not change value during program execution. All constants are assumed to be positive unless assigned negative values. Integers can be written with or without a decimal point, but all fractions must be expressed in decimal form. Very small or large numbers can be written in exponential form, and depending upon their size and the system under which BASIC is being run, they must be written this way. This is how all numbers with decimals in BASIC are internally stored by the computer. Basically, the number is rewritten as a number raised to an appropriate power of ten.

Expressing Numbers in Exponential Form

Number	Scientific Notation	Exponential Form
2320	2.320×10^3	2.320E3
.00325	3.25×10^{-3}	3.25E$-$3

Thinking of the number in scientific notation helps determine the correct value to follow E. This value reflects the number of places the decimal point has been moved to the right or the left. Moving the decimal to the right results in negative exponents, while the opposite holds for movements to the left.

The values of *variables* are free to change during program execution. In the computer's memory, storage locations are reserved for all of the variables found in the program. The values of these variables are either input or calculated during program execution. In BASIC, all variable names must be either a single alphabetic letter or a letter followed by a single numeral. For example, S, R and H1 are all valid variable names; S might represent salary, R stand for rate, and H1 be the symbol for hours.

Arithmetic operators are symbols used to indicate how variables and constants are to be combined. Five arithmetic operators are available for computational purposes.

Arithmetic Operators

Operation	Symbol	Example	Interpretation
Addition	+	A+B	A plus B
Subtraction	−	A−B	A minus B
Multiplication.........	*	A*B	A times B
Division.................	/	A/B	A divided by B
Exponentiation	** or ↑	A*2	A raised to the 2nd power

Computations in BASIC follow these rules:
1. All quantities within parentheses are evaluated first, starting with the innermost parentheses.
2. Exponentiation is performed before multiplication, division, addition, or subtraction.
3. Multiplication and division are performed before addition or subtraction.
4. In case of computational ties, computations proceed on a left to right basis.

The implications of how computations are performed in BASIC should be briefly explored. For example, consider the following expression:

$$(D3-A)/B^{**}C$$

where D3 = 12
     A = 3
     B = 3
     C = 2

First, the value for A will be subtracted from the value for D3 ($12 - 3 = 9$) because of the parentheses. Then B will be raised to the C power ($3^{**}2 = 9$), since exponentiation is next in the processing hierarchy. Finally, division takes place ($9/9 = 1$). If there had been ties in the order in which the computations were to be performed (for example, two addition operations), computations would have been performed on a left to right scan. Shown below are some examples of how arithmetic expressions should be written in BASIC.

Examples of Arithmetic Expressions in BASIC

Expression	In BASIC
$(A + B)^2$	(A+B)**2
$\dfrac{A + B}{C1}$	(A+B)/C1
$\dfrac{A + BC^T}{4T}$	(A+B*C**T)/(4*T)

In addition to arithmetic operators, *relational operators* are also used in BASIC. These operators are shown below. Their role in BASIC will be explored later.

Relational Operators

Operator	Symbol	Example	Interpretation
Equals............................	=	A=B	A equals B
More than.......................	>	A>B	A is more than B
More than or equal to	>=	A>=B	A is more than or equal to B
Less than.......................	<	A<B	A is less than B
Less than or equal to	<=	A<=B	A is less than or equal to B
Not equal.......................	<>	A<>B	A is not equal to B

Substitution Activities

In computer programming the equals (=) sign has an interpretation somewhat different than it has in mathematics. It actually represents a *substitution activity* which says to assign to the variable on the left-hand side of the arithmetic expression the value determined from the right-hand side. In many instances, this seems quite normal. For example, the statement of line 10:

$$10 \ A=P*R**2$$

would mean that in the storage location for A (area) place the value of (P*R**2) (πr^2, the area of a circle.) In other cases, such as with a counter variable, the equals sign does not make algebraic sense. An example is the statement of line 20:

$$20 \ J=J+1$$

Viewed as a substitution activity this statement says to place in the storage location for J the previous value of J plus 1. In the flowcharts seen previously an arrow ($\leftarrow$) was used to represent a substitution activity, but in BASIC an equals (=) must be used.

LET Statement

The LET statement in BASIC performs substitution activities. It takes the general form shown below. In this and other illustrations of the general form for BASIC programming statements, boldface is used to indicate the invariant portion of the statement.

LET   variable name   =   arithmetic expression

An example of the LET statement is shown by line 25.

25 LET A=B+C

The use of LET is optional with many BASIC language translators, and in such cases it can be dropped from the coding. For example,

25 A=B+C

is all that is required with many computer systems. Such is the case with the CDC 6000 Computer Systems we are patterning our BASIC language on, so the word LET is excluded from the programming illustrations.

Input

Though not much flexibility is available, the input of data in BASIC is quite simple in comparison to that used in other programming languages. Data can be included with the program that is written, or it can be input by the user during program execution. In either case, there is no concern over such matters as whether the data is in decimal or integer form.

READ and DATA Statements.   The READ and DATA statements are used in combination to input data *with the program.* The READ statement specifies the variables for which data are to be input, and the DATA statement specifies the actual variable values. For example,

10 READ X1,X2
20 DATA 100,200

causes 100 and 200 to be stored in the computer memory locations reserved for X1 and X2, respectively. If desired, one DATA statement can serve two or more READ statements. For example,

10 READ X1,X2
20 READ Y1,Y2
30 DATA 100,200,500,600

results in 100 being stored for X1, 200 for X2, 500 for Y1 and 600 for Y2. All of the data specified by DATA statements are placed in an *array* (i.e., a sequential string of storage locations) by the computer. As variables are encountered in the READ statements, the data in the array are "picked off" and stored in the memory locations for the variables. If more data are specified in the DATA statements than are requested by the READ statements, the unused data are ignored. On the other hand, if all of the data have been exhausted and there are still more READ instructions, program execution stops after the printing of an error message unless the RESTORE statement is used. RESTORE causes the first DATA statement(s) to be used again. For example,

```
10  READ X
20  DATA 10
30  RESTORE
40  READ Y
```

results in both X and Y taking on the value of 10.

It is usually a good practice to place input statements near the beginning of the program. This ensures that all of the variable values are specified by the time they are needed in the program. In addition, it separates the entering of data from the main program logic.

Input Statement. The INPUT statement can be used to supply data to the program *while it is running*. The general form of this statement is:

INPUT variable list

An example is:

10 INPUT I,H,R

When the computer encounters an INPUT statement during program execution, a question mark (?) is printed. The user must then enter data for all of the variables specified in the INPUT statement. Program execution continues once the variable values have been input.

One problem in using the INPUT statement is that the computer assumes the user knows all of the variables for which values must be input and the order in which these inputs are to be entered. Unless the user is quite familiar with the program, he will have to consult the program in order to decide which variable values to enter. There is a way around this inconvenience, however, and it will be considered during the discussion of literal data.

In many instances the preparer of a program is not the sole or major user. Also, at the time the program is written, the input values may not be known with certainty. The INPUT statement is much more convenient to use in these cases than the READ-DATA combination. However, the INPUT statement is usually not desirable if large amounts of data must be entered.

Output

The PRINT statement in BASIC has a large number of uses. It can be employed to skip a line (by printing a blank), provide column headings, and output variable values.

FIGURE 6–4
Division of a Print Line into Output Fields

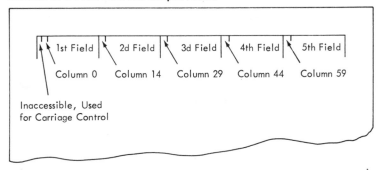

While it is very simple to output in BASIC, relatively little flexibility is afforded. The output page is usually divided into five *fields* (a group of columns considered together is referred to as a field) of 15 columns each. The first column in the first field is used by the computer for output carriage control and is inaccessible to the user. Consequently, the first field has only 14 effective columns. The columns accessible to the user are numbered 0–73, with the first data output starting in column 0, the second in column 14, and so on through the fifth field, which starts in column 59. If more than five data output items are included in a PRINT statement, the additional items are placed on the next line. Figure 6–4 illustrates the division of a print line into output fields.

When the user wants to output variable values, the PRINT statement followed by the variable names separated by commas is used. For example,

$$10 \text{ PRINT A,B,C}$$

causes the values of A, B, and C stored in the computer's memory to be output, starting in columns 0, 14, and 29, respectively.

Actually, the user can exercise more control over the output than has been indicated so far. The width of the output fields, and, hence, the number of variables that can be output per line, can be changed by using semicolons instead of commas to separate the variables in the PRINT statement. The field width is shortened to 6 spaces for numbers of one to three digits, 9 spaces for numbers of four to six digits, and 12 spaces for numbers of seven to nine digits. For over nine digits, the normal 15-column field is used. Commas and semicolons can be intermixed in PRINT statements.

The PRINT statement can also be used to output the results of arithmetic computations. For example,

20 PRINT A1+A2

results in the sum of A1 and A2 being output.

In order to have an attractive, readable output, it is usually necessary to include column headings or comments on the printout. In programming, this type of output is known as *literal data*. Literal data are included in a PRINT statement by placing quotation marks around the desired output. For example,

40 PRINT "GROSS SALARY"

causes GROSS SALARY to be printed out starting in the first output field.

Two or more literals can be included in a single PRINT statement. For example,

50 PRINT "ID","HOURS","RATE","SALARY"

would provide column headings for the outputted values for ID, HOURS, RATE, and SALARY, starting in columns 0, 14, 29, and 44, respectively.

Both literal and numeric data output can be requested in a single PRINT statement. For example,

45 PRINT "GROSS SALARY =",S

would result in an output such as

GROSS SALARY = 88

assuming that 88 was stored in S.

Perhaps you can now guess how literal data can be integrated with the INPUT statement to help clarify exactly what variable values must be entered. The following statements,

20 PRINT "INPUT VALUE FOR X"
22 INPUT X

would result in

INPUT VALUE FOR X
?

being printed out at the user's terminal. Thus it should be clear what needs to be input by the user.

The BASIC language translator always tries to provide output that is as precise as possible. This results in numeric data sometimes appearing as an integer (a whole number such as 20), a decimal (such as 2.5), or in exponential form (4.3E6). The programmer has no control over this aspect of the output.

END Statement

The END statement is the last programming statement in a BASIC program. With some computer systems this statement is optional. When required, however, the END statement must be given the highest line number in the program. For example,

190 PRINT X,Y
200 END

STOP Statement

A STOP statement can be placed anywhere in a program. When it is encountered, program execution terminates. For example,

150 STOP

stops the running of the program at line 150. STOP statements are sometimes used when there are multiple points in a program where the programmer wants program execution terminated.

REM Statement

It is considered good practice to include documentation for any program that is written. Much of this documentation can be included with the program itself through the use of remark statements. In BASIC, a REM statement is employed to include remarks with the program. For example, a program that computes a project's internal rate of return might have the following as its first programming statement.

10 REM THIS IS AN INTERNAL RATE OF RETURN PROGRAM

RUN,BASIC

Once the user is ready to execute his program, RUN,BASIC is typed.[3] This is a *systems command* (not a BASIC language statement) which instructs the computer system to run the program that has been entered. It comes directly after the END statement. Later in the chapter systems commands are discussed in greater detail, but at this point it is sufficient to indicate that systems commands supply instructions to the computer about what to do with the program that is being entered or has been entered. Since systems commands are not programming statements, they are not given line numbers. The following illustrates how the RUN,BASIC command might appear:

---

[3] With many computer systems, RUN rather than RUN,BASIC is sufficient.

120 END
RUN,BASIC

An Illustration

In Figure 6–3 above, a BASIC program was shown for the flowchart presented in Figure 5–3 from the preceding chapter in order to provide a general impression of what a BASIC program run from a terminal looks like. Now that some of the BASIC programming statements have been discussed, you should give Figure 6–3 further study. It can help you see how the elements presented so far are integrated into an executable program.

Branching

In general, programming statements are performed sequentially according to increasing line number. It is possible, however, to program the computer to branch to another point in the program. The GO TO and IF–THEN statements are used in BASIC for branching.

GO TO Statement. The GO TO statement results in an unconditional transfer of control. The line number indicated in the GO TO statement is always executed next. For example,

40 GO TO 80

results in the programming statement associated with line 80 being performed next.

An illustration of the use of the GO TO statement can be provided by a BASIC program for Figure 5–5. This program is presented in Figure 6–5. The way the program in Figure 6–5 is written, data will continue to be processed until the user stops supplying input data. The END statement is never reached because of the GO TO instruction. Endless loops of this type should, in general, be avoided. Much computer time is wasted because of the careless use of GO TO statements.

FIGURE 6–5
A BASIC Program for Figure 5–5

```
10 REM COMPUTES WORKERS' SALARIES
20 PRINT "ID","HOURS","RATE","SALARY"
30 INPUT I,H,R
40 S=H*R
50 PRINT I,H,R,S
60 GO TO 30
70 END
RUN,BASIC
```

FIGURE 6-6
A BASIC Program for Figure 5-4

```
10 REM COMPUTES A WORKER'S SALARY CONSIDERING OVERTIME
20 PRINT "ID","HOURS","RATE","SALARY"
30 READ I,H,R
40 DATA 220,43,3.40
50 IF H<=40.0 THEN 80
60 S=40.0*R+(H-40.0)*1.5*R
70 GO TO 90
80 S=H*R
90 PRINT I,H,R,S
100 END
RUN,BASIC
```

IF–THEN Statement.   BASIC allows a conditional transfer of control in its IF–THEN statement. The general form of this statement is:

IF arithmetic expression relational operator arithmetic expression
THEN line number

Branching takes place to the specified line number when the IF portion is true. However, when the IF is false, the line number after the IF statement is executed. An example of the IF–THEN statement is:

15 IF X>X1 THEN 30

If X is greater than X1, line 30 is performed next; if not, the line number after 15 is executed.

The IF–THEN statement can be made up of constants, variables, and arithmetic expressions. Examples include,

126 IF 2*X>=Y THEN 10
130 IF 5*X2=Y2 THEN 145

Any of the relational operators that were presented earlier can be used in IF–THEN statements. When used in IF–THEN statements, the equals sign has the conventional meaning from mathematics.

The flowchart of Figure 5-4 provides a good vehicle for illustrating the IF–THEN statement. The BASIC program for Figure 5-4 is presented in Figure 6-6. Note the use of the GO TO statement to avoid the incorrect recomputing of S.

Looping

A loop causes a series of statements to be repeated a number of times. In BASIC, the FOR–TO–STEP and NEXT statement combination results in looping. Such a capability usually reduces greatly the required number of programming statements. The general form of the statement is shown below:

FOR variable name=arithmetic expression **TO** arithmetic
.   expression **STEP** arithmetic expression
.

.

NEXT variable name

An example is:

10 FOR I=1 TO 100 STEP 1

.

.

.

50 NEXT I

The easiest way to understand the FOR–TO–STEP and NEXT statement combination is to think of it as a loop with a counter as described in Chapter 5 (see Figure 5–6). The variable associated with FOR serves as a counter variable. This variable is initialized to the value of the expression on the right-hand side of the equals sign. Looping continues until the counter variable exceeds in value the expression to the right of the TO portion of the statement. After each pass through the loop the counter variable is incremented by the value of the expression following STEP. If the increment is 1, "STEP 1" can be omitted, since the computer will assume an increment of 1.

The bottom of the loop is indicated by the NEXT statement. It is at the bottom of the loop that the incrementing is performed. After looping has been performed the specified number of times, control passes to the statement following NEXT. For example,

10 FOR J=1 TO 4

.

.

.

20 NEXT J

will cause the programming statements with line numbers between 10 and 20 to be repeated four times. After the fourth time through the loop, J is incremented to 5, which causes control to pass out of the loop. Other valid loops include,

15 FOR K=X TO Y STEP 2

.

.

.

30 NEXT K

75 FOR M=A1+3 TO A2 STEP 5

    .
    .
    .

80 NEXT M

It is also possible to program *nested loops* — loops written within loops. An illustration is:

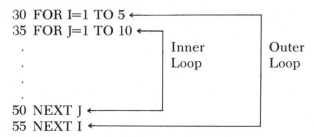

30 FOR I=1 TO 5
35 FOR J=1 TO 10
    .   Inner   Outer
    .   Loop   Loop
    .
    .
50 NEXT J
55 NEXT I

The first time through the loop, I and J are set equal to 1. When line 50 is encountered, control passes back to line 35 and $I = 1$ and $J = 2$. After the inner loop has been passed through ten times, line 55 is executed, which results in a branch to line 30 and the setting of $I = 2$ and $J = 1$. With the nested loops presented above, looping occurs $10 \times 5 = 50$ times in the order (1,1) (1,2) . . . (1,10), (2,1), (2,2) . . . (5,10).

Nested loops always vary through the innermost loop first and then work outwards. They must not intersect each other. For example, the following statements would result in an error message.

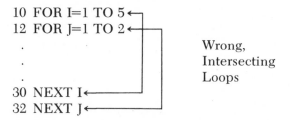

10 FOR I=1 TO 5
12 FOR J=1 TO 2
    .   Wrong,
    .   Intersecting
    .   Loops
30 NEXT I
32 NEXT J

Systems Commands

As has been mentioned previously, computer systems have a set of systems commands that instruct the computer what to do with the program that has been or is being entered. One of these, the RUN, BASIC command, has already been discussed. Several others that are available with most computer systems are quite useful. Their exact form differs from system to system.

In entering a program from a terminal, mistakes are common,

because of either a typing error or a programming error. As long as the RETURN key has not been pressed, mistakes on a line can be erased from computer storage by backspacing to the point of error. A line for which the RETURN key has already been pressed can be erased by retyping the line number along with the correct programming statement. Lines can also be deleted with the DELETE statement. The exact form of the DELETE statement depends very much upon the particular computer system being used, but its function is to delete one or more lines of a program that has been entered. The DELETE statement, as with all systems commands, requires no line number.

Often a user will want a current listing of the program that has been entered, either for his permanent records or, as is frequently the case, because he wants to know exactly what is stored in the computer's memory. This situation often develops because by the time much of the program has been entered, several (if not many) changes and corrections have been made. The LIST statement provides a partial or complete listing of the program. Its exact format, as with all systems commands, can be found by consulting the manufacturer's user's manual.

The material on the BASIC language and systems commands that has been presented thus far must be practiced if it is to be mastered. The assignments that immediately follow provide this experience. BASIC has additional capabilities which are quite useful, some of which are covered in later sections of this chapter. It is now time for you to master the fundamental concepts, however.

ASSIGNMENTS (BASIC CONCEPTS)

6-1. Determine whether the following BASIC programming statements are correct:

a. 100 RUN

b. 80 X=(X1(X2+X3)°5)

c. 90 XA=XB

d. 15 X=Y/−2

e. 30 LIST

f. 42 INPUT X,X1

g. 19 1X=Y°°2

h. 20 DATA 2,2.7E6

i. 82 LET S=5

j. 14 READ 5,6

k. 20 PRINT M,N,M+N

l. 30 PRINT C,D,"TOTAL"

m. 40 GO TO 50

n. 45 IF X=2 THEN GO TO 75

o. 50 FOR I=2 TO 10 STEP 2

.

.

.

60 NEXT STEP

p. 72 IF X1>=X2 THEN 60

q. 20 FOR J=1 TO 5

.

.

.

25 NEXT J

r. 15 DELETE 30,31,22

s.   10 FOR I=1 TO 10
      11 FOR J=1 TO 10

       .
       .
       .

      20 NEXT I
      21 NEXT J

6-2.   Prepare a BASIC program based upon the program flowchart in Figure 5–7 in Chapter 5. The following employee records are to be processed:

ID	HOURS	RATE
560	40	4.00
620	40	3.60
531	40	3.80
195	45	4.00

Include appropriate column headings to enhance the readability of your output.

6-3.   In Chapter 5, Figure 5–8 was presented to illustrate a loop with an accumulator. Prepare a BASIC program from the flowchart to process the following data. Provide column headings for your output.

ID	Hours	Rate
1153	42	3.60
823	42.5	3.60
21	40	4.00
532	40	4.20
458	41	3.40

6-4.   Assignment 5-6 in Chapter 5 involved preparing a flowchart for determining a customer's water bill. Process the following data through a BASIC program based upon that assignment:

ID	GAL
52310	480
55314	732
60241	500
42186	320

6-5.   If the principal is $1,000, the interest rate is 6 percent per year, and the money is invested for ten years, how much is the investment worth after each of the ten years? Base your analysis upon a BASIC program written from the flowchart of assignment 5-7 in Chapter 5.

6-6.   In assignment 5-8 in Chapter 5, a flowchart was requested for the processing of students' test scores. Write a BASIC program based upon this assignment and process the following data inputs:

ID	TSCORE
03	85
15	96
12	60
07	75
01	77
13	88

09	92
08	38
02	81
14	72
06	83
23	88
04	75
05	75
10	90

ADVANCED CONCEPTS IN BASIC

*Subscripted Variables[4]

In BASIC, a single alphabetic character must be used to represent a subscripted variable. The subscript itself can be a constant, variable, or simple arithmetic expression. All of the following are valid subscripted variables:

$$A(3)$$
$$S(X)$$
$$T(2*Y+3)$$

The only requirement is that the subscript must be an integer. If the subscript is a noninteger, the computer converts it into an integer through *truncation* — the dropping of the decimal portion.

The computer automatically sets aside ten storage locations for any singly subscripted variable. For example, $S(J)$ would have the following array of locations reserved for it:

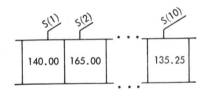

All of these locations may not be needed, but they are available. If more storage is necessary, a dimension statement, DIM, must be used. This causes the computer to set aside the amount of storage specified in the dimension statement. For example,

5 DIM S(100)

provides 100 locations for $S(J)$, from $S(1)$ to $S(100)$. The DIM statement is nonexecutable and can appear anywhere in the program.

---

[4] Sections and assignments dealing with subscripted variables are indicated with an asterisk.

FIGURE 6–7
A BASIC Program for Figure 5–10

```
10 REM DETERMINES WORKER WITH HIGHEST SALARY
20 READ N,I(1),H(1),R(1),I(2),H(2),R(2),I(3),H(3),R(3)
30 DATA 3,1702,40,3.20,1063,44,3.30,1112,40,3.60
40 T=0
50 FOR K=1 TO N
60 S(K)=H(K)*R(K)
70 IF S(K)<=T THEN 100
80 I1=I(K)
90 T=S(K)
100 NEXT K
110 PRINT I1,T
120 END
RUN,BASIC
```

As an illustration of subscripted variables in a BASIC program, consider Figure 6–7, which presents a program written from the flowchart of Figure 5–10. The program assumes that there are only three employee records.

Figures 5–10 and 6–7 should be closely studied. They show how subscripted variables and loops can be integrated to provide a powerful computational capability. The integration occurs when the value of the counter variable of the loop is also used as the subscript value for the subscripted variables.

Strings

To this point the discussions and examples have been limited to the processing of numeric data; for example, workers have been identified by their identification numbers rather than by their names. In BASIC it is possible to process alphabetic and special characters by using *character strings*. A character string is formed by combining numeric, alphabetic, and special characters in a desired order. The string can be from 1 to 72 characters in length. The character string formed is assigned to a *string variable*.

A string variable is represented by a single alphabetic character followed by a dollar ($) sign. The following are valid string variables:

A$,R$,T$

Each string variable used in a program must be dimensioned (with a DIM statement) if it has a length of more than one character. The DIM statement defines the maximum length of the character string; for example, a string variable storing a character string of five characters would require a DIM statement such as:

10 DIM C$(5)

A string variable can be assigned character strings that are shorter than that which has been dimensioned.

Character strings can be assigned to a string variable in a number of ways. For example, a LET statement can be used:

25 LET M$="WILSON"

The quotation marks around the character string are required. As might be guessed from the previous material on the LET statement, the use of LET with string variables is optical with many computer systems.

An INPUT statement can also be used to assign a character string, for example,

15 INPUT H$,R$

The user, upon request (indicated as usual by a ?), can input for each variable as many characters as have been dimensioned. The inputs must be in quotation marks and separated by commas. However, if only one string is input, the characters need not be in quotes.

The READ-DATA statement pair can also be used, for example,

10 READ A$,B$
20 DATA "TED","JIM"

Regardless of the number of strings in the DATA statement, each must be in quotation marks.

In order to output a string variable, the PRINT statement is used. For example,

135 PRINT W$

would cause the character string associated with W$ to be printed.

It is possible to compare character strings assigned to string variables. The IF–THEN statement is used for this purpose. Shown below are valid IF–THEN statements involving string variables.

10 IF A$=B$ THEN 30
25 IF T$="LAST CARD" THEN 200
30 IF M$<>N$ THEN 65

In such statements a character-by-character comparison is made of each character string to see whether the same characters are contained. Based upon this comparison, an appropriate branch is made.

More could be said about character strings and string variables, but such a discussion would take us beyond the introductory bounds of this book. Furthermore, these extensions are of greater interest to computer specialists than managers.

Functions and Subroutines

There are certain computations that are required many different times and in many different applications, such as, finding the square root of a number. In order to facilitate computer usage, computer manufacturers have written program segments that perform these frequently needed computations. These *library functions* are stored within the computer system as part of the operating system and are available to the user. Some of the most commonly available and useful library functions in BASIC are shown below:

Selected Library Functions

Library Function	Application	Example
ABS(X)	Absolute value of X	ABS(−6)=6
LOG(X)	Natural logarithm (base e) of X	LOG(3.2)=1.16315
SQR(X)	Positive square root of X	SQR(25)=5
RND(X)	A uniform random number between 0 and 1	RND(5)=.125
INT(X)	The largest integer value not greater than X	INT(3.62)=3 INT(−4.2)=−5

The *argument* of the function is that which is within the parentheses and is to be evaluated. This can be a constant, a variable, or an arithmetic expression. Examples of using a library function include:

$$10 \ X=SQR(25)$$
$$15 \ X2=LOG(X)+4$$
$$20 \ Y=INT(2*T-2)$$

It is also possible to define one's own function. If a computation is to be made several times, it may be easier to define the function once and use the defined function thereafter rather than to repeat the computation with a programming statement every time it is needed. There are certain restrictions on functions, however. They can use only one line, must employ no other user-defined functions, and cannot contain subscripted variables. A function is defined by the DEF statement. For example,

$$10 \ DEF \ FNA(X)=X**2+3$$

defines the function FNA. The function's name must contain three letters, the first two being FN. On the right-hand side is the arithmetic expression which will be needed repeatedly. The expression can contain constants and operators, but only the variable that is the argument of the function (X in this case).

In order to use the function, a programming statement is written such as that shown below:

120 Y=FNA(5)

The computer treats the argument of FNA (in this case 5), as the value of X to be evaluated in the function:

FNA(5)=5**2+3 = 28

The value 28 is stored in the computer's memory for Y. If the argument had been T + 3, with T previously defined as 4, Y would have taken on a value of 52.

FNA(T+3) = FNA(4+3) = 7**2+3 = 52

Subroutines offer more flexibility than functions. With a subroutine it is possible to leave the main program, make some needed computations, and return to the departure point. The BASIC programming statement that causes a branch to a subroutine is:

GOSUB line number

An example is:

10 GOSUB 200

The programming statements that make up the subroutine start at the line number defined by the GOSUB statement. The last statement in the subroutine is RETURN, which transfers control back to the statement following GOSUB. For example, as shown below, control goes from line numbers 10 to 200, 200 through 220, and then back to 20.

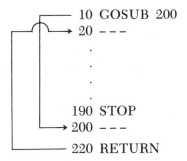

Care in programming subroutines must be taken to ensure that all of the variables in the subroutine have defined values before control passes to the subroutine.

BASIC is not a difficult programming language to learn. However, as with all programming languages, practice is required in order to determine what can and what cannot be done with the language. The best way to see whether or not a program is correct is simply to run it. By starting with simple programs, such as for the previous assignments, and working up to more complex assignments, it is surprising how quickly programming skills can be learned. The assignments that follow provide opportunities for mastering the advanced concepts that have just been presented.

ASSIGNMENTS (ADVANCED CONCEPTS)

6-7. Determine whether the following BASIC programming statements are correct:

a.	60 A2=A(2)	g.	15 INPUT A1(5)
b.	20 INPUT M$	h.	130 PRINT A$,B(2)
c.	25 Y=FNA(5)	i.	114 X=ABS(T)
d.	32 GOSUB 10	j.	300 RETURN
e.	18 S=FAB(6)	k.	18 FNA(X)=X**2
f.	35 DIMENSION A(50)	l.	45 DEF FNB(T)=3**T+4

°6-8. The following data are to be processed:

ID	HOURS	RATE
21	40.0	$4.20
86	40.0	3.65
923	40.0	3.00
865	44.0	5.50
714	40.0	3.50
553	40.0	3.50
597	40.0	3.75
928	40.0	4.10
122	42.0	3.60
281	40.0	3.90

Use the flowchart prepared for assignment 5-9 (Chapter 5) as the basis for coding a BASIC program to process the data given above.

6-9. In Chapter 5, a program flowchart was requested in assignment 5-5. Prepare a BASIC program based upon that assignment to process the following data.

Name	Degree	GPA
WILSON, MARK	1	3.61
ADAMS, SUE	4	2.41
MATSUDA, LAURA	3	2.05
PORTWOOD, CHUCK	2	3.12

6-10. The following expression can be used to sample values from a uniform distribution that has a lower limit of A and an upper limit of B.

$$S=A+R*(B-A)$$

The variable R is a uniform random number that can be obtained from the library function RND(X). The variable S is the sampled valued from the uniform distribution defined by A and B.

a. Prepare a user-defined function that obtains values for S. Assume a value of 5 for A and 10 for B. Show any other BASIC statements that are needed to support your function. Experiment with your computer system to determine the effect of using different values for X in RND(X).

    b. Repeat part *a* but use a subroutine in place of the function.

6-11. Select a BASIC programming application related to your professional area of interest. For example, one application might be computing average and marginal costs from a schedule of total costs at various levels of output. Include program documentation for the application you have selected.

REFERENCES

Books

Control Data CYBER 70 Computer Systems, Models 72, 73, 74 6000 Computer Systems, BASIC Language Reference Manual. Minneapolis: Control Data Corporation, 1972.

Farina, Mario V. *Programming in BASIC.* Englewood Cliffs, N.J.: Prentice-Hall, 1968.

Gately, W. Y. and G. G. Bitter. *BASIC For Beginners.* New York: McGraw-Hill Book Co., 1970.

Kemeny, J. G. and T. E. Kurtz. *BASIC Programming.* New York: John Wiley & Sons, 1967.

Deck Makeup

Positioning the Code

A Sample Program

FORTRAN Statements

Characters, Arithmetic Assignment Statement, Input/Output
Statements, STOP and END Statements, An Illustration,
Branching, Looping

Assignments (Basic Concepts)

Advanced Concepts in FORTRAN

Subscripted Variables, Input/Output with the A Format,
Subprograms

Assignments (Advanced Concepts)

References

More colleges of business administration teach FORTRAN than any other
programming language. A primary reason for this is that FORTRAN is possibly the most popular language in use today. The material in this chapter
will have to be studied carefully and then practiced. Learning the FORTRAN
language is definitely not a spectator sport.

7

The FORTRAN Programming Language

The FORTRAN programming language was developed and introduced in the late 1950s by IBM, working in conjunction with several major computer users. Today, almost all computer systems have the capability for processing FORTRAN programs. The FORTRAN language is particularly well suited for applications that require numerous, complex mathematical and statistical calculations. Because of its usage in disciplines that rely heavily upon quantification, FORTRAN is probably the most widely used programming language. With the increasing movement to the quantification of business problems, it is an especially appropriate language for students of business administration. More colleges of business administration teach FORTRAN than any other programming language.

Many different versions of FORTRAN have evolved, with increasing capabilities — FORTRAN, FORTRAN II, and FORTRAN IV. Even with the same FORTRAN version slight differences exist among the language translators developed by the various computer manufacturers. These differences among *compilers* (a FORTRAN language translator is more specifically referred to as a FORTRAN compiler) sometimes require minor modifications when existing FORTRAN programs are switched from one computer system to another. Normally, however, this is more of a problem for computer specialists than for managers, since most of the differences involve special capabilities that are not usually required by the casual user.

The material on FORTRAN presented in this chapter should be studied in conjunction with the program flowcharting concepts presented in Chapter 5. A FORTRAN program is simply a coded version of the algorithm that is expressed in the program flowchart. And as you learn more about developing algorithms, you will increasingly need and appreciate the capabilities of the FORTRAN language.

The FORTRAN programs that you write will probably be key-punched on cards and then entered to the computer via a card reader. Most universities use card-oriented systems in their introductory computer courses. The specific computer system that the illustrations in this chapter refer to is the IBM System/360—a very common system. It should be stressed, though, that almost all other systems accept FORTRAN programs and that media and input devices other than cards and card readers can normally be used.

DECK MAKEUP

People who are learning FORTRAN are often confused over what types of cards are required and their relative placement in a program deck. Figure 7–1 illustrates a sample deck makeup.

At the front of the deck are *job control cards* (sometimes also referred to as *systems* control cards). The exact form of these cards depends upon the operating system, the available computer hardware and software, and local computer center specifications. The purpose of job control cards is to provide the computer with information necessary in processing the program and data. Typically, the job control cards carry information to the computer such as the name of the job, the user's name and account number, the job class, and the language translator to be used. After the job control cards comes the user's FORTRAN program, which contains all of the instructions the user wants the computer to follow. Any subprograms are placed after the main program (or before it). Subprograms, which are sometimes used to make computations outside of the main program, are discussed later in the chapter. More job control cards are placed next in order to designate the end of the main program and any subprograms. After these control cards come the data that are to be processed by the FORTRAN program. At the end of the data deck are the final job control cards which mark the end of the data and the job.

FIGURE 7–1
Sample Deck Makeup

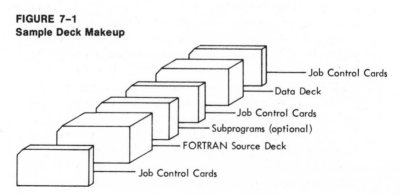

- Job Control Cards
- Data Deck
- Job Control Cards
- Subprograms (optional)
- FORTRAN Source Deck
- Job Control Cards

POSITIONING THE CODE

A keypunch card has 80 columns that can be used for communicating data or instructions to the computer. (Instructions for preparing a punched card on a keypunch machine are provided in Appendix C.) When reading a card the computer looks at predefined *fields* (groups of related columns) for certain pieces of information. In order to help ensure that the desired symbols are placed in the proper columns, FORTRAN coding sheets (as shown in Figure 7–2) are commonly used in preparing FORTRAN programs. Keypunching is then performed, using the coding sheets as the instructions source.

The directions that follow for positioning programming code apply only to FORTRAN statements. Job control cards are not FORTRAN programming statements. Job control statements have their own set of specifications that must be followed, and since the specifications vary with the computer system, they are not discussed here and must be learned from your instructor. The material that follows also does not apply to data cards. As we will see later in the chapter, the programmer must communicate to the computer how the data are placed on the data cards. What we are presently concerned with is the positioning of FORTRAN statements.

Column 1 can be used to designate a comment card. This designation is made by placing a "C" in column 1, as illustrated in Figure

FIGURE 7–2
FORTRAN Coding Sheet

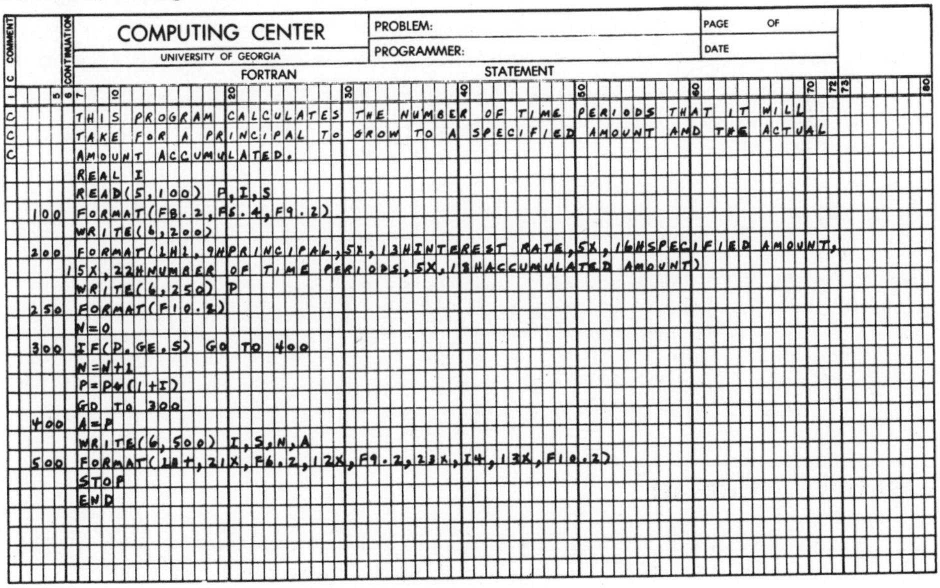

COMPUTING CENTER
UNIVERSITY OF GEORGIA
PROBLEM:
PROGRAMMER:
PAGE OF
DATE
C COMMENT | CONTINUATION | FORTRAN STATEMENT

```
C     THIS PROGRAM CALCULATES THE NUMBER OF TIME PERIODS THAT IT WILL
C     TAKE FOR A PRINCIPAL TO GROW TO A SPECIFIED AMOUNT AND THE ACTUAL
C     AMOUNT ACCUMULATED.
      REAL I
      READ(5,100) P,I,S
  100 FORMAT(F8.2,F5.4,F9.2)
      WRITE(6,200)
  200 FORMAT(1H1,9HPRINCIPAL,5X,13HINTEREST RATE,5X,16HSPECIFIED AMOUNT,
     15X,22HNUMBER OF TIME PERIODS,5X,18HACCUMULATED AMOUNT)
      WRITE(6,250) P
  250 FORMAT(F10.2)
      N=0
  300 IF(P.GE.S) GO TO 400
      N=N+1
      P=P*(1+I)
      GO TO 300
  400 A=P
      WRITE(6,500) I,S,N,A
  500 FORMAT(1H+,21X,F6.2,12X,F9.2,23X,I4,13X,F10.2)
      STOP
      END
```

7–2. A *comment card* is a means for including descriptive material with the program, which otherwise can look rather unfathomable. The compiler ignores all comment cards when translating the FORTRAN program but does include them in the program listing on the printout. Comment cards are commonly used for documentation, explaining the program's logic, or simply improving the program's readability through spacing (e.g., a C followed by blanks).

Columns 1–5 are used for program statement numbers. A *statement number* serves as a label for the particular programming statement to which it is assigned. Not every programming statement needs a statement number, but any statement that is referenced by another statement in the program must be given a number. There is no significance to the specific numbers assigned to the statements, since they are used solely as a source of identification. The numbers do not influence the order in which the programming instructions are executed by the computer.

In some instances a FORTRAN statement will not fit on a single card and must be continued on one or more additional cards. If any character other than a zero or a blank is placed in column 6, the computer is told that the card contains a continuation of the previous programming statement rather than a new one.

Columns 7–72 are reserved for FORTRAN programming statements. It is here that the instructions for reading the data, making computations, and so on are written.

The remaining columns, 73–80, are not considered by the compiler when translating the FORTRAN program. They are either left blank by the programmer or used for identification. Some programmers use this *identification field* to number the cards in their program. If any of the cards get out of order, they can then be easily placed in the correct sequence. Any identification placed in columns 73–80 is included in the program listing on the printout.

In summary, the columns are used as indicated below:

Column	Use
1	By placing a C in column 1, comments can be included with the program.
1–5	A statement number used to identify a particular statement.
6	By placing a character other than a zero or a blank in column 6, the compiler is told that the statement is a continuation of the previous one.
7–72	The FORTRAN statement.
73–80	Either left blank or used for identification.

A SAMPLE PROGRAM

Before turning to specific FORTRAN programming statements, you should study the complete program provided in Figure 7–3. In-

FIGURE 7-3
A FORTRAN Program for Figure 5-3

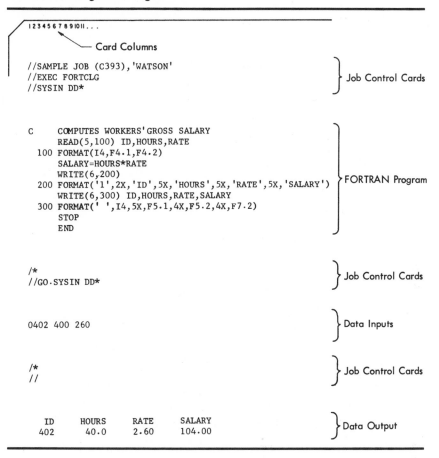

cluded are job control cards, a FORTRAN program, sample data inputs, and the resultant data output. The program was written from the flowchart of Figure 5-3.

FORTRAN STATEMENTS

Whether the programming statements are *executable* or *non-executable*—that is, whether they direct program action or simply supply information needed in the translation of the program—they are the means through which the computer is given specific information and processing instructions. The FORTRAN statements embody the logic developed in the program flowchart.

Characters

The following set of characters can be used in developing FORTRAN statements:

Numeric .... 0 through 9
Alphabetic .... A through Z and $
Special characters .... blank , . + − ° / () = '

Any FORTRAN statement, other than a WRITE-FORMAT statement combination with literal data (which is discussed later), is limited to these characters.

Arithmetic Assignment Statement

The power of the FORTRAN language lies in its capability for making numerous, complex calculations. An *arithmetic assignment statement* such as shown below is used for this purpose.

ASALES=TSALES/TPERD

This expression might be used to determine the average sales per time period (ASALES), computed by dividing the number of time periods (TPERD) into total sales (TSALES). The equals sign in FORTRAN means to assign (or substitute) the value of the right-hand side of the expression into the storage location reserved for the variable on the left-hand side. With the above example, ASALES is assigned the value found by dividing TSALES by TPERD.

There are many programming situations where the assignment interpretation of the equals sign must be strictly used in order to gain a correct understanding of the operation. For example,

BAL=BAL+ORDER

is a valid programming statement. It says to substitute, in the storage location reserved for BAL (balance), the current value for BAL plus the value for ORDER. Perhaps you can now appreciate why the arrow symbol is used in flowcharting, while the equals symbol is used in programming. The arrow symbol emphasizes the substitution nature of the computer's operations. An earlier use of the equals sign might have created confusion because of its ingrained meaning from mathematics.

All arithmetic assignment statements are made up of constants, variables, and operators, as shown on the following page:

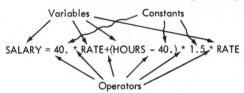

Constants are numbers that do not change value during program execution. All constants are assumed to be positive unless specifically given a negative sign. In FORTRAN a distinction is made between decimal and integer constants.[1] A *decimal constant* is one that contains a decimal point; for example, 25.2, −512.83, or 87.0. An *integer constant* can only be a whole number and does not include a decimal point; for example, 3, −27, or 500. The maximum allowable size on decimal and integer constants depends upon the computer being used, but most business applications do not approach the upper limits.

The values of *variables* are free to change during program execution. Two types of variables are used in FORTRAN — decimal and integer. A *decimal variable* is one whose possible values contain a decimal point, while an *integer variable* can only assume a whole-number value. The reason for distinguishing between decimal and integer quantities is that they are stored and manipulated differently within the computer. It will soon become clear why it is important to keep this distinction in mind.

Depending upon the compiler, a variable name can usually contain only up to six characters. The first character must be a letter, but the remaining characters can be either letters or numerals. No special characters are allowed in variable names. Any name that starts with either I, J, K, L, M or N is *implicitly* assumed by the compiler to be of integer mode (the type of variable it is). An easy way to remember what letters define an integer variable is to think of the first two letters in the word INteger. The I and N are the first and the last of the range of letters that indicate integer mode. All of the other variables in a FORTRAN program are assumed to be of decimal mode — those variables that start with the letters A through H or O through Z and $.

A variable's mode can also be *explicitly* specified. A statement with the words REAL or INTEGER, followed by a variable list, specifies the listed variables' mode. For example, the statement

---

[1] Decimal constants and variables are also referred to as *real* or *floating point*, while integer quantities are often called *fixed point*. The terms "decimal" and "integer" are more natural for students of business administration.

REAL IVORY,NORM

causes the variables IVORY and NORM to be processed as decimal variables.

Examples of valid and invalid variable names and, if valid, whether the variable is integer or decimal, are shown below:

Examples of Valid and Invalid Variable Names

Name	Valid or Invalid	If Valid, Mode	Discussion
A..................	Valid	Decimal	
2DOL............	Invalid		Must start with a letter
NCARD.........	Valid	Integer	
N+	Invalid		Cannot use special characters

Arithmetic operators are symbols used to indicate how variables and constants are to be combined. The following arithmetic operators are available in FORTRAN for computational purposes:

Arithmetic Operators

Operation	Symbol	Example	Interpretation
Addition...............	+	ORDER+BAL	ORDER plus BAL
Subtraction...........	−	GROSS−TAXES	GROSS minus TAXES
Multiplication	*	USALES*PRICE	USALES times PRICE
Division	/	TCOST/USALES	TCOST divided by USALES
Exponentiation	**	STDEV**2	STDEV to the 2nd power

Arithmetic expressions in FORTRAN are evaluated according to the following rules:

1. All quantities within parentheses are evaluated first, starting with the innermost parentheses.
2. Exponentiation is performed before multiplication, division, addition, or subtraction.
3. Multiplication and division are performed before addition or subtraction.
4. In case of computational ties, computations proceed on a left to right basis.

To illustrate, assume that an arithmetic expression is to be written to calculate a new product's break-even point expressed in dollars of total sales. The following FORTRAN arithmetic statement accomplishes this objective.

BEVEN=SPRICE*FCOST/(SPRICE−VCOST)

When executed, first the per-unit variable costs (VCOST) would be subtracted from the selling price (SPRICE), because of the parentheses. The next operation would be the multiplication of the selling price (SPRICE) times the total fixed costs (FCOST), because of the left to right processing sequence when there are ties in the computational order. And finally, the result of the multiplication is divided by the result of the subtraction operation. The result is placed in the storage location labeled BEVEN. For practice, decide what the processing sequence would be if the parentheses were left out of the arithmetic expression.

Before the topic of arithmetic computations in FORTRAN can be completed, some additional comments regarding decimal and integer quantities must be made. Not all compilers permit what is known as *mixed mode* arithmetic—arithmetic expressions made up of both decimal and integer quantities. Consequently, on some computers a programming statement such as

$$A=NCARDS+2.$$

would not be acceptable, since NCARDS is integer mode and 2. is decimal mode. It is good practice to learn to program without mixing modes.

The comments about mixing decimal and integer quantities apply only to the terms on the right-hand side of the equals sign, not to the variable on the left of the equals sign. For example, it is perfectly acceptable to have all integer quantities (i.e., variables and constants) on the right-hand side and a decimal variable on the left-hand side, or vice versa. The computer will transform the result of the computation (after the computation has been made) into whatever is the mode of the left-hand side of the expression. For example,

$$TOTAL=NCARDS+5$$

where NCARD has a value in memory of 95, would result in the decimal value 100. being stored as the value for TOTAL.

There are special considerations in mixing modes for exponentiation. A decimal quantity can have an integer exponent, such as

$$A=2.3**N$$

However, because of the way that the computer performs arithmetic, an integer cannot be raised to a decimal power. For example, the following expression is invalid;

$$M=N**2.2 \quad \text{(Invalid)}$$

Some additional aspects of integer arithmetic should be discussed. An expression such as,

$$NVAL=ASOLD/2.$$

where ASOLD equals, for example, 11., would result in a value of 5 being substituted in storage for NVAL. Dividing ASOLD by 2. equals 5.5, but since NVAL is of integer mode, the .5 is truncated (i.e., dropped off) and a value of 5 results for NVAL. If the expression had been,

$$NVAL=NQUAN/2$$

the result would still have been a value of 5 for NVAL, but in this case the truncation would have occurred as soon as NQUAN was divided by 2, since both are of integer mode.

Input/Output Statements

One of the biggest obstacles in learning the FORTRAN language is the writing of input and output statements. These statements require great care because many details are involved. The beginning programmer will probably have to refer back to this section of the book quite frequently.

Input. Two statements must be used together in order to input data to the computer. These statements are the READ and FORMAT statements. Shown below is an example of a READ-FORMAT statement pair.

$$READ(5,10)\ TOTAL,VALUE$$
$$10\ FORMAT(2F.5.2)$$

These statements communicate many things to the computer — what is to be done (the input of data), the input device to be used, the variables that are involved, and how the data are located on the input medium.

READ instructs the computer that data are to be read in. The first item within the parentheses of the READ statement gives the number of the input device that is to be used. In the above example, an input device numbered 5 is to be used (here assumed to be a card reader). The appropriate input/output equipment numbers depend upon the manufacturer of the computer and local computer center designations. The second item within the parentheses provides the statement number of the FORMAT statement which describes how the data are placed on the data card, in this case, statement no. 10. The list of variables that are to be input is placed after the parentheses, each variable being separated by a comma. The above READ statement indicates that the values for TOTAL and VALUE are to be input.

Used in conjunction with a READ statement is a FORMAT statement that indicates how the data are placed on the input medium (data card or cards, in our example). There is a direct correspondence between the sequencing of variables in the READ statement and the specifications in the FORMAT statement. The above example illustrates the use of the F format, one of several formats that can be used in writing FORTRAN programs.

The *F format* is used only with decimal variables and takes the following general form,

$$\textbf{n}\textbf{F}\textbf{w}.\textbf{d}$$

In this and other discussions of the general form for FORTRAN programming statements, boldface is used to indicate the invariant portion of the statement. In the F format statement, n is the number of times the format is to be repeated; w is the width of the field on the data card; and d is the number of columns that are to the right of the decimal point. Referring to the previous example for the input of TOTAL and VALUE, the 2F5.2 specification tells the computer that the F5.2 format is to be used twice, and in this case the values being input each take up five columns on the data card, and the last two columns in each field should be interpreted as being to the right of the decimal.

The data might appear on a data card for the current example as shown below.

The values being input would be 37.66 for TOTAL and −2.40 for VALUE. The computer interprets all blank columns to the right of the decimal point as being zeros, so data should be *right justified* (i.e., placed as far to the right as possible) in their fields.

There is an override condition for the F format which some programmers prefer to use. If the decimal point is punched on the data card, its punched position is used, rather than what is specified in the F format. This approach seems to reduce many careless input errors. In counting the field width preparatory to writing the F format, whether the override provision is used or not, it is necessary to include in the count a column for the decimal point and another column when a minus sign is used. For example, if −32. were to be input, the specification would have to be at least F4.0, whether the decimal was going to be punched or not.

Whereas the F format is used with decimal variables, the *I format* must be employed with integer variables. Its general form is as shown below,

$$\textbf{n}\textbf{I}\textbf{w}$$

where n is the number of times the format is to be repeated, and w is the width of the field on the data card. For example, assume that a value of 32 is to be input for a variable named ITEM, and the data card is punched such as shown below:

An appropriate READ-FORMAT statement pair for this example would be:

READ(5,100) ITEM

100 FORMAT(I2)

In determining the field width for I formats there is no need to allow for a decimal point, since integer variables do not have one, but a position must be provided for any minus sign.

So far in our examples only a single data card has been input by a single READ–FORMAT statement pair. However, it is possible to have a READ–FORMAT statement pair input data from more than one data card. When more variables are specified in the READ statement than formats in the FORMAT statement, the computer encounters the right parenthesis of the FORMAT statement and then begins reading the next data card, using the specifications in the FORMAT statement once again. For example,

READ(5,25) A1,A2,A3

25 FORMAT(F5.2)

would result in A1 being read from the first data card, A2 from the second, and A3 from the third—all under a F5.2 format.

A slash (/) placed in a FORMAT statement also causes the computer to move to the next data card. For example,

READ(5,35) IDA,A,B

35 FORMAT(I4,/,2F4.2)

results in the reading of IDA from the first data card under an I4 format, and A and B from the next card under an F4.2 format. The commas around the slash are optional and can be omitted.

READ–FORMAT statements pairs do not have to be placed sequentially in the program, since FORMAT statements are referenced by their statement numbers. Consequently, many programmers place all of their FORMAT statements at the beginning of the program to remove them from the main program logic. Conversely, some programmers place all of their FORMAT statements at the end of the program for the same reason. However, most students initially find it most logical to group their READ–FORMAT statements together.

It is possible for several READ statements to use the same FORMAT statement. Of course, the format for the READ statements must be the same.

Output. Output in FORTRAN is performed using the WRITE–FORMAT statement pair. There are many similarities between the methods for input and output in FORTRAN. An illustrative pair of output statements is shown below:

WRITE(6,200) BAL,NTIMES
200 FORMAT('1',F8.2,I2)

The WRITE statement indicates that an output device numbered 6 should receive the output. Once again, the specific number depends upon the manufacturer of the computer, the desired output form (printout, magnetic tape, and so on) and the local computer center's designations. Here it will be assumed that the number 6 refers to a printer. The second number within the parentheses, 200 in this case, is the statement number of the FORMAT statement that defines the format for the output. Following the parentheses is the list of variable values that are to be output—BAL and NTIMES in this case.

The FORMAT statement provides the output specifications for the variables. Two of the major forms are the F and I formats, whose use parallels that for the input of data. The field width on the F format should include provisions for a possible minus sign and a decimal point. The decimal point is always printed when the F format is used. The I format does not have to allow for a decimal point, but a column for a minus sign should be included. If the values for BAL and NTIMES (for the current example) are 64.8 and 9, respectively, the printout would appear as shown below. For the time being ignore the 1 in the FORMAT statement. This specification controls the vertical spacing of the output, a point which is discussed later.

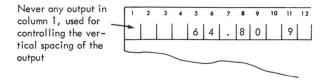

Never any output in column 1, used for controlling the vertical spacing of the output

Notice that all of the output values are right justified in their fields. When the output values do not use all of the columns that have been specified in the FORMAT statement, two things occur; blanks are placed in all of the columns that are to the left of the decimal, and zeros are placed in all of the empty columns to the right of the decimal. This effect can be seen in the output given for BAL and NTIMES.

The readability of an output can frequently be enhanced by spreading the output across the printout. The number of output columns available on the printer varies with the equipment, but in general it is around 132. One way to spread out the output is to make the field widths much larger than necessary. This approach, however, is not very precise or convenient. A preferred alternative is to use the *nX specification* in the FORMAT statement. This specification instructs the computer to skip n columns before printing. For example,

WRITE(6,75) NBUYS
75 FORMAT('1',10X,I2)

where NBUYS equals 18, would appear on output as shown below:

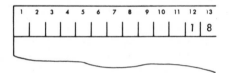

The nX specification can also be used with READ–FORMAT statement pairs when the data are spread across the data cards.

In order to have an attractive, readable output, it is usually necessary to include column headings or comments on the printout. This type of output is known as *literal data*. The easiest way to generate literal data is to place that which is to be outputted within single quotes in the FORMAT statement. For example, assume that you want to output the literal data, INVENTORY LEVEL IS, and then the current inventory level. The following WRITE–FORMAT statement pair accomplishes this objective.[2]

WRITE(6,5) INVEN
5 FORMAT('1',4X,'INVENTORY LEVEL IS ',I3)

When the value of INVEN is 120, the output would appear as shown on the following page.

---

[2] The Hollerith specification, nH, where n specifies the number of characters to be printed, is used on some computer systems. The current example would appear as 5 FORMAT(1H1,4X,19HINVENTORY LEVEL IS ,I3).

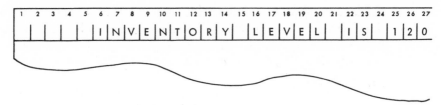

One final aspect of outputting must be considered—the vertical spacing of the lines on the printout. This spacing is not performed automatically and must be planned for by the programmer.

Control over vertical spacing is directed by what is placed in the first output column. If a blank is to be output in the first column, one line is skipped before printing; a 0 results in two lines being skipped, a 1 tells the computer to advance to the next page, and a + to suppress any advancement.

Control over Vertical Spacing

Carriage Control Character	Paper Advance before Printing
blank	1 line
0	2 lines
1	Advance to next page
+	Suppress advancement

No matter what is "scheduled" to be output in the first column, nothing is actually printed on the page in this column. This explains why actual output never begins until column 2. The first column is used exclusively for carriage control on the printer. It is up to the user to plan the output in such a way that the desired spacing is realized. As an example of controlling the output's vertical spacing, consider the following statements:

WRITE(6,60) COUNT
60 FORMAT('0',F10.3)

The 0 in the FORMAT statement results in two lines being skipped before the value of COUNT is output. The 0 is not actually printed, however; it is only used for carriage control.

STOP and END Statements

The end of a program is signaled by the STOP and END statements. The STOP statement, whenever encountered, terminates program execution. It marks the *logical* end of the program. The

END statement must physically be the last card in the program deck. It is a nonexecutable statement which indicates the *physical* end of the program.

An Illustration

A sample of a complete FORTRAN program was presented in Figure 7–3. It represents the FORTRAN equivalent of the flowchart of Figure 5–3. All of the FORTRAN statements necessary to fully understand this program have now been presented. It would be worthwhile to carefully study the program before proceeding.

Branching

Usually it is necessary to transfer control from one point in a program to another. The GO TO statement in FORTRAN causes an unconditional transfer of control. Its general form is:

GO TO statement number

An example is:

GO TO 30

When this instruction is encountered, control is passed to the statement number specified. The only restriction (and it applies to all transfer of control statements) is that the statement branched to must be executable. For example, it would be incorrect to try to branch to a FORMAT statement.

The computed GO TO statement is used to pass control to one of several possible points in a program. The specific branch point is determined by the value of an integer variable. The general form of this statement is:

GO TO(statement number $_1$, statement number$_2$, . . . statement number$_n$), integer variable

If the value of the integer variable is 1, control is transferred to the first statement number within the parentheses. When the variable value is equal to 2, the instruction associated with the second statement number is performed, and so on for the other statement numbers. For example,

GO TO(10,50,40,30), J

results in statement no. 40 being performed next when J has a predefined value of 3.

An IF statement can also be used to transfer control. Two forms of this statement are commonly available – the arithmetic and logical IF.

With the *arithmetic IF*, branching takes place based upon whether an arithmetic expression is less than zero, zero, or greater than zero in value. Its general form is,

IF(arithmetic expression) statement number$_1$, statement number$_2$, statement number$_3$

When the arithmetic expression's value is less than zero, control is passed to the first statement number; if equal to zero, to the second statement number; and when greater than zero, to the third statement number. For example, for the statement shown below,

IF(BAL-80.) 15,30,25

when BAL equals 80., control passes to the instruction associated with statement no. 30 (since 80. − 80. = 0.).

The *logical IF* statement is a very useful statement, but it is not available with all compilers. When available, it can be used to test the relationship between two arithmetic expressions. If the test proves true, the programming statement associated with the IF statement is performed; if false, control passes to the next statement. The relational operators shown below are used with the logical IF statement:

Relational Operators

Operator	Symbol	Example	Interpretation
Equals......................	.EQ.	A.EQ.B	A equals B
Greater than..............	.GT.	A.GT.B	A is greater than B
Greater than or equal to................	.GE.	A.GE.B	A is greater than or equal to B
Less than..................	.LT.	A.LT.B	A is less than B
Less than or equal to................	.LE.	A.LE.B	A is less than or equal to B
Not equal.................	.NE.	A.NE.B	A is not equal to B

The logical IF statement takes the following general form:

IF(arithmetic expression.relational operator.arithmetic expression) programming statement

For example,

IF(COUNT.GE.10.0) GO TO 30

would result in an unconditional transfer of control to statement no. 30 if the value of COUNT is greater than or equal to 10.0. Consider another example:

IF(2.*A+B.EQ.TOT) VAL=A

This statement results in the value of A being assigned to VAL if $2*A+B$ is equal to TOT. Control then passes to the next sequential statement.

FIGURE 7–4
A FORTRAN Program for Figure 5–4

```
C COMPUTES A WORKER'S SALARY CONSIDERING OVERTIME
      READ(5,200) ID,HOURS,RATE
  200 FORMAT(I4,F4.1,F4.2)
      IF(HOURS.LE.40.) GO TO 300
      SALARY=40.*RATE+(HOURS-40.)*1.5*RATE
      GO TO 400
  300 SALARY=HOURS*RATE
  400 WRITE(6,500)
  500 FORMAT('1',1X,'ID',6X,'HOURS',5X,'RATE',5X,'SALARY')
      WRITE(6,600)ID,HOURS,RATE,SALARY
  600 FORMAT('0',I4,5X,F5.1,4X,F5.2,4X,F7.2)
      STOP
      END
```

The flowchart of Figure 5–4 provides a good illustration of the use of the logical IF statement and the unconditional GO TO statement. The FORTRAN program for Figure 5–4 is presented in Figure 7–4.

Looping

A loop causes a series of instructions to be repeated. An interesting application of a loop was shown in Figure 5–8, which presented a flowchart for computing workers' gross salaries and accumulating

FIGURE 7–5
A FORTRAN Program for Figure 5–8

```
C COMPUTES AND ACCUMULATES WORKERS' GROSS SALARIES
      WRITE(6,50)
   50 FORMAT('1',7X,'ID',5X,'HOURS',7X,'RATE',5X,'SALARY')
      READ(5,100) N
  100 FORMAT(I4)
      J=1
      TOTSAL=0.
  150 READ(5,200) ID,HOURS,RATE
  200 FORMAT(I9,F5.2,F4.2)
      SALARY=HOURS*RATE
      TOTSAL=TOTSAL+SALARY
      WROTE(6,300) ID,HOURS,RATE,SALARY
  300 FORMAT('',I9,4X,F6.2,7X,F4.2,4X,F7.2)
      J=J+1
      IF(J.GT.N) GO TO 350
      GO TO 150
  350 WRITE(6,375)
  375 FORMAT('0',3X,'TOTSAL')
      WRITE(6,400) TOTSAL
  400 FORMAT('',F9.2)
      STOP
      END
```

a salary total. Control over the number of times through the loop was provided by a counter variable and a decision point. When the counter's value exceeded the specified number, the decision point transferred control outside the loop. A FORTRAN program can be written from this flowchart, drawing heavily upon the logical IF statement's capabilities. This program is presented in Figure 7–5.

While counters and IF statements can be used in constructing loops, the DO statement in FORTRAN provides the same capabilities, yet more efficiently. The general form of the DO statement is shown below.

DO statement number integer variable = integer quantity, integer quantity, integer quantity

The statement number specified in the DO statement is the last statement in the loop. The integer variable (the loop variable) serves as a counter. The first integer quantity is the initial value of the loop variable. Looping continues until the loop variable exceeds in value the second integer quantity. After each pass through the loop, the loop variable is incremented by the amount specified by the third integer quantity. For example,

DO 50 I=1,10,1

results in all of the programming statements between the DO statement and statement no. 50 being performed 10 items (as I is incremented from 1 to 10 by 1). Valid and invalid DO statements are illustrated below:

Examples of Valid and Invalid DO Statements

Example	Valid or Invalid	Discussion
DO 100 NAME=1,30	Valid	An increment of 1 is assumed when the third integer quantity is omitted
DO 15 I=J,K,L	Valid	
DO 5 COUNT=3,20,3	Invalid	Must be an integer loop variable

There are certain restrictions on the last instruction in a DO loop — it must be executable, but not a transfer of control statement. Rather than remembering a list of acceptable and unacceptable statements, many programmers find it convenient to end all DO loops with a CONTINUE statement. This statement simply instructs the computer to move on to the next statement in the program.

It is also possible to have loops within loops — referred to as *nested loops*. The inner loop is said to be nested within the outer loop. An illustration of this concept is shown below on the following page:

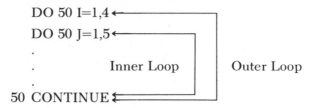

Nested loops vary through the innermost loop first and then work outwards. With the loops presented above, looping occurs $4 \times 5 = 20$ times in the order $(1, 1), (1, 2) \ldots (1, 5), (2, 1), (2, 2) \ldots (4, 5)$. The loops must not intersect, but they can have the same terminal point. It is possible to have many levels of nesting—loops within loops, within loops, and so on.

At this point you have been exposed to the basic FORTRAN statements and their use. Now you can test your understanding of FORTRAN and begin writing simple programs. The assignments that follow are designed to satisfy these objectives. After mastering these assignments, you should study the more advanced FORTRAN statements and concepts that are presented later in the chapter. You will then more fully appreciate the computational power of FORTRAN.

ASSIGNMENTS (BASIC CONCEPTS)

7-1.   Shown below are a number of valid and invalid FORTRAN statements. The arithmetic expressions in these statements involve the use of the variables AVALUE, BVALUE, ITEM, JOE, and TOTAL. The values stored in the computer's memory for these variables are 10.5, 100.0, 5, 10 and 200.0, respectively. Determine whether the following statements are valid or invalid, and if valid, the value stored for the variable on the left-hand side of the expressions.

  a.   CVALUE=AVALUE+BVALUE
  b.   DVALUE=AVALUE+4
  c.   APPLE=ITEM−JOE
  d.   VAL2=JOE°ITEM
  e.   VAL−3=JOE/ITEM
  f.   N=(6+ITEM)/JOE
  g.   TOM=BVALUE(TOTAL°.01)
  h.   I=ITEM°°2
  i.   AVALUE=AVALUE+TOTAL
  j.   SAMPLE=2.°°ITEM
  k.   NOW=(2.3°BVALUE/JOE)/(ITEM°°2−2.)
  l.   TVALUE=0.5+AVALUE/BVALUE
  m.   CABLE=BVALUE°°2/TOTAL−100

7-2. A data deck contains the data presented below:

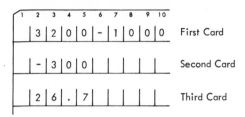

Determine whether the following READ–FORMAT statement pairs represent valid or invalid statements, and if valid, the values stored in the computer's memory.

a.   READ(5,50) A,I
    50 FORMAT(F5.2,I5)
b.   READ(5,100) A
    100 FORMAT(F5.2)
c.   READ(5,80) ALPHA,BETA,GAMMA
    80 FORMAT(F5.2)
d.   READ(5,5) COUNT,BILL
     5 FORMAT(F5.2,/,F5.2)
e.   READ(5,600) N
    600 FORMAT(/,/,I5)
f.   READ(5,20) F2
    20 FORMAT(5X,F3.1)

7-3. The following variables and their values are stored in the computer's memory:

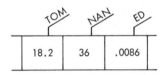

Determine whether the following WRITE–FORMAT statement pairs represent valid or invalid statements, and, if valid, how they would present the output:

a.   WRITE(6,1) TOM
     1 FORMAT('0',F4.1)
b.   WRITE(6,50) NAN
    50 FORMAT(5X,'THE VALUE OF NAN IS',NAN)
c.   WRITE(6,25) TOM,ED
    25 FORMAT(F4.1,F9.2)
d.   WRITE(6,30) ED
    30 FORMAT(10X,F8.2)

e.   WRITE(6,15) TOM
   15 FORMAT('+',F7.3)
f.   WRITE(6,45) NAN
   45 FORMAT('1',F4.0)

7-4. Determine whether the following FORTRAN statements are valid:

a. GO TO ITEM
b. IF(X°°2.GE.100.) Y=CHI
c. IF(SAM+BILL) GO TO 100
d. GO TO(5,15,25), APPLE

e. GO TO 50
f. IF(3°A2–A3) 10,15,20
g. IF(X.LT.Y), Z=2°X

7-5. Determine whether the following FORTRAN statements are valid or invalid:

a.   DO 50 I=1,5
         .
         .
         .
      50 CONTINUE
b.   DO JOE MIKE=I,J,K
         .
         .
         .
      JOE CONTINUE
c.   DO 100 MIKE=MOE,MEL
         .
         .
         .
      100 CONTINUE
d.   DO 60 J=1,100,5
         .
         .
         .
      60 GO TO 70

e.   DO 50 M=1,5
      DO 55 N=1,6
         .
         .
         .
      50 CONTINUE
      55 CONTINUE
f.   DO 15 I=1,N,5
      DO 15 J=1,N,1
      DO 15 K=1,N,1
         .
         .
         .
      15 CONTINUE

7-6. In Chapter 5, a loop with a counter was illustrated in Figure 5–6. Prepare a FORTRAN program based upon this flowchart. Use the following data inputs with your program:

N	ID	Hours	Rate
4	367	40.0	3.50
	1338	40.0	3.85
	26	42.0	4.00
	555	40.0	3.50

7-7. The flowchart of Figure 5–7 illustrated a loop with a last-record check. Prepare a FORTRAN program, including appropriate headings for your output, to process the following data cards:

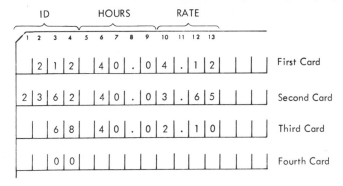

7-8. Assignment 5-6 required the preparation of a program flowchart for computing a customer's water bill. Prepare a FORTRAN program from the flowchart you prepared for this assignment. Use the following data inputs with your program:

ID	GAL
272983606	536.0
302023419	162.0
286353812	405.0

7-9. Assignment 5-8 required the preparation of a program flowchart to compute and output the mean test score and the identification number and score of the student with the highest test score. Prepare a FORTRAN program based upon this flowchart and then process the following data inputs through your program.

ID	TSCORE
386	86
312	92
365	93
342	76
350	84

ADVANCED CONCEPTS IN FORTRAN

*Subscripted Variables[3]

The major difference between simple and subscripted variables is that *subscripted variables* have a string of memory locations reserved for their values (this string is frequently referred to as an *array*), while *simple variables* require only a single memory location. In FORTRAN it is necessary to communicate to the computer the number of storage locations to reserve for each subscripted variable. This

---

[3] Sections and assignments dealing with subscripted variables are marked with an asterisk.

information is provided by the DIMENSION statement, an example of which is shown below.

DIMENSION AVALUE(50),BVALUE(25)

With this DIMENSION statement, the computer reserves 50 locations for AVALUE (AVALUE(1), AVALUE(2), ... AVALUE(50)) and 25 locations for BVALUE (BVALUE(1), BVALUE(2), ... BVALUE(25)).

A specific element of a subscripted variable can be referenced by an integer constant, integer variable, or simple arithmetic expression (i.e., must be of integer mode, cannot involve division or exponentiation). Examples of valid subscripted variables are presented below:

A(3)
BELOW(J)
NOW(2*K+3)

The input and output of subscripted variables can be accomplished in a number of ways. One way, though somewhat inefficient, is to specify each element of the subscripted variable; for example,

READ(5,500) A(1),A(2),A(3),A(4),A(5) } 1 data card required
500 FORMAT(5F8.4)

Another approach is to employ a loop; for example,

DO 5 I=1,5
READ(5,400) A(I)   } 5 data cards required
400 FORMAT(F8.4)
5 CONTINUE

Notice in this case that each value for A(I) must be on a separate data card. The specific element of the subscripted variable being input is determined by the current value of the loop variable, I.

Perhaps the easiest input procedure is to draw upon the implied DO loop features of the FORTRAN language. The following READ–FORMAT statement pair results in the input of A(I).

READ(5,300) (A(I),I=1,5) } 1 data card required
300 FORMAT(5F8.4)

In this example, all of the values for A(I) would be on a single data card. In order to distinguish the implied DO loop specification from a list of variable names that usually appear in a READ statement, parentheses must be placed around the DO loop specification.

An illustration of the use of subscripted variables was provided in Figure 5–10. A FORTRAN program for this flowchart is shown in Figure 7–6.

FIGURE 7-6
A FORTRAN Program for Figure 5-10

```
C DETERMINES WORKER WITH HIGHEST SALARY
      DIMENSION ID(10),HOURS(10),RATE(10),SALARY(10)
      READ(5,50) N
   50 FORMAT(I4)
      READ(5,100) (ID(J),HOURS(J),RATE(J),J=1,N)
  100 FORMAT(I4,F4.1,F4.2)
      TOPSAL=0.
      DO 200 K=1,N
      SALARY(K)=HOURS(K)*RATE(K)
      IF(SALARY(K).LE.TOPSAL) GO TO 200
      IDTOP=ID(K)
      TOPSAL=SALARY(K)
  200 CONTINUE
      WRITE(6,250)
  250 FORMAT('1','IDTOP',4X,'TOPSAL')
      WRITE(6,300) IDTOP,TOPSAL
  300 FORMAT('0',1X,I4,4X,F6.2)
      STOP
      END
```

Input/Output with the A Format

Considerable attention has been devoted to the input and output of data, but all of it has been directed toward numeric data. No mention has been made of the input and output of nonnumeric data in FORTRAN. This important capability of the language must be discussed, because there are many business applications that require the processing of alphabetic and special character data. For example, payroll programs must process employees' names and addresses, end-of-term grade reports contain substantial alphabetic data, and order-processing programs must accommodate the customer's name and address.

The *A format* is especially designed for use with alphabetic and special character data. This format can also be used with numeric data, but the data cannot be subjected to normal arithmetic operations. In other words, numeric data can be input with the A format, but it can then only be output. The A format takes the following form,

$$nAw$$

where n is the number of times the format is to be repeated, and w is the field width. There is an upper limit on the field width, w, that varies with the computer. On the IBM System/360 the upper limit is 4. This limitation is due to how data are stored when input under an A format. Shown below is the input of the alphabetic data, TOM, for the variable called NAME.

READ(5,100) NAME
100 FORMAT(A3)

In a similar manner, data can be output with a WRITE–FORMAT statement pair. A significant difference between output under the A format compared to other formats is that the output is left justified in its field. Consider, for example, how the following WRITE–FORMAT statement pair presents the data.

WRITE(6,200) NAME
200 FORMAT ('1',4X,A4)

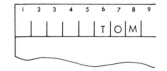

The data, TOM, is output left justified in its field.

There might be some reservations as to the usefulness of the A format if it can store, say, only four characters. Though it is not particularly convenient, there is a way around the problem. Essentially what is involved is breaking the data into sets of four characters and storing each set in a different variable. For example, consider inputting the following name and address:

JONES 152 HIGH ST.

This data input can be divided into four sets of four characters and one set of two characters (counting the blanks, which are, you will recall, characters).

READ(5,75) N1,N2,N3,N4,N5
75 FORMAT(4A4,A2)

These statements result in JONE being stored in N1, S 15 in N2, 2 HI in N3, GH S in N4, and T. in H5.

In an analogous manner, the data can be output. Notice once again how the output is left justified.

WRITE(6,200) N1,N2,N3,N4,N5
200 FORMAT('1',5A4)

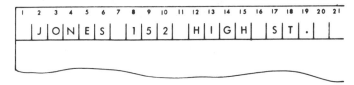

Subprograms

Subprograms can be grouped into two major categories — functions and subroutines. Functions can be further classified into library, arithmetic, and FORTRAN functions. Regardless of the classification, subprograms are designed to supply certain computational results to a *main program* — that part of the program which provides the primary thrust for accomplishing the data processing objective.

There are at least several reasons for using subprograms. One is to avoid repeating one or more programming statements a large number of times. This occurs when the same computations are required several times in the same program. Rather than writing the required programming statements each time the computations are required, a subprogram that performs the computations can be written once and then be "called" each time it is needed.

Subprograms can also be used to reduce the time it takes to complete a large programming assignment. Rather than having a single programmer perform the entire task, a team is assigned to the project. The project is then broken down into component parts, with each programmer in the team being responsible for completing one or more of the parts. Each part is then prepared as a subprogram to the main program, and the main program is little more than a "skeleton" on which to "hang" the subprograms.

With this introduction to the use of subprograms, we can consider their various forms. The most commonly used type is the library function. A *library function* is a set of programming statements that already have been written, are stored as part of the operating system, and are available to the user. The functions that are stored are those for performing computations that are needed in a wide variety of applications; for example, finding the absolute value or square root of a number. Some of the most commonly available and useful library functions in FORTRAN are as follows:

Selected Library Functions

Library Function	Argument Type	Application	Example
ABS(X)	Real	Absolute value of X	ABS(−18.3) = 18.3
IABS(I)	Integer	Absolute value of I	IABS(−5) = 5
AMAX0($I_1,I_2, \ldots ,I_n$)	Integer	The largest value of I_i	AMAX0(3,−2,8) = 8
AMAX1($X_1,X_2, \ldots ,X_n$) ..	Real	The largest value of X_i	AMAX1(326.,32.) = 326.
SQRT(X)	Real	The square root of X	SQRT(36.) = 6.

That which is within the parentheses of the function, X or I in the examples, is referred to as the *argument* of the function. The argument can be a constant, a variable, or an arithmetic expression. The argument is evaluated in the function and is then placed in the programming statement in which the function appears. For example, consider the following FORTRAN statements, which contain library functions.

$$VAL=SQRT(88.2)$$
$$NUMBER=IABS(N)+55$$

In these examples, VAL would be assigned a value equal to the square root of 88.2, and NUMBER would take on a value equal to the absolute value of N plus 55.

A programmer can define his own function. The simplest type of user-defined function is the *arithmetic statement function*. Its use is limited, though, to computations that can be performed in a single programming statement. Shown below is an illustrative arithmetic statement function named TITLE.

$$TITLE(A,B)=2.^{*}A+B^{**}3$$

The statement is similar to an arithmetic assignment statement, but its form defines a function. The appearance of the name of the function (TITLE), the dummy argument list (A and B), and the function $(2.^{*}A+B^{**}3)$ are sufficient to identify the statement as a *function-defining statement*.

In order to use a function that has been defined, it is only necessary to place the function in a programming statement—as is the case with a library function. Consider the following programming statement,

$$BOAT=24.0+TITLE(SCORE,3.0)$$

In this example the actual argument list for TITLE is SCORE and 3.0. The dummy arguments, A and B, were simply "holding" a place for the actual quantities (SCORE and 3.0, respectively). In the computer's memory location for BOAT is stored 24.0 plus the value of the function named TITLE when evaluated with the value of SCORE in place of the dummy argument A and 3.0 in place of the dummy argument B. This computation results in a value of 39.0 for BOAT when SCORE has a value of 3.0.

$$BOAT = 24. + 2.^{*}3. + 3.^{**}3 = 39.0$$

In general, it should not be expected that any of the variable names found in the actual and dummy argument lists will be the same. The function is usually written for use in more than one place, and there is no reason to tie it to any particular set of variable names. It is necessary, though, that the actual and dummy arguments agree in number, mode, and sequence.

Another type of function is the *FORTRAN function*. It is used when one or more programming statements are required to make the desired computations, and when only one computational result is returned to the main program. Unlike library and arithmetic statement functions, FORTRAN functions are essentially programs in their own right. They are even located separately from the main program, as shown in Figure 7-1.

As an example of a FORTRAN function, consider the problem of calculating a salesman's commission when the commission is a function of the markup (i.e., selling price minus cost). More specifically, assume that the commission is 5 percent of the markup when the markup is $100 or less, and 7.5 percent otherwise. The following main program statement would call the FORTRAN function named SCOM:

$$COM=SCOM(SPRICE,COST)$$

The function itself might appear as shown below:

```
    FUNCTION SCOM(SPRICE,COST)
    MARKUP=SPRICE−COST
    IF(MARKUP.GT.100.) GO TO 50
    SCOM=.05*MARKUP
    GO TO 100
 50 SCOM=.075*MARKUP
100 CONTINUE
    RETURN
    END
```

The name of the function (SCOM) and its actual argument list (SPRICE and COST) can be used in any main program statement. The statements that comprise the function are located separately from the main program (see Figure 7-1). The first programming statement in the function must name the function and all of its dummy arguments. If the function is to return a decimal or integer value, it must be given a decimal or integer name. While in our example the actual and dummy arguments are the same, this need not be the case as long as they agree in number, mode, and sequence. Another requirement is that at least one arithmetic assignment statement in the function must contain the name of the function on the left-hand side of the equals sign. It is in this manner that the function obtains its value to pass back to the main program. In our example, the sales commission, SCOM, is calculated in one of two possible places, depending upon the markup. The value found for SCOM is ultimately passed back to the main program and is assigned to the variable named COM. A FORTRAN function must contain a RETURN and an END statement. The RETURN statement returns control to the main program, while the END statement marks the physical end of the function.

The final type of subprogram is the *subroutine*. Like the FORTRAN function, it is similar in appearance to a completely independent program and is physically placed outside of the main program. A subroutine does differ, however, from a FORTRAN function. Most importantly, it has the capability for returning more than one computational result to the main program.

As an illustration, consider a subroutine that calculates the total, mean, and standard deviation from a set of observations. In our example, it is workers' gross salaries that are to be analyzed. In order to call the subroutine into action, a CALL statement such as that shown below is used.

CALL STATS(N,SALARY(I),TOTAL,MEAN,STDEV)

The call statement transfers control to the subroutine—the one that is named by the CALL. In our example it is the subroutine named STATS. The CALL statement also must specify the actual argument list. And it is here that subroutines once again differ from functions. In a subroutine, the actual arguments pass the data to the subroutine, but they also are the mechanism for passing the computational results back to the main program. This point is illustrated in our example. The actual arguments, N and SALARY(I), are used to carry the number of workers and workers' gross salary into the subroutine while TOTAL, MEAN, and STDEV are used to communicate back to the main program the results of the subroutine's computations.

The subroutine named STATS might appear as shown below:

```
      SUBROUTINE  STATS(N,X(I),TOTAL,MEAN,STDEV)
      DIMENSION  X(100)
      XSUM=0.
      XSQSUM=0.
      DO  100  I=1,N
      XSUM=XSUM+X(I)
      XSQSUM=XSQSUM+(X(I)**2)
  100 CONTINUE
      TOTAL=XSUM
      MEAN=XSUM/N
      STDEV=SQRT((XSQSUM-XSUM**2/N)/N)
      RETURN
      END
```

The SUBROUTINE statement identifies that which follows as being a subroutine. The name of the subroutine follows all of the restrictions associated with variable names, but the mode does not matter because no values are ever associated with the subroutine name. The dummy argument list comes next in the SUBROUTINE statement and must agree in number, mode, and sequence with the actual argument list. The variable names in the actual and dummy argument lists may or may not be the same. In our example all are the same, with the exception of SALARY(I), which goes with X(I). After the SUBROUTINE statement come the statements that comprise the subroutine. Notice that X(I) is dimensioned. All subscripted variables used in a subroutine must be dimensioned, since a subroutine is translated separately from the main program. A RETURN and an END statement mark the logical and physical end of the subroutine, respectively. When the RETURN statement is encountered, control passes back to the main program. And with this return are the values that have been computed for TOTAL, MEAN, and STDEV (the actual variable names). These values can then be used in the main program as would any variable value.

We have now completed our introduction to the FORTRAN programming language. More could be said about the language, but it would take us beyond what most managers ever need to know. The assignments that follow will reinforce the advanced concepts and programming statements that have just been presented. In addition, the assignments that follow the chapters on computer-assisted decision making and routine data processing applications will enhance your knowledge of FORTRAN as well as indicate possible areas of application. In general, the more programs you write, the better you will understand FORTRAN and its capabilities and limitations.

ASSIGNMENTS (ADVANCED CONCEPTS)

7-10. A data deck contains the data presented below:

1	2	3	4	5	6	7	8	9	10	11	12	13	14	15	
		4	0	0		-	3	0	0			7	0	0	First Card
1	9	.	3	0	.	6	2	8	.	2					Second Card
.	0	0	3												Third Card

The following FORTRAN statements are designed to input data from the data cards. First, determine whether or not the programming statements are valid, and if they are valid, what values are input into the computer's memory.

a.   READ(5,1) S(1),S(2),S(3)
      1 FORMAT(F5.2,F5.2,F5.2)

b.   50 FORMAT(F4.2)
      READ(5,50) TOT(1),TOT(2)

c.   DO 25 I=1,3
      READ(5,15) VAL(I)
   15 FORMAT(F5.2)
   25 CONTINUE

d.   READ(5,100) (BILL(I),I=1,3)
  100 FORMAT(F5.2,F5.2,F5.2)

e.   READ(5,105) (ITEM(J),J=1,3)
  105 FORMAT(3F5.2,/,3F4.2,/,F5.2)

*7-11. Assignment 5-9 (Chapter 5) required the use of subscripted variables in accumulating a salary total for all workers. Prepare a FORTRAN program based upon your flowchart and process the following data inputs.

ID	Hours	Rate
518	40.0	$4.05
036	40.0	3.85
511	46.0	3.50
212	48.0	4.35
586	40.0	3.70
135	42.5	3.70

*7-12. Assignment 5-10 (Chapter 5) called for preparing a program flow-chart which enters employee identification numbers, departmental code numbers, and gross earnings as subscripted variables and then totals the gross earnings in each department. Prepare a FORTRAN program based upon your flowchart and process the following data inputs through your program.

ID	Code	Gross
386	3	$160.00
419	3	182.25
860	2	143.25
136	1	160.00
156	3	187.50
189	2	175.00
263	1	160.00
341	2	160.00

*7-13. Each inventory item (ITEM(I)) has a safety stock level (SLEVEL(I)). Whenever the inventory (ILEVEL(I)) level drops below the safety stock, an order is placed for a predetermined quantity (ORDER(I)), plus the amount that the inventory balance has dropped below the safety stock. Prepare a FORTRAN program that inputs SLEVEL(I), ORDER(I), and ILEVEL(I) and computes the size of the order to be placed (PORDER(I)). Output from your program should be ITEM(I) and PORDER(I). Process the following data inputs. Include appropriate column headings for your output.

ITEM(I)	SLEVEL(I)	ILEVEL(I)	ORDER(I)
200	100	120	100
360	200	185	150
480	100	95	105

7-14. In Chapter 5, a program flowchart was requested in assignment 5-5 for students' names, degrees, and GPAs. Prepare a FORTRAN program based upon that assignment to process the following data.

Name	Degree Code No.	GPA
Worthly, Bill	1	3.62
Farmer, Shirley	3	2.85
Sturgen, Mark	2	3.05
Bozeman, Ann	4	2.60

7-15. The following assignments require writing subprograms.

  a. Write an arithmetic statement function that calculates the end-of-week inventory balance (EBAL). Its value is equal to the beginning-of-week balance (BBAL), plus any shipments received (SHIP), minus the current week's sales (SALES).

  b. A bank computes the service charge (CHARGE) on checking accounts in the following manner. If the minimum balance (MINBAL) in a customer's account during the past month is equal to or greater than $250, there is no service charge. However, if the balance dips below $250, the customer is charged $.50 plus $.08 for each check written (CHECKS). Prepare a FORTRAN function that computes customer service charges.

  c. The same bank discussed in part *b* wants to enlarge its FORTRAN function into a subroutine. Specifically, it wants the subroutine to return, through its dummy argument list, the customer's end-of-month balance and the month's service charge (still CHARGE). Obviously, the subroutine has to have passed to it total monthly deposits (TOTDEP), total monthly withdrawals (TOTWIT), previous end-of-month balance (PBAL), and the number of checks written (still CHECKS).

7-16. Prepare a subprogram called SOCSEC which computes an employee's social security withholding. The dummy argument list should include FICA (the amount of social security withheld), SALARY (the gross earnings for the current pay period), and GROSS (the cumulative gross earnings through the last pay period). Social security taxes are withheld at a rate of 5.85 percent of gross earnings on the first $15,300 earned each year. Nothing is withheld on earnings over $15,300.

REFERENCES

Books

Couger, J. Daniel and Loren E. Shannon   *FORTRAN IV: A Programmed Instruction Approach.* Homewood, Ill.: Richard D. Irwin, 1972.

Ford, Donald H.   *Basic FORTRAN IV Programming.* Rev. ed. Homewood, Ill.: Richard D. Irwin, 1974.

McCameron, Fritz A.   *FORTRAN IV.* Rev. ed. Homewood, Ill.: Richard D. Irwin, 1974.

McCracken, D. D.   *A Guide to FORTRAN IV Programming.* New York: John Wiley & Sons, 1972.

Silver, G. A.   *Simplified FORTRAN IV Programming.* New York: Harcourt Brace Jovanovich, 1971.

Common Business Applications

Sales Order Processing, Inventory Control, Customer Billing,
Accounts Receivable, Accounts Payable, Other Applications

Routine Data Processing Programs

The Edit Program, The Update Program, The Register
Program, The Action-Document Program, The Summary
Program

The Payroll Application

Payroll Master File, Payroll Master File Update, Inputs to the
Payroll Application, The Payroll Edit Program, The Payroll
Register Program, The Payroll Check Program, The Payroll
Journal Program, Periodic Reports, Summary

Assignments

Commonly Required Algorithms

Sorting, Sequence Checking, Table Lookup, Subtotals,
Summary

Assignments

References

This is the first of two chapters which focus on specific computer applications. In this chapter the most common data processing applications are briefly examined. Then the preparation of the organization's payroll is considered to illustrate the detail associated with routine data processing applications. And finally, examples of the algorithmic logic commonly used in developing applications of this type are given.

8 Routine Data Processing Applications

For conceptual purposes, the major uses of the computer can be dichotomized into *computer-assisted decision making* and *routine data processing* applications. In computer-assisted decision making the computer is used to help analyze complex decision-making situations. Management science techniques and models are commonly integrated with the computer in order to generate needed information. It is becoming increasingly important for managers to be aware of and comfortable with computer-assisted decision making, and the next chapter looks at this topic in detail. It will also surface again when the integration of management science models into information systems is considered.

The most important use of the computer, however, is for routine data processing applications. This use includes applications such as payroll preparation, customer billing, inventory recordkeeping, and so on. It is routine data processing that keeps most large organizations from being drowned in a sea of paperwork.

This chapter considers many facets of routine data processing. It briefly examines those applications that are found in most organizations. Since these applications are so pervasive, students of business administration should be familiar with their use. The applications discussed include sales order processing, inventory control, customer billing, accounts receivable, and accounts payable. Most of these routine data processing applications require several kinds of computer programs to accurately and effectively accomplish their objectives, and the edit, update, register, action-document, and summary programs are discussed. Also present is an in-depth examination of probably the most pervasive of all data processing applications—the preparation of the organization's payroll. This application is usually one of the first "put on the machine." While reading the discussion of this application you should become aware that even the most routine data processing application is more involved than you might imagine. This chapter will illustrate why routine data processing applications are best left to computer specialists.

The final portion of this chapter examines the mini algorithms that are used in many routine data processing applications. The algorithms illustrate the sorting of data, checking to see that data are in correct sequence, looking up a value from a "table," and computing subtotals. While this coverage is far from exhaustive, it is representative of some of the more commonly used data processing techniques. The assignments that follow provide additional experience in developing program flowcharts and computer programs.

COMMON BUSINESS APPLICATIONS

There are a number of data processing applications that usually pave the way for the introduction of the computer into the organization. Some of these applications include: (1) payroll, (2) accounts receivable, (3) customer billing, (4) accounts payable, (5) inventory control, and (6) sales analysis. If it were not for these applications, far fewer organizations would have need for a computer.

Because these basic applications are so common, computer manufacturers and software specialty firms have developed generalized programs for performing them. While the software specialty firms charge for these programs, some computer manufacturers provide them free of charge with their equipment. Firms that follow this practice are said to *bundle* their software with their hardware. Other manufacturers, most notably IBM, *unbundle* their hardware and software; in other words, the hardware and software are sold separately. A middle ground is the position of some firms, which provide a limited amount of software free but add charges beyond some point. Manufacturers that do provide free software are engaging in a form of nonprice competition.

Organizations that do not receive applications programs with their hardware and do not elect to purchase them from outside sources must obviously prepare their own. Even if applications programs are obtained from outside the organization, a certain amount of work is required to fit them into a particular organizational setting. Job assignments of this type are given to computer specialists rather than managers. As will be shown in the payroll application, a considerable amount of knowledge about data files and computer software and hardware is required in order to develop and implement most routine data processing applications. However, it is important for managers to have an appreciation of what applications are most commonly performed by the computer and what is involved in their functioning. Given this information, the manager is in a position to evaluate the applications that are currently being performed and to decide what other applications might be computerized. Furthermore, a knowledge of what is involved in developing a new application is valuable in that it provides a basis for evaluating what resources (e.g., personnel, time, money) would be required. Some of the most common business applications are discussed below.

Sales Order Processing

Customers' orders are taken or received in several ways—through salesmen's calls, by mail, by telephone. In most systems the order is recorded on a *sales order form* and later put in machine-readable form. In processing the sales order, a computerized *customer master file* is used which contains data on each customer, such as the customer's name, address, credit rating, credit limit, and special handling requirements.

Listings of the processed sales orders are output. These listings provide an *audit trail* (i.e., a series of documents that allow auditors to verify the accuracy and appropriateness of the organization's accounting practices), and they are also used for internal control purposes. Also output are notices to be sent to customers to acknowledge the receipt of the order. Usually the notice is one of acceptance, but occasionally orders are rejected. For example, the customer might be requesting a credit sale and management may have decided against extending any additional credit to this customer.

Sales order processing is usually linked to the inventory control system. The accepted sales orders become an input to the inventory control system, and orders are filled from inventory as provided by the accepted sales orders.

Inventory Control

Inventory control is necessary to ensure that customers' orders are quickly and accurately filled. In addition, the system should be designed to assist in keeping inventory costs as low as possible by minimizing carrying, ordering, and stockout costs. There are several inputs to the inventory control application. The accepted sales orders from the sales order processing system have already been discussed. Also input are notices of new stock received by the receiving department. Then too, there are necessary adjustments to the inventory records for reasons such as stock being lost, stolen, damaged, or returned.

Two important files are used in inventory control. One is the *inventory master file*, which contains data on the items carried in inventory, including current inventory levels. The second file is for recording *back orders*. These are orders that cannot be currently filled because of stockouts but customers are willing to wait until the ordered items become available.

One output from the inventory control application is listings of the inventory transactions which are used in monitoring the inflow and outflow of inventory goods. Another output is information on filled orders for the billing department. The billing department uses this information in billing customers for their purchases. This illustrates how an output from one application frequently becomes an input to another. This same relationship also holds for the information that is given to the purchasing department.

Orders for items that are either low or out of stock are placed by the purchasing department, based upon a report from the inventory control system. If the item is manufactured by the firm rather than purchased, the information is sent to the production department instead. The inventory control system also generates reports for management's use. Many of these are *management exception reports* — so called because they indicate exceptional conditions that warrant management's attention. Examples of this type of report include *slow-moving stock* and *out-of-stock reports*.

Customer Billing

After the filling of the customer's order is reported by the inventory control system, the customer's bill — the *invoice* — is prepared. The major input to this application is, of course, information on orders that have been filled. In preparing the customer's invoice, the customer master file, which was updated with any necessary changes when the sales order was first received, comes into use. This file contains information on the customer that is needed in completing the billing and shipping of the order, such as shipping addresses and special handling requirements. In some systems a *sales summary file* is also found. This file contains current and past sales data and is used in supplying management with sales analyses for use in performing the marketing function.

Customers' invoices are obvious outputs from the billing application. Summary lists of these invoices are also prepared for control purposes. You can probably gather by this point that routine data processing applications have many controls built into them. The billing system also generates necessary *shipping documents*, such as *shipping labels*, that are needed before the order can be shipped. One more output that is very important is the summary information on each invoice that is supplied to the accounts receivable department so that this information can be included on the customer's monthly billing statement.

Accounts Receivable

The accounts receivable application prepares customers' end-of-the-month billing statements and provides information that is useful to collection personnel who are responsible for collecting outstanding debts. There are three major inputs to the accounts receivable application: (1) the invoice summary data provided by the customer billing system, (2) data on cash payments made by the customers (payments for goods purchased previously and now paid for), and (3) changes to the customers' accounts for management-approved adjustments. These might include adjustments for discrepancies between warehouse records on the goods shipped and the customer's records on the goods received, and allowances to the customer for spoiled, damaged, or returned goods.

The *accounts receivable file* plays an important role in the accounts receivable application. It records and maintains the amount owed by each customer and serves as the central depository for all new charges, payments, and adjustments. The customer master file is also used once again, to supply information needed in preparing customers' statements (e.g., mailing addresses).

Output from the application are summary listings of the cash payments and the amount still owed — once again for control purposes. The monthly billing statements are also prepared and sent to customers. Normally the statements are prepared and sent just before the first of the month, to increase the likelihood of prompt payment. Another output from the accounts receivable application is the *aged trial balance* (or *aging schedule*), a document which shows, by account, the length of time payments are overdue, and by what amount. This information is very useful to collection personnel in focusing their collection efforts.

Accounts Payable

An organization's accounts payable represent what it owes for its purchases. In order to maintain good relationships with suppliers, to ensure a good credit rating, and to take advantage of price discounts for prompt payment, the organization should pay its bills on a timely and accurate basis. The accounts payable application is designed to accomplish this objective while maintaining appropriate financial controls.

One type of data input to the system is invoices from suppliers. Before an invoice is paid, however, it must be verified that the billed items were actually ordered and then later received. Copies of the *purchase order* from the purchasing department and a *receiving report* from the receiving department satisfy these needs. *Vouchers* from the accounting department are also an input to the system. A voucher is commonly used in situations where a payment is due but there is no invoice (e.g., reimbursing an employee for travel expenses).

The accounts receivable application employs an *accounts payable master file*. This file maintains an up-to-date record of the amount owed on each account. Listings of transactions that have taken place are output and are used for control purposes. An important output is the checks for the invoices and vouchers that have been approved for payment. Most applications also output a number of reports for management's use, such as a listing of the unpaid invoices and vouchers. Other output include summary data which become inputs to the organization's general accounting system.

Other Applications

Some of the most common routine data processing applications have been described — sales order processing, inventory control, customer billing, accounts receivable, and accounts payable. There are others that could be discussed, such as production control and general ledger accounting, and another important application — preparing the payroll — will be examined more closely below. These applications tend to reduce clerical expenses and supply management with needed information. Though the specifics of each application vary from organization to organization, in general they function as described above.

ROUTINE DATA PROCESSING PROGRAMS

In the discussion above, which was designed to provide a general understanding of the most common business applications, no attempt was made to show how each is actually performed. The reason is that the detail involved in each application is substantial. Nevertheless, there are many similarities in these applications, particularly in the similar types of computer programs that are used. It is useful to describe these programs through the following classification system: (1) edit programs, (2) update programs, (3) register programs, (4) action-document programs, and (5) summary programs.[1] A knowledge of the function of these programs must be developed before the payroll application is considered.

---

[1] This classification system is suggested in A. L. Eliason and K. D. Kitts, *Business Computer Systems and Applications* (Chicago: Science Research Associates, 1974), p. 20.

The Edit Program

Nearly all basic applications are designed to accurately, effectively, and efficiently process new data. But before the data are processed, checks must be made on the accuracy of the data inputs. The edit program performs this function by checking both the quantity and quality of the data to be processed. The quantity check involves comparing the actual against the planned number of data inputs. For example, if it is known that 25,000 meter readings are to be input into the electric company's billing program, a check should verify that exactly 25,000 inputs do exist—not 24,999 or 25,001. The edit program does this checking. It also attempts to control the quality of the data by considering the reasonableness of each data input. In this way obvious errors can be detected. For example, if a company's Eastern and Western sales regions are character coded by a 1 and a 2, respectively, any character other than a 1 or a 2 is an obvious error which needs to be corrected before processing proceeds. The output from the edit program is a *transaction file*. This file contains the edited transaction data that will be further processed.

The Update Program

The update program serves two important functions. First, it enters additional data into the transaction file that has been created by the edit program. The data that are entered are obtained from a *reference file* which supports the particular application. For example, in a manufacturing firm with a computerized system for costing the products it produces, one set of data inputs for this application would be standard labor cost figures. This data would be obtained from the reference file and entered into the transaction file by the update program.

The second important function performed by the update program is to make appropriate changes to any master files. A master file contains both permanent and temporary data that are important to a particular application. For example, as we have seen, an accounts receivable master file contains permanent data such as the customer's address, and temporary data such as the amount owed. The update program modifies the master file with the edited data from the transaction file.

The Register Program

The register program provides a complete, permanent record of the data inputs being processed. In accounting, such a listing is referred to as a *register*. There are several reasons why such records are needed. They provide the opportunity for a visual check on the accuracy of the data; a human inspection sometimes detects errors that cannot be found any other way. The records also make it possible to check at a later date on the processing of any particular transaction. Such records are required by auditors when verifying the accuracy and appropriateness of the organization's accounting practices. In some applications, computations are also performed by the register program. As will be seen, such is the case with the payroll application.

The Action-Document Program

From every computer application there are certain output documents that are the main reason for its existence. The output might be billing statements, listings of items to order for inventory, paychecks, and so on. It is the action-document program that provides this output.

The Summary Program

Nearly all computer applications output summary reports, which are prepared by the summary program. This program consolidates the details of the transaction data that have been processed into summary figures, and these figures typically then become inputs to other applications. For example, summary reports from the accounts payable application usually become inputs to the organization's general accounting system.

We will now consider an application and its programs in detail. As noted above, the application to be examined is that of preparing the organization's payroll.

THE PAYROLL APPLICATION

One of the oldest and most common data processing applications is preparing the payroll. In many organizations this is the first application that is computerized. As long as organizations have been paying their employees, there have been payrolls to prepare. Prior to the introduction of the computer, many firms used punched card calculators to compute the payroll and tabulating machines to print it. These business machines provided a bridge between clerical and computerized systems.

A computerized payroll system basically performs the same functions as a clerical system. However, the speed and accuracy with which these functions are carried out are much greater. In addition, many special reports can be generated by the payroll system that would be quite time-consuming to prepare otherwise.

The primary function of the payroll system is to calculate employ-

FIGURE 8–1
Systems Flowchart for the Payroll Application

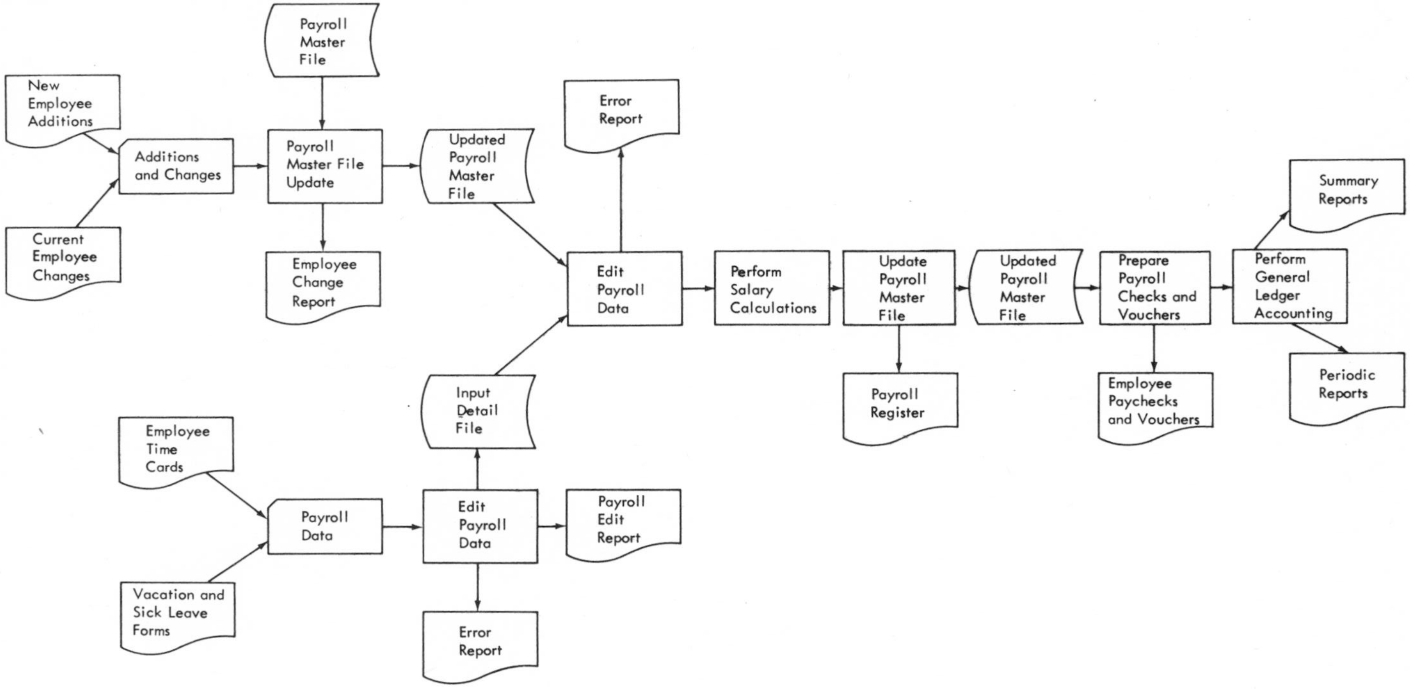

ees' salaries accurately. This task requires consideration of factors such as the number of hours worked, the wage rate, and necessary deductions (e.g., union dues, state and federal taxes, health plans). Paychecks are prepared after the appropriate calculations have been made.

Summary information from the payroll data is required throughout the organization's accounting system. For example, the total wages paid is used in preparing the firm's income statement.

In many payroll systems the data used to prepare the payroll also goes into the various information systems throughout the organization. For example, consider a job shop which works on several different orders during a particular pay period. In order to determine the cost for each job it is necessary to know the labor charges incurred. This information can be obtained as a by-product of the payroll system if the workers are required to indicate the number of hours worked on each job on their time cards.

Many of the reports and statements that employers are legally required to supply are provided by the payroll system. Quarterly and end-of-the-year reports on taxes and social security withholdings must be filed with the government. Employees must be given statements each pay period and summary statements at the end of the year.

Thus it can be seen that a payroll system serves many functions. Figure 8–1 shows how a typical payroll system operates with a systems flowchart for the entire payroll application.

Payroll Master File

For each employee a considerable amount of data are stored — name, address, social security number, number of tax exemptions, and so on. As discussed in Chapter 1, each of these items is a data element. The sum of the data elements for each employee constitutes a single record, and all of the employee records together form a file. When the file is used in calculating the payroll, it is commonly referred to as the *payroll master file*. The master file is normally stored on magnetic tape or disk. The payroll master file usually contains permanent and current information. The permanent portion includes items such as the employee's name, social security number, and year-to-date figures such as total wages paid. The current portion contains data from the current pay period.

Payroll Master File Update

Before data from the current time period are processed it is first necessary to *update the payroll master file*. This update, which is performed by the *update program*, is required to add new employees

FIGURE 8–2
Form for Additions to the Payroll Master File

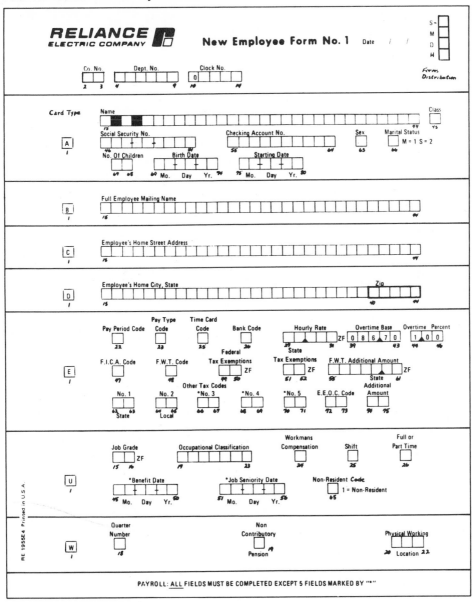

to the payroll file or make changes to existing employee records. Possible changes include corrections (such as for misspelled names), new home addresses, changes in the number of tax exemptions claimed, and so on. Changes or additions to the master file are first recorded on forms such as the one shown in Figure 8–2. Separate but similar forms are usually used for new employees and for reporting changes. These forms are then sent to keypunching. After keypunching, the master file is updated.

Inputs to the Payroll Application

There are several inputs that are required in preparing the payroll. One of these has just been discussed — the updated payroll master file. Another is a record of the number of hours worked by the hourly workers, information which is commonly provided by *employee time cards*. An example of a time card is shown in Figure 8–3. The time

FIGURE 8–3
Employee Time Card

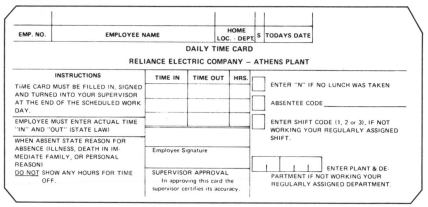

card contains data such as the employee's name, identification number, departmental code number, time period covered, regular hours, overtime hours, time spent on different jobs, and so on. After the time card is signed by the employee and his supervisor it is submitted to keypunching. Salaried employees do not turn in time cards; at most, special forms are submitted to keypunching when vacation or sick leave is taken. Otherwise, all of the requisite data for the salaried employees are contained in the payroll master file.

The Payroll Edit Program

The *payroll edit program* checks the validity of the data inputs. It screens the inputs for errors, such as overtime hours that should have been reported as regular hours. If errors are detected, an *error report* is printed and further processing stops until the errors are corrected.

The final outputs from the edit program are a *payroll edit report* and an *input detail file*. The edit report permits a visual inspection of the data inputs that have been entered. For each employee, the data inputs contained on the data cards are shown. The input detail file contains the validated payroll data for the organization's employees. The detail file is stored on secondary storage (usually magnetic tape or disk) and becomes the input to the next program, the register program.

The Payroll Register Program

The *payroll register program* integrates the data contained in the input detail file with the payroll master file. Additional data validity checks are made, and the salary computations are performed. For example, each record in the detail file is further checked for accuracy. This is the first opportunity in the payroll system where the master file can be used to verify the current data inputs. For example, it might be discovered that an employee has already used up all of his sick leave and cannot claim any more. Errors of this type result in an error report being printed.

FIGURE 8–4
Payroll Register

		PAYROLL REGISTER						DATE 7/27/--	
PAY PERIOD 27		PERIOD ENDING 07/05/--						PAGE 5	
EMPL NO.	EMPLOYEE NAME ITEM DESCRIPTION	PER.	GROSS EARNINGS	FEDERAL W/TAX	FICA TAX	STATE TAX	DESCRIPTION ACCT CD HOURS	RATE	AMOUNTS
33104	D. GORDON								
	PREV YTD	26	5,325.68	1,065.14	234.33	53.27			
	SALARY	27					0314954		223.00
	ALLOWANCE	27					0314964		2.50
	DEPS. 03 SUMMARY	27	225.50	42.00	9.90	4.46		TOTAL TAX	56.36-
	HOSP INS	27					0314200		11.21-
	UNITED FND	27					0314210		1.00-
	286-09-4549 NEW YTD	27	5,551.18	1,107.14	244.23	57.73		NET PAY	156.93
33126	J. GOSSELIN								
	PREV YTD	26	5,850.00	1,462.50	257.40	58.50			
	EARNINGS	27					0314854	40.0 5.72	228.80
	OVERTIME	27					0314874	2.0 5.72	22.88
	DEPS. 01 SUMMARY	27	251.68	62.97	11.08	2.52		TOTAL TAX	76.57-
	HOSP INS	27					0314200		5.80-
	CRED UNION	27					0314205		10.00-
	UNITED FND	27					0314210		4.00-
	453-07-8877 NEW YTD	27	6,101.68	1,525.47	268.48	61.02		NET PAY	155.31
33148	G. GRAHAM								
	PREV YTD	26	6,219.96	1,243.99	273.68	62.20			
	EARNINGS	27					0314874	40.0 5.03	201.20
	DEPS. 02 SUMMARY	27	201.20	40.24	8.85	2.01		TOTAL TAX	51.10-
	HOSP INS	27					0314200		2.90-
	UNION DUES	27					0314215		5.00-
	139-01-4113 NEW YTD	27	6,421.16	1,284.23	282.53	64.21		NET PAY	142.20
	FINAL TOTALS CURRENT		61,931.85						
	FIT		11,012.71						
	FICA		2,420.68						
	STATE		6,193.19						
	OTHER		4,214.91						
	NET PAY		38,090.36						

Source: *Management Reports in Today's Business* (White Plains, N.Y.: IBM Corporation, 1973), p. 18.

It is the register program that actually performs the salary calculations. The hours worked are translated into dollars and cents, and appropriate deductions are made. The register program uses data from both the input detail file and the payroll master file. For example, social security withholdings depend upon both current wages and year-to-year withholdings. The former data come from the detail file, while the latter are in the master file.

The results of the payroll calculations are entered into both the current and permanent portions of the payroll master file. The current portion receives entries such as gross pay, regular hours, overtime hours, and so on. The permanent portion of the file receives additions to its year-to-date totals. From the updated master file a *payroll register* is prepared (see Figure 8–4) which provides a permanent payroll record for the pay period.

The Payroll Check Program

The major function of the *payroll check program* is to print the employee's paychecks. Along with the paychecks, payroll vouchers which show many of the data elements from the payroll master file are prepared. These elements include items such as hours worked, gross earnings, federal taxes withheld, and so on. A typical paycheck and voucher are shown in Figure 8–5.

FIGURE 8–5
Paycheck and Voucher

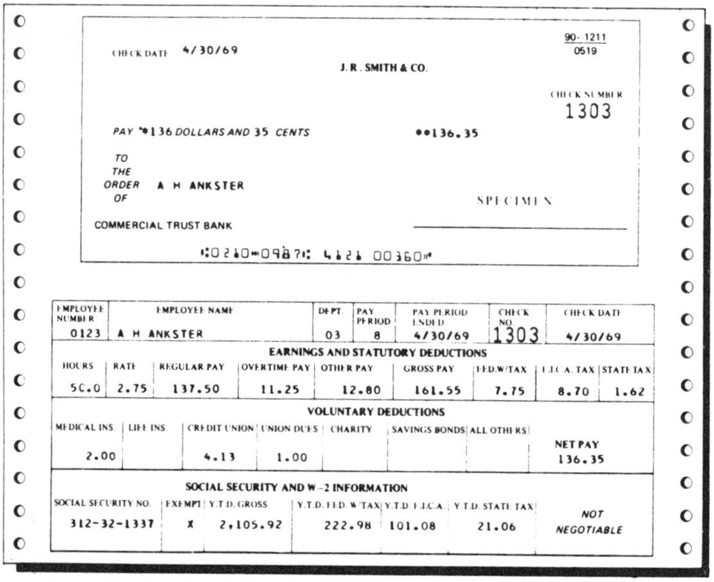

CHECK DATE 4/30/69

90-1211
0519

J. R. SMITH & CO.

CHECK NUMBER
1303

PAY **136 DOLLARS AND 35 CENTS **136.35

TO THE ORDER OF A H ANKSTER

SPECIMEN

COMMERCIAL TRUST BANK

0210-0987 4121 00360

EMPLOYEE NUMBER	EMPLOYEE NAME	DEPT.	PAY PERIOD	PAY PERIOD ENDED	CHECK NO.	CHECK DATE
0123	A H ANKSTER	03	8	4/30/69	1303	4/30/69

EARNINGS AND STATUTORY DEDUCTIONS

HOURS	RATE	REGULAR PAY	OVERTIME PAY	OTHER PAY	GROSS PAY	FED.W/TAX	F.I.C.A. TAX	STATE TAX
5C.0	2.75	137.50	11.25	12.80	161.55	7.75	8.70	1.62

VOLUNTARY DEDUCTIONS

MEDICAL INS.	LIFE INS.	CREDIT UNION	UNION DUES	CHARITY	SAVINGS BONDS	ALL OTHERS	NET PAY
2.00		4.13	1.00				136.35

SOCIAL SECURITY AND W-2 INFORMATION

SOCIAL SECURITY NO.	EXEMPT	Y.T.D. GROSS	Y.T.D. FED. W/TAX	Y.T.D. F.I.C.A.	Y.T.D. STATE TAX	
312-32-1337	X	2,105.92	222.98	101.08	21.06	*NOT NEGOTIABLE*

Source: *IBM System/3: Guide to Payroll* (White Plains, N.Y.: IBM Corporation, 1971), p. 19.

The payroll check program does not make any of the computations that are required to determine an employee's salary. These computations have already been made in the register program and the results are stored in the payroll master file. The output from the payroll check program is based upon the payroll file's contents.

The Payroll Journal Program

The *general ledger* is an organization's final, consolidated accounting document. It contains summaries of all of the organization's financial transactions — including payroll transactions. The payroll data inputs to the general ledger are provided by the *payroll journal program*. This program summarizes payroll data such as wages paid, social security withholdings, sick leave, and so on. The data for the payroll journal program come from the payroll master file.

Periodic Reports

An organization must file several periodic reports with state and federal governments. One of these is the Internal Revenue Division's *941 quarterly report* of social security withholdings, which is prepared from the payroll master file. Two approaches can be used in preparing this report. One alternative is to set up special fields in the payroll master file for recording quarterly data. With this approach current data are added each pay period to the quarter-to-date totals. After the 941 report has been prepared at the end of the quarter, the special fields are reset to zero so that the next quarter's activities can be recorded. There is another option that does not require establishing special quarterly fields. Instead, a copy of the payroll file from the preceding quarter is retained. The difference between the current and past quarter's year-to-date records provides figures for the most recent quarter's activities.

Another periodic report involves the preparation of the Internal Revenue's *W-2 forms* for all individuals employed by the organization during the past year. This end-of-the-year report indicates the employee's gross pay, federal tax withholdings, state tax withholdings, social security withholdings, and so on (see Figure 8–6). The program that prepares the reports obtains its data inputs from the year-to-date portion of the payroll master file. After the W-2s have been prepared, the year-to-date fields in the payroll file are reset to zero so that data can be recorded for the coming year. The records of employees no longer employed with the organization are deleted from the master file.

FIGURE 8-6
W-2 Forms

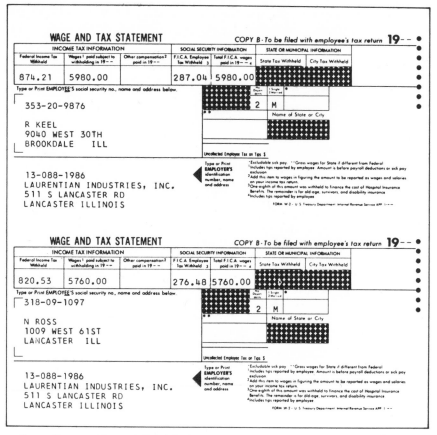

Source: *Management Reports in Today's Business* (White Plains, N.Y.: IBM Corporation, 1973), p. 20.

CONCLUDING REMARKS

You can see that preparing the payroll requires quite a few steps — probably more than you might have imagined. It would be a good idea to look back at Figure 8-1 and review the entire process. Actually, the payroll illustration presented here was simplified somewhat; for example, several additional checks on the validity of the data inputs and the accuracy of the data processing results were not mentioned. As it is, you might feel that you have learned more about payroll than you really wanted to know.

The lasting impression you should gain from this section is that routine data applications can become quite involved — not so much in terms of complex programming but in regards to data inputs, data files, hardware, validity checks, and so on. It is for this reason that we say routine data processing applications should be performed by experienced, competent systems analysts and programmers.

Following this section are assignments that will test and expand your knowledge of routine data processing applications. The chapter does not end at this point, however. Following these assignments are examples of algorithmic logic which are commonly used in developing routine data processing applications. This material and the assignments at the end of the chapter should provide additional insights into the flowcharting and programming of basic business applications of the computer.

ASSIGNMENTS

8-1. Distinguish between computer-assisted decision making and routine data processing applications. Give examples of each.

8-2. Consider the characteristics of the following two computer applications. Which one would you classify as computer-assisted decision making and which one as routine data processing?

Application 1

a. Relatively little data input.
b. Numerous and frequently complex computations—employing the "number crunching" capability of the computer.
c. Relatively little concern over programming efficiency, since the programs are run infrequently.

Application 2

a. Voluminous files of data.
b. Relatively simple computations.
c. Periodic program runs.
d. Considerable concern over programming efficiency.

8-3. Discuss what most managers do and do not need to know about routine data processing applications.

8-4. What does the sentence, "Manufacturers that do provide free software are engaging in a form of nonprice competition" mean? What other forms of nonprice competition are engaged in by computer manufacturers?

8-5. Discuss the data inputs, master files, and data output that are associated with the following routine data processing applications:

a. Sales order processing   d. Accounts receivable
b. Inventory control   e. Accounts payable
c. Customer billing

8-6. Discuss the function of the edit, update, register, action-document, and summary programs.

8-7. Discuss the following in regards to payroll preparation.

    a. The advantages and disadvantages of obtaining payroll programs:
       (1) From outside the organization.
       (2) Through internal development.
    b. The functions performed by the master file update.
    c. The inputs to the payroll system.
    d. The functions performed by the edit program.
    e. The functions performed by the register program.
    f. The functions performed by the paycheck program.
    g. The functions performed by the journal program.
    h. The periodic reports that are generated.

8-8. Contact a computer manufacturer's sales representative or data processing specialist to learn about other basic applications. Prepare a short report on an application you learn about.

COMMONLY REQUIRED ALGORITHMS

There are certain techniques (or mini algorithms) that are used frequently with routine data processing applications. Some of these have been encountered in previous chapters, such as using header and trailer card control on input loops or employing accumulator variables to obtain totals. While these techniques are not used exclusively with routine data processing applications, it is in this area that their use predominates. In addition to the techniques presented above there are others that are worthy of discussion. They include sorting, sequence checking, table lookup, and computing subtotals.

Sorting

With many applications there is a need to *sort* alphabetic or numeric data into ascending or descending order. While such programs are usually supplied by the computer manufacturer and are stored as part of the operating system, it is useful to have insights into how such a program might operate.[2] In addition there are instances when one might want to develop his own program, as when no other program is easily obtainable.

Consider a situation in which three job applicants have taken a screening exam and the personnel manager wants the test scores listed in descending order. Figure 8–7 presents a program flowchart that accomplishes this data processing objective.

The first step is to input the three test scores (SCORE1, SCORE2, and SCORE3) that are to be sorted. A comparison is then made to

---

[2] The sorting routine presented here is very simple. Those that are sold commercially for sorting large quantities of data employ highly sophisticated logic.

FIGURE 8–7
Sorting Test Scores in Descending Order

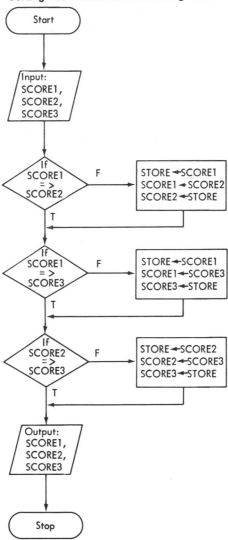

determine if SCORE1 is equal to or greater than SCORE2. If this test proves true, SCORE1 is already in its correct position relative to SCORE2. In this algorithm SCORE1 ultimately stores the highest score, SCORE2 the next highest, and SCORE3 the smallest. If the test between SCORE1 and SCORE2 proves false, the values for these two variables need to be reversed. Since the values can not be reversed simultaneously, one of the values must be stored temporarily. The variable named STORE is used for this purpose. The second decision point under consideration compares the values for SCORE1 and SCORE3. Keep in mind that SCORE1 contains the highest of the first two test scores. If SCORE1 is equal to or greater than SCORE3, it is known that the value for SCORE1 is the largest of the three. However, if the test proves false, the values for SCORE1 and SCORE3 must be reversed. Once again the variable STORE is used in the reversing process. The final decision involves comparing the values of SCORE2 and SCORE3. Based upon the same type of logic used previously, the values of SCORE2 and SCORE3 are placed in the correct order. The descending listing of test scores is then output, and processing stops.

Sequence Checking

To the extent that it is practical and feasible to do so, internal checks should be built into computer programs. In other words, specific checks designed to detect obvious errors should be included in the program's logic. While many checks of this type are used in routine data processing applications, a common one involves checking to determine if data inputs are in the *correct sequence*. For example, assume that inventory data are to be processed. On each data card is listed the item's part number (NUMBER) and the current inventory level (LEVEL). The program that later processes the inventory data assumes that the data are being entered according to increasing part number. A program flowchart that verifies whether or not the data inputs are being entered correctly is shown in Figure 8–8.

The key variable in the sequence-checking routine is CHECK. If it ever has a value larger than the value for NUMBER, the data inputs are out of order. Consider the algorithm's logic. Initially CHECK is assigned a value of zero, which assures that the value of CHECK is less than any part number. Then the first data card is input. Since the first card is not the trailer card, the first decision point tests false. The second decision point also tests false, since CHECK has been initialized with a value less than any part number. After both tests, CHECK is assinged the value of NUMBER, the first part number. Then the next data card is input. If the test of whether or not the value of CHECK (the past part number) is greater than the value of NUMBER (the current part number) proves true, the cards are out of order. An appropriate error message is output, and further processing stops. However, if the test proves false, the next card is input and tested. If this testing of whether CHECK > NUMBER continues to prove false, the data inputs are in the correct sequence. Eventually the trailer card is encountered, and the remainder of the program is executed.

FIGURE 8–8
Sequence Checking of Data Inputs

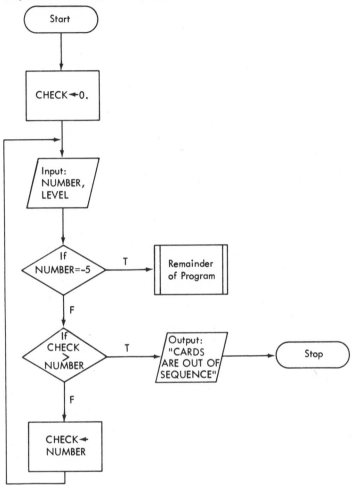

Table Lookup

Many data processing applications require that numbers be obtained from a table of values. Programs of this type employ what is commonly referred to as a *table lookup*. The values selected from the table depend upon the data being processed.

As an example of a table lookup, consider the problem of calculating a salesman's commission when the commission depends upon the markup realized on the sale. The markup is defined as the difference between the item's selling price and its cost to the seller. Selling prices are frequently negotiated. In general, the higher the item's list

FIGURE 8-9
Table Lookup for Determining Sales Commissions

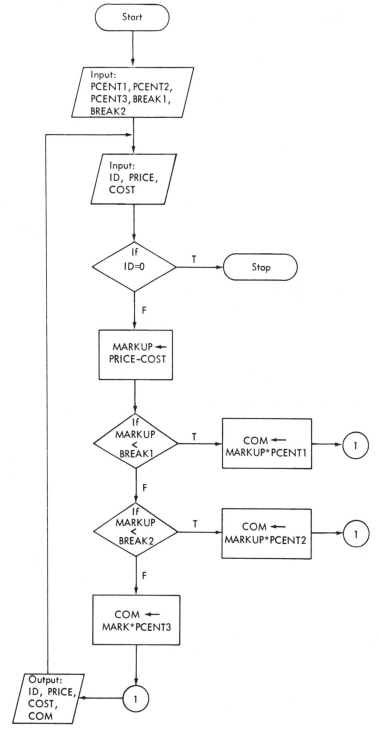

price, the greater is the likelihood that the buyer actually ends up paying less than the price asked. The purchase of new cars provides a good example. In car business jargon, a customer who pays the list price for a car that could have been purchased for less is humorlessly referred to as a "barefoot Pilgrim." The salesman's objective is to obtain the highest markup possible on each sale. In order to foster this objective, sales commissions are commonly based upon the markup realized.

Figure 8–9 illustrates a situation where the salesman's commission is a percentage of the markup. However, the percentage is not a constant. It can be either PCENT1, PCENT2 or PCENT3, depending upon the markup. These values are input, along with the markup break points (i.e., those points where the percentages change) on the commission structure (BREAK1, BREAK2). Each transaction card supplies the salesman's identification number (ID), the item's selling price (PRICE), and its cost (COST). The value for PCENT1 is used whenever the markup (MARKUP=PRICE–COST) is less than the first break point (BREAK1) in the commission structure. If the value of MARKUP is between the value of BREAK1 and BREAK2, the value for PCENT2 is used in calculating the salesman's commission (COM). If the markup exceeds the second break point, the top percentage (PCENT3) is used.

The table lookup in this illustration involves selecting the appropriate percentage to use in calculating the commission. As can be seen from Figure 8–9, a table, as it is commonly known, is not used. Rather, a series of decision points is used to branch to the right percentage figure (the right table value). This is how most simple table lookup routines function. Figure 8–9 processes all of the sales transactions, outputting the values for ID, PRICE, COST, and COM. Processing stops when the trailer card is encountered.

Subtotals

In processing data there is frequently a requirement for *computing subtotals*. This requirement implies that there are one or more attributes which categorize the data. The subtotals are computed on the basis of these categories.

Consider the objective of computing sales subtotals on a regional basis. In other words, management wants sales totals for all of the firm's marketing regions. The flowchart of Figure 8–10 accomplishes this objective.

A key to understanding the flowchart is a knowledge of how the data cards are sequenced. All of the inputs for a particular sales region are placed together. At the end of each region's inputs is placed a card with −50. as the figure for SALES. This card marks the end of the data

FIGURE 8–10
Calculating Sales Subtotals on a Regional Basis

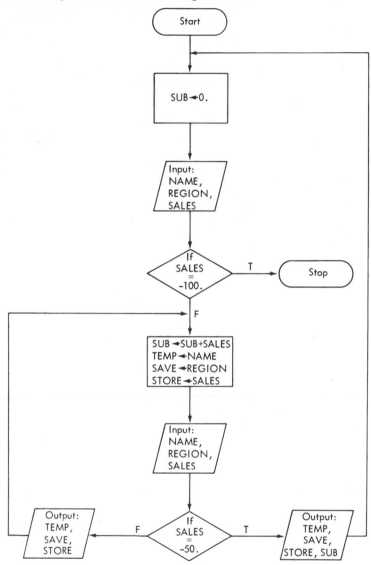

inputs for each region. The last card in the deck is the trailer card, with −100. as the value for SALES.

The first step indicated by the flowchart is initializing the variable SUB with a value of 0. This is an accumulator variable used in computing the subtotals. The data card for the first salesman is then input. It contains his name (NAME), marketing region (REGION), and sales total (SALES) for the preceding time period. As is usually the case, the trailer card test follows the input. The value for SALES is added to the accumulator variable SUB, and the values for NAME, REGION, and SALES are stored in the temporary storage locations TEMP, SAVE, and STORE, respectively. The need for this last step will become apparent later. The next data card is then input. It should be kept in mind, however, that the values for NAME, REGION, and STORE on the previous card are not lost, since they have been temporarily stored elsewhere. A test is then made to see whether or not the card just input marks the end of the records for the first sales region. If this test proves true, the values for TEMP, SAVE, STORE, and SUB are output. The current values for NAME, REGION, and SALES should *not* be output, since they store whatever was on the trailer card. The last salesman's record is stored in TEMP, SAVE, and STORE. The logic then flows to the top of the flowchart, where the process repeats itself for the next region. However, if the aforementioned test proves false, the latest input contains data that belongs with the current region. The values for TEMP, SAVE, and STORE are output and control loops back to the temporary storing and accumulating operations.

Summary

The illustrations for sorting, sequence checking, table lookup, and computing subtotals indicate the general nature of the specialized logic that is used in routine data processing applications. While none of the techniques are especially hard to understand and program, they do reflect clever algorithmic thinking. The computer specialist quickly becomes familiar with this type of logic.

ASSIGNMENTS

8-9. Develop a computer program based upon the sorting routine presented in Figure 8–7. Process the following data inputs through your program:
SCORE1=86
SCORE2=93
SCORE3=72

8-10. Modify the sorting algorithm of Figure 8–7 so that an ascending listing of test scores is provided. Prepare a computer program for your flowchart and process the following data inputs:
SCORE1=63
SCORE2=78
SCORE3=58

8-11. The sorting algorithm of Figure 8–7 does not keep track of the applicants' names, only their test scores. Develop a flowchart that outputs the applicants' names as well as their test scores. Process the following data through a computer program based upon your flowchart.

Name	Test Score
CROW	47
SING	95
REED	82

8-12. Prepare a computer program based upon the sequence-checking algorithm of Figure 8–8. Process the following two data sets in the order shown through your program.

Data Set 1		Data Set 2	
Number	Level	Number	Level
38	100	38	100
42	150	63	60
63	60	42	150
88	35	88	35

8-13. Figure 8–9 presented an illustration of a table lookup algorithm. Prepare a computer program based upon the flowchart and run the program with the following data inputs:

BREAK1	BREAK2	PCENT1	PCENT2	PCENT3
$100.00	$500.00	0.20	0.22	0.24

ID	PRICE	COST
5	$ 525	$ 300
3	2,200	1,500
12	125	80
3	750	500

8-14. The program flowchart shown in Figure 8–9 calculates sales commissions. Modify the flowchart so that it outputs only the accumulated sales commissions for each salesman (assume that there are three salesmen). Prepare a computer program based upon your flowchart, and process the following data inputs.

BREAK1	BREAK2	PCENT1	PCENT2	PCENT3
$200.00	$400.00	0.30	0.33	0.36

ID	PRICE	COST
1	$ 800	$ 500
1	1,200	1,000
3	500	250
2	2,000	1,500
3	200	100

°8-15. Modify the program flowchart presented in Figure 8–9 so that it allows for N − 1 price breaks and N percentages. Accomplish this objective by changing BREAK1 and BREAK2, and PCENT1, PCENT2, and PCENT3 to subscripted variables. Prepare a computer program based upon your flowchart, and process the following data inputs.

° Assignments dealing with subscripted variables are indicated by an asterisk.

BREAK(1)	BREAK(2)	BREAK(3)	PCENT(1)
$100.00	$300.00	$500.00	0.18
PCENT(2)	PCENT(3)	PCENT(4)	
0.22	0.26	0.30	

ID	PRICE	COST
5	$ 325	$ 250
8	2,500	1,800
3	800	600
5	1,300	900
3	1,100	800
8	350	250
8	1,000	750

8-16. The flowchart of Figure 8–10 computes sales subtotals on a regional basis. Prepare a computer program based upon this flowchart, and process the following data inputs.

Name	Region	Sales
MIX	1	$120,000
ABLE	1	82,500
GATES	2	214,000
TERSINE	2	64,000
LEDVINKA	3	75,250
MARK	3	93,500
KANG	3	104,750

8-17. Modify the flowchart of Figure 8–10 so that in addition to computing subtotals, the total for all regions is computed and output. Also include an error detection scheme for ensuring that all of the data inputs are in the right order—all of the region 1s are together, and so on. Prepare a computer program based upon your flowchart, and process the data of assignment 8-16 twice, once with the data inputs in the right order and once with them out of order.

8-18. The Home Lighting Company manufactures lamps for the home. Orders for the lamps are received either from the company's salesmen or from retail establishments. No lamps are sold directly to the public. Currently the company manufactures five lamps, with code numbers 1–5. The prices of these five lamps are $19.95, $24.95, $39.95, $49.95 and $69.95, respectively. A 5 percent discount is given for all orders of $200 or more. The manufacturer pays the shipping costs. Prepare a computer program that computes the bill to send each customer. Process the following orders through your program:

Customer's Name	Lamp Code Number	Quantity Ordered
ABLE	4	2
GRAY	1	4
	2	3
PANG	1	2
	2	2
	3	2
	4	2
	5	2

8-19. The county wants a computer program written that computes home-owner's real estate taxes. Recorded on each data card will be the homeowner's name, address, and property valuation. Real estate taxes are assessed according to the following schedule:

Property Valuation	Real Estate Tax as a Percent of Property Valuation
$0–10,000	1
10,000–30,000	1.5
30,000–75,000	2
Over 75,000	2.5

Prepare a computer program that computes the homeowner's real estate tax and outputs this information, as well as the homeowner's name, address, and property valuation. Process the following data inputs through your program:

Name	Address	Property Valuation
SIMKIN	220 TERRACE ST.	$43,500
WILLIAMS	6315 DERAMUS AVE.	37,000
ANTHONY	CHEROKEE RD.	64,000
WORTHLEY	2340 AHAMELE PL.	18,750

REFERENCES

Books

Dock, V. Thomas and Edward Essick *Principles of Data Processing.* Chicago: Science Research Associates, 1974.

Eliason, A. L. and K. D. Kitts *Business Computer Systems and Applications.* Chicago: Science Research Associates, 1974.

O'Brien, James A. *Computers in Business Management: An Introduction.* Homewood, Ill.: Richard D. Irwin, 1975.

Schriber, T. J. *Fundamentals of Flowcharting.* New York: John Wiely & Sons, 1969.

Silver, Gerald A. and Joan B. Silver *Data Processing for Business.* New York: Harcourt Brace Jovanovich, 1973.

Spencer, Donald D. *Introduction to Information Processing.* Columbus, Ohio: Charles E. Merrill Publishing Co., 1974.

Vazsonyi, Andrew. *Introduction to Electronic Data Processing.* Homewood, Ill.: Richard D. Irwin, 1973.

Modeling

  Systems Thinking, Characteristics of Mathematical Models

Packaged Programs

Classical and Modern Aids to Decision Making

  Classical Method, Modern Method

Computer Search for Optimality

Simulating Managerial Thought

Assignments

References

Some of the most exciting computer applications involve the use of management science models. The integration of models with the computer often results in information that could not be obtained in any other way. You will have to study each illustration of a computerized model presented in this chapter carefully—much in the same way that programming languages, accounting, statistics, and mathematics are studied.

9

Computer-Assisted
Decision Making

It can be said that at the heart of managing is decision making, and a manager's performance is largely evaluated on the basis of the quality of the decisions he makes. Good decisions usually result in advancement for the individual and efficient operations for the organization.

Since World War II, increasing emphasis has been placed on the use of *management science* models (also referred to as *decision* models) to assist in decision making. These models have emerged in response to complex real-world problems, such as the optimal location of a firm's warehouses or the planning and controlling of large projects.

Before the widespread availability of the computer, many managers were unable to derive benefit from these new methods; the mathematical and statistical skills required for their use were frequently just too great. To some extent this problem is being rectified as colleges of business administration are providing their graduates with better management science backgrounds. It also helps that many of the methods of analysis are now explained and illustrated in books that are more readable than the original presentations. Without the availability of the computer, however, these methods would be either prohibitively difficult or time-consuming for most managers to use.

The use of management science models with the computer has been facilitated by the increasing availability of preprogrammed software support packages which contain the logic embodied in the model. Essentially all the manager must do to employ the model is enter the data in the specified form. The packaged model then performs the analysis, using the preprogrammed logic. The computer has also influenced the development of management science models. Increasingly, the computer's computational power is being utilized, rather than developing models that use sophisticated mathematical and statistical formulations.

In summary, decision making is becoming more of a science and less of an art as management science techniques evolve, managers become more familiar with the new methods, and the computer is made available to perform the analysis.

The primary objective of this chapter is to illustrate how models and the computer can be used to supply information to support decision making. This use of the computer, which is referred to as *computer-assisted decision making,* involves an integration of management science models with the computer to provide information to assist the manager in fulfilling decision-making responsibilities. The chapter will also serve to enhance the flowcharting and programming skills developed in preceding chapters.

For this chapter, unlike others in the book, you must have a basic background in mathematics and statistics, since management science techniques do involve the use of mathematical and statistical techniques. Some care has been taken, however, to include illustrations that minimize the need for previous coursework in mathematics and statistics. If certain examples are not fully understood with the first reading, do not be overconcerned. Learning management science techniques, and hence computer-assisted decision making, requires careful study, an opportunity to ask questions, and practice. Your instructor and the assignments at the end of the chapter should provide all of these. When you have completed this chapter you should have an appreciation of how decision models and the computer can be used to support decision making.

MODELING

The use of models is inseparable from computer-assisted decision making. In fact, computer-assisted decision making implies using a computerized model to provide management with the information needed to support decision making. In general, a *model* is a representation of reality. Obviously, this definition includes many different types of models. While many classification systems for models are possible, the one presented in Figure 9–1 is particularly useful.[1]

The first distinction is between physical and symbolic models. As the names imply, *physical models* are physical representations of reality, whereas *symbolic models* use symbols to represent reality.

Physical models can be further divided into iconic and analog models. An *iconic model* looks like the represented reality; for example, a photograph is an iconic model. An *analog model* acts like the represented reality. For example, before a chemical plant is constructed, a miniature, working replica is frequently built. Because the

---

[1] This classification system is suggested by Clifford H. Springer, Robert E. Herlihy and Robert I. Beggs, *Advanced Methods and Models* (Homewood, Ill.: Richard D. Irwin, Inc., 1965), pp. 7–10.

FIGURE 9-1
Classification System for Models

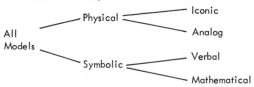

miniature plant behaves like the proposed larger plant, the miniature plant is properly described as an analog model. However, the miniature plant is also considered to be an iconic model if it looks like the proposed larger plant. The model classifications are not mutually exclusive—a particular model can fall into more than one category.

Symbolic models can be divided into verbal and mathematical models. *Verbal models* use words to represent reality, while *mathematical models* use mathematical symbols. Verbal models are used every day. For example, a marketing manager discussing a sales promotion plan for a new product is using a verbal model. The words used in describing the plan are a model of the future reality. However, it is primarily mathematical models that interest us in this book. Computer-assisted decision making involves the integration of mathematical models with the computer.

Systems Thinking

Before discussing modeling in greater detail, it is necessary to consider the relationship between "systems thinking" and modeling, since good modeling requires a systems orientation. A *system* can be defined as a set of interrelated elements that function in a purposeful manner. *Systems thinking* involves looking at a situation from a systems point of view. In examining a situation with the intention of modeling it, a systems orientation focuses attention on the system's major elements, the relationships between the elements, and possible boundaries on the system for modeling purposes. It is a holistic orientation which recognizes that things seldom occur in isolation in a system. A change in one part of the system usually has rippling effects that are felt throughout the entire system. It is up to the model builder to detect these interrelationships so they can be included in the model.

Characteristics of Mathematical Models

Not all mathematical models have the same characteristics; they differ in *purpose, mode, randomness* and *generality*. A framework for considering these differences is shown in Figure 9-2.

The purpose of a mathematical model can be optimization or description. An *optimization model* is one that seeks points of maximization or minimization. For example, in many business problems management wants to know what actions will lead to a profit maximization or a cost minimization. Optimization models provide this information.

A *descriptive model* describes the behavior of the system. It is not the purpose of this type of model to output values that will suggest how to make the modeled system function most efficiently; a descriptive model simply describes how the system operates. There are

FIGURE 9–2
Classification System for Mathematical Models

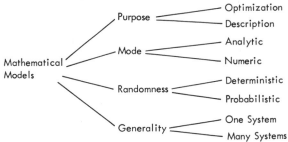

Source: Suggested in part by Claude McMillan and Richard F. Gonzalez, *Systems Analysis: A Computer Approach to Decision Models,* 3rd ed. (Homewood, Ill.: Richard D. Irwin, Inc., 1973), pp. 1–16.

several reasons for building such a model, one of which is to provide a better understanding of the operations of complex systems. If a model does not correctly describe the behavior of the system, it is unlikely that the model builder fully understands the system.

Even if the model does seem to possess good descriptive powers, this is no guarantee that the modeled system is fully understood. Newtonian physics provides a good case in point. Newton's models were largely unchallenged until 1905, when Albert Einstein published his famous theory of relativity. When subsequent research tended to support Einstein's theories, it was realized that Newton's models were oversimplifications. However, even as oversimplifications, they were useful (and still are today) in explaining the world in which we live. Furthermore, they provided a starting point for the development of more complete models.

A descriptive model is also useful in answering "what if" questions. For example, a marketing model might supply the answer to the following question: "What will be the effect on total sales if advertising expenditures are increased by 10 percent?" Obviously, it would be advantageous to be able to answer questions like this without actually exposing the firm to real-world dangers.

The mode of operation of mathematical models can be either analytic or numeric. The *analytic mode* involves using traditional mathematical and statistical techniques to perform the analysis (e.g., differential calculus, matrix algebra, or linear combination of variables). A *numeric mode* of analysis replaces these frequently complex mathematical and statistical operations with a very large number of simple computations. The analytic mode should be used whenever possible, since it is more precise and efficient. However, some situations that cannot be analyzed by analytic methods can be handled by numeric techniques. In general, the more complex the system and the more detailed the model, the greater is the likelihood that a numeric method of analysis will have to be employed. Later in this chapter both numeric and analytic methods of analysis are illustrated.

In relation to randomness, nearly all systems are *probabilistic.* That is, the behavior of the system cannot be predicted with certainty —a degree of randomness is present. A *probabilistic model* attempts to capture the probabilistic nature of the system by requiring probabilistic data inputs and generating probabilistic output. Even though most systems are probabilistic, most models are *deterministic. Deterministic models* employ single-valued estimates for the variables in the model and generate single-valued output. The primary reasons that deterministic models are more popular than probabilistic ones are that they are less expensive, less difficult, and less time-consuming to build and use, and they often provide satisfactory information to support decision making.

In terms of generality, a mathematical model can be developed for use with only *one system* or be made applicable to *many systems.* Other things being equal, the more general the model, the less specific the level of detail. However, a general model has the advantage of being transferable from one situation to another.

The actual modeling of a system begins with a realization that certain information about the behavior of the system is needed, or is at least desirable, to support decision making. As has been suggested, a systems orientation should be taken in developing the model. The final version of the model is seldom the same as the initial one. In testing a model it is usually found that revisions must be made. The objective is to develop a valid model that generates the desired information.

In the sections of the chapter which follow the use of management science models is illustrated, with emphasis on models used for computer-assisted decision making.

PACKAGED PROGRAMS

The most common use of management science models to support decision making involves the utilization of *packaged* (or *canned*) *programs*.[2] These are programs that have been previously written, usually by someone else, to perform a desired analysis. The programs themselves are frequently already stored within the computer system on a secondary storage medium. In order to use a packaged program it is only necessary to "call" the appropriate program and supply the data inputs according to the specified format. The manager receives as output the analysis needed to support decision making.

Most computer facilities have canned programs that are both local and national in origin. The local programs have been written by employees and users of the local computer facility. Many business firms have programs of this type for analyzing situations they encounter frequently, such as sales forecasting. Documentation of the programs varies. Some packages of programs, such as the Biomedical (BMD) Computer Programs developed at the University of California at Los Angeles, are well documented and widely distributed. Almost all major universities and research centers have packaged programs like the BMD series. Included are programs for simple data description, principal-component analysis, simple linear regression, and similar purposes.

The following example demonstrates the use of packaged programs. The Energy Conversion Company (ECC) produces three different types of electrical generators, A, B, and C. The contribution to profits from producing generators A, B, and C is $500, $650, and $450, respectively. In a world of unlimited resources and consumer demand, ECC would manufacture an unlimited quantity of each. Unfortunately, however, ECC operates in a world of constraints in regard to previous commitments, potential demand, skilled labor, machine time, raw materials, and so on.

ECC has agreed to supply customers with a minimum of two each of type A, B, and C generators during the next time period. Consequently the production of each must be at least two. ECC's salesmen have indicated that the maximum possible sales for type A generators is 20 units; for type B, 10 units; and for type C, 30 units. In other words, there is an upper limit to demand. A specific machine is used in producing each type of generator. Each type A generator produced requires two hours on this machine; each type B generator, three hours; and each type C, one hour. During the next time period this machine will be available 60 hours. The final constraint involves a component part that is in critically short supply. Only 60 will be

---

[2] This material is taken from Hugh J. Watson, "Computers Can Reduce Management Risks," *Journal of Systems Management*, December 1971, pp. 13–17.

available during the next time period. Three of these parts must go into each generator A, two into each B, and two into each C. These constraints are believed by management to be the most potentially binding and hence are included in the analysis.

The decision-making situation just described can be analyzed by a management science technique known as *mathematical programming*. This technique is appropriate for problems where scarce resources are to be allocated in an optimal manner. For mathematical programming to be employed it is necessary to express the problem in mathematical form. First, the objective must be stated in what is known as the *objective function*. For ECC it would appear as shown below:

$$\text{Contribution to profits}_{max} = \$500 \, X_A + \$650 \, X_B + \$450 \, X_C.$$

This statement shows that the total contribution to profits, which is to be maximized, is equal to $500 times the number of type A generators sold, plus $650 times the number of type B generators sold, plus $450 times the number of type C generators sold. The *constraints* must also be expressed mathematically, as below:

Constraints	Explanations
(1) $X_A \geq 2$	
(2) $X_B \geq 2$	Previous commitments to customers
(3) $X_C \geq 2$	
(4) $X_A \leq 20$	
(5) $X_B \leq 10$	Upper limits on demand
(6) $X_C \leq 30$	
(7) $2X_A + 3X_B + 1X_C \leq 60$	Availability of machine time
(8) $3X_A + 2X_B + 2X_C \leq 60$	Availability of parts

Constraints 1–3 express the commitment to produce at least two generators of type A, B, and C. The limitation due to demand is shown by expressions 4–6. Constraint 7 reflects the limitation upon available machine time, while constraint 8 indicates the number of component parts that can be obtained. The objective function and constraints, considered together, are a complete mathematical statement of ECC's situation. Any problem that can be analyzed by mathematical programming must have a similar structure—an objective function and constraints.

There is an algorithm (recall that an algorithm is a series of steps that lead to a solution) known as the *simplex method* which can be used to analyze problems like ECC's. On small problems, like the one presented here, the simplex method can be performed easily by hand. However, as the problem becomes more complex the use of a canned simplex program becomes almost mandatory. It is the technique of how to use a canned program that interests us here, not the simplex method itself.

As mentioned previously, every mathematical programming problem has a similar structure. All that is necessary to use a packaged program is to input the specific mathematical characteristics of the situation under investigation. For example, in our problem the coefficients on the variables in the objective function are $500, $650, and $450. These values, along with a statement that maximization is desired, are inputs to the packaged program. The coefficients on the variables in the constraint equations must also be stated, as must the nature of the constraint equation, whether it be less than, equal to or less than, equal to, equal to or more than, or more than. And finally, the right-hand side values of the constraint equations must be supplied. Given these inputs in the proper format, the packaged program performs the analysis using the simplex method. Actually, the manager needs to know very little about the actual workings of the simplex method (a very easy algorithm to forget). He only needs how to spot possible areas of application, properly structure the problem, and enter the required inputs to the packaged program.

The above problem was analyzed using a packaged program called from a terminal. Among the information generated was the following:

VARIABLE	VALUE
X(1)	2
X(2)	10
X(3)	17

OPTIMAL VALUE OF OBJECTIVE FUNCTION IS 15150

This information indicates that ECC will optimize its contribution to profits if it produces 2 type A, 10 type B, and 17 type C generators. ($X(1)$ corresponds to X_A, $X(2)$ to X_B and $X(3)$ to X_C.) This feasible production mix will lead to a profit contribution of $15,150. Management obtained this information by recognizing its problem as being suitable for analysis by mathematical programming, properly structuring the problem, and supplying it to the computer in the proper format. Many other types of problems can be analyzed by following analogous procedures.

CLASSICAL AND MODERN AIDS TO DECISION MAKING

The computer has considerably influenced the development of management science models. Previously, most new models relied upon increasing mathematical and statistical sophistication. More and more, however, the newer models are drawing upon the computational power of the computer. This is a favorable trend for the multitude of managers who are not rigorously trained in mathematics and statistics.

It also should be mentioned that the new computer-oriented aids to decision making provide greater flexibility for modeling the real world. In order to clearly demonstrate the differences, two variant approaches to inventory analysis are presented. The first is a classical approach which requires a knowledge of differential calculus to completely understand it (not to actually use it, however) and which offers relatively little flexibility. The second is a Monte Carlo inventory simulation model.

Classical Method[3]

Inventory in itself does not create value. It simply creates a cost, albeit a necessary one, that is associated with producing a product or providing a service. The objective of management, therefore, is to keep inventory costs as low as possible.

It is meaningful to classify the costs of inventory as (1) carrying costs, (2) ordering costs, or (3) stockout costs. *Carrying costs* are the costs of physically having the item in inventory. These are the costs of warehousing, insurance, obsolescence, spoilage, tied-up capital, and so on. *Ordering costs* are the costs associated with ordering a quantity of an item for inventory. The major component costs are for clerical and materials handling expense. *Stockout costs* are the costs of not having an item on hand when there is a demand for it. When the unavailable item is for final sale, the costs include the opportunity cost of the foregone sale and the possible loss of future sales because of lost customer goodwill. If the demanded item is not for final sale but, say, supplied to an internal production process, there are the costs of disrupted production activities.

The classical approach to the inventory problem uses differential calculus to determine the optimum quantity and time to order for inventory. Underlying the analysis are the assumptions that the demand for the item is constant and known with certainty and that the delivery time after ordering is known with certainty. Figure 9–3 depicts a situation where, at time zero, an order for inventory of size Q (the order quantity) has just arrived. This inventory is consumed as a constant, known rate over time. When L units (the order point) remain in inventory, an order is placed for Q more units. These Q units arrive just as the previous inventory is depleted. Then the cycle is

---

[3]This material is taken from H. J. Watson and R. J. Tersine, "Computer Assisted Decision-Making: Inventory Analysis," *Cost and Management*, November–December 1973, pp. 30–34.

FIGURE 9–3
Amount in Inventory as a Function of Time

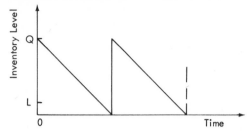

repeated. The problem is to determine what value of Q minimizes inventory costs and then to calculate the optimal order point, L.

Assuming a known demand, D, per unit of time, a carrying cost, K_c, per item per unit of time, and an ordering cost, K_o, per order, it is possible to find the value of Q that minimizes the total inventory costs, TC. There is no need to consider stockout costs, since the assumptions of certainty on demand and delivery time rule out the possibility of a shortage.

We will first consider the total carrying costs. The greatest number of items ever in inventory is Q, the smallest is zero. Since demand is constant, the average inventory level is $Q/2$. If K_c is the carrying cost per item, the total carrying cost for an average of $Q/2$ items must be:

$$K_c \frac{Q}{2}$$

If D is the demand per unit of time, and Q units are ordered at a time, D/Q must be the number of orders placed per unit of time. When the cost per order is K_o, the result is a total ordering cost of:

$$K_o \frac{D}{Q}$$

The total cost of inventory, TC, is the sum of the carrying and ordering costs:

$$TC = K_c \frac{Q}{2} + K_o \frac{D}{Q}$$

In order to find the value of Q that minimizes TC, a first derivative of TC with respect to Q is taken:

$$\frac{dTC}{dQ} = \frac{K_c}{2} - \frac{K_o D}{Q^2}$$

This expression is then set equal to zero and solved for Q, in order to find the value of Q that minimizes TC.[4]

$$\frac{K_c}{2} - \frac{K_oD}{Q^2} = 0$$

$$\frac{K_c}{2} = \frac{K_oD}{Q^2}$$

$$Q^2 = \frac{2K_oD}{K_c}$$

$$Q = \sqrt{\frac{2K_oD}{K_c}} \qquad (9\text{--}1)$$

This expression is the famous *economic order quantity* formula, which reveals the optimum number of items to order for inventory. Given the demand, carrying costs, and ordering costs, the optimum order quantity is easily determined. An example is:

$$Q = \sqrt{\frac{2(20)(1000)}{4}}$$

$$= 100 \text{ units per order}$$

when
$$D = 1{,}000 \text{ units per year}$$
$$K_c = \$4 \text{ per year per item}$$
$$K_o = \$20 \text{ per order}$$

If 1,000 units are used per year and it takes two weeks for an order to arrive, an order should be placed when only two weeks' supply remains in inventory.

$$L = \frac{1{,}000(2)}{52}$$

$$= 39 \text{ units}$$

To account for the uncertainty that actually exists in the real world in regards to demand and delivery time, most firms provide a safety stock. The actual order point is then the L value computed, plus the desired safety stock.

It would be inappropriate to overemphasize the difficulty of developing, understanding, and applying the classical economic order quantity formula. It might be better to point out the shortcomings of

---

[4] Only the positive square root of $2K_oD/K_c$ need be considered, since an order for inventory must be for one or more units. A second derivative test reveals that Equation 9–1 does provide a minimum.

the model in terms of its depiction of the real world. It obviously is somewhat unrealistic because it assumes certainty for demand and delivery time. It is not impossible to include uncertainty in an analysis and develop an appropriate inventory model by analytical methods, but this requires a considerable degree of mathematical and statistical sophistication. The Monte Carlo inventory simulation that follows is relatively simple to understand and apply, and it does provide a more valid representation of the real world.

Modern Method

In business systems modeling, a *simulation* is a mathematical model that represents the behavior of a system over time. It provides management with the opportunity to observe how alternative policies, conditions, and strategies might affect a system without incurring real-world risks. Because the arithmetic computations required for practical problems are ordinarily too great for hand analysis, the computer is usually employed.

The inventory simulation that follows employs the *Monte Carlo method.* While this name might conjure up visions of gambling, excitement, and romance, it actually refers to a method of randomly sampling values from a probability distribution. Some of its applications are rather exciting, however. By employing the Monte Carlo method it is possible to analyze probabilistic situations that would be almost impossible to investigate using standard mathematical and statistical techniques.

The specific steps to follow in order to perform a Monte Carlo inventory simulation are as follows:

1. Construct cumulative frequency distributions for the probabilistic variables.
2. Associate random numbers with the cumulative frequencies.
3. Set reasonable values for Q and L.
4. Simulate activity and resultant costs.
5. Calculate the average cost for the simulated time period.
6. Repeat steps 3–5 with Q and L set at all reasonable combinations.
7. Compare cost averages.
8. Determine the best values for Q and L.

Assume that the following empirical data on demand and delivery time are available. The data reflect the company's historical experience during the past year. The reason the demand history covers 50 rather than 52 weeks is due to the fact that the company ceases operations two weeks a year for a companywide vacation. During last year's operations the number of times the inventory item under analysis was ordered was ten. Hence the historical data on delivery time include ten observations.

Historical Data on Demand and Delivery Time

Demand/Week	Frequency	Relative Frequency	Cumulative Relative Frequency	Random Numbers
0.........................	2	.04	.04	01–04
1.........................	4	.08	.12	05–12
2.........................	14	.28	.40	13–40
3.........................	20	.40	.80	41–80
4.........................	8	.16	.96	81–96
5.........................	1	.02	.98	97–98
6.........................	1	.02	1.00	99,00
	50	1.00		

Delivery Time (weeks)	Frequency	Relative Frequency	Cumulative Relative Frequency	Random Numbers
1.........................	6	.60	.60	01–60
2.........................	3	.30	.90	61–90
3.........................	1	.10	1.00	91–99,00
	10	1.00		

If it is believed that the future will be like the past, the relative and cumulative frequencies can be interpreted as probabilities. For example, the probability that demand is equal to three in any week is 0.40. Random numbers are then associated with the possible values for demand and delivery time in such a way that the number of random numbers assigned to each variable value is proportional to its probability of occurrence. In this illustration a total of 100 random numbers are possible, 00–99. And 40 of the 100 have been assigned to a demand of 3, since its probability of occurrence is 0.40. At this point after all of the random numbers have been associated with variable values, the first two steps in the Monte Carlo inventory simulation have been completed.

A reasonable Q and L combination must next be selected. A "reasonable combination" is one that the decision maker believes might minimize inventory costs. In this illustration a Q of 5 and an L of 3 are used; an order for five units is placed whenever three or less units are remaining in inventory. Later in the analysis other Q and L combinations are simulated.

The simulation is most easily understood by considering how a worksheet similar to that in Table 9–1 might be used. It should be noted that a column is included for stockout costs. With a probabilistic model the possibility of a shortage must be considered. It will be assumed that a stockout condition has a cost of $20 per unit, and the potential buyer will not wait until more items arrive. Carrying costs

TABLE 9–1
Worksheet for a Monte Carlo Inventory Simulation

Weeks Simulated	Random Numbers		Simulated Activity				Simulated Cost			
	Demand	Delivery Time	Demand	Order Placed	Order Received	Balance	Carrying Cost	Order Cost	Stockout Cost	Total Cost
0						5				
1	.19	20	2	5		3	$ 6	$10	$ 0	$16
2	.45		3		5	5	10	0	0	10
3	.99	13	6	5		0	0	10	20	30
4	.80	14	3	5	5	2	4	10	0	14
5	.15		2		5	5	10	0	0	10
6	.34	61	2	5	5	3	6	10	0	16
7	.10		1			2	4	0	0	4
8	.74		3		5	4	8	0	0	8
9	.02		0			4	8	0	0	8
10	.10	39	2	5	5	2	4	10	0	14

are assumed to be $2 per item per week, and ordering costs are $10 per order.

The simulation begins with an order arriving in week 0, which places a balance of five units in inventory. For week 1, a random number is selected from a table of uniform random numbers, and this number is then associated with a demand level. The frequency distribution for demand shows that the number selected, 19, should be interpreted as a demand for two units. This demand drives the inventory balance down to three units, and an order is placed for five more units because the order point ($L = 3$) has been reached. Another random number is then needed to simulate when the ordered items are delivered. From the frequency distribution for delivery time it can be seen that the next random number drawn, 20, should be interpreted as a one-week delivery time. This means that the items will be delivered and ready for sale next week. The costs for week 1 are as follows: $6 for carrying costs ($2 × 3); $10 for ordering costs (one order placed); and $0 of stockout costs. The total cost thus is $16.

In week 2 a demand for three units develops (random number = 45). Available for sale are the three units in inventory plus the five units that arrive because of last week's order. This development leaves five units in the inventory balance, and no new orders need be placed. The total costs are $10 + $0 + $0 = $10.

The demand in week 3 is for six units. This demand is for one more unit than is available in inventory, and a stockout cost of $20 is incurred. An order is placed for five more units; these units arrive next week (random number = 13). The total costs in week 3 are $0 for carrying costs, $10 for ordering costs, and $20 for stockout costs.

The simulation should be carried out through a large number of weeks so that a representative average can be computed. The average, found by summing the total costs for the simulated weeks and then dividing by the total number of weeks simulated, provides an unbiased estimate of the average weekly cost of ordering five units whenever the inventory balance is three or less.

There is no guaranty that the Q and L combination tried first is the best one. For this reason step 6 in the Monte Carlo model calls for simulating other reasonable Q and L combinations. Table 9–2 shows the matrix of cost averages that resulted from trying different combinations of Q and L. On the basis of this matrix, management would probably decide to order a quantity of five units whenever the inventory balance dropped to three, because $11.73 is the lowest cost figure in the matrix.

The figures presented in Table 9–2 were not obtained by hand computations, as can probably be guessed. Instead, a flowchart and computer program were developed for this purpose. An assignment

TABLE 9–2
Matrix of Costs for Different Q and L Combinations

Order Quantity, Q	Order Point, L				
	2	3	4	5	6
2	$33.92	35.17	20.02	34.91	34.32
3	23.79	26.27	18.91	26.72	17.55
4	19.63	17.65	18.59	20.08	17.07
5	20.05	11.73	13.04	14.48	13.68
6	17.73	19.44	15.33	14.19	14.24
7	20.11	12.99	13.92	13.17	15.68

at the end of the chapter which requires the preparation of a similar program is an interesting and challenging task.

COMPUTER SEARCH FOR OPTIMALITY

There are many business problems in which the objective of an analysis is to identify an optimal, or nearly optimal, solution from a large number of alternatives. Many management science algorithms represent a specific response to this type of problem. These algorithms specify a sequence of steps that lead to a satisfactory, if not optimal, solution. In many instances it is necessary to enlist the aid of the computer to follow the sequence of steps, since the number of steps is frequently quite large and many computations are required at each step.

The problem discussed previously which concerned the Energy Conversion Company's decision of how many type A, B, and C generators to produce in the next time period provides a good case in point. There are a large number of feasible solutions to the production mix problem but only one is optimal. The optimal solution was found earlier by a procedure which involved (1) identifying the problem as being amenable to analysis by the simplex method of mathematical programming, (2) mathematically specifying the problem in the proper format, and (3) performing the analysis by a packaged simplex program. The packaged program carried out the sequence of steps that make up the simplex algorithm. Many mathematical programming problems are sufficiently large that they are prohibitively difficult to solve by hand, and so a computer must be used.

There are certain problem situations in which either no appropriate algorithm exists or it is unknown to the manager. Since a decision must usually be arrived at by some means, the manager should consider developing his own algorithm. At first glance this possibility might be considered to be beyond most manager's capabilities, but this need not be the case. An algorithm does not necessarily have to be complex in order to analyze a real-world situation. The ECC's problem will be used to demonstrate this contention.

Developing an algorithm begins with considering an appropriate sequence of steps for performing the problem analysis. Probably several different approaches will be tried before a satisfactory one is found. Initially, the solution procedure will be very loosely stated, such as the following for ECC's problem: determine a feasible solution, calculate its value, and compare the values of other feasible solutions in order to find the optimal solution. Assuming that this procedure appears potentially fruitful, a more specific series of steps can be outlined:

1. Determine a reasonable solution.
2. Test the feasibility of the solution.
3. Compute the solution's value.
4. Compare the solution's value with the best previous alternative.
5. Store the best solution.
6. Generate another reasonable solution.
7. Repeat steps 2–6.

Before the algorithm can be applied it is necessary to supply limits to the "reasonable solution." The constraint equations are presented once again in order to help you follow the analysis:

Constraints

$$(1) \quad X_A \geqq 2$$
$$(2) \quad X_B \geqq 2$$
$$(3) \quad X_C \geqq 2$$
$$(4) \quad X_A \leqq 20$$
$$(5) \quad X_B \leqq 10$$
$$(6) \quad X_C \leqq 30$$
$$(7) \quad 2X_A + 3X_B + 1X_C \leqq 60$$
$$(8) \quad 3X_A + 2X_B + 2X_C \leqq 60$$

It is easily seen from constraints 1–3 that a lower limit of two units exists for each type of generator. It can also be determined that no more than 17 type A, 10 type B, and 25 type C generators can be produced and sold. We will consider how the upper limit for type A was determined, since the same procedure was followed for types B and C. Constraint 4 shows that no more than 20 units of A can be made. If constraint 7 is analyzed with B and C set equal to 2 (the minimum number of each that can be produced) it is possible to

FIGURE 9–4
Flowchart for Optimal Production Mix Determination

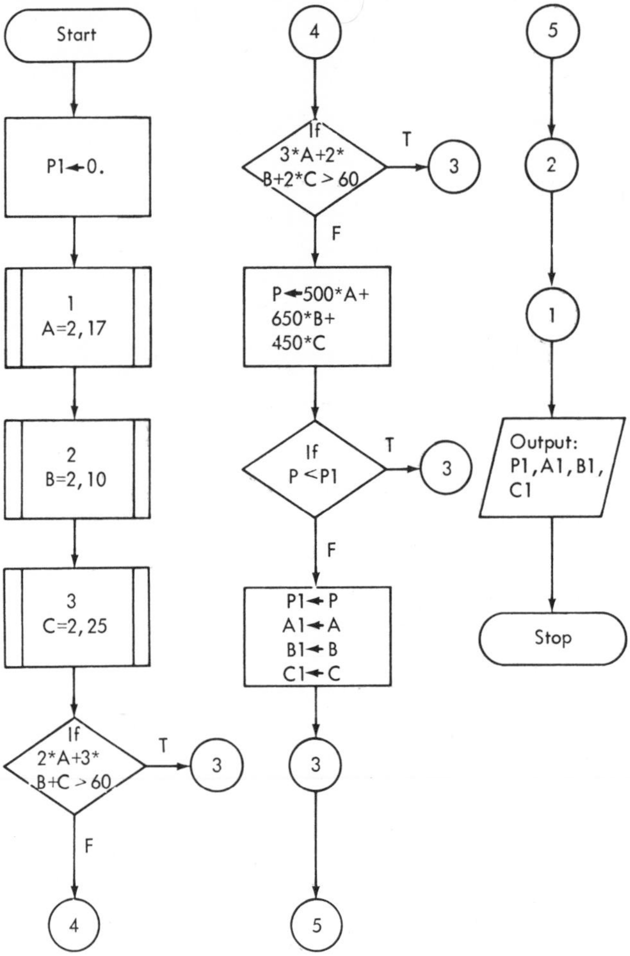

determine the maximum number of units of A that can be made while still satisfying constraint 7. This analysis shows that no more than 26 units of A can be made. A similar analysis applied to constraint 8 reveals that only 17 units of A are possible; this is the most limiting constraint. In programming the computer's search, therefore, there is no need to consider producing more than 17 units of A.

An appropriate next step is to develop a flowchart from which a computer program can be written. The flowchart details the sequence of steps designed to analyze management's problem (see Figure 9–4). An assignment at the end of the chapter asks you to write a computer program based upon this flowchart.

The variable P1 is used in Figure 9–4 to compare alternative profit figures. Initially it is set equal to zero, implying no production of units of A, B, or C. Nested loops are employed to rotate through the possible combinations of A, B, and C. The upper and lower limits for A, B, and C reflect the analysis that was performed before preparing the flowchart. The possible combinations are tested to see whether or not they actually satisfy the constraint equations. If a particular combination is not feasible, control passes to the end of the loop—equivalent to rejecting the possibility and starting on another combination. When a particular combination does satisfy the constraints, the associated profit is computed. Next, this profit is compared to the best previous profit figure. If less in value, control passes to the end of the loop. If better, the profit figure and the A, B, and C combination are stored in memory locations reserved for P1, A1, B1, and C1, respectively. These variables always store the best profit figure and the best A, B, and C combination found to date. After all of the possible combinations have been tried, the values for P1, A1, B1, and C1 are output, thus completing the analysis.

SIMULATING MANAGERIAL THOUGHT

Some managerial positions require that a substantial portion of each working day be spent making routine, repetitive decisions. For example, bank officers daily have to decide upon the final disposition of checks written against insufficient funds. Credit managers have to decide for each applicant whether or not to issue a credit card. Personnel managers must screen everyone seeking employment with the organization. While decisions of this type are not overly complex, they are costly to the organization in terms of the man-hours required to make them. When this type of decision making can be modeled and computerized, personnel can be freed for other activities. In addition, a computerized model does not suffer from any lack of internal consistency, as a human decision maker might.

This section presents a model designed to simulate a particular bank officer's processing of overdrafts.[5] Procedures similar to those discussed here can be followed to model and computerize routine decision-making tasks of low to moderate complexity.

There are a number of approaches that have been developed for handling overdrafts (bad checks). A common way is to have the bank officer decide upon their final disposition. The bank officer decides which checks to immediately honor (pay) or not honor, and those which require a personal call to the depositor before a decision is

---

[5] This material is based on H. J. Watson and H. W. Vroman, "A Heuristic Model for Processing Overdrafts," *Journal of Bank Research*, Autumn 1972, pp. 186–88.

made. Consequently, there are three decision alternatives. Even relatively small banks receive up to several hundred bad checks a day.

The bank officer who deals with these checks on a day-to-day basis develops a sensitivity to the appropriate disposition of any particular check. Some checks, because of the known integrity of their writers, are honored almost routinely. Other checks, say from notoriously careless depositors, may not be paid. In other words, the bank officer accumulates a wealth of information about the bank's customers. In addition, he develops an efficient set of *heuristics* (rules-of-thumb)

FIGURE 9–5
Bank Officer Charles Burch Processing Overdrafts

that define how he will probably act in a given situation. Any system that replaces the previous one should maintain the professional expertise gathered by the bank officer over time.

The building of the model began with the bank's officer, Charles Burch of the First National Bank of Athens, Georgia, working in conjunction with the model builders to develop a list of those variables that were thought to be the most important in the decision-making process. The initial list contained 14 variables, including the dollar amount of the check, to whom the check was written, and the credit worthiness of the depositor. The initial list of variables even indicated that the bank officer was more likely to honor a check written by a University of Georgia coed than a male student.

The next step in the model-building process was to observe Burch at work and record appropriate empirical data (see Figure 9–5). It was found that a number of variables which, were originally considered to be important actually were not and could be discarded (e.g., to whom the check was written). From the empirical data a model that simulated Burch's thought processes was built. Not surprisingly, since the model was built from the data, it accurately predicted the actions Burch did take.

The analysts then collected more data to try to validate the model. The validation employed was to compare Burch's decisions with those predicted by the model. During the validation process, it became clear that parts of the model had to be changed; for example, the need for a procedure for handling multiple overdrafts (several by the same person) became apparent. This process of data collection, model testing, and model revision was repeated until a model had been developed that closely described Burch's actions. The final testing of the model revealed that it correctly predicted these actions over 95 percent of the time.

An analysis of the remaining 5 percent resulted in the conclusion that some of the factors responsible for the errors were inherent in the human variable—Burch. It was noticed that Burch became weary and distracted by customer calls toward the end of the day and tended to adopt a harsher attitude toward overdrafts. In this regard the model was more internally consistent than Burch was.

Even when the model was in error, it did not err diametrically. There were no instances, for example, where the model predicted that Burch would honor a check and he actually did not. The errors that occurred were of the type where Burch decided to pay the check, while the model predicted that he would "hold and call."

The model that was finally built contained five variables. The type of account—regular or special—was one of the factors considered by Burch. Another variable was whether the existing balance was already negative, a consideration which was necessary for handling multiple overdrafts. Burch's subjective evaluation of the person's general credit worthiness—whether it was good, bad, or unknown—was also important. To the extent it was known, this factor included the depositor's past history of overdrafts, his place of residence in the city, property ownership, employment record, savings account balance, and so on. Another variable was the magnitude of the overdraft compared to the current balance. This consideration was quantified by dividing the difference between the check's amount and the account's balance by the account's balance (check-balance/balance). The final variable was the amount of the check. Overdrafts for small amounts are usually paid.

The model which contained the five variables was formulated as a tree diagram. The *tree diagram* shows all of the possible variable interactions and the resultant courses of action. Figure 9–6, for example, is one branch of the tree diagram (the tree diagram contains many similar branches). This branch shows that a check for $50.00 or less which is not a multiple overdraft and was written by a depositor with a good credit rating is paid by Burch. The model does not claim that Burch should act this way; rather, it indicates that he *does* act in this manner.

The model developed for the First National Bank of Athens is probably appropriate only for that bank. Other bank officers might employ a different set of decision criteria in judging overdrafts, and even if the same variables are used, the tree diagram formulated

FIGURE 9–6
Sample Branch of the Tree Diagram

would probably be different. This likelihood is not surprising, because people preceive things differently, operating conditions vary from bank to bank, and the implications of the social milieu vary from community to community.

Computerization does not completely release Burch from the task of handling overdrafts. There are still some customers categorized as "to call" by the model, and these will have to be handled by Burch or some lesser official. In addition, regardless of how their checks are handled, there will be some customers who feel their overdrafts are the result of a unique situation and should be handled that way. Burch can treat these people in an unhurried manner, thus avoiding possible customer complaints of such bureaucratic dysfunctions as categorization and impersonality. Burch's psychological set is to treat customers as individuals. When he was alternating his overdraft task with customer relations, the mental chore of switching psychological sets was necessary. This is costly to the individual because it is tiring, and costly to the organization because as time progresses the switching becomes inconsistent.

The heuristic model developed for the bank was easily computerized. The equivalent of a week's overdrafts could be processed in less than a minute. The only information required by the model that was not readily available in the bank's accounting system was the depositor's credit worthiness. Over time this information can be built into the system. In the meantime, the "unknown" branches of the tree diagram still permit the computer to process the checks.

The computerized model just described should provide some insight into the potential of the computer for affecting managers' jobs. While there is considerable controversy over the extent to which the computer will assume managerial functions, there is no doubt that it will continue to have an increasing impact on them. This topic is considered in more detail in Chapter 12, "The Impact of the Computer on Management."

ASSIGNMENTS

9-1. Equipment *downtime* is the length of time required between when a piece of equipment fails and when it is repaired and operating again. Obviously, management's desire is to minimize downtime as much as possible. In order to analyze downtime, management has collected the following data.

Downtime (*in minutes*)

23	26	06	44	25
16	28	24	63	46
52	51	18	41	24
42	62	13	51	21
10	25	29	27	05
44	30	16	46	19
36	35	27	33	52
52	31	72	35	17
18	39	46	38	35
49	82	25	29	33

Statistically analyze the downtime data using a packaged program. To the extent possible with the available program, compute the mean, standard deviation and place the data into a frequency distribution with five classes.

9-2. Management is interested in developing a demand forecasting model for an item stocked in inventory. It is planning to use a model of the form:

$$X = T + S + I$$

where X is the forecasted demand
    T is the trend in demand
    S is the seasonal factor in demand
    I is a random demand element

The historical demand per quarter for the item is shown below:

Quarter	Demand
1	100
2	96
3	122
4	165
5	132
6	154
7	160
8	213
9	180
10	160
11	200
12	252
13	232
14	240
15	240
16	292

Plot the data to convince yourself that there is a linear upward trend in the demand for the item. Run the data through a packaged linear regression analysis program in order to obtain a trend equation for the forecasting model. Compute seasonal adjustment factors for each of the year's four quarters (average deviations of the actual data from the trend line). Using the trend equation and seasonal adjustment factors, predict the demand in quarter 20.

9-3. A furniture company makes three types of beds—king, queen, and regular. The contribution to profits from each bed are $150, $100, and $75, respectively. The same cutting machine is used in making each type of bed, and it is only available 80 hours during the next time period. Each king, queen, and regular size bed requires four, three, and two hours, respectively, on the cutting machine. Skilled labor is also in short supply. During the next time period only 160 hours will be free for making beds. Each king, queen, and regular size bed requires eight, five, and four hours, respectively, of skilled labor. During the next time period the maximum potential demand for king, queen, and regular size beds is 15, 30, and 40 beds, respectively. How many of each type of bed should be made in order to maximize the total contribution to profits? Use either a packaged program or a computer search for optimality for your analysis.

9-4. This chapter has presented the following mathematical models:
  a. Mathematical programming for optimum production mix determination.
  b. A classical model for inventory analysis.
  c. A Monte Carlo inventory simulation.
  d. A computer search for optimal production mix determination.
  e. A simulation of the processing of overdrafts.
  Classify each of these models in terms of Figure 9–2.

9-5. The economic order quantity formula can be used to determine the optimal number of items to order at a time (Q). After this value has been determined the order point (L) can be calculated. Write a program that management can easily use to find Q and L. Inputs to the program will be the demand per year (D1), the delivery time (D2), the carrying costs (K1) expressed in dollars per item per year and the ordering costs (K2) expressed in dollars per order. Run your program with the following data inputs:

$D1 = 500$ $K1 = \$1.20$
$D2 = 1$ week $K2 = \$15.00$

9-6. The vendor who supplies the inventory items discussed in assignment 9-5 is willing to offer a price discount on large orders. More specifically, a discount (D) is offered off the price (P) on any orders of size S or more. Write a program that decides whether or not it would be more economical for management to order the economic order quantity, Q, or, alternatively, S, the minimum order size to qualify for the price discount. (Hint: Compare the annual costs for the two alternatives.) Run your program with the data presented in 9-5, along with the following two sets of data. Once again make sure that your program is easy for management to use.

	Set 1	Set 2
S	100	150
P	$10.00	$10.00
D	2%	2%

9-7. The flowchart in Figure 9–4 presented a computer search for optimality algorithm to determine the optimal production mix. Prepare and run a computer program based upon this flowchart. Where are your data inputs?

9-8. Pricing the product is an important marketing decision. A common objective is to select the price that maximizes profits. The mathematical model shown below is designed to help the manager in his pricing decision.

$$P = S \,^\circ\, O - V \,^\circ\, O - F$$

where P = Profit
    S = Selling price
    O = Units produced and sold
    V = Variable costs per unit
    F = Fixed costs

The number of units that can be sold is related to the selling price. The demand schedule for a particular product is presented below:

S	O
$4.00	500,000 units
4.50	475,000
5.00	450,000
5.50	400,000
6.00	350,000

Relevant cost data are also available:

$$V = \$.50/\text{unit}$$
$$F = \$1,000,000$$

Prepare a flowchart and a computer program that computes the profit associated with each selling price and outputs every P, S, O, V, and F combination.

9-9. Referring to problem 9-8, modify the flowchart and program so that only the P, S, O, V, and F associated with the best selling price selection is output.

9-10. The exponential smoothing model is widely used for predicting future observations (such as the level of sales for an item stocked in inventory). Its general form is,

$$\overline{X}_i = A \circ X_i + (1 - A) \circ \overline{X}_{i-1}$$

where $\overline{X}_i$ = The exponentially smoothed average through period i
 A = The smoothing constant $(0 \leq A \leq 1)$
 X_i = The observation from period i
 $\overline{X}_{i-1}$ = The exponentially smoothed average through period $i-1$

The value of $\overline{X}_i$ is used to predict X_{i+1}. Write a program that accepts corresponding sets of part numbers (Ps), As, $X_i s$, and $\overline{X}_{i-1} s$ as data inputs, and calculates $\overline{X}_i s$. Output should be the values of P and $\overline{X}_i$. Process the following data. Include appropriate column headings for your output.

P	A	X_i	$\overline{X}_{i-1}$
365	0.80	320	300
28	0.75	100	90
412	0.60	460	400
1313	0.80	36	25

9-11. The fundamentals of a Monte Carlo inventory simulation model have been discussed and illustrated in this chapter, but no flowchart or computer program has been presented. While the task is not particularly simple, see if you can develop a flowchart and computer program to perform the type of analysis illustrated by Table 9–1. Use the demand, delivery time, and cost data presented in the example.

9-12. A local bank officer spends a substantial portion of each working day processing charge card applications. He has expressed an interest in the possibility of computerizing his decision-making process. Based upon your discussions with him, it appears that three variables are of critical importance in the decision-making process: Previous credit record—excellent, good, fair or bad; income—over $10,000 or under $10,000; marital status—married or single. The bank officer has three decision alternatives available to him. He can issue no card, issue a card with a $300 credit limit, or issue a card with a $700 credit limit. Using the sample data presented on the next page, prepare a tree diagram that describes the bank officer's decision-making process.

Case	Previous Credit Record	Income	Marital Status	Decision
1.........	Fair	Over $10,000	Married	Card–$300
2.........	Poor	Under $10,000	Single	No Card
3.........	Fair	Over $10,000	Single	Card–$300
4.........	Excellent	Over $10,000	Married	Card–$700
5.........	Good	Under $10,000	Single	Card–$300
6.........	Good	Over $10,000	Married	Card–$700
7.........	Poor	Over $10,000	Married	No Card
8.........	Fair	Under $10,000	Single	No Card
9.........	Fair	Under $10,000	Married	Card–$300
10.........	Good	Over $10,000	Single	Card–$700
11.........	Excellent	Over $10,000	Single	Card–$700
12.........	Excellent	Under $10,000	Married	Card–$700
13.........	Good	Under $10,000	Married	Card–$700
14.........	Excellent	Under $10,000	Single	Card–$700

Prepare a computer program for your tree diagram. (Hint: Code Excellent, Good, Fair, Poor as 1, 2, 3, 4; Over $10,000, Under $10,000 as 1,2; and Married, Single as 1, 2, respectively.) Process the following charge card applications through your program. The program output should be the applicant's name and the decision made.

Name	Previous Credit Record	Income	Marital Status
HALL	Good	Over $10,000	Single
LEE....................	Poor	Over $10,000	Single
CASE	Excellent	Under $10,000	Married
HILL...................	Fair	Over $10,000	Married
MIX	Fair	Under $10,000	Married
PAGE	Good	Over $10,000	Married

9-13. It has been suggested that decision-making processes of low to moderate complexity can be simulated. This type of modeling has been illustrated by the overdraft processing problem. What other decision-making processes might be simulated? Would the modeling be of value to the organization? Why or why not?

REFERENCES

Books

Clarkson, P. E. G. *Portfolio Selection: A Simulation of Trust Investment.* Englewood Cliffs, N.J.: Prentice-Hall, 1962.

Feigenbaum, E. A. and J. Feldman *Computers and Thought.* New York: McGraw-Hill Book Co., 1963.

Levin, R. I. and C. A. Kirkpatrick *Quantitative Approaches to Management.* New York: McGraw-Hill Book Co., 1971.

McMillan, Claude and Richard F. Gonzalez *Systems Analysis.* 3rd ed. Homewood, Ill.: Richard D. Irwin, 1973.

Meier, R. C., W. T. Newell and H. L. Pazer *Simulation in Business and Economics.* Englewood Cliffs, N.J.: Prentice-Hall, 1969.

Springer, Clifford H., Robert E. Herlihy and Robert I. Beggs *Advanced Methods and Models.* Homewood, Ill.: Richard D. Irwin, 1965.

Springer, Clifford H., Robert E. Herlihy and Robert I. Beggs *Probabilistic Models.* Homewood, Ill.: Richard D. Irwin, 1968.

Articles

Watson, Hugh J. "Computers Can Reduce Management Risks." *Journal of Systems Management,* December 1971, pp. 13–17.

Watson, Hugh J. "Simulating Human Decision Making." *Journal of Systems Management,* June 1973, pp. 24–27.

Watson, H. J., T. F. Anthony and W. S. Crowder "A Heuristic Model for Law School Admissions Screening." *College and University,* Spring, 1973, pp. 195–204.

Watson, H. J. and R. J. Tersine "Computer Assisted Decision-Making: Inventory Analysis," *Cost and Management,* November–December, 1973, pp. 30–34.

Watson, H. J. and W. H. Vroman "A Heuristic Model for Processing Overdrafts." *Journal of Bank Research,* Autumn 1972, pp. 186–88.

Wiest, J. D. "Heuristic Programs for Decision Making." *Harvard Business Review,* September–October 1966, pp. 129–43.

Informal Information Systems

Formal Information Systems
The Computer's Role, Data, Data Sources, Data Hierarchy

Progress in Information Systems

Management Information Systems
An Integrated Data Base, A Hierarchial Information Structure,
A Decision-Support Orientation

Decision-Support Systems

Information System Evolution

Management's Information System Responsibilities

Assignments

References

The next four chapters deal directly with management's relationship to the computer. After finishing these chapters, you should have a better understanding of how the computer is used to supply information, how it affects the organization and the management group, and what management's responsibilities are in regards to the computer. The present chapter explores both the technology and the performance capabilities associated with information systems. You should gain a better appreciation of what an information system is, how it functions, and management's role in regards to the system.

10

Information Systems and Management

An *information system* can be defined as a set of interrelated elements composed of personnel, data, and equipment which process data into information. Though the use of the term "information system" is relatively new, organizations have always had systems for supplying information. An accounting system is just one type of information system which has been common in business organizations for many years.

Computers and their attendant technology have supported the emergence of information systems with capabilities that surpass those developed previously. The large storage capacities and processing speeds of computers make it possible to do many things that are not feasible with systems that are manual or business machine oriented. As a result of the use of the computer, the quality of management practice has been upgraded, and some of the ways that managers manage have been affected.

Sophisticated information systems have not evolved independent of need. As organizations have become increasingly complex, management has demanded the availability of better and more comprehensive information. Improved technology has been combined with the efforts of information specialists and management to create information systems that are more responsive to management's needs.

Managers become involved with information systems in many ways. Some of the major ways include supplying data inputs, using the information that is generated, participating in the systems' design, controlling the systems' operation, and so on. This chapter discusses these and other considerations in managements' relationship to information systems.

INFORMAL INFORMATION SYSTEMS

Informal information systems operate in all organizations to disseminate information from person to person, without using formal communication channels. Frequently they are referred to as the grapevine because of the way they twist and wind their way throughout the organization. The secretaries who eat lunch together, the riders in a carpool, and the members of the company softball team all participate in informal information systems. The information the members exchange is outside of the organization's planned, formal communication channels.

To management, informal information systems can be both a source of irritation and a blessing. Consider a situation in which management has learned that within a couple of hours there will be a surprise visit from members of the board of directors. To foster the objective of showing the board members that the organization is operating effectively and efficiently, management decides to alert employees about the surprise visit. But the formal information system would probably be too slow to do this in time, and a formal announcement might be interpreted as an indication that the organization does not usually function smoothly. Therefore management decides to take advantage of the informal information systems in the organization by informing key members in the grapevine of the surprise visit and counting on them to spread the news. One of the most notable attributes of the grapevine is the speed with which it communicates information.

Informal information systems can also cause considerable consternation, since they are largely outside of management's control. Erroneous information is frequently transmitted, and information that management is not ready to disseminate becomes known and spread by the grapevine. Because of occurrences such as these, informal information systems are not wholeheartedly appreciated by management.

FORMAL INFORMATION SYSTEMS

While informal information systems are interesting, this book is concerned with *formal information systems*, which are established by the organization to collect, record, and process data into timely, meaningful information.

Most organizations have many formal information systems. Usually each functional area (accounting, marketing, production) has its own information system or systems. Some systems, such as that for the organization's accounting function, cross over functional lines and span the different managerial levels. The current trend is to integrate the many information systems most organizations have into fewer and more inclusive systems. This development is emerging as the result of computer hardware and software advances, accumulated experience in developing information systems, and management's need for better information.

The Computer's Role

A frequent question is whether or not an information system has to be *computer based*, that is, whether it must employ a computer. From a theoretical point of view, the answer to this question is no. Many small organizations have adequate, or better than adequate, information systems that do not involve computers. This can be true as long as the demands placed on the information system are not too great. However, nearly all information systems found in medium- to large-sized organizations are computer based. In general, discussion of information systems assumes the availability of a computer. This book also makes this assumption, but much of the discussion applies equally well to noncomputerized systems.

Data

Data usually have only limited value until they are combined with other data and processed into information. Consider a single sales transaction, such as the sale of ten refrigerators by a manufacturer to a wholesaler. The recording of this single *transaction* (e.g., to whom sold, number sold, amount received) is relatively unimportant, other than for bookkeeping purposes. Management becomes more interested when this transaction is combined and processed with similar transaction data to provide output such as monthly sales summaries. And the processing usually does not stop at this point. The sales summaries are then perhaps fed into a sales forecasting model, whose output in turn is used by a production scheduling program. Thus information that is generated by processing data can itself become data for further processing.

Data Sources

Data can be thought of as the "fuel" that powers information systems. Without data, no information can be provided. However, management's information requirements dictate what data are collected and stored. No data should be maintained only for the sake of having it.

An organization can collect data from many different sources. Most of the data are generated within, or are *internal to,* the organization, but other data come from outside, or *external* or *environmental*, sources. Examples of internal data include sales records, payroll figures, inventory records, and so on. Internal data result from the organization's operations. On the other hand, external data are not a direct consequence of the organization's activities. The data are generated outside of the organization — though the organization might be highly interested in the data. Examples of external data include vendor's price lists, trade association data, governmental unemployment forecasts, tax schedules, and so on.

Data include not only *objective* data such as the number of items sold but also *subjective* or *judgmental* data such as management's expectations as to the number of units of an item that will be sold next year. Most of the information provided by an information system is the result of processing objective data, but many important and difficult business decisions depend as much or more upon subjective data.

Data are acquired from both *planned* and *incidental* or accidental data gathering efforts. The organization's accounting system provides an excellent example of an information system in which the collection of data is highly planned and structured. By contrast, an employee learning on the golf course that a competitor is planning to develop a new product line illustrates an accidental, but nevertheless important, data source.

Data Hierarchy

An individual piece of data (datum) is referred to as a *data element*. Examples include an item's part number, the number of units sold in a sales transaction, the number of exemptions claimed by an employee for tax purposes, or a customer's savings account balance.

Data elements must be organized in a logical, systematic manner in order to be located and used easily. For example, it is useful and meaningful to organize together all of the recorded data on an item carried in inventory. The data elements might include the item's part number, order point, order quantity, inventory balance, and so on. Data elements organized together are referred to as a *record*.

A distinction is made between the physical and logical organization of data. The *logical organization* is concerned with linking specific data elements together in a purposeful and useful manner. As an example, all the data on a customer's savings account are usually organized into a single record. The *physical organization* refers to how the data are physically stored. For example, the same data stored on different storage media (magnetic disk, data cell) have different physical organizations.

Records that are logically and physically related constitute a *file*.

For example, all of a firm's inventory records are usually organized into a single file. Other files are usually set up for payroll, accounts receivable, accounts payable, vendors, and customers.

As computer applications have increased in scope and become better integrated, the term *data base* (also *data bank*) has come into usage. In a narrow sense, the term is employed to describe those files that are related and tend to be used together. For example, the firm's production department might have its own data base. Some of the files in this base might include an inventory file, vendor file, customer order file, and many more. With this interpretation of a data base, organizations can be said to have several data bases, frequently one for each functional area.

Another interpretation sees the data base in a broader context which considers any data stored by the organization as part of its data base, whether or not they are logically organized, linked, or integrated. In this interpretation the organization has only a single data base which includes any data that are available to it.

Figure 10–1 illustrates a *data hierarchy* for inventory data. The term "data hierarchy" refers to the relationship between data elements, records, files, and base. The data elements for this example

FIGURE 10–1
An Inventory Data Hierarchy

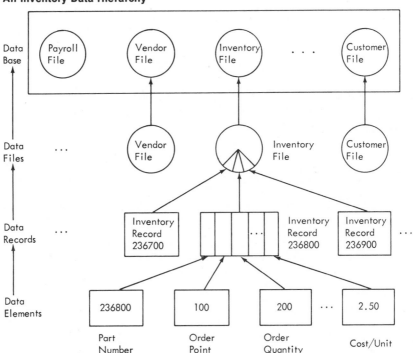

include the item's part number, order point, and so on. All of the relevant data elements are combined to form a record. The inventory records together are organized into an inventory file, and the inventory file is one of the files that make up the data base.

PROGRESS IN INFORMATION SYSTEMS

Manual- or business-machine-oriented information systems have been in existence for many years. If the organization remains relatively small and stable and the demands placed on the information system are not too great, many manual systems perform quite well.

When computers were first commercially introduced in the 1950s, organizations such as banks which must process considerable amounts of data began to purchase or lease computers. The computer, with its attributes of speed, accuracy, and large storage capacity, was a natural investment for organizations such as these. The cost of the computer, support equipment, and personnel was usually justifiable on the basis of increased accuracy and decreased clerical expenses (on a cost-per-transaction basis).

The first information systems were what might be called *basic data processing* systems, in which each data processing task is performed independently of other tasks. For example, preparing the payroll might be separate from the personnel department's recordkeeping. Today, basic data processing systems are usually found only in smaller organizations.

Over time, many basic data processing systems evolved into *integrated data processing* systems, in which the tasks performed are integrated. In operational terms this is to say that many tasks share the same data files, and the same input data are often used in more than one application. For example, the same production data might be used in inventory recordkeeping and materials requirements planning. Integrated data processing systems are fairly common.

While the introduction of basic and integrated data processing systems did facilitate the processing of transaction data, they did not provide management immediately with better information. Initially, the computer-based information systems provided only *scheduled reports*, which are prepared on a periodic basis and are largely intended to summarize the transaction data that have been processed. Examples of scheduled reports include monthly sales summaries, inventory status reports, and daily production reports. Management does benefit from such computer-prepared reports, but in many instances they do not contain the type of information needed to support decision making. In addition, the timing of the receipt of the scheduled reports frequently does not fit into the manager's decision-making time frame.

Reprinted by permission of NEA.

Over time, the need to develop information systems that truly support decision making became apparent to management and information specialists alike. These systems, which are oriented to supplying
management with information, are referred to as *management information systems.*

MANAGEMENT INFORMATION SYSTEMS

Few topics generate as much controversy among information specialists as management information systems (MIS). There are considerable differences of opinion as to what an MIS is, who has one,
and why they have it. At one extreme are those who view an MIS,
at least in operational terms, as being little more than the processing of transaction data and the preparation of an expanded set of
scheduled reports. If this limited concept of what constitutes an MIS
is acceptable, it can be concluded that many organizations have one,
and its existence can be justified on the basis of reduced clerical
expenses. At the other extreme is the idea that an MIS should provide
all organizational elements with the information needed to function
effectively. Typically, special attention is focused upon supplying the
upper managerial levels with information to support their decision-
making efforts. Justification for the cost of such a system has to go
beyond simple clerical displacement savings to a basis of improved
decision making and other factors that are difficult to measure. The
more ambitious concept results in the conclusion that few, if any,
organizations currently have a total MIS.

We lean toward the more ambitious MIS concept, even though
most organizations are only at the rudimentary MIS level. Given the

FIGURE 10–2
Visual Model of a Management Information System

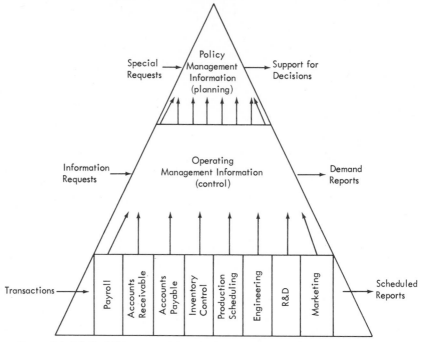

Source: Robert V. Head, "Management Information Systems: A Critical Appraisal," *Datamation*, May 1967, pp. 22–27.

creative nature of most information specialists, improved technology, and encouragement from management, MIS development should continue along the lines suggested by Walter Kennevon's definition:

> A management information system is an organized method of providing past, present and projection (*sic*) information relating to internal operations and external intelligence. It supports the planning, control and operational function of an organization by furnishing uniform information in the proper time-frame to assist the decision-maker.[1]

This definition stresses that an MIS should be able to summarize past and present data, make projections into the future, utilize both internal and external data, support the most fundamental managerial functions, and have a decision-support orientation. Given the breadth of these requirements, it is easy to understand the skepticism with which some people view the MIS concept. Few current information

---

[1] Walter Kennevon, "MIS Universe," *Data Management*, September 1970, pp. 62–64.

systems can claim to satisfy all the requirements suggested by Kennevon.

An excellent visual model of the broad concept of MIS has been developed by Robert Head (see Figure 10–2). It suggests three major features of an MIS: (1) an integrated data base, (2) a hierarchical information structure, and (3) a decision-support orientation. Each of these features merits consideration in detail.

An Integrated Data Base

Associated with increased computer capabilities has been the development of large, on-line secondary storage mediums and software systems for managing the data stored in them. Today, for example, magnetic disks and drums can store millions of characters of data in machine-readable form. A management information system must have a large storage capacity in order to handle the vast quantities of data needed by the various functional areas. Equally important is a software system that allows data to be easily and efficiently stored and retrieved. These software systems are referred to as *data base management systems, file management systems, generalized information systems,* and so on. Their function is to provide efficient data storage, linkages, retrieval, and report generation. These systems are highly sophisticated and almost always are purchased from an outside vendor.

As an organization's data base becomes better integrated, the potential increases for greater efficiencies and capabilities. For example, integration reduces the need to redundantly store and maintain data. Instead of keeping separate data for each application, much of the data are stored and maintained centrally, and many programs draw from the same data base.

Another force in the development of integrated data bases has been management's growing demands for information that requires integration. This requirement is particularly true in regards to the upper managerial levels. Whereas the boundaries of decision making at the lower managerial levels are usually contained within a particular functional area, when one considers decision making at higher levels the distinction between functional areas tends to blur. Top management must view the organization as a total system rather than a group of disjointed functional areas. Consequently, the information needed to manage effectively at this level has to be system oriented and able to cut across functional areas. An integrated data base makes data from throughout the organization available in a centralized location.

Developing an integrated data base is a difficult, expensive, time-consuming endeavor that demands the attention and support of top management. Managers in the functional areas are seldom anxious to relinquish control over the data in their particular areas, and they must be convinced that they will continue to be supplied with the data and information they need. If the system does not live up to this expectation the functional areas will begin to store data redundantly — a natural but expensive reaction.

The conversion to an integrated base must be carefully planned. Normally it is done in stages, with the organization's *lifeline* or *key-task* (i.e., most critical to success) areas converted first. With this approach the greatest benefits are realized at an early stage. In later stages peripheral areas are converted until the desired degree of conversion has been realized.

A Hierarchical Information Structure

Managers throughout an organization have varying information requirements, which is understandable in light of the differences between managerial positions. Consequently, an MIS must be carefully designed to serve management's wide spectrum of information needs.

The lower levels of management are deeply involved in what is commonly referred to as *operational control*, for which Robert Anthony supplied a useful definition: "Operational control is the process of assuring that specific tasks are carried out effectively and efficiently."[2] It is through the exercise of operational control that management ensures that the organization's basic activities are being carried out as planned. Examples of operational control include monitoring the activities of salespeople in the field, the tellers in a bank, and the output from a production system. To a large extent the information required to perform operational control is provided by scheduled reports based upon the processing of transaction data.

Middle management also receives and benefits from scheduled reports but also must be able to obtain reports upon demand. This capability facilitates middle management's performance of *management control*. Anthony's definition is: "Management control is the process by which managers assure that resources are obtained and used effectively and efficiently in the accomplishment of the organization's objectives."

Middle management, which is charged with the responsibility for planning and controlling the use of the organization's resources,

---

[2] Operational control, management control, and strategic planning are defined and discussed in Robert N. Anthony, *Planning and Control Systems — A Framework for Analysis* (Cambridge, Mass.: Division of Research, Graduate School of Business, Harvard University, 1965).

frequently must have reports upon demand. Examples of *demand reports* include a report on the number of minorities currently employed by the organization and a listing of customers with savings account balances of $50,000 or more. If the document is in report form and is supplied only when demanded rather than on a scheduled basis, it is a demand report.

Top management has the most diverse and difficult information needs because this level has *strategic planning* responsibilities. According to Anthony, "Strategic planning is the process of deciding on objectives of the organization, on changes in these objectives, on the resources used to obtain these objectives, and on the policies that are to govern the acquisition, use, and disposition of these resources." The unstructured nature of the strategic planning function makes it difficult to plan in advance what information will be required. While the MIS must supply top management with scheduled reports and other reports on demand, it should also be quick to respond to specific information requests. For example, the MIS might be designed in such a way that it can indicate the market share of a product the firm produces and sells.

The type of information upper management needs must frequently draw upon more than transaction data and include external and subjective data as well. Since these types of data are not "naturally" stored by the organization, considerable planning is necessary to ensure their availability. Simply storing the data is not enough; a sophisticated data base management system must also be available to quickly and easily retrieve the data requested.

A Decision-Support Orientation

As has been seen, an MIS must serve the organization's hierarchy of information needs. In general, the information is used to support decision making, which can be viewed either as a separate managerial function, or as an activity which underlies the major managerial functions of planning, organizing, controlling, and so on. Indeed, it is this decision-support orientation that largely distinguishes the MIS concept.

In order to support decision making the MIS must generate scheduled reports, reports on demand, and responses to specific information requests, as we have noted. These capabilities are being realized through improved computer hardware and software technology, encouragement from management, and accumulated experience in developing the systems. Nevertheless, there are many information requests that are difficult for an MIS to satisfy quickly. For example, most MISs cannot respond quickly or accurately to a request for information on the cost of producing a new product. Only tentative, highly speculative estimates can be quickly supplied for a request of this type. Even more difficult is a request for information as to how the new product might affect production schedules, administrative expenses, warehousing needs, and so on. The more unstructured management's information needs are, the more difficult it is for the MIS to respond.

DECISION-SUPPORT SYSTEMS

Management science models used in conjunction with the computer can supply management with information that is extremely useful in supporting decision making, as was noted in Chapter 9. Unfortunately, however, these models have not been as operationally useful as one might expect. There are far too many situations in which well developed, carefully tested models have fallen into disuse. It is not that the decision models lack mathematical rigor, sophistication, or usefulness. Rather, it seems that too little attention has been devoted to considering their relationships to data and the decision makers who use the models.

For decision models to live up to their potential, they should be integrated into the information system in such a way that they are accessible to management and easy to use. In this case the models themselves no longer are the primary focus of attention but are viewed as part of a larger system which includes the decision models, the data, and the decision maker (see Figure 10–3). Information systems with this design philosophy have started to appear in just the past few years under the name of "decision-support systems." A *decision-support system* is oriented to decision support and integrates the decision maker, data, and decision models into an effective and efficient system.

The decision models in a decision-support system are similar to those discussed in the preceding chapter, including both packaged and user-prepared models. A variety of models is usually required to support the wide spectrum of decision making encountered in the

FIGURE 10–3
An Enlightened View of the Use of Decision Models

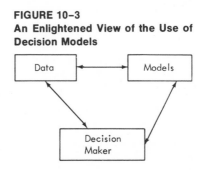

various functional areas and at the different managerial levels of the typical organization.

The models designed to support top management's strategic planning responsibilities are commonly referred to as strategic models. *Strategic models* are useful in helping formulate an organization's basic objectives and defining broadly stated plans of action. For example, many organizations have models to evaluate the possible consequences of introducing a new product. The model provides a mechanism for systematically processing management's subjective judgments, marketing research data, cost data, and the like.

Tactical models are usually included in a decision-support system to support the management control responsibilities of middle management. These models are used in planning and controlling the allocation of the organization's resources. The mathematical programming model presented in the previous chapter to illustrate how a model can be used to assist in determining the optimal production mix is a good example of a tactical model.

The inventory control and overdraft-processing models presented in the preceding chapter illustrate another class of models found in a decision-support system. These *operational models* are used to analyze and solve the relatively highly structured and narrowly defined problems that are frequently encountered at the lower organizational levels.

An efficient data base management system is a necessity in a decision-support system. The data base management system allows data to be easily entered, maintained in the data base, and later retrieved for use with the decision models. Because the decision maker must be provided with fast and easy access to the data and the models, the availability of computer terminals, a conversational programming language, and on-line access to the data and the models is also helpful.

In addition to a variety of models and modeling capabilities, a decision-support system requires a comprehensive data base. The data base must include transaction data, other internal data, and external data, and not only objective data but subjective data. The strategic models in particular have demanding data requirements. Most of these models rely heavily upon subjective and external data. Great care must be taken in designing the data base to ensure that these types of data are included.

Decision-support systems are difficult and expensive to develop. They require highly sophisticated hardware and software technology. The designers of the system must comprehend the nature of decision making throughout the organization, time and care must be taken in planning and obtaining the data for the data base, and the users of the system must thoroughly understand its capabilities and how to use it. Considering all these factors, it is easy to see why decision-support systems are currently still largely at the prototype stage. In the future, however, they should become increasingly common.

INFORMATION SYSTEM EVOLUTION

Many of the topics discussed in this and other chapters—computer hardware and software, computer generations, types of information systems, management's information needs, decision models, and the like—are important considerations in deciding how an organization's information systems can, and should, evolve. We will briefly review, slightly expand, and integrate these topics through the medium of the *information system evolution matrix* shown in Figure 10–4. The rows in the matrix indicate possible technological positions, while the columns show the possible performance levels that can be realized by a specific information system. Since some row, column positions are more desirable than others, the matrix provides a useful vehicle for considering the evolution of information systems. It should not, however, be interpreted in a rigid manner. Each cell in the matrix represents only a *general* relationship between technology and performance states of evolution.

Information systems technology has two major components—computer hardware and software. In general, the systems technology rows correspond with the standard delineations among computer generations, based on such generic attributes of the system as speed,

FIGURE 10–4
Information System Evolution Matrix

Systems' Technology Dimension	Systems' Performance Dimension			
	Basic Data Processing (N,1)	Integrated Data Processing (N,2)	Management Information Systems (N,3)	Decision-Support Systems (N,4)
1st Generation (1,M)	X	Y	Y	Y
2nd Generation (2,M)	Z	X	Y	Y
3rd Generation (3,M)	Z	Z	X	Y
Evolving 4th Generation (4,M)	Z	Z	Z	X

storage capacity, input/output, languages, applications programs, and software.

The system performance dimension marks some rather distinct stages in the continuum of information system evolution. The four stages named reflect type of tasks performed, nature of the data base, type of information generated, use of decision models to generate information, and managerial levels served by the information system. Figure 10–5 summarizes these stages.

A basis for examining the evolution matrix in Figure 10–4 can be found in a study of the performance dimensions presented in Figure 10–5 and a review of the technology characteristics of computer generations which were summarized in Table 3–1 (Chapter 3). The point of emphasis in this examination will be on the cost effectiveness of each matrix position and how this consideration affects the evolution of information systems.

In general, information systems should evolve along the principal diagonal (marked by Xs) in the matrix. This diagonal indicates that as technology increases, system performance also increases. However, this increase is due not only to technological factors but also to the encouragement of management and efforts of information specialists within the organization. The improved technology *facilitates* improved system performance but does not guarantee it.

Other positions in the matrix are also possible. Consider, for example, the lower left portion (indicated by Zs). In general, these positions are marked by heavy commitment to technology but relatively little return in regards to system performance. Consequently, systems in these positions tend to be inefficient. The further the distance from the principal diagonal, the less efficient the system. For example, position (3,1) is less efficient than (2,1).

Unfortunately, Z positions are not at all uncommon. They occur when management has been "sold" more technology than is currently needed in the organization, or when the computer and information specialists are either too few in number or do not possess the requisite skills to utilize the available technology. Some organizations may temporarily be in a Z position, since the upgrading of information systems takes time.

The Y positions in the matrix are less common but are also possible. They represent attempts to push system performance beyond that which might be expected, given the available technology. In order to achieve these positions, the system's designers must expand existing state-of-the-art technology. In other words, they must develop the technology that is required, and such attempts incur heavy start-up or "pioneering" costs. Many organizations have been disappointed in the consequences of trying to move into (1,2) or (2,3) positions. Not all attempts have been unsatisfactory, however; there is the

Basic Data Processing (N,1)

Only basic data processing tasks are performed, and each task is a self-contained job (e.g., payroll). No common data base exists, since a separate file is maintained for each job. The outputs from the information system are summary reports which reflect the transaction data that have been processed. The reports are available to all managerial levels but are of limited value to middle and top management because of the nature of their decision-making responsibilities (i.e., management control and strategic planning). Typically, no decision models are used.

Integrated Data Processing (N,2)

In this stage data processing tasks become integrated. Many of the tasks use more than one data file, and the same input data are often used by more than one application. However, almost all data processing activities still involve the processing of transaction data and the generation of reports which primarily support lower management decision making. Simple decision models such as for inventory control begin to be used.

Management Information Systems (N,3)

There are differences of opinion as to what constitutes a management information system. At one extreme are those who view an MIS as being little more than the processing of transaction data and the preparation of an expanded set of scheduled reports. At the other extreme are those who believe that an MIS should provide all organizational elements with the information needed to function effectively. Somewhere in between is what most people mean by an MIS. In this middle position the information system has the beginning of an integrated data base. Demand as well as scheduled reports are generated and begin to serve the information needs of middle and top management. Active attempts are made to structure appropriate information flows to the upper managerial levels. Decision support models are commonly used, but they are not well integrated into the information system.

Decision-Support Systems (N,4)

A decision-support system, rather than stressing structured information flows, focuses on the use of decision models to support decision making. In order to support such systems, it is necessary to maintain an enhanced data base—one that retains subjective, external, and internal data, as well as transaction data. The availability of such data makes it possible to "fuel" the decision models that are integrated into the information system. These systems also require mechanisms to provide easy access for the user to the decision models and the data base. In general, decision-support systems feature an integrated system composed of decision models, data base, and decision maker in order to support decision making at the various managerial levels.

potential in some such situations for big rewards. For example, the system might provide a unique competitive advantage for the organization, or elements of the system might be marketable as packaged software. In general, it can be said that the Y positions can return big rewards, but they are also high risk and can place great demands upon the organization's resources. Any organization contemplating moving to a Y position should ask itself if breaking new technological ground is a valid objective.

MANAGEMENT'S INFORMATION SYSTEM RESPONSIBILITIES

Managers must be cognizant of their responsibilities regarding the organization's information system and take an active interest in it, since all managers must interface and interact with the information system in one way or another. For most organizations a computer-based information system represents a substantial financial investment which must be carefully managed. Because the capabilities, efficiency, and accuracy of the computer-based system also bear heavily upon the organization's ultimate success, management has a strong impetus to see to it that the system is utilized with maximum effect.

At least three different types of relationships can exist between the manager and the organization's information system. In the first case, the manager is organizationally located in the data processing department. Here he is a computer specialist who more than likely has moved up from the ranks of programmers and systems analysts. In this role, the manager (perhaps his title is manager of data processing) assumes the daily responsibility of satisfying the information needs of the total organization.

In another type of relationship, the manager serves as a representative from his functional area. In this role the manager is providing a liaison service; his responsibility is to assure that the information system serves the needs of the functional area he represents. In fulfilling this responsibility, he may be a member of a *steering committee*, an advisory group usually composed of representatives of the various functional areas of the organization, or he may be temporarily assigned to the staff of the data processing department. This is not uncommon when management is making significant changes in its information system and there is an important need for organizational support, assistance, coordination, and cooperation.

The final type of relationship occurs when the manager is primarily a user of the output from the information system. Even in this role the manager has responsibilities; he must supply much of the data that go into the information system and must work closely with the computer specialists to specify information requirements. In most cases the computer specialist knows best what information can be provided, but the manager is in the best position to know what information is needed to perform his job.

Wherever the manager is positioned in the organization, a relationship is created which requires the manager to exercise responsibility. At least it should be, because management must be actively involved if the most effective systems are to be designed and operated on a continuous basis.

Since computer-based information systems are destined to become increasingly important in almost all types of organizations, it is imperative that students of business administration be aware of the capabilities and limitations of these systems and, most importantly, of management's responsibilities in supporting them. The purpose of an information system is to support management in performing its managerial functions, but management must continually help shape and support the system.

ASSIGNMENTS

10-1. Distinguish between informal and formal information systems. From your experiences, list examples of each.

10-2. What sources of data are there? Consider yourself as the president of a university and give examples of the data that would be available to you. Include an example from every basic data source.

10-3. Support one of the three following positions in regard to subjective and objective data.

   a. Subjective data are not reliable, since two managers can look at the same situation and arrive at different subjective estimates. Consequently, subjective data are not reliable for decision-making purposes.

   b. Even though a manager might feel somewhat uncomfortable using subjective data, this does not really matter. A decision has to be made, and subjective data are better than no data.

   c. Subjective data are superior to objective data because they reflect the manager's subjective beliefs. It is his decision and he will be held accountable for it, so the decision should reflect the manager's feelings.

10-4. What is meant by a data hierarchy? Give an example of a data hierarchy from the marketing area.

10-5. What are the major features of an MIS? Why is each feature important?

10-6. Consider a chain of supermarkets and identify what might be the lower, middle, and top management levels. What are some of the information needs at each level?

10-7. Some people interpret the MIS in a very broad context, while others have a much more limited concept of what constitutes an MIS. Would those who interpret MIS broadly be likely to consider decision-support systems as a separate stage of information system evolution? Why?

10-8. Go out into the community and locate an organization that is willing to discuss its information systems with you. Prepare a report based upon what you learn. Discuss where the organization would be currently located in an information system evolution matrix.

10-9. Discuss with a manager in an organization with a computer-based information system how the system evolved. What sort of cost-benefit analysis was performed along the way? Prepare a report based upon your conversation.

10-10. What are the different types of relationships that a manager can have with the organization's information system? Discuss management's responsibilities in each of these roles.

REFERENCES

Books

Anthony, Robert H. *Planning and Control Systems: A Framework for Analysis.* Cambridge, Mass.: Division of Research, Graduate School of Business, Harvard University, 1965.

Emery, J. C. *Organizational Planning and Control Systems.* New York: Macmillan Co., 1969.

Morton, M. S. *Management Decision Systems: Computer Based Support for Decision Making.* Cambridge, Mass.: Graduate School of Business, Harvard University, 1971.

Voich, Dan, Jr., H. J. Mottice and William A. Shrode *Information Systems for Operations and Management,* Cincinnati: South-Western Publishing Co., 1975.

Articles

Ackoff, R. L. "Management Information Systems." *Management Science,* December 1967, pp. B147–56.

Argyris, Chris "Management Information Systems: The Challenge to Rationality and Emotionality." *Management Science,* February 1971, pp. B275–92.

Canning, R. L. "What's the Status of MIS?" *EDP Analyzer,* October 1969.

Dearden, John "MIS Is a Mirage." *Harvard Business Review,* January–February 1972, pp. 90–99.

Harold, Terrence "An Executive View of MIS." *Datamation,* November 1972, pp. 65–71.

Head, Robert V. "The Elusive MIS." *Datamation*, September 1970, pp. 22–27.

Kennevon, Walter "MIS Universe." *Data Management*, September 1970, pp. 62–64.

King, W. R. "The Intelligent MIS: A Management Helper," *Business Horizons*, October 1973, pp. 5–12.

McFarland, W. F. "Problems in Planning the Information System." *Harvard Business Review*, March–April 1971, pp. 75–89.

Olle, T. W. "MIS: Data Bases." *Datamation*, November 1970, pp. 47–50.

Sprague, R. H. and H. J. Watson "MIS Concepts: Part I." *Journal of Systems Management*, January 1975, pp. 34–37.

Sprague, R. H. and H. J. Watson "MIS Concepts: Part II." *Journal of Systems Management*, February 1975, pp. 35–40.

Rappaport, Alfred "Management Misinformation Systems: Another Perspective." *Management Science*, December 1968, pp. B133–36.

Zani, W. M. "Blueprint for MIS." *Harvard Business Review*, November–December 1970, pp. 95–100.

General Thoughts on Planning

Management Planning for Computers
Gaining Management Support, Planning for the Total Effort

Conducting the Feasibility Study
Need for a Study, Nature of Feasibility Studies, Steps in the Feasibility Study

Computer System Selection
Rent, Lease, or Purchase, Other Approaches

Preparing Organizational Resources for Change
Personnel, Physical Arrangements

Systems Design and Programming

Installing Equipment

Appraisal, Follow-up, and Review

Concluding Remarks

Assignments

References

This management-oriented chapter introduces the process of planning for the selection and implementation of computer systems. It is hoped that you will gain some notion of the managerial complexities involved in conducting a feasibility study, making a choice as to computer system, preparing organizational resources for change, and systems design and programming.

11 Planning for, Selection, and Implementation of Computer Systems

Though you should have some appreciation of the computer's role in business by now, most of the knowledge and skills you have gained may appear miniscule when you consider how to introduce and manage a computer system. There are ways to take advantage of the computer other than actually acquiring its hardware, but in this chapter we will assume that an organization is going through the process of deciding upon a computer-based data processing system which involves the actual acquisition and implementation of computer hardware. Techniques such as using the extra time available on a computer owned by a large firm or employing a service bureau are indeed options, and we will examine them in this chapter. In general, however, we will consider what is involved in the actual decision to acquire computer hardware and the problems associated with its implementation.

An important dimension which must be considered is organizational size. While many business students will be taking jobs in organizations in which computer facilities already exist, there are a number of smaller businesses whose operations have not yet been computerized and in which planning considerations will be more important. In any event, a discussion of planning, selection, and implementation should make you aware of the enormity of this critical task.

A number of important topics will be discussed in this chapter. Some general thoughts on the planning process and, specifically, on management planning for computers will be treated first. Then the main emphasis will be on the process involved in deciding whether a computer should be introduced into the organization and what implementation considerations are important once such a decision has been made.

For discussion purposes this decision process will be broken down into the formulation stage and the implementation stage. Considerably more emphasis will be placed in this chapter on the formulation stage of introducing a computer into the organization. The ultimate success or failure of the effort hinges on the preliminary decisions that are made. In addition, formulation is concerned with the *planning orientation* which characterizes the managerial activities discussed in the chapter.

GENERAL THOUGHTS ON PLANNING

Planning has been defined as anticipatory decision making, or thought activity which anticipates future events. The direct association between planning and organizational success has been established in management literature and practice. Indeed, planning has been called preventive (as opposed to curative) decision making because it is designed to prevent undesirable organizational consequences from occurring. Planning may also be thought of as helping to create a desired future. As such, it involves the assessment of probabilities of future environmental conditions and then managerial action to ensure that the most favorable organizational consequences occur.

Because experience has suggested to managers that employing computers can be in the best long-range interests of the organization, they have given favorable consideration to computerized data processing as a viable option for handling certain kinds of work. The decision concerning the adoption of a computer calls for extensive managerial planning effort aimed at answering such questions as: Could our organization benefit from a computer? In what specific areas could we benefit? What are the associated costs and benefits of computer use? What are the keys to management success with computers? How can a firm fail in its efforts to implement computer use? What planning steps must be engaged in to properly implement computerized system usage? Questions such as these are at the heart of management interest in planning for computers.

MANAGEMENT PLANNING FOR COMPUTERS

Installing a computer system is not a simple task. Since a computer cannot think like humans do, it cannot be expected to provide much help in the initial stages. The task of planning for a computer is a vital and difficult managerial responsibility which is fraught with uncertainties at best. These planning efforts are paradoxical; while planning is difficult because of all the uncertainties associated with computerization, that is precisely *why* it is necessary to engage in planning for it.

Management planning for the computer is a time-consuming and pervasive decision-making process which cuts across organizational lines and touches practically everyone in the organization. Therefore it requires a kind of administrative overview that is not commonly found in organizations and a special kind of integrative, coordinative thinking which can only be applied from a high-echelon position within the organization. Having top-management support from the outset, therefore, is a key factor in the decision-making process. The interdependence of departments within an organization makes it necessary to create a data base broad enough to supply all operational levels with their information needs, so high costs will necessarily be associated with data processing systems. This is especially true in the case of the management information systems discussed in Chapter 10. The complexity and costs of most data processing systems demand that top-management participation in the planning process be gained at the outset and retained throughout the implementation phase.

Gaining Management Support

You might rightly question why management support would not be taken for granted in a decision of such mammoth size. Ideally, top managers would always be involved in a decision of this magnitude, but organizations seldom operate ideally. In fact, experience has demonstrated that decisions of this nature are occasionally left to members of the organization who are lower in the hierarchy. At one time computers were considered to be simply bookkeeping machines and consequently were limited in scope and application. Today, such a comparison is absurd. Computers are a major investment that typically exceeds most organizational purchases in complexity and potential ramifications. Small business computers require investments of as much as several thousand dollars up to about $50,000 and rent for about $300 to $1,000 per month. Medium-sized computers sell for as much as $200,000 to $1 million and rent for about $4,000 to $20,000 per month. Large computer systems, of course, exceed these costs.

Managerial failure at any level can spell disaster to a project of the size of computerization. Therefore managerial support from all levels is mandatory in planning for computer systems. Several surveys have revealed that success in matters such as computer acquisition is highly questionable without management support. One expert asserts that "without meaningful top management support and the discipline of proper planning, the contribution of the whole data processing program may be nullified."[1] Another case supporting involvement of management which has been presented is as follows:

> If EDP is to be responsive to the total needs of top management, it demands total involvement on the part of that management. The executive look at EDP has got to be more than a glance through the plate glass window. They have to grasp the significance of a dynamic EDP operation.[2]

A research study by McKinsey & Company lends credence to this statement with the finding that firms with the most successful computer operations were those in which top managers participated actively in the function. In many cases, management's lack of interest and involvement is traceable to apprehension about the computer.[3] This is understandable because many executives with no training in use of the computer or exposure to its potentialities view it as a powerful device which can be understood only by highly skilled computer specialists. Resistance to change (to be discussed more fully later) often emanates from managerial offices as well as other areas of the organization.

High-level managers typically will not fully support anything they are apprehensive about or know little about, but their support must be gained during the preliminary planning stages for computerization. Their involvement can make them feel an obligation to and identification with the project, and their support must be fully behind the effort from the beginning because the success of the effort depends initially on the authority and commitment that emanate from high-echelon offices. Therefore the gaining of managerial support is one of the key elements in the initial planning process.

As an example of top management's support—or lack of it—and related problems of computerization, consider the case of a company encountered in a management consulting experience of one of the authors. A small-company president was interested in buying a computer. Instead of authorizing a study to determine feasibility and consider costs versus benefits, the president instructed his son-in-law (a lower level supervisor in the company) and the plant manager to take charge of the purchase. After seeing what computers were available, they decided on equipment valued at approximately $150,000, though neither of the two involved in the selection process knew much about computers. It was not until over a year after purchase

[1] F. Roodman, "Helping Management Manage," *Journal of Data Management*, August 1965, p. 12. Also see "Developing an ADP Plan," *Computer Decisions*, January 1975, pp. D2–D4.

[2] A. E. Keller, "EDP—Power in Search of Management," *Business Automation*, June 1966, p. 31.

[3] Peter P. Schoderbek and J. D. Babcock, "At Last—Management More Active in EDP," *Business Horizons*, December 1969, p. 55.

and delivery that the company even hired someone to direct the computer operation, and then this individual concluded that the company had purchased equipment with much more capability than was needed.

The president's role in the entire decision process was to select the colors of the carpeting to be installed in the data processing room. Meanwhile the data processing manager cannot get his equipment installed and running because the president has the workmen who are supposed to be completing the computer room working on a house he is building. The consultant had been called in to work on another management problem, and the company apparently still does not know that it has a problem in the computer area. Of course such fiascoes do not occur all the time in computerization, but more frequently than you might think.

"I THINK WHAT WE NEED NOW IS SOMEONE CALLED A COMPUTER PROGRAMMER."

© Datamation ®

Planning for the Total Effort

In the general process of initiating a study to consider the adoption of a computerized system, there are many variables that impinge on how the process evolves and how much time and resources are eventually committed to it. This section will outline and discuss the process as it often occurs.

Planning for the total effort involves certain steps which must be undertaken by an organization considering the adoption of a computer system. In cases where an organization already has a computer system and is interested in upgrading the existing system, a modification of the approach presented below may be necessary. Assume for purposes of general discussion, however, that we are describing a firm that does not presently have a computer.

Figure 11–1 shows the two major stages in the process of introducing a computer into the organization—the formulation stage and the implementation stage. The *formulation stage* entails such preimplementation considerations as conducting the feasibility study, which involves analyzing the organization's data processing needs and

FIGURE 11–1
Introducing a Computer into the Organization

STAGE

ACTIVITIES

Formulation Stage

Implementation Stage

1. Conducting the Feasibility Study

   Setting up the feasibility group

   Assessing organization's EDP needs (initial systems analysis)

   Analyzing and improving existing systems (initial systems design)

   The feasibility group's recommendations

2. Computer System Selection

   Rent, lease, purchase

3. Preparing Resources for Change

   Personnel, physical space

4. Systems Design and Programming

   In-depth systems investigation and analysis

   In-depth systems design and development

   Programming the applications

   Implementing the applications

5. Installing Equipment

6. Appraisal, Follow-up, and Review

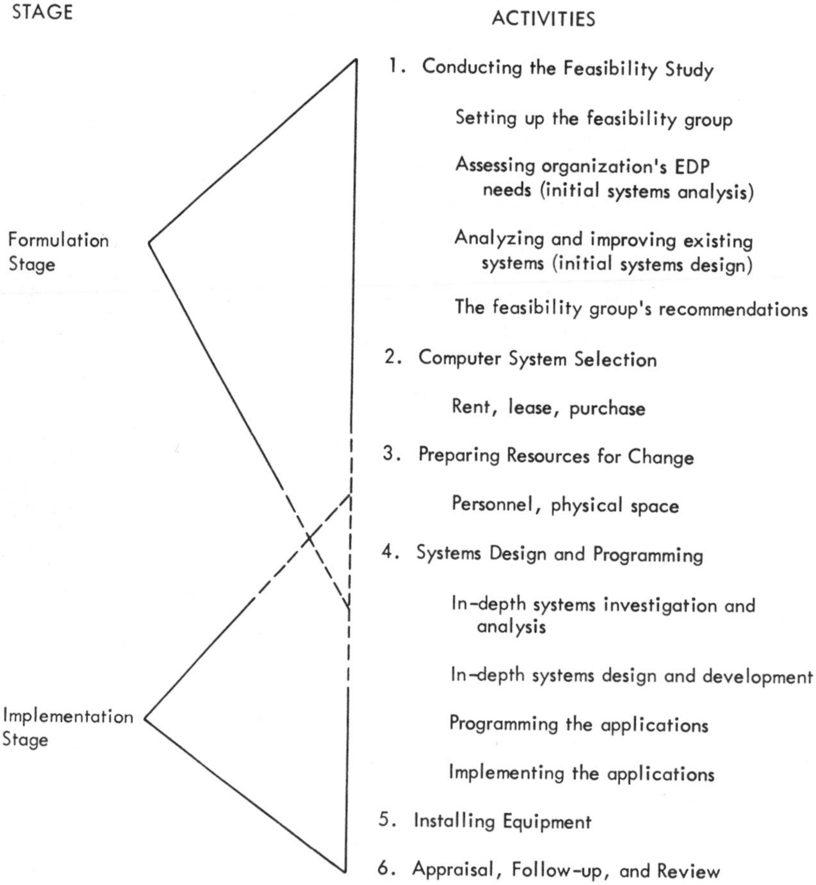

analyzing and improving the organizations' existing systems (initial systems analysis and design). Additionally, the formulation stage involves computer system selection and preparing organizational resources for change. The *implementation stage*, which overlaps the formulation stage somewhat (as Figure 11–1 illustrates), entails a more intensive systems analysis and design and also includes programming and implementing the applications. Installing the equipment is part of this stage, as is appraisal, follow-up, and review.

These stages will become clearer as they are discussed individually. The process of introducing a computer into an organization could be described in various ways, and the steps presented here should be considered as only representative of the process.

CONDUCTING THE FEASIBILITY STUDY

Although some preliminary thinking always takes place before a study is initiated to determine the feasibility of adopting a computer system, this is the first formal step in the process. A *feasibility study* is a systematic evaluation and appraisal of the organization's characteristics and needs to determine whether a computerized system is merited from both technological and economic points of view. This is a study which takes the *individual organization's* needs into account, and it must be viewed from this perspective. Some experts today question whether the study should be called a feasibility study, since practically anything is feasible with today's offerings of computer hardware, software, and price ranges. They argue that the study ought to be called a *justification study* because in effect what management is determining is whether the firm can justify the installation of computer equipment. This is a good argument, and no effort will be made to refute it. However, for the sake of convention we will continue to employ the more standard term.

Need for a Study

The need for a feasibility study is justified from the four standpoints discussed below:

1. There is a tendency for some managers or organizations to want to adopt a computer simply because it has status, that is, it is the fashionable thing to do. Perhaps this is the reason the small-company president in the example discussed previously wanted a computer. Hopefully, a rigorous, objective appraisal of feasibility will keep management realistic.

2. A considerable investment is involved, in terms of not only direct outlays but also other organizational resources — managerial time, personnel, and the indirect costs associated with organizational

FIGURE 11–2
Time and Expense Associated with Completing a Computer Project

PHASE	EXPENSE	TIME
I. Preliminary analysis	2%	5%
II. Feasibility assessment	5	10
III. Analysis and design	10	15
IV. System engineering	8	10
V. Programming and procedures	45	40
VI. Installation	30	20

Source: "The Computer/Cost Confrontation." *ADP Newsletter*, vol. 15, no. 6 (March 22, 1971).

change. Therefore, it is imperative not only that a feasibility study be conducted but also that a definite decision concerning the computer be made as early as possible. Xerox Corporations' cost and time estimates for major phases of introducing a computer (see Figure 11–2) demonstrate the importance of making a definite decision as early in the development cycle as possible. The feasibility study is designed to help the firm make this decision.

3. The feasibility study can help management get its thinking in order so that major pitfalls or problems can be avoided. Management may be inclined to engage in a crash program of computerization or be so anxious that it buys the computer hardware first and then tries to build a system around it. Such a tail-wagging-the-dog approach is not entirely uncommon. In the example cited previously, the individual who was hired to manage and operate the computer installation was frustrated in his efforts to mesh the company's requirements with the purchased computer's capabilities.

4. The feasibility study can identify frailties in existing data processing and information handling systems. In the experience of most organizations, numerous weaknesses in present systems, such as inadequacies and redundancies in paper work, information flows, and reporting requirements, surface as a result of the feasibility study. Since part of the feasibility study is to determine which possible computer applications are feasible in the organization, this is not surprising.

Nature of Feasibility Studies

Not only must the feasibility study be conducted from the specific viewpoint of the concerned organization, as noted earlier, but key organizational personnel must be intimately involved in the study if it is to be of greatest value. Furthermore, the feasibility study can be an exciting educational venture for those who are chosen to comprise the investigatory group.

There is often a tendency to call in a computer manufacturer's representative early in the process, but this should be avoided, to maintain objectivity. While it would seem that tapping the knowledge of manufacturers' representatives would provide an important source of information, experience has indicated that these individuals (each strongly motivated to represent his own company's products) should not be brought in until the organization has *independently investigated* and developed its own specifications. This is an important task of the feasibility study—to determine the organization's data processing needs independent from salesmen or others who have honest motives which nevertheless are sometimes inconsistent with the interests of the study group.[4]

One pitfall which must be avoided at all costs is purchasing computer hardware first and then designing the organization's information system to fit it. This is a typical procedure when the manufacturer's representative is called in before the study group has identified a detailed set of specifications. Computer salesmen seem to have an uncanny ability to always have "just the right system" for the company that is approached on this basis. The representatives of the computer manufacturers, therefore, should be brought in after the feasibility group has identified the organization's needs.

Though it is unwise to bring computer company representatives into the feasibility study too early, the services of independent systems or computer consultants are a reservoir of resource knowledge. Independent consultants can provide a dispassionate "outsider" perspective to enhance the study group's investigation and analysis. One of their weaknesses, however, is that on occasion they get "wedded" to particular hardware they can use comfortably and let this familiarity with a particular system affect their impartiality in the advisory process. This possibility must be kept in mind by the manager.

Outside observers also can assume the role of disinterested arbiter when changes are to be made in the organization. Feasibility investigations often hit upon organization "sore points," or internal jurisdictional disputes may arise when suggestions are made that certain organizational changes are necessary. It is quite likely that as a consequence of the study changes in organizational structure, authority, jurisdiction, or reporting flow will be deemed necessary, whether computers are introduced or not.

---

[4] For an in-depth discussion of the employment of in-house personnel to select hardware, see D. S. Farbman, "A Team Approach to Hardware Analysis," *Computer Decisions*, November 1974, pp. 63–65.

Steps in the Feasibility Study

Figure 11–3 defines the various steps needed in a typical feasibility study, and they are discussed below.

Setting up the Feasibility Group. The composition of the feasibility group is an important preliminary decision. While top-management support must be present from the outset, it is not recommended that the chief executive be an active member of this group. This is primarily because of the overwhelming influence he would bring to bear on the group's decision process (though not necessarily intentionally) and the amount of time he would have to take from other responsibilities. If the group is to render a truly objective appraisal of the organization, the persuasive power of the top manager is best kept apart. Nevertheless, the chairman of the feasibility study will undoubtedly report to the chief executive. Because sensitive organizational exigencies are under examination, the committee's efforts must be legitimized by top-management authority.

The group should be comprised of responsible people from the various functional areas of the organization, including representatives from all areas which it is anticipated will be affected greatly by the group's decision. The size of the organization under consideration will have an important bearing on the size of the group. Since there is no optimal size for a group of this kind, this decision will rest largely with top management.

The specific purpose of the feasibility committee is to recommend a decision to top management as to whether or not the organization should *at this time* invest in a computerized data processing system. If the recommendation is affirmative, then implementation decisions such as what, when, and how become imperative.

Assessing the Organization's Data Processing Needs. One of the single most important mandates of the feasibility group is to assess the organization's data processing requirements. This entails a survey of the present situation to develop a fairly representative picture of the organizations' existing information systems.

The depth to which the feasibility group goes in assessing needs varies considerably from organization to organization. In any case,

FIGURE 11–3
Steps in the Feasibility Study

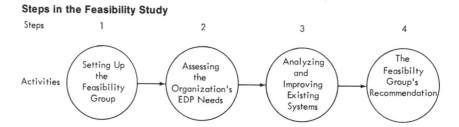

the group has a responsibility during this assessment to probe the firm's internal systems and develop an accurate appraisal of the organization's data processing needs. This preliminary systems analysis must penetrate through the formal and informal systems to reveal information strengths and inadequacies.

While this investigation of the organization is somewhat short of an intensive systems study, for purposes of indicating computer feasibility it usually suffices. Specifically, the feasibility group is expected to carefully identify necessary data inputs, processing, and information outputs in the information flow. The purpose at this stage is to determine, through a kind of cost-benefit appraisal, whether the existing system is better than a proposed system. This study requires consideration of financial, economic, and physical factors in an effort to determine the various areas of organizational operations in which a computer system might be effectively applied.

After a preliminary investigation has taken place, it may be indicated that potential net savings and operating benefits are sufficient to justify a more intensive systems analysis. What happens at this juncture varies from organization to organization. In some, a go–no-go recommendation is made based upon this preliminary study, and in others a more intensive analysis is undertaken. In any event, one sure outcome of this investigation is an analysis of the organization's information systems and suggestions for improving them.

Though we have been assuming that the organization is considering the initial acquisition of computer capability or upgrading existing facilities, companies that take a close look at their data processing requirements occasionally find that they could *downgrade* rather than upgrade their computer operations. There has been a recent noticeable trend for top executives to question whether they are getting their money's worth out of their company's computer systems, due to the overcomputerization which has occurred in recent years.

Francis J. Melly, president of FMS Management Services, Inc., estimates that the "average company with sales of $100 million annually is overcomputerized by 20 percent."[5] He attributes this to a number of factors, among the most consequential of which are the tendency of data processing professionals to build computer empires, and business managers who do not ask "What are our company's *real* EDP needs, and can we justify them?" Regarding the first point, he suggests that "It's simply not in the nature of highly trained, intelligent specialists to seek ways to reduce their programs, equipment—and, yes, their power."[6]

---

[5] Francis J. Melly, "Report on the Computer Backlash," *Advanced Management Journal*, vol. 39, no. 2 (April 1974), pp. 11–12.

[6] Ibid., pp. 11–13.

Though Melly's first observation points up the problems of over-computerization, it is his second point that is important here, since we are discussing the assessment of the organization's data processing needs. Melly's message should be underscored: Management frequently misses the critical point that the purpose of a computer capability is to fulfill the company's real data processing needs, not to put the company in the forefront of computer development by acquiring new equipment or continually upgrading existing systems.

Analyzing and Improving the Organization's Present Systems.   The next step in the feasibility study is often the intensive study of selected key areas of possible computer applicability and the subsequent recommendation of alterations to be made in present methods. Key areas are chosen for more intensive study to determine the possible improvements that computerization could make in present systems. These areas are usually the ones that are most important to the organization and involve a large number of repetitive transactions. The areas chosen for study also are those in which the operational manager is predisposed to success of the project.[7]

A computerized data processing system is more than just the old system with a computer added to it. The whole orientation of the system and the data processing methods employed in the organization must be changed. At this point in the feasibility study it is likely that work simplification or job improvement techniques can be applied to existing systems. Eventually this will have to be done, whether at this time or later when a more thorough systems analysis is undertaken in the implementation stage. In the typical situation, detailed specifications for computer applications cannot be stated until present methods have been improved. To do otherwise would be to build into a new system all of the weaknesses and inadequacies of the former one. It is better that information, work, and reporting flows be logically and rigorously subjected to close scrutiny and modification before a computer system is implemented than to wait until afterward and then make the needed modifications. At this point the question is whether specifications can be generated as a result of the preliminary study, or more intensive systems analysis, modifications, and improvements are needed.

The Feasibility Group's Recommendation.   At the moment of decision for the feasibility group a recommendation must be made to management. It is assumed that the group has weighed the costs and benefits associated with the decision and is now in a position to recommend whether or not the projected computer applications are

---

[7] For a more in-depth discussion see W. A. Bocchino, *A Simplified Guide to Automatic Data Processing*, 2d ed. (Englewood Cliffs, N.J.: Prentice-Hall, Inc., 1972), p. 228.

justified. The recommendation may be negative or it may be a "tentative go," pending further investigation of the available equipment. In any event, while the general position of the group can be stated at this time, there are many details still to be worked out by studying equipment characteristics, considering the rent, lease, or buy decision, and so on.

COMPUTER SYSTEM SELECTION

It may seem that the bulk of the work has been done once specifications for computer hardware and software have been established by the feasibility investigation group, but only the tip of the iceberg has been exposed. Computer system selection is an extremely complicated process, and numerous considerations enter into the selection decision.

Many of the considerations which must now be examined are tangible; such equipment characteristics as hardware capacity, price, and efficiency can be examined quantitatively. There are numerous other factors, however, which do not lend themselves so neatly to ready comparisons among equipment manufacturers. These factors include the reputation of the manufacturer for complying with delivery dates, service provided, and so forth. Often it is the latter type of criteria upon which ultimate decisions depend.

Equipment appraisal and selection were somewhat less involved when there were fewer manufacturers and options from which to choose. In today's market, in which various configurations of main and peripheral equipment have proliferated, the selection decision is immensely more complex. There are also numerous factors to consider, such as hardware characteristics (speed, storage capacity, flexibility), economic considerations (initial costs, operating costs, return on investment), and service aspects (programming assistance, timeliness of service, maintenance, training support), so care must be exercised in the evaluation process. Figure 11–4 summarizes a number of factors which impinge on computer system selection.

A typical approach to the selection process is to issue to a number of manufacturers the specifications that have been established during the feasibility study. It may be advisable at this point to distribute the criteria to only a few (three or four) suppliers rather than to all who may be interested. It is then likely that a conference will be held at which the decision specifications are elaborated upon for the equipment representatives. The next step would be for each equipment supplier to work up a proposal and a bid for the company's business.

A number of simulation models have been developed to provide firms with a more objective appraisal of how different types of equip-

FIGURE 11–4
Sampling of Factors Impinging on Computer System Selection

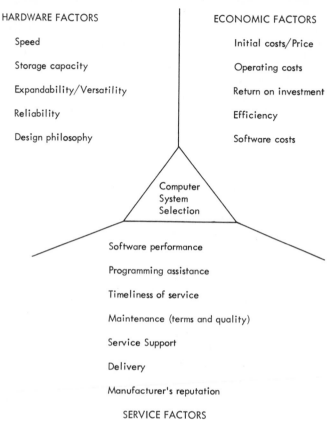

HARDWARE FACTORS

Speed

Storage capacity

Expandability/Versatility

Reliability

Design philosophy

ECONOMIC FACTORS

Initial costs/Price

Operating costs

Return on investment

Efficiency

Software costs

Computer
System
Selection

Software performance

Programming assistance

Timeliness of service

Maintenance (terms and quality)

Service Support

Delivery

Manufacturer's reputation

SERVICE FACTORS

ment perform in regard to stated performance criteria. Thus a computer can be used to help make a decision about a computer! A program that is representative of these simulations is the SCERT program. The function of SCERT (*S*ystems and *C*omputers *E*valuation and *R*eview *T*echnique) is to contrast input, output, and processing times on various computers.[8]

Once the feasibility group has received proposals from the interested vendors, their responsibility is to evaluate the proposals in light of the stated specifications. It is not always the lowest bidder in dollar terms that gets the contract. The important considerations of service and manufacturer reputation (e.g., its record of keeping promises) are also examined. The proposals must be scrutinized

---

[8] SCERT, Comress, Inc., Washington, D.C.

carefully because the tendency of each competing company will be to make its own equipment seem the ideal choice.

Rent, Lease, or Purchase

The *form* of the relationship of the computer facility to the organization—whether it should be rented, leased, or purchased—is another important decision that must be made in regard to the choice of equipment. There are many advantages and disadvantages in each of these contractual arrangements, and they should be analyzed by a specialist who is familiar with the company's financial situation and the accounting and tax implications associated with the decision. Some of the characteristics of these arrangements are discussed briefly below.

1. *Rent option.* In the rent arrangement, the company pays the computer manufacturer a minimum monthly fee for a term spanning less than three years. The basic fee includes an amount to cover maintenance, insurance, and so on, and computer usage is most often billed on an hourly basis.[9] Hence, over a long period, this would be a very costly arrangement. It does have the obvious advantage of flexibility, and it insulates the company against technological obsolescence.

2. *Lease option.* The lease option differs from the rent option in that it frequently involves leasing from other than the manufacturer, though this is not always the case. Additionally, it is a longer term agreement, lasting over three years, and billing is not based on usage. Many specialized leasing companies exist independent of computer manufacturers. In the lease option the user does not have the wide choice of equipment he would have were he dealing directly with the manufacturer, and to overcome this disadvantage some companies participate in a *sale and leaseback* arrangement whereby a client company goes to a manufacturer and purchases a specific system, sells it to a leasing company, and then leases it back from the leasing company. In this way the user can get the kind of equipment it wants without having to buy it.

3. *Purchase option.* The purchase option is straightforward; the company simply contracts to buy the equipment. Though there are numerous disadvantages to this option, such as initial capital outlay required, technological obsolescence, and additional maintenance fees, there are also advantages, especially if the equipment is kept over a long period of time. Certain tax advantages accrue to the purchaser that would not under a leasing arrangement. Over the years,

---

[9] Bocchino, *Simplified Guide to Automatic Data Processing*, p. 236.

the federal government itself has moved toward the purchase option after a rather intensive study of the options available. The government, however, is the largest computer user in the world, and it is not suggested that its situation is comparable to that of most business firms.

To a certain extent, specific manufacturers have some influence over whether leasing or purchasing is the most favorable option. They can exercise this control by strategically altering the benefits associated with purchasing versus renting their particular equipment. Firms with large, successful renting or leasing operations may set their purchase price arbitrarily high to discourage purchasing, and smaller companies may react in an opposite manner.

The choice of equipment is complicated not only by the variety of equipment and services available but also by the necessity to make a fundamental choice as to purchasing, leasing, or renting. Experts knowledgeable in accounting and taxation matters must help make these kinds of decisions. The acquisition of hardware is only one step in the total installation process.

Other Approaches

Though we have been assuming in this chapter that the firm is considering the actual acquisition of a computer, a number of other approaches to acquiring computer resources are currently being employed. A company can get access to computer time for processing some of its data by renting excess time on the computers of large firms (e.g., banks). *Service bureaus* which specialize in data processing can take over some or all of the company's data processing chores. Service bureaus may be independent firms, subsidiaries of computer

FIGURE 11–5
Summary of Options for Acquiring Computer Resources

HARDWARE ACQUISITION OPTIONS
1. Rent
2. Lease
3. Buy
4. Facilities management (assumes firm has hardware)

OTHER OPTIONS
5. Service bureaus
   a. Independent firms
   b. Subsidiaries of computer manufacturers
   c. Service divisions of other firms with excess computer time to sell
6. Large firms that have excess computer time to sell but do not have officially established service branches or bureaus
7. Cooperative computer centers established by small companies based upon mutual needs

---

manufacturers, or service divisions of other firms with excess computer time to sell. In recent years small firms with mutual data processing needs have joined together to form *cooperative computer centers.*

One of the most interesting recent developments has been the creation of *facilities management firms.* This alternative is being chosen by increasing numbers of companies which realize they can take care of their data processing needs by transferring complete responsibility for computers to these specialized, outside agencies. Some facilities management firms estimate that they can save a company 10 to 40 percent of its computer budget. Facilities management contracts may call for taking over a firm's computers, the computer room, and everyone in it to the transference of limited control.[10] Figure 11–5 summarizes the main options for acquiring computer resources.

PREPARING ORGANIZATIONAL RESOURCES FOR CHANGE

One of the last major responsibilities in the formulation stage is the preparation of organizational resources for the pending introduction of the computer. Since this is a transitional step that is taken after some initial decisions have been reached and before others are made, in ways it overlaps into the implementation stage. Certain preparatory actions can be taken immediately, while others are contingent upon later decisions. The chief organizational resources that must be prepared are personnel and physical arrangements, including certain technical properties.

Personnel

Personnel preparation is a vital step in the introduction of computerization in an organization. It includes not only the selection and hiring of managerial personnel to manage the installation but staffing the installation with specialists such as systems analysts, computer operators, programmers, and keypunch operators. Depending on the size of department to be established, this responsibility could involve selection techniques for new employees, personnel testing and screening, hiring, and training.

Another important class of personnel preparations that must simultaneously take place is in the group of existing managers and em-

---

[10] "More Companies Hire Specialized Concerns to Run Their Data-Processing Operations," *The Wall Street Journal*, November 29, 1973, p. 36.

ployees who will be affected by the changes. It is indeed rare that existing employees are unaffected by changes that are as dramatic as those affecting information processing and flows. The introduction of technological change into the organization is certain to have an impact on existing authority structures and patterns, and consideration must be given to all those departments, functions, and persons that will be influenced by the impending changes. Some have suggested that preparing the people who will be affected by the changes is the most difficult part of installing a computer. Compared with human resources, selection of hardware is no problem.[11] It should not be surprising, therefore, that *resistance to change*, on the part of both managerial and staff personnel, is likely to be exhibited during this preparatory period and for some time afterward.

Management experience has demonstrated that one of the immediate results of a change decision, no matter how minor, is an actual or perceived change in organizational relationships. As a general rule, if preventive measures are not taken, such changes will inevitably result in resistance on the part of organizational members. Resistance usually results because the following types of changes associated with implementing new technology will have an effect on personnel:

1. Changes affecting a worker's job content or pay.
2. Changes that reduce authority or freedom of action.
3. Changes that disrupt established work routines.
4. Changes that rearrange formal and informal group patterns.
5. Changes that are forced without explanation or employee participation.[12]

These effects are usually associated with new-systems introductions unless management takes actions to prevent them. This is what is meant by preparing existing personnel for change. An example of an action that could be taken to offset this resistance is to announce, early in the change process, a policy of retraining existing personnel, upgrading present skills, or teaching new skills. Employees do not like uncertainty, and such efforts could reduce their fears about what impact computer acquisition will have on their jobs and their continued employment with the company.

Increasingly, managers chosen to implement computer systems have had to give greater consideration to the human resource in their change efforts. One good example of the extent to which some experts

---

[11] M. W. Cashman, "Studies in Small-Scale Computing," *Datamation*, June 1974, pp. 42–47.

[12] B. J. Hodge and H. J. Johnson, *Management and Organizational Behavior* (New York: John Wiley & Sons, Inc., 1970), pp. 432–33.

are moving in this direction is provided by the experiences of J. W. Lawrie, J. M. Ryan, and A. Carlyle in their experiments with a large Midwestern bank.[13] This bank was interested in installing computer terminals to be used by its tellers, and in addition to cost-benefit analyses to evaluate the probable economic impact of the terminals, it also wanted some consideration of the possible psychological and motivational effects of the introduction on the people who would be affected by the installation.

To determine what effects or consequences the installation might have on the morale, attitudes, and behavior of the work force, the bank proceeded to gather relevant data. Seven branches of the bank had already installed terminals on a pilot basis, and the idea was to determine if any significant differences existed between the terminal sample and the nonterminal sample on key variables. If such differences did exist the bank would consider this information in its efforts to make installations in the rest of the bank. As it turned out there was "no evidence that the terminal significantly changes absenteeism or turnover," and "Overall the terminal neither helps nor hurts tellers' feelings about the job." The bank did find, however, that "the terminal is associated with more positive feelings about 'co-workers' and the teller's feelings about being 'responsible for work.'"[14]

With this data at its disposal, the bank was able to plan the transition from a human resource perspective more rationally than if all they had were speculations about the "people impact" of the installation. Since computer installations do affect workers so directly—by creating changes in supervisory-subordinate relationships, displacing workers, changing their job content, requiring higher level skills, and so on—managers must demonstrate sensitivity to the interface between human systems and computer systems.[15]

In sum, it can be seen that the effects on personnel of introducing a computer system can be numerous and intensive. It is management's responsibility to manage the change by preparing for it rather than taking the action and then trying to cope with the consequences.

Physical Arrangements

Another crucial element that must also be considered is the physical space that will be needed to install the computer and its

[13] J. W. Lawrie, J. M. Ryan, and A. Carlyle, "Terminals and Their Impact on Employee Motivation," *Datamation*, August 1974.

[14] Ibid., p. 62.

[15] E. A. Tomeski, "Job Enrichment and the Computer: A Neglected Subject," *Computers for People*, November 1974, pp. 7–11.

related equipment. At this stage the company will ordinarily have the expert assistance of the computer manufacturer's representatives in preparing the site. The computer vendor can be expected to supply the purchaser with technical assistance and planning guidelines to help in site choice and preparation, including consideration of such relevant factors as layout, temperature control, dust control, power availability, and special flooring. It is stressed that "site preparation must begin as early as system selection, sometimes earlier."[16]

SYSTEMS DESIGN AND PROGRAMMING

Figure 11-1 showed systems design and programming as the first part of the implementation stage, but the activities listed in the figure should not be considered as taking place at discrete times. There is considerable overlap among them — for example, some of the systems analysis work is done during earlier parts of the feasibility study, and equipment installation takes place while systems analysis, design, and programming are going forward. The essential objective of systems design and programming is to analyze existing systems (e.g., payroll, accounts receivable), design them to be optimal in terms of existing resources and constraints, and develop a series of programs to handle specific applications. Specifically, the activities involved in this step include:

1. Systems investigation and analysis (more in depth than in the formulation stage).
2. Systems design and development.
3. Programming the applications.
4. Implementing the applications.

The company's personnel may receive assistance from the vendor in handling these activities. When the computer system is purchased as a "bundle" or package, a vendor representative is usually assigned to work with the company on a full-time basis until the programs are prepared and running.

INSTALLING EQUIPMENT

The bulk of the responsibility for actual equipment installation rests with the vendor, working closely with company personnel. Getting the actual equipment installed is one step; however, having it fully coordinated with the organization's other systems is more complex indeed. For some time during and after the installation period

---

[16] D. A. Reisman, "Facilities Planning," *Datamation*, November 1974, pp. 55–59. See this article for an in-depth discussion of site selection and preparation.

parallel operations will be necessary. Due to the intracacies associated with the conversion process, there will be a transition period during which the operation will not run smoothly. This will likely precipitate second thoughts on the part of some managers as to whether computerization was a good decision. After the process of initial *debugging*, or detection and removal of mistakes in routines or malfunctions in the computer, the system should function smoothly and the manager should be reassured.

APPRAISAL, FOLLOW-UP, AND REVIEW

Appraisal, follow-up, and review ideally are a continuous process. As management gains experience with the new system, alterations and modifications will undoubtedly be made. A continuing appraisal of the system is necessary to ensure that the organization is gaining optimal benefits from it. The appraisal is designed to make certain that equipment options and new applications are being considered, costs and benefits are being monitored, and feedback is being systematically received and reviewed. Continuous consideration must be given to this multitude of factors if the operation is to continue to yield benefits to the organization. Since the many phases of installing and operating a computerized system are interrelated and interdependent, it is necessary that a continuing information systems audit be made.

CONCLUDING REMARKS

Out of necessity we have treated the computer planning, selection, and implementation process in a rather brief fashion. In actuality it is a complex management decision process entailing a considerable expenditure of time and resources. You can surmise the numerous details associated with each individual case of computer installation; we have described the procedure and its characteristics in rather general terms.

It has been suggested that top-management support is needed from the outset in an effort of this size. The success of a computer installation is traceable in no small part to the extent and quality of management leadership and continuous involvement. Computer installation is a process which has a beginning but no end, and the continuing support and guidance of management are necessary to maintain an effective and truly integrated management information system. Indeed, a continual management audit of the data processing department should be a regular, necessary management function.

It should be stressed that many of the steps involved in the procedure of introducing computerized data processing into an organiza-

tion take place simultaneously. The process begins with a feasibility
study, computer system selection, and preparation of organizational
resources for change. These elements constitute what may be called
the formulation stage. Once these activities have been completed
and a decision has been made to go ahead with the installation, implementation considerations come into play. These include systems
design and programming, the actual installation of equipment, and
appraisal, follow-up, and review. In addition, numerous operational
considerations enter the picture which have not been discussed in
this chapter. Among these factors are: the control function, computer
effectiveness studies, continual training of personnel, expansion of
applications, and institutionalization of work procedures and guidelines.[17]

ASSIGNMENTS

11-1.   In what ways is planning difficult? Why should a company engage
        in planning? How can planning ease implementing a computer sys-
        tem?

11-2.   What problems could be encountered if a computer system did not
        have management support? How could these problems be overcome?

11-3.   What are the two major stages in introducing a computer into the
        organization, and what do these stages entail?

11-4.   How is a feasibility study used? What factors are considered in such
        a study?

11-5.   Why is it important to make the go–no-go decision concerning a
        computer as early as possible?

11-6.   When should a manufacturer's representative from a computer com-
        pany be called in? What pitfalls should be avoided at all costs when a
        system is being considered? How can information on systems be
        obtained?

11-7.   What steps should be included in a feasibility study? How does each
        step contribute to the decision?

11-8.   What important considerations should be examined in making a
        decision on the right computer for a company? In what ways can the
        selection process be narrowed down? How could SCERT be in-
        volved in the decision-making process?

---

[17] To this point we have been discussing planning for the computer. However,
the topic of planning by the computer is of increasing concern to corporate managers.
For an excellent treatment of this topic see The Diebold Group's "ADP Planning in an
Uncertain World," *Computer Decisions*, January 1975, pp. D1–D8.

11-9. In preparing for the changes the computer will bring about, how can the company help make sure the computer will be accepted by personnel with the least amount of problems? What is the management challenge in this change process?

11-10. Why should a continual information systems audit take place? How do you feel this should be accomplished?

REFERENCES

Books

Bocchino, W. A. *A Simplified Guide to Automatic Data Processing.* Englewood Cliffs, N.J.: Prentice-Hall, 1972.

Brandon, D. H. *Management Planning for Data Processing.* Princeton, N.J.: Brandon/Systems Press, 1970.

Clifton, H. D. *Systems Analysis for Business Data Processing.* Princeton, N.J.: Auerbach Publishers, 1969.

Ditri, A. E., J. C. Shaw, and W. Atkins *Managing the EDP Function.* New York: McGraw-Hill Book Co., 1971.

Elliott, C. Orville and Robert S. Wasley *Business Information Processing Systems: An Introduction to Data Processing,* 4th ed. Homewood, Ill.: Richard D. Irwin, 1975.

Kanter, Jerome *Management Guide to Computer System Selection and Use.* Englewood Cliffs, N.J.: Prentice-Hall, 1970.

Krauss, L. I. *Administering and Controlling the Company Data Processing Function.* Englewood Cliffs, N.J.: Prentice-Hall, 1969.

Joslin, E. O. *Computer Selection.* Reading, Mass.: Addison-Wesley Publishing Co., 1968.

Lundell, E. D. and E. J. Bride *Computer Use: An Executive's Guide.* Boston: Allyn & Bacon, 1973.

Massey, L. D. and J. Heptonstall *EDP Feasibility Analysis.* Braintree, Mass.: D. H. Mark Publishing Co., 1968.

Articles

Blackman, Maurice "A Specification for Computer Selection." *Data Processing,* vol. 15, no. 6 (November–December 1973).

Borovits, Israel "Purchase or Produce?" *Data Processing,* vol. 15, no. 5, (September–October 1973).

Bucci, Robert A. "Avoiding Hassles with Vendors." *Datamation,* July 1974, pp. 68–72.

Cashman, Michael William "Studies in Small-Scale Computing." *Datamation,* June 1974, pp. 42–47.

"The Computer/Cost Confrontation." *Automatic Data Processing Newsletter,* vol. 15, no. 6, March 22, 1971.

Gardner, W. David   "Upgrading—One Company's Experience." *Datamation*, February 1974, pp. 65–66.

"Managing Software: It Can Be Done." *Infosystems*, November 1973.

Nolan, Richard and K. Eric Knutsen   "The Computerization of the ABC Widget Co." *Datamation*, April 1974, pp. 71–76.

Schoderbek, Peter P. and Babcock, J. D.   "At Last—Management More Active in EDP." *Business Horizons*, December 1969.

"Software: The Make or Buy Decision." *Infosystems*, April 1973.

Computer Impact on the Managerial Environment

The Computer and Managerial Functions

The Computer's Impact on Lower Management

The Computer's Impact on Middle Management
  Results of Some Studies

The Computer's Impact on Top Management
  A Disparaging View, The Manager's Planning Horizon

Concluding Remarks

Assignments

References

This chapter is concerned with the computer's impact on management. In particular, it examines the consequences of the presence of a computer for lower, middle, and top management levels. You should gain an appreciation of the usefulness of computers at each level and an understanding of their impact on job scope and content, decision making, numbers of personnel, and the general task environment.

12

The Impact of the Computer on Management

Management is a pivotal factor in the search for effective methods of utilizing the world's scarce resources. It can either stimulate or deter the progress of a society, depending upon how well it meets that society's changing expectations of it. Throughout the adjustment process by which management attempts to fulfill societal needs in general and organizational needs in particular, management is constantly barraged with technological change which simultaneously makes its work more productive and more complex. Management's task is to adapt to changing societal needs and technological advances in such a way that its work will be accomplished most effectively.

The introduction of the digital computer is one of the most profound technological changes that has ever confronted the managers of organizations. Before it became available business for hundreds of years had found the processing of data a difficult and time-consuming task. Like most technological changes, computer capability entails certain implications and impacts which must be considered by its users. The effects and changes that are brought about by the introduction of technological innovations are also social and economic in nature. The primary concern here, however, will be with the organizational and managerial consequences of computerization.

A distinction can be made between the impact of computers on management and the impact of computers on the organization. The present chapter will concentrate on the computer's effect on management, in particular the consequences it can have for the management *group* in an organization and its impacts at each of the various levels of management—lower, middle, and top. The next chapter will be oriented toward the impact of the computer on the organization, in particular on the organization's *structure*. This distinction is based on the notion that the management *process* (an activity carried out by people) is distinguishable from the organization's *structure* (the framework within which management activity takes place).

Included in the present chapter will be a discussion of the following topics:

1. The computer's impact on the managerial environment.
2. The computer and managerial functions.
3. The computer's impact on lower management.
4. The computer's impact on middle management.
5. The computer's impact on top management.

The primary emphasis of this chapter is on the last three topics. In particular, each managerial level will be examined in terms of the computer's impact on decision making, the number of jobs, the content and nature of jobs, and general changes in the environment at that level.

COMPUTER IMPACT ON THE MANAGERIAL ENVIRONMENT

Since the end of World War II, many innovations have brought about substantial changes in the management of businesses. Radical advances in the behavioral and quantitative sciences have forced managers to abandon ideas and concepts they had come to depend upon. Methodologies and techniques based upon the scientific method of problem solving provided the management group with more sophisticated computational approaches to decision making, and these quantification-based approaches to management problem solving were enhanced by the vast potential of the electronic computer. Both computers and management sciences have come of age, almost hand in hand, and both have become characteristics of the contemporary environment of management. While the computer is not a necessity in the case of quantitative approaches to decision making, its capabilities and potential have encouraged and facilitated the use of management science techniques.

Probably the most important activity managers engage in is decision making, and the computer's greatest impact has been in this area. In the most literal sense, the computer's greatest contribution has been its ability to process large amounts of data with unprecedented speed and efficiency. This facility has immeasurably improved the decision-making process by giving managers an ability to gather, analyze, and reproduce quantities of data which can make their problem-solving capacities more diverse, more precise, and more sophisticated. Since the human mind is limited in its ability to digest and analyze large quantities of data, the computer provides managers with an indispensable decision-making tool. Rather than replacing man as a decision maker, the computer's effect has been to extend the manager's repertoire of skills in the decision process.

The computer has also had a profound influence upon managers' thought processes. Computerization must be credited with playing an important role in the evolution of what has come to be known as the systems approach to management. The use of a logic-based instrument such as the computer implies a thought process which is rigorous, analytical, and oriented toward understanding the relationships between causes and effects. Such an approach views the organization as a system or as an assemblage of component subsystems which are intimately related and interdependent. The computer, therefore, has aided and supported systems thinking. In particular it has facilitated the design and utilization of complex information systems, which have required managers to formalize authority flows, information needs, and reporting relationships. Thus, the computer has affected managerial relationships in a rather direct way through its systems orientation.

THE COMPUTER AND MANAGERIAL FUNCTIONS

The functions of management are those activities in which managers typically engage. Since the most pervasive managerial function is decision making, it characterizes the managerial environment within which the organization operates. Computer-assisted decision making was discussed in Chapter 9. A closer examination of the decision-making task, however, indicates that it can be more definitively characterized as involving planning, organizing, staffing, directing, and controlling. Although these functions do not provide an exhaustive description of what the manager does, they do represent the areas most affected by the computer. Other managerial activities such as leading, communicating, and motivating are not discussed here because they have not been as dramatically influenced by the computer's presence. Since organizing involves creating structure and framework, it will be discussed in the next chapter, which is concerned with the computer's impact on the organization.

Specific examples of how the computer has affected planning and controlling were given in Chapter 2, "Business Applications of the Computer." There we discussed how the managerial processes are affected in such functional areas as manufacturing, marketing, finance, and accounting. It is worth considering, however, how the computer has resulted in alterations of managers' jobs at the various hierarchical levels in a typical business organization.

The management structure of the typical business organization has been traditionally defined as having three layers or levels, which can be referred to as lower management, middle management, and

FIGURE 12–1
The Managerial Levels

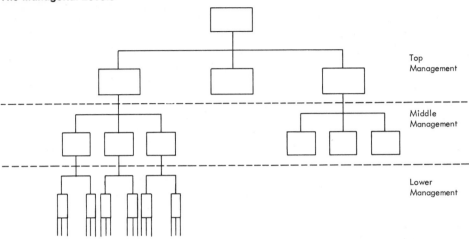

top management. As organizations experience growth and become more complex, it is increasingly difficult to distinguish between these levels of management. In general, however, the three levels may be portrayed as shown in Figure 12–1.

THE COMPUTER'S IMPACT ON LOWER MANAGEMENT

In large, complex structures, several levels of management may be encompassed within each of the three broad categories of management. In our interpretation, lower level management includes first-line supervisors or foremen. These are the individuals who represent the administrative group at the lowest possible level and who interface with the workers on a daily basis.

In order to demonstrate the impact of computers on this level, it is first necessary to clarify the nature of the work carried out by these managers. For the most part, first-line managers are concerned with the daily planning, execution, and control of the organization's work. They manage workers who carry out the most basic activities of the firm—the production of a product, sales or service, the preparation of a payroll, or other such fundamental elements of work.

With the exception of human relationship activities such as leading and motivating, the manager's task at the lower level entails making decisions of a highly programmable nature. *Highly programmable* activities are those that occur frequently, are rather homogeneous in nature, and are of routine importance. They are so repetitive, in fact, that the organization develops systematic procedures or ways of handling them. Most management decisions at the lower level are highly programmable. It should be stressed that we are using the term "programmable" in a different sense than that of programming the computer.

Because these kinds of decisions are repetitive, managers have had an incentive to develop decision rules for handling them. For example, the demand for raw materials and supplies frequently occurs at a predictable rate, and over time specific reordering quantities and times can be easily identified. The manager knows that when inventories reach a certain triggering point (the order point), he should automatically submit purchase orders. In a retail business, the manager in charge of putting prices on products has a relatively systematic procedure for calculating markups and discounts and thus engages in a highly programmable activity.

The computer has a tremendous capacity for handling routine tasks—the monitoring of inventory levels, the preparations of large payrolls, the systematization of purchase orders, or the pricing of products. Thus it facilitates the handling of highly programmable activities. Since the first-line manager is at the interface of daily organizational work, the computer can be used advantageously at this operational level.

Ever since Frederick W. Taylor introduced the concepts of scientific management,[1] managers have extended the specialization of labor, particularly at the lower level. This specialization process has resulted in the typical task being broken down into smaller and smaller parts, thus making work processes highly repetitive. The repetitive nature of a task makes it more subject to systematic analysis and simplification. As a result of these techniques, some jobs have been automated or taken over by machines, and others have been highly programmed.

The overall effect of these trends has been to reduce the amount of discretionary judgment the first-line manager must exercise on a daily basis. Since most of the decisions the manager faces at this level are of a recurring nature, unique decisions seldom have to be made. This is not to say that such situations never occur, however. Exceptions do arise which require the manager's attention, and the "exception principle" dictates that attention be devoted to these exceptional problems.

Since so much of the first-line manager's task entails highly programmed activities, the computer's use at this level is widespread. The decisions he engages in are characterized by homogeneity, repetitiveness, and volume, and thus he can effectively utilize the

---

[1] Frederick W. Taylor, *The Principles of Scientific Management* (New York: Harper & Bros., 1911).

computer's capacity for speed and accuracy. The manager's job is to supply pertinent inputs to the various computerized systems he interfaces with and then to use the computer's output to aid his daily task of short-range scheduling, establishment of work priorities, and coordination of effort. In sum, the computer takes unorganized data and generates useful information which aids the manager at this level in his planning, execution, and control functions.

Computerization seems to diminish somewhat the number of first-line supervisors because it gives a single manager the ability to handle a larger job scope, that is, an increased number of operations and activities. There is the probability, however, that staff or supportive functions are created by virtue of the computer's presence, and the ultimate impact on the total number of first-line jobs may be negligible. What is affected, therefore, is the relative mix of line versus staff managers.

It should be noted that although the computer has extended the first-line manager's capabilities, it also has created additional problems in the human sphere. As work becomes more automated and systematized, the chances for conflict and friction between people increase. The primary conflict arises in the repetitive and routine nature of the work and the employee's typical resistance to mechanized job tasks.

THE COMPUTER'S IMPACT ON MIDDLE MANAGEMENT

To discuss the impact of the computer upon middle management as if the computer existed in isolation from other technological advances is probably unfair. It is much easier, and considerably more realistic, to speak of the computer in conjunction with several other elements of technology. It has been noted, for example, that concomitant with the use of the computer in business has been the adoption of quantitative methods of analysis and decision making. Management information systems, which are usually computer based, have also had an impact upon the manager and his job.

As a consequence, an analysis of the computer's impact upon management must be taken to mean the computer and all of the attendant technology which has evolved. While this is true for management in general, it is especially applicable to the middle- and top-management levels in the organizational hierarchy, for it is at these levels that less programmed decision making takes place.

Middle-management activity can be said to be less programmed than that at lower levels. Considerably more heterogeneity characterizes the nature of middle management work; since middle managers occupy higher positions in the administrative echelon, it is

TABLE 12–1
Managerial Impacts of the Computer

Management Level Affected by Computer	Number of Companies Reporting Impact
Middle management	9
Middle and lower management	2
Middle and top management	3
Supervisors (lower management)	1
Top management	1
All levels	1

Source: Thomas L. Whisler, *The Impact of Computers on Organizations* (New York: Frederick A. Praeger, Inc., 1970), p. 83.

understandable that their work is more comprehensive, less routine in nature, less structured, and flavored with more variety. As Figure 12–1 above illustrates, middle managers are "managers of other managers."

If it can be said that work must be programmable in order to be computerized, relatively less of middle management's work is conducive to computerization. However, numerous inroads are being made into programming certain aspects of the middle manager's job. For those decisions these managers engage in that are routine or repetitive, specific decision rules can be designed to simulate the manager's decision processes with a high degree of accuracy and reliability. Thus, the computer can be instructed to take data, subject it to necessary computations, make comparisons with predefined decision criteria, and generate optimal (or acceptable) courses of action.

This sort of mechanization of the decision process, of course, applies only to those aspects of middle-management work that are highly structured. When it is used in conjunction with quantitative techniques such as mathematical programming, a considerable number of middle management decisions can be facilitated. Middle management decisions such as determining optimal inventory requirements, equipment selection, and scheduling of work lend themselves to programming. Thus the computer provides information to the middle manager which supports his decision making activities.

Considerable controversy surrounds the issue of how much impact the computer has had on middle management. It is agreed, in general, that middle management has been more affected by the computer and its technology than lower or top management has. Table 12–1 summarizes the findings of a recent study in which companies were requested to indicate which level of management had been most affected by the computer in terms of decision making. The findings indicate that the middle-management level is far more subject to computer impact than the other levels are. The precise nature of the impact, however, is at the center of the controversy.

The debate over the impact of the computer upon middle management was begun in 1958 when Harold Leavitt and Thomas L. Whisler set forth a set of predictions in their much quoted and now famous article, "Management in the 1980s." Their prognostications included the following statement pertaining to the impact of the computer upon middle-management jobs:

1. Jobs at today's middle-management level will become highly structured. Much more of the work will be programmed, i.e., covered by sets of operating rules governing the day-to-day decisions that are made.
2. A radical reorganization of middle-management levels should occur, with *certain classes* of middle-management jobs moving downward in status and compensation (because they will require less autonomy and skill), while other classes move upward into the top-management groups.
3. The line separating the top from the middle of the organization will be drawn more clearly and impenetrably than ever, much like the line drawn in the last few decades between hourly workers and first-line supervisors.[2]

Leavitt and Whisler made some additional predictions about the computer's impact on organization structure, but those will be treated in the next chapter.

The predictions of these authors forecast some interesting consequences for middle management. However, they were not alone in their speculations. In 1962, Donald Michaels anticipated that the computer would lead to mass unemployment as the "monster machine" took over the decision-making process from managers.[3] He asserted that a drastic reduction in numbers of middle managers was inevitable and that the consequences of this trend would be social unrest and a widespread feeling of dissatisfaction with work and skepticism about organizational loyalty.

According to Michaels, eventually an elite class of employees would emerge, a class much like the innovative type of personnel Leavitt and Whisler also predicted would emerge. This group would be comprised of the computer-oriented professionals who would dominate organizations as a consequence of their specialized expertise.

Most recent evidence does not suggest that the trends predicted

---

[2] Harold J. Leavitt and Thomas L. Whisler, "Management in the 1980's," *Harvard Business Review*, vol. 36 (November–December 1958), pp. 41–48.

[3] Donald N. Michaels, "Cybernation: The Silent Conquest," *Computer and Automation*, March 1962, pp. 26–42.

by Leavitt, Whisler, and Michaels are entirely accurate, although the 1980s have not yet arrived.[4] Leavitt and Whisler's projections about the highly structured nature of middle-management jobs are apparently based upon the assumption that most middle-management decision making is programmable; that is, that management decisions at this level are repetitive, routine, predictable, and amenable to specific operating decision rules. Where this is true, a machine could probably take over a considerable number of middle-management decisions. So, if a particular middle manager's primary task is to make routine decisions, the computer can probably assume many facets of his or her job. It would be inaccurate to state, however, that this is a characteristic of the typical middle manager's job. In general, the typical middle manager is confronted with numerous nonprogrammed, novel, complex decisions which are not conducive to computerization.

While the computer has tended to take over some of the average middle manager's decisions, this does not mean that it is *displacing* middle managers. More to the point, it means that the time formerly required at the middle-management level for programmable decisions will be released. Consequently, the middle manager will have more time at his disposal to engage in other management activities such as dealing with employees, motivating workers, leading, counseling, planning, or maintaining better contacts with customers. Once freed of routine tasks by the computer, the middle manager will be able to spend more time on the creative activities he ought to be doing. Thus the computer's impact, rather than making the middle manager a kind of outdated, useless functionary, should broaden his job scope and enrich his responsibilities with more meaningful work experiences.

Results of Some Studies

Research studies of the impact of computers on middle management provide evidence upon which to assess the controversy over the probable fate of middle managers. One study by Joseph Schwitter which was reported in the middle 1960s examined the impact of computers on middle management in 47 organizations. Schwitter found that there were more increases than decreases in middle managers' job scope (i.e., the range of tasks in the job) and content. In general, Schwitter reached the conclusion that middle-management jobs in the future would call for greater initiative, vision, and

---

[4] For example, see J. G. Hunt and P. F. Newell, "Management in the 1980's Revisited," *Personnel Journal*, vol. 50 (January 1971), pp. 35–43.

knowledge. Thus his study rejects the notion that middle-management jobs will become more programmed and automated.[5]

A study conducted by Donald R. Shaul confirms, in general, the study cited above. Shaul studied middle and top managers and predicted that middle managers would experience an expanded job scope. Sixty percent of the managers he interviewed stated that their experiences with electronic data processing equipment had been favorable; they could spend more time on planning activities than they could before, and they had more time to consider new opportunities. In addition, the managers interviewed indicated that they felt they made better decisions with computers, and they did not feel

TABLE 12–2
Changes in Skill Level of Jobs at Different Organizational Levels

Organizational Level	Percent of Computer-Affected Departments in Which It Is Reported That:		Percent of Reported Changes in Skill Level (Col. A) in Which Skill Went:	
	(A) Skill Changes Occurred	(B) No Skill Changes Occurred	(C) Up	(D) Down
Clerical	90	10	70	30
Supervisory	87	13	93	7
Middle management	56	44	92	8
Top management	41	59	94	6

Source: Thomas L. Whisler, *The Impact of Computers on Organizations* (New York: Frederick A. Praeger, Inc. 1970), p. 140.

their status had been lowered. Most managers also responded that their jobs had become more complex and they were using more judgment and experience in their decision-making processes.[6]

A study conducted by Thomas Whisler revealed some interesting findings pertaining to the computer's effect on job skills at different organizational levels. His findings are presented in Table 12–2. This study confirms that one certain effect upon middle management (as well as all organizational jobs) is an upgrading of the skills necessary to carry out the various job-level functions. Skill changes are most pervasive at the clerical level and diminish at each successive higher

[5] Joseph P. Schwitter, "Computer Effect upon Managerial Jobs," *Academy of Management Journal*, vol. 8 (September 1965).

[6] Donald R. Shaul, "What's Really Ahead for Middle Management?" *Personnel*, November–December 1964, pp. 8–16.

TABLE 12–3
Assessment of Predictions and Trends of Computer Impact on Management

Prediction	Leavitt and Whisler	Michaels	Chicago Seminar	Present Trends
Reduced number of total managers..............	Yes	Yes	Yes	No
Reduced number of middle managers..........	Yes	Yes	Yes	No
Emergence of elite class....................	Yes	Yes	Yes	Partially
Improved status of innovative, creative, and mathematically oriented personnel	Yes	Yes	Yes	Yes

Source: Based on J. L. Gibson et al., *Organizations: Structure, Process, and Behavior* (Dallas, Texas: Business Publications, Inc., 1973), p. 145, as adapted from J. G. Hunt and P. F. Newell, "Management in the 1980's Revisited," *Personnel Journal,* vol. 50 (January 1971), pp. 35–43.

level, and the effect in all cases is understood to be an upgrading of required job skills.[7]

A seminar held at the University of Chicago which considered the impact of the computer upon organization and management produced a number of predictions which were similar to those set forth earlier by Leavitt, Whisler, and Michaels. These predictions were assessed by J. G. Hunt and P. F. Newell. Their conclusions as to present trends compared with the various predictions are presented in Table 12–3.[8]

As the data in Table 12–3 illustrate, all of the trends and predictions concerning the computer's impact on management have not materialized. In summary, however, it can be acknowledged that middle management is a level at which computer influence has been considerably felt. The chief consequence of computerization has been to extend the middle manager's capabilities by relieving him of the necessity to make tedious, routine, programmable types of decisions.

THE COMPUTER'S IMPACT ON TOP MANAGEMENT

Many of the impacts of the computer which have been discussed so far apply to all levels in the management hierarchy. For example, the fact that the computer is an extension of the decision maker's

[7] Thomas L. Whisler, *The Impact of Computers on Organizations* (New York: Frederick A. Praeger, Inc., 1970), p. 140.

[8] Hunt and Newell, "Management in the 1980's Revisited."

capabilities rather than a replacement for him holds true at all managerial levels. Further, the relative skill mix of managers at all levels is affected by the computer's presence in the organization.

Before we can make definitive statements about the computer's impact on top management in the typical organization, we must first briefly explain what top management is and what its functions are. As was seen in Figure 12–1, top management is comprised of those individuals who occupy the major positions in the organizational pyramid. Typically, top management either refers to the president of the organization or the president and the top organizational vice presidents. In addition, the board of directors is often considered to be a part of top management. Top-management group membership will vary with the size of the firm. For purposes of discussion, top management is defined here as including the company president and vice presidents.

Top management is the major policymaking body in the typical business enterprise. This level of management makes the major decisions about the company's basic purpose—its goals. In establishing goals top management must make strategic choices as to what line of business the firm will be in, what major products or services it will sell, in what major markets it will compete, and what methods of operation will be utilized.

Because they are at the interface between the organization and the external environment, top managers have the dual responsibility of monitoring and assessing external market opportunities and relating these opportunities to the company's resources and capabilities. The decisions they make are strategic in nature—that is, they are long range in perspective and comprehensive in scope. Top managers engage in strategic long-range planning much more than middle and lower level managers do, and this is one area where the computer has assumed an important role.

In the long-range planning efforts of top managers, there are certain aspects that will be influenced by the computer and others that will be unaffected. Aspects of their jobs that are probably not affected include the determination of basic company purpose, identity, and philosophy. Neither will success in the top manager's job be directly affected, because top management is evaluated on its accomplishment of stated goals, such as profitability, organizational growth, and market share. Consequently, the fundamental task of top management is not likely to be changed by computerization.

At each successively higher level in the organization structure, a greater proportion of the manager's decisions are nonprogrammable. Figure 12–2 illustrates how the mix of programmable versus nonprogrammable decisions varies at different levels in the organization. Because top managers engage in relatively few programmable

FIGURE 12-2
Mix of Decisions in the Managerial Levels

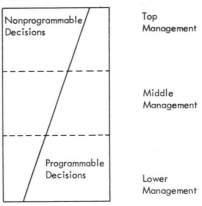

decisions, it might be concluded that the computer has limited applicability to top management. This is not entirely true. In the evolution of the computer over the past 20 years, managers have found that decisions that were once based solely upon intuition, judgment, experience, and rules of thumb can be made amenable to computer application. It is not anticipated that the point will ever be reached where there no longer exists a need for judgment and intuition. Nevertheless, experience indicates a growing sophistication in the ability to quantify decision variables that were once thought to be unquantifiable.

With the computer at his disposal, the top manager is able to simulate market conditions, project company resources, and define economic parameters so that some of the unknowns of the past become known. As mathematical models are developed which depict real-world conditions more realistically, the capabilities of the top manager are extended. For example, some managers presently have the ability to look into the future via a computer simulation of product performance. The advantage in making strategic planning decisions is obvious.

Since the groundwork for strategic top-management decisions has often been handled by middle managers, it is anticipated that the computer skill requirements for top managers will not necessarily be as great as those for middle managers. It can be postulated that the computer skill requirements for the various managerial levels are as depicted in Figure 12-3.

As time passes, and as the younger candidates for top management come to occupy the top slots, the relative skill requirements may

FIGURE 12–3
Computer Skills and Managerial Level

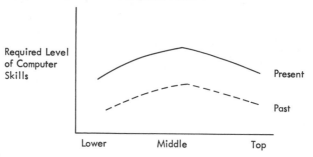

change. At the present, however, it seems that the bulk of computer expertise resides in the middle management ranks, particularly among the specialized staff group of managers.

A Disparaging View

Though the computer is employed by many top-level managers, a few chief executives today suggest that it has failed to assume a prominent role in their work. They stress that though the computer is an important business tool, it has a minimal role in meeting their informational needs. (We suggest that it has a more important role than they realize, because they receive considerable data input from middle and first-line managers who employ the computer in much of their research.) Typical of the response to computerization reported by a number of top-level executives is that of Chairman D. C. Burnham of Westinghouse Electric Corporation, who stated:

> We moved into this new building four years ago and we said, "Well, this is the computer age, when chief executives will have computer terminals and be able to push buttons to see how things are here and there." But, it hasn't come. We wired the building so I could have a computer terminal, but it has never been plugged in.[9]

Table 12–4 reports a sampling of negative statements from top-level executives regarding their use of the computer. Certainly not all executives assume this viewpoint, but as the table indicates, top-level managers from several of the country's largest firms do not view the computer as a necessity in their positions.

---

[9] "People Contact Counts More than Computers," *Business Week*, May 4, 1974, p. 80.

TABLE 12–4
Executive Comments on the Computer—The Negative Viewpoint

Executive	Title and Company	Quotation
J. F. Alibrandi	President, Whittaker Corp.	"How many executive offices have you been in lately where there's a big box behind the desk with thick IBM runs that no one has ever looked at?"
W. Thomas Beebe	Chairman, Delta Airlines, Inc.	"I haven't been in the computer room for two years."
Thomas V. Jones	Northrup Corporation, Chairman	". . . would rather talk to the people who use the computer and get their judgments."
C. Peter McColough	Chairman, Xerox Corporation	"If I see one [a printout] on my desk, I won't read it."

Source: "People Contact Counts More than Computers," *Business Week*, May 4, 1974, p. 80.

The Manager's Planning Horizon

One of the greatest changes we see in the top manager's job pertains to the information he has at his disposal, not only for strategic decisions but also for operational decisions, and not only the quantity of information but the timeliness of that information. Since the computer can quickly gather, summarize, and analyze data, top management can be apprised at a moment's notice of the daily operations of the firm, and thus can be in a position to exercise immediate control where necessary. Traditionally, the chief top-management problem has been that facts could not be assembled and summarized quickly enough to be useful for decision-making purposes. Large-scale computerized information systems have helped resolve this problem, and high-echelon managers now are able to have facts and figures at their disposal much more quickly.

This availability of information, enhanced in terms of quantity, quality, and timeliness by the computer, has a definite impact on the planning task, which takes up a significant part of executive time. The net effect of the computer's presence is to improve the quality of planning and to increase the number of time periods in the future into which managers can look. Without the computer, the planning function operates slowly, and information is delayed en route to top management. Information cannot be gathered, assimilated, and communicated as it is generated but has to filter upward, allowing successive levels of management to digest it. Thus operational reports are slow in making it to the top, and consequently top-management response time to changes is slow. As a result of this sluggish movement of information, there is usually a considerable lag time between when something happens and when management can respond—often months or years.

The effect of computer-based information systems has been to considerably shorten the time between when data are generated and when top management has information at its disposal for decision-making purposes. Furthermore, we suggest that as computerized systems further develop, it will become fairly common to gather data as it is generated (real time), condense the data into pertinent form for decision making, and communicate it to all relevant managerial levels. Hence information flow time will substantially decrease, and the executive's response time in converting plans to operations will be shortened. Thus top managers will be able to respond more quickly with timely managerial action.[10]

CONCLUDING REMARKS

The computer will continue to have a marked impact on the management of organizations—whether they be business, governmental, or educational in nature. We have discussed the effect of the computer on the management of business enterprises because it represents the most general usage. Figure 12–4 summarizes the major computer impacts at each of the managerial levels.

Although it is difficult to discuss the long-range effects of computer technology on the management of organizations, a number of short-range effects have been identified. There is no solid evidence to indicate that the numbers of managers at the various organizational levels have changed or will do so. The manner in which managers make decisions has changed, however, with programmable decisions being increasingly taken over by the computer. The computer has been seen as an extension of the manager's decision-making capabilities rather than a replacement for her or him. Aided by a systematic, analytical frame of reference, mathematical models and techniques, and an initiative to explore alternate uses of the computer, modern managers should be able to use the computer to find new, more efficient, and less time-consuming ways to accomplish their tasks. The computer is designed to complement and supplement managerial experience, intuition, and judgment, not to replace these traditional talents or traits.

Very little has been said thus far about how the computer and its attendant technology will affect managers personally. We have

---

[10] For an elaborate discussion on the impact of the computer on planning horizons see F. G. Withington, "The Long Range Effect of the Computer," in *The World of the Computer*, ed. John Diebold (New York: Random House, 1973), pp. 100–119.

FIGURE 12-4
Computer Impacts at Three Managerial Levels

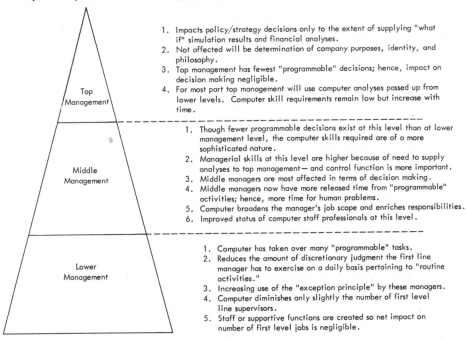

Top
Management

1. Impacts policy/strategy decisions only to the extent of supplying "what if" simulation results and financial analyses.
2. Not affected will be determination of company purposes, identity, and philosophy.
3. Top management has fewest "programmable" decisions; hence, impact on decision making negligible.
4. For most part top management will use computer analyses passed up from lower levels. Computer skill requirements remain low but increase with time.

Middle
Management

1. Though fewer programmable decisions exist at this level than at lower management level, the computer skills required are of a more sophisticated nature.
2. Managerial skills at this level are higher because of need to supply analyses to top management — and control function is more important.
3. Middle managers are most affected in terms of decision making.
4. Middle managers now have more released time from "programmable" activities; hence, more time for human problems.
5. Computer broadens the manager's job scope and enriches responsibilities.
6. Improved status of computer staff professionals at this level.

Lower
Management

1. Computer has taken over many "programmable" tasks.
2. Reduces the amount of discretionary judgment the first line manager has to exercise on a daily basis pertaining to "routine activities."
3. Increasing use of the "exception principle" by these managers.
4. Computer diminishes only slightly the number of first level line supervisors.
5. Staff or supportive functions are created so net impact on number of first level jobs is negligible.

purposely not discussed this topic because there are too many diverse personal reactions to the introduction of computers in organizations. Numerous illustrations could be given of the efforts to resist change that have focused on the computer, but this reaction is typical for all new technology. It should be expected that some resistance mechanisms will be utilized by managers as well as nonmanagers when computers are introduced into organizations. Time has told the story, however, that in most cases the benefits to management and all organizational personnel have easily exceeded the costs, both economic and personal, of computerization of the data processing function in organizations.

In the computer age management will find that it has been relieved of a considerable number of routine activities and thus is able to focus on the multitude of human, social, and political issues that increasingly plague organizations. Managers will direct their attention to problems they ought to be considering but which are ill-defined, unstructured, and heuristic in nature. These problems require experience, intuition, judgment, perception, and sensitivity — characteristics good managers must possess, even more so in the future.

ASSIGNMENTS

12-1. Why must the impact of the computer on management be considered separately from the computer's impact upon the organization? Is the distinction real or imaginary?

12-2. Some management theorists have defined the management process as decision making. Others have defined it as planning, organizing, controlling, staffing, and directing. How are these two approaches similar? Different? Which of these two approaches is more conducive to discussing the computer's role in management?

12-3. Are computer science and management science the same fields of study? How are they related? How are they different?

12-4. What are the computer's most significant benefits to management? Interview a manager (or administrator) of a business firm, a governmental agency, and an educational institution and ask this same question. If the answers differ, offer plausible reasons for the differences noted.

12-5. How can a computer simulate a manager's thought processes? What kinds of management thinking cannot be simulated by the computer?

12-6. Is the computer related to the systems approach to management? Discuss.

12-7. How do computer capabilities aid the functions of planning and control? In marketing? In production management? In financial management?

12-8. What are the various managerial levels in a typical business firm? How do they differ? How are they similar? How do these similarities or differences relate to the computer's impact on the various levels?

12-9. Differentiate between a programmable decision and a nonprogrammable decision. Give illustrations of each from your personal life experience. What is the relationship between the computer and each of these decision types?

12-10. Which level of management has been most affected by the computer? Explain.

REFERENCES

Books

Albrecht, L. K.   *Organization and Management of Information Processing Systems.* New York: Macmillan Co., 1973.

Hodge, Billy J. and Herbert J. Johnson   *Management and Organizational Behavior.* New York: John Wiley & Sons, 1970.

Martin, James and Adrian R. D. Norman *The Computerized Society.* Englewood Cliffs, N.J.: Prentice-Hall, 1970.

Parkman, Ralph *The Cybernetic Society.* New York: Pergamon Press, 1972.

Reif, W. E. *Computer Technology and Management Organization.* Iowa City: College of Business Administration, University of Iowa, 1968.

Shultz, George P. and Thomas L. Whisler *Management Organization and the Computer.* Glencoe, Ill.: Free Press, 1960.

Steiner, George A. *Top Management Planning.* London: Collier-Macmillan Limited, 1969.

Stewart, Rosemary *How Computers Affect Management.* London: Macmillan & Co., 1971.

Whisler, Thomas L. *Information Technology and Organization Change.* Belmont, Calif.: Wadsworth Publishing Co., 1970.

Whisler, Thomas L. *The Impact of Computers on Organizations.* New York: Frederick A. Praeger, 1970.

Wren, Daniel A. and Dan Voich, Jr. *Principles of Management.* New York: Ronald Press, 1968.

Articles

Carroll, Archie B. and Hugh J. Watson "The Computer's Impact Upon Management," *Managerial Planning,* May–June, 1975, pp. 5–9; 19.

Brady, R. H. "Computers in Top Level Decision Making." In *The Impact of Information Technology on Management Operation,* ed. W. C. House. Princeton, N.J.: Auerbach Publishers, 1971.

Hunt, J. G. and P. F. Newell "Management in the 1980's Revisited." *Personnel Journal,* vol. 50 (January 1971), pp. 35–43.

Karp, William "Management in the Computer Age." *Data Management,* December 1970.

Larson, Harry T. "EDP: A 20 year Ripoff," *Infosystems,* November 1974, pp. 26–30.

Leavitt, Harold J. and Thomas L. Whisler "Management in the 1980's." *Harvard Business Review,* vol. 36 (November–December 1958), pp. 41–48.

Michaels, Donald N. "Cybernation: The Silent Conquest." *Computer and Automation,* March 1962, pp. 26–42.

Moan, Floyd E. "Does Management Practice Lag behind Theory in the Computer Environment?" *Academy of Management Journal,* vol. 16, no. 1, (March 1973), p. 7.

"People Contact Counts More than Computers." *Business Week,* May 4, 1974, pp. 80–81.

Schwitter, Joseph P. "Computer Effect upon Managerial Jobs." *Academy of Management Journal,* vol. 8 (September, 1965).

Shaul, Donald R. "What's Really Ahead for Middle Management?" *Personnel,* November–December 1964, pp. 8–16.

Organizational Structure and Technology

Organizational Location of the Computer

Location 1: Accounting or Payroll Department, Location 2: Specific Operating Department, Location 3: An Independent Department

Organization of the Data Processing Function

Span of Control and Levels of Management

Departmental Impacts and Alterations

Creation of New Departments, Elimination of Old Departments, Modification of Existing Departments

Line versus Staff Authority of the Computer Department

The Centralization-Decentralization Issue

Bases for Examining the Issue, Determining the Extent of Centralization

Preparing for Organizational Change

Assignments

References

Whereas the previous chapter surveyed the computer's impact on management, this chapter concerns its impact on the organization. It introduces the organizational location decision, span-of-control impacts, departmental impacts, and the important issue of centralization versus decentralization. The case study in Appendix D should be studied and analyzed after you have completed this chapter.

13

The Impact of the Computer on the Organization

The computer and its attendant technology have had a vast influence on managerial processes and organizational structure, and they will continue to do so. The preceding chapter examined selected issues pertaining to the computer's impact on management and decision making at various managerial levels. This chapter will discuss the computer's influence on the organization. A number of attributes of organization will be examined, including the organizational structure and technology, organizational location of the computer, and organization of the data processing function. In addition, the following computer impacts will be studied: span of control and levels of management, departmental impacts and alterations, line versus staff authority departmentation, and the centralization-decentralization issue. The chapter will conclude with a brief discussion of preparation for organizational change.

ORGANIZATIONAL STRUCTURE AND TECHNOLOGY

It might at first appear that there is no need to define organizational structure, but experience indicates that organizations and organizational structure have different meanings for different people. Depending upon one's outlook and experience, organizations can be perceived in a considerable number of different ways. Economists, accountants, sociologists, or behavioral scientists would perceive an organization's structure in different lights, based upon their interpretation of how and why the organization evolved in the way it did. In addition, each might feel that his particular speciality had had an especially profound impact upon the organization.

Organizational structure can be defined as the pattern of relationships existing between people within the context of an organizational

323

system. This pattern of relationships may be viewed in pictorial form in an organization chart such as Figure 12–1 in the preceding chapter. In business terms, the organizational structure illustrates the formal authority relationships, reporting flows, and communication patterns that management feels will be optimal for accomplishing the goals of the organization. Thus, when we refer to the computer's impact upon organizational structure, we are referring to the structural decisions of management which are influenced by its presence in the organization.

It should be made clear at the outset that the computer is a technological advancement, like many others that have influenced organizations. Technology may mean new machinery, as in the case of automated assembly lines which make up the heart of our mass production society, or new knowledge and techniques which may not themselves be physical pieces of equipment, such as new skills, mental processes, knowledge of the universe, and so on. The computer might be said to be technology which represents both of these; it is equipment and machinery, but it also has fostered a new way of thinking (i.e., total systems concepts).

History suggests many examples of how new technology has required organizational adaption. The railroads, air transportation, the telephone, assembly-line production techniques, and the space program have all involved new technologies which have had tremendous organizational repercussions. The computer and its peripheral equipment are just another in a long procession of technological advancements which require organizational adaptation of structure and process.

The computer is not unique in its impact on organizations, but it is of recent vintage compared to some other technological advances. It is suggested, consequently, that as you study computers you should be aware of the parallels between computer impact and other technological impacts on organizations, processes, and people. This should make you appreciate more fully that the computer is but one link—although an extremely important one—in the chain of technological progress.

ORGANIZATIONAL LOCATION OF THE COMPUTER

One of the most specific impacts the computer has had on organizational structure pertains to the position it occupies in the organizational framework. As all other organizational activities, it must have a place in the scheme of things. The location it occupies is to a large extent an indication of how the computer is viewed by management.

Three alternative organizational locations of the computer are worth examining: the computer may be located in the accounting or payroll department, subsumed under a specific operating department, or exist as an independent department which operates on the same level as the other major departments of the organization. Though these three locations do not necessarily exhaust all the possible places within the organizational framework in which the computer may be positioned, they do represent the three most general cases.

Location 1: Accounting or Payroll Department

Historically, the computer was frequently placed in the accounting or payroll department of the organization, and it has characteristics that help explain this placement. The initial applications of the computer were often in the payroll or perhaps bookkeeping department. Since these departments typically deal with financial data in mass quantities, the computer "felt at home" in this organizational location (see Figure 13–1).

The accounting department has also been a natural location for housing the computer. Even today many organizations choose to retain it in the accounting, finance, or controller's department. The advantages of handling financial transactions in a central location are great, and this logic argues that the computer should be located "where the data are," so to speak.

Though this location does have the advantage of physical proximity to data, a likely drawback is the parochial viewpoint that could be

FIGURE 13–1
Data Processing within Accounting Department

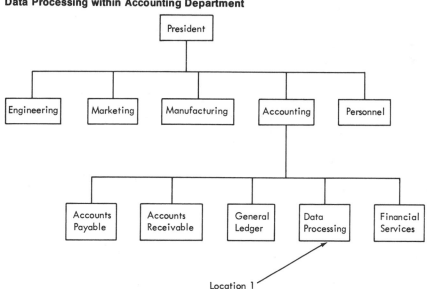

engendered which might limit possible alternate uses of the computer for the rest of the organization. If caution is not exercised by management, the computer could easily become self-serving to the interests of the accounting, payroll, or finance departments. In addition, the development of alternative uses and applications may be stifled if the computer is not readily accessible to other departments. When it is under the authority of the accounting or payroll department manager, other departments might be deterred from finding ways to use it. The net effect would be that the computer would have limited applications and uses in the organization and would directly affect only the department in which it is located.

Though some organizations do maintain their computer facilities within the accounting, payroll, or finance departments today, indications are that this type of location is becoming less prevalent.

Location 2: Specific Operating Department

The second location the computer frequently assumes is in some specific operating department of the organization other than the accounting or payroll-type departments mentioned in location 1. Actually, location 1 is just a special case of location 2, but it has been a frequent one. A good example of location 2 would be placing a computer in the policyholder service department of a large insurance company, as illustrated in Figure 13–2.

FIGURE 13–2
Data Processing within a Specific Operating Department

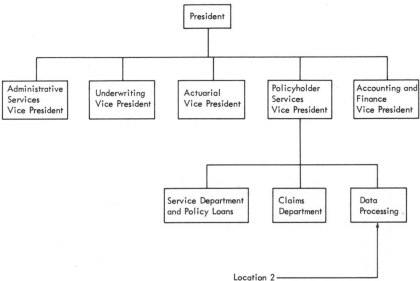

The policyholder service department in this company is the dominant user of the computer, and it can readily be seen why it would be located there. From a broad organizational point of view, the chief disadvantage of this setup can also be easily seen. The computer in this instance is likely being used in a suboptimal fashion. While it may be providing a necessary benefit to the particular department in which it is housed, the total organization is not receiving all the advantages it has to offer.

It is natural that in this type of location the tendency will be for the policyholder service department to place higher priorities on its own work than on the work of other user departments or of the company as a whole. The host department in this case will receive favorable treatment, and it is likely that there will be a reluctance to employ the computer in a decision-support role which is foreign to policyholder service work.

Location 3: An Independent Department

One of the most enlightened organizational positions for the computer locates it independent of but equal to the operating departments of the organization. Figure 13–3 illustrates this independent but equal status on a typical organization chart. In this position, the data processing manager reports to top management of the organization. Placing the computer department in a status equal with other departments recognizes the units neutrality and independence from other groups in the organization.

At this level the data processing manager is considered a high-level executive in his own right. He is at a policymaking level where he can exercise considerable influence over the long-range role of computer systems in the organization. From this perspective he can assure that decisions are made in the interest of the entire organization rather than favoring an individual operating department. Though some of

FIGURE 13–3
Data Processing as an Independent Department

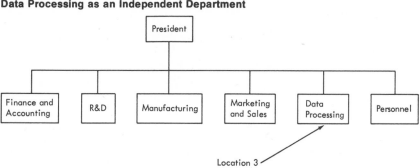

the organization's departments will doubtless receive higher priorities for their applications, it is more' likely that the decision will be made on the basis of overall organizational needs.

One caveat worth mentioning with respect to this third location of the computer is the possibility that the computer will be placed in such a position that it becomes an end in itself. Although this is not likely on a large scale, it is possible that particular computer activities will become ends in themselves if careful scrutiny is not given to them. Cautious and continuous systems analysis should prevent this kind of diversion from organizational goals, however.

The acid test of the computer's use and position in the organization will be top management's attitude toward it. Placing the computer department in a prominent and visible location such as location 3 makes explicit top management's recognition of its critical role and position. The organization should be expected to profit from the status and availability of the computer in this location. In the final analysis, however, the success of the firm's computer-based activities will not be primarily contingent upon the computer facility's location in the organizational structure. Location is only one factor which can help determine the success of computerization, albeit an important factor. Management must create and support an environment which is conducive to dynamic growth in the computer's role and influence.

ORGANIZATION OF THE DATA PROCESSING FUNCTION

In addition to the location of data processing in the organization, another relevant issue is the organizational structure of the data processing department itself. The topic of what structural arrangements should be employed within the data processing department is a highly specialized subject, and the authority and labor-division relationships that can exist between people in a data processing organization take numerous forms.

Thomas Gildersleeve suggests that the data processing function can be organized into four types: (1) application organization, (2) functional organization, (3) project-functional, and (4) project-staff.[1] A slightly different schema is set forth by Frederic G. Withington, who suggests the pooled organization, functional organization, and project organization.[2] Each of these is an organizational arrangement that may be found effective, depending upon the size, mission, and

---

[1] Thomas R. Gildersleeve, "Organizing the Data Processing Function," *Datamation*, November 1974, pp. 46–50.

[2] Frederic G. Withington, *The Organization of the Data Processing Function* (New York: Wiley-Interscience, 1972), pp. 11–33. Withington provides a number of excellent illustrations of representative data processing organizations on pages 81–96.

FIGURE 13–4
Organization Chart for a Typical Data Processing Department

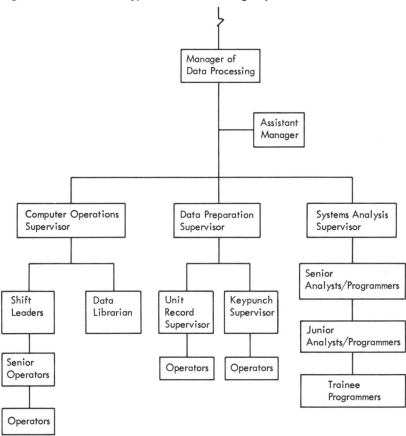

philosophical orientation of the organization and its management. If you are interested in the management of a data processing component of a larger organization, you should study these two sources. Here we only want to demonstrate the organizational considerations that must be examined by management and to make the distinction between the location of the department *within* the parent organization as contrasted to the organization *of* the department clear. Figure 13–4 presents an organization chart of a typical data processing department.

SPAN OF CONTROL AND LEVELS OF MANAGEMENT

By considering the computer's impact on the span of control and the number of levels of management simultaneously, we can demon-

FIGURE 13–5
Span of Control and Levels of Management

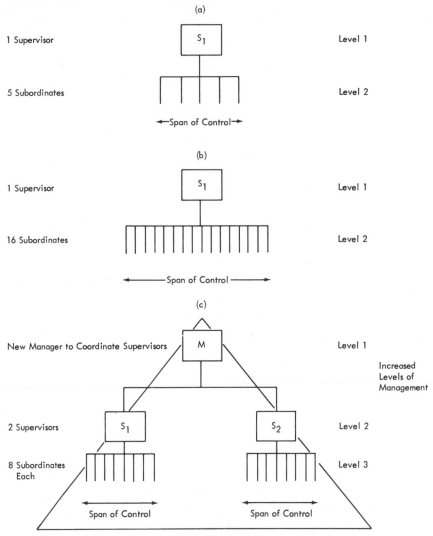

(a)

1 Supervisor S_1 Level 1

5 Subordinates   Level 2

←—Span of Control—→

(b)

1 Supervisor S_1 Level 1

16 Subordinates   Level 2

←————Span of Control————→

(c)

New Manager to Coordinate Supervisors   M   Level 1

                                                                                                      Increased
                                                                                                      Levels of
                                                                                                      Management

2 Supervisors S_1 S_2 Level 2

8 Subordinates   Level 3
Each

Span of Control   Span of Control

strate how the organization's shape or configuration has been affected by the computer's presence. A manager's *span of control* (also
called span of management) refers to the number of subordinates he
can effectively supervise. As an organization grows, the manager's
span of control typically widens to a point beyond which he can no
longer effectively manage—because there are too many subordinates
reporting to him.

When this point is reached, his managerial job will have to be divided, usually into two parts. As this growth process continues, additional *levels of management* are eventually created, and scalar growth occurs. For example, assume that a supervisor initially had five subordinates reporting to him. As the organization grows, he eventually has 16 subordinates reporting to him. Since his mental and physical capabilities are limited, management decides to divide his job into two parts, thus creating two supervisory positions with a span of eight subordinates each. At a higher level it may then become necessary to create a new managerial position to coordinate the activities of the two supervisors, and a new level of management is created. Figure 13–5 illustrates how these change processes affect the organizational structure.

Thus the span of control characterizes the horizontal dimension of the organization, and the number of levels characterizes the vertical dimension of the organization. It can be seen from the triangle imposed on part c of the figure why the typical organization structure is said to be pyramidal in shape.

Probably one of the most dramatic speculations concerning the computer's impact on organization structure was that made by Harold Leavitt and Thomas Whisler in their "1980s" article, discussed in Chapter 12.[3] They predicted the virtual disappearance of the middle-management part of the structure, so that the organization structure would look much like a football balanced on top of a bell, rather than a pyramid (see Figure 13–6).

This structure is, of course, in radical contrast to the organizational pyramid created by the conventional span of control and scalar growth process. However, very little evidence exists to indicate that this kind of effect actually results from the computer's impact upon organizations. In fact, the sparse research data available on this subject, data reported by Whisler himself in 1970,[4] reveal relatively few changes in span of control and number of organizational levels. The evidence indicates that only slight changes in the number of levels of management are brought about, usually in the direction of slightly decreasing the number of levels. A research study conducted by Whisler found both decreases and increases in the number of levels in insurance companies, but the number of decreases was over double the number of increases. About all we can conclude from this is that if any changes in the number of levels are to occur, they will more likely mean a reduction in the number of levels. This could be due to the increased span of control made possible by the computer.

---

[3] Harold J. Leavitt and Thomas L. Whisler, "Management in the 1980's," *Harvard Business Review*, vol. 36 (November–December 1958), pp. 41–48.

[4] Thomas L. Whisler, *The Impact of Computers on Organizations* (New York: Frederick A. Praeger, Inc., 1970).

FIGURE 13–6
Bell-Football Organization Structure

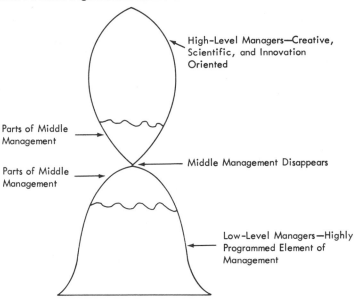

High–Level Managers—Creative,
Scientific, and Innovation
Oriented

Parts of Middle
Management

Parts of Middle
Management

Middle Management Disappears

Low–Level Managers—Highly
Programmed Element of
Management

The ongoing processes of organizational change make it almost impossible to determine what the true impact of the computer is on structure. Since organizational growth or decline is constantly taking place, it is difficult to assess which changes are brought about by the computer's presence and which ones occur because of these organizational changes. In addition, the organizational effects felt during a computer installation period might vary from the effects that will be brought about after the computer has been installed and everyday operations have resumed.[5]

Numerous factors affect an organization's span of control, such as similarity of functions, proximity of subordinates, complexity of work, and coordination requirements of subordinates. It is extremely difficult to isolate one factor and determine its effect on span of control. Research conducted by Whisler, however, seems to indicate that some small effect on span of control is caused by the computer.

In an examination of insurance company departments Whisler found that organization charts exhibited a decrease in the span of control when computers were introduced in 40 percent of the cases examined, and an increase in span of control in 31 percent of the cases,

---

[5] For an excellent analysis of the computer's impact relative to organizational growth, see C. F. Gibson and R. L. Nolan, "Managing the Four Stages of EDP Growth," *Harvard Business Review*, January–February 1974, pp. 76–88.

with no change occurring 29 percent of the time.[6] This is not conclusive evidence that the computer will have a predictable impact on span of control; unfortunately, too many variables affect span of control to make it possible to single out the computer as a cause of a specific kind of alteration. As time passes, however, more conclusive evidence may become available on the computer's impact in this sphere.

Whisler is not the first to predict that the organizational pyramid structure would disappear, "crumble," or change shape as the consequence of newly induced variables such as the computer. However, little present evidence exists to indicate that such variables have the potency to alter the traditional organizational shape. For the time being, and at least into the foreseeable future, the conventional organizational configuration is likely to withstand pressures for major change in a most stubborn fashion. A possible exception might be the project management or task force arrangements which have been used with success in a few industries amenable to this kind of structure. In general, however, it was not because of the computer's presence that these organizational accommodations were made.

DEPARTMENTAL IMPACTS AND ALTERATIONS

Since there is a limit to the number of subordinates a manager can effectively supervise, organizations have had to employ the concept of *departmentation*, or the grouping of employees into departments of manageable size. The typical organization chart demonstrates that companies have chosen to create departments based upon different common denominators, so that departmentation may be on a functional, territorial, or product basis.

Regardless of the basis, there is evidence that introduction of the computer has affected company departments in several ways. These include (1) the creation of new departments, (2) the elimination of old departments, and (3) the modification of existing departments.[7]

Creation of New Departments

The creation of new departments as a consequence of computerization is understandable, since organizational units often must be established to "house" the computer and its peripheral equipment, along with personnel and other associated resources. The introduction of a computer into a large organization might create the need for

---

[6] Whisler, *Impact of Computers on Organization,* p. 53.

[7] For a more elaborate discussion of these alterations and data reporting actual findings, see Whisler, *Impact of Computers on Organizations,* pp. 57–63.

specific departments such as data processing, systems analysis and design, keypunch and tape operations, and programming. Such additions represent major commitments by the managers of organizations, and they cannot take the addition of new departments lightly.

Considerable thought must go into the organizing decision which determines the particular authority, information, and reporting flows that will exist *within* the computer area, and also with respect to the computer area vis-à-vis the rest of the organization's departments. This is the basic location decision discussed in the first part of the chapter.

Elimination of Old Departments

It may also become necessary, as a consequence of the computer's introduction, to eliminate existing departments. For the most part, this organizational "pruning" process will be necessary only when a department becomes obsolete, such as a department that had been using outdated tabulating machines and processes. In reality, however, people or departments are seldom eliminated. Rather, their role usually changes, or departments are modified.

Modification of Existing Departments

Whereas the elimination of old departments probably represents the extreme of departmental alterations, modification of existing departments is commonplace when the computer is introduced. These modifications take place in a number of ways, one of the most common being the transfer of certain data processing activities. If a new computerized data processing department is created, for example, there will likely be a transfer of data processing activities from existing departments into the new one. The reason for these transfers, of course, is the many advantages that are available through the aggregation and consolidation of computer-associated activities in one central location. As a consequence of this transfer of responsibilities, it is possible that remaining departments will become so small they must be consolidated or merged with other departments. Other departmental alterations that may occur are splits and reorganizations within departments.

The particular departmentation approach management chooses to employ with regard to the computer is a critical organizational decision. Essentially, it represents the division-of-labor choice made by management in an effort to ensure effectiveness and efficiency in the computer function. Although this may at first appear an easy decision to make, it frequently is quite complicated. Any effort to introduce change into an organization is bound to meet systematic resistance from those affected or those who perceive they will be affected; in this case, jurisdictional disputes among departments are likely to occur. If departmentation decisions are made only after all of the factors impinging on the decision have been considered, disputes and conflicts can be minimized.

LINE VERSUS STAFF AUTHORITY OF THE COMPUTER DEPARTMENT

With respect to the departmentation decision, another important question can be raised. In a sense this is simply an elaboration on specific aspects of the computer location decision, which was introduced in the first part of the chapter. The question concerns what kind of authority will be granted to the computer department in the organizational structure, and it pertains to the nature of authority relationships — the issue of line versus staff.

Although much confusion and disagreement exist in this area, the basic concepts of line versus staff are clear. *Line departments* are usually defined as those that have an explicit and direct responsibility for accomplishing the objectives of the organization. *Staff departments,* on the other hand, are usually defined as those that help the line departments in the accomplishment of organizational goals. Therefore, staff departments are supportive in nature.

In the typical manufacturing firm, for example, production would be termed a line function, as would sales. These departments deal directly with the manufacture and sale of the firm's products. Such activities as personnel, accounting, and data processing are termed staff departments. It may not seem to matter whether a department is called line or staff, since these names simply describe what the departments have to do with the firm's major objectives. Where it does matter, however, is in the kind of *authority* emanating out of line and staff departments. Since line departments are the major ones, their authority is usually absolute, whereas the authority emanating out of a staff department is really not authority at all but advisory or consultation rights.

Therein lies the problem; if the computer department is labeled a staff function, it is viewed as supportive in nature — a service department. Service departments are often viewed with such connotations as supportive, auxiliary, or, in general, second class. Although management may not intend to view these departments as secondary in importance, frequently the treatment they receive indicates that this is the case.

We maintain that the role played by a data processing or computer department should not be viewed as secondary in importance. To a great extent, a computer department provides the coordinating mechanism whereby the firm can continue to operate effectively. Information requirements are so great in the typical organization today that the success of the central computing department or computerized information system to a great extent will dictate the success of the organization — regardless of its objectives. Even though the computer facility does assume a service role as a facilitator of information provision, we do not think it should be viewed in a secondary light. Indeed, the information and control needs of the typical business firm, which can be largely met by the computer, are two of the most important functions determining organizational success.

To qualify the idea that service functions carry little authority and are advisory and supportive in nature, some enlightened managers have adopted the concept of *functional authority*. Functional authority allocates to a staff department the final authority over a decision which falls within the realm of its departmental expertise. For example, a centralized data processing department would be given the authority to stipulate the particular forms to be used or reporting requirements to which other departments must adhere. This authority would recognize the need for data to be reported and processed in uniform ways to facilitate decision making and control. With such authority, the staff manager would have decision-making rights over other line managers with respect to certain specific decisions. Functional authority has problems, of course, the most obvious being the conflict that may result from line and staff jurisdictional disputes. However, there are advantages that can accrue to the firm through the proper use of functional authority.

Another line versus staff effect that will manifest itself in the organizational structure is the relative mix of line and staff departments. With the increasing specialization of knowledge, more staff departments are appearing on the typical organization chart. There are many managerial implications of this trend. The potential for line and staff authority conflict increases, allocation of resources becomes a source of friction, control of administrative overhead costs is an issue, and the debate over centralization or decentralization of organizational functions is heightened. We will not discuss all these here, but the centralization-decentralization question receives further consideration in the section below.

In general, it must be said that technological advances like the computer have caused a kind of "blurring" of the distinction that was once clear between line and staff departments. As increased specialization occurs in the form of specific departments within organizations, this clear-cut distinction will diminish. The business environment is becoming more complex, and organizations are becoming increasingly dependent on highly specialized operations. Thus it is increasingly more awkward and unrealistic to argue that line departments, as they have been traditionally defined, are more important than staff departments. Without the expertise of such critical staff departments as data processing, long-range planning, research and development, market research, industrial relations, and many others, most firms could not survive in today's competitive business environment.

THE CENTRALIZATION – DECENTRALIZATION ISSUE

One of the most controversial issues in the debate over the computer's impact upon management and organization involves the trends toward centralization or decentralization in organizations. *Centralization* means bringing together into a central location certain organizational activities or authority over these activities. *Decentralization* refers to moving activities away from a central location (frequently high up in the organization) and dispersing them throughout the organization. Numerous observers have argued both sides of these issues; one school sees trends toward centralization, and another sees trends toward decentralization. It is possible that they are both correct, but neither has specified very clearly to which aspects of computers they are referring. Frequently they use the term "the computer" as if it specifies clearly the activities to which reference is being made.

Bases for Examining the Issue

We suggest examining the centralization-decentralization issue by considering three distinct dimensions of the computer's relationship to organizations:

1. Where the data are *stored* in the organization.
2. Where *processing* of the data takes place.
3. Where *decision making* occurs.

Examining each of these dimensions makes it possible to identify centralization-decentralization trends more precisely.

Where Data Are Stored. When we discuss where data are stored in the organization, we are referring to the physical location of the data used in compiling reports, supporting decision making, and so on. Before computers, data were typically stored where they were used. Some data were kept in (or routed to) a central location – such as data necessary to compile annual profit and loss statements, balance sheets, and other company reports. Other data which were used by various operating divisions of the firm – marketing, engineering, production, personnel, research and development – were typically stored by the users of the data. For example, the production department might keep extensive data on inventory—inventory master file, transaction records, filled orders, back orders, and re-order points, and these data would be housed in the production department.

After the computer became available, the trend was to large centralized data bases, with use of secondary storage media such as magnetic disks and drums and the development of data base management systems. Computer economics and technological advances are the primary reasons for this move toward centralized data bases. Managers can access these data through a number of ways, so all they have to keep in their own departments are operating data which for one reason or another are not centrally stored. In terms of where the data are stored, the trend has been from decentralization to centralization employing a centralized data base.

Where Data Are Processed.   When we discuss where data are processed, we are in effect asking where the central processing unit (CPU) is located. Before computers became available, some data were processed centrally, but most were processed where they were located—dispersed throughout the organization. Computers made processing capability available in a centralized location. The advent of minicomputers now has made it possible for some computerized processing to take place on a decentralized basis. In addition, "intelligent terminals" now locate processing away from the mainframe computer. A remote intelligent terminal has processing capabilities that permit some of the menial tasks (e.g., error detection, data editing) to be handled in the decentralized location of the terminal. As in any other system, however, careful planning and thought must go into the decision to employ intelligent terminals.[8]

With recent hardware developments, therefore, data are processed in a central location, to the extent that data are there. But data are processed on a decentralized basis if gains are possible from minicomputers, which may or may not be linked to the main computer.

Where Decision Making Occurs.   This crucial issue in the centralization-decentralization debate is frequently neglected. Before computers some decision making did take place on a centralized basis, but the trend was for decisions to be made where the data were. This meant that, particularly in large companies where timeliness is crucial, decisions had to be made by the managers closest to the data. No capability existed for the kind of data summarization and analysis that is possible today, and top managers did not have access to data in a single place. Consequently, top managers had little

---

[8] For an excellent discussion see R. B. Ritchie, "Intelligent Terminals and Distributed Processing," *Computer Decisions*, February 1975, pp. 36–40.

choice but to let decision making take place where the data were gathered, in dispersed parts of the organization.

With the advent of the computer, it became feasible to bring into one location the previously dispersed data for decision making. From a feasibility perspective, central management was able to do something they could not prior to computerization—have access to data upon which decision making could be based. The important gain made available by this was that management now could have access to data from across functional departments for decision-making purposes.

The factor of economics also encouraged the centralization of decision making. In order to achieve the full potency of a computerized system, it was necessary to develop a centralized, comprehensive data base. If cost were no factor, each operating department could develop its own system, but the parallel costs with such an arrangement would make the computer system clearly uneconomical. Therefore, the tendency toward centralizing the data base was in part a response to the exorbitant costs of redundant systems spread throughout the organization. Centralized locations for aggregating data for decision making are logical, particularly from a cost standpoint.

Operating managers were led to believe that centralization was simply an economically necessary move which would make all data available to all managers. In some cases they failed to see the loss of control which would inevitably occur with the centralization of the data bank; in others, they saw it coming but had little power to prevent it, since it was necessary from a cost point of view. What happened was that when top management had all of this previously unavailable data at its fingertips, they could make more of the operating decisions that once were made at lower levels. Thus the level of decision making rose in the organization as a consequence of the computer's introduction.

As later generation computers have become available, in particular with the advent of terminal access to data bases, a trend toward decentralized decision making has occurred. Managers in decentralized parts of the organization now have instantaneous access to centrally stored data, and decentralized types of decisions are occurring with increasing frequency. Figure 13–7 provides a summary of this discussion.

Determining the Extent of Centralization

In the final analysis, the extent to which an organization is centralized or decentralized will be determined by top-management philosophy, tempered by its experiences, successes, and failures in the area. Varying industries and companies within industries have had radically different experiences with this issue. Basically, there

FIGURE 13–7
Impact of Computers on Centralization and Decentralization: Summary of Trends

		With Computers		
Issue	*Before Computers*	*Before Terminals*	*With Terminals*	*With Minis*
Where the data are *stored*	Largely decentralized	Largely centralized	Largely centralized	Largely centralized
Where the data are *processed*	Largely decentralized	Largely centralized*	Largely centralized	Centralized/ decentralized
Where *decision making* occurs	Largely decentralized	Largely centralized	Decentralized	Decentralized

* See the discussion on intelligent terminals in the text.

are a large number of options on the centralization continuum from which management can choose, and there are many advantages and disadvantages of each one. Management may wish to centralize some decisions and not others, or centralize some functions and not others. Quality, quantity, time, and cost considerations of data processing may dictate different approaches in different decision areas.

Large, complex, multidivision firms, for example, have found it necessary to create computer or data processing components within each main division, while retaining a centralized computer division. Figure 13–8 illustrates the decentralized computer units on the same chart with the centralized data processing unit. Such a system becomes necessary as an organization grows and its information processing needs become complex. In large firms it is not uncommon for individual divisions to have their own computer and data processing facilities, as well as systems analysts, programmers, and other key computer personnel.

In general, it is risky to say that either highly centralized or highly decentralized organizational structures will achieve optimal computer usage. Many firms have gone overboard in their moves toward either extreme, and the consequences have been disappointing. Among the many factors which must be considered are the following:

1. Implications for the development of managerial personnel.
2. Uniformity of company policy.
3. Economic size of the firm.
4. History of the enterprise.
5. The firm's stage in its information systems evolution (see Chapter 10).
6. Managerial philosophy.
7. Necessity for control.
8. Environmental influences (the nature of the task environment the firm faces).

FIGURE 13–8
Multidivision Organization with Various Computer Facilities

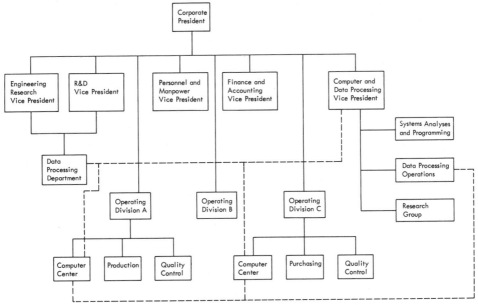

A final point deserves special mention. In a recent analysis of the centralization-decentralization issue and its relation to organizational structure, Daniel Robey suggests that the important dimension of the organization's task environment has been typically neglected and concludes that "under stable conditions, computers tend to reinforce centralization . . . under dynamic conditions, computers reinforce decentralization."[9] His most important point, however, is that "we may regard computerized, information technology as a flexible mechanism which can facilitate either form of structure (decentralized or centralized) depending on the more basic requirements which the task environment imposes."[10]

Thus it is difficult to generalize on the issue of whether centralization or decentralization trends dominate. A contingency approach is recommended whereby management makes the decision based upon the particulars of its own situation. Some choice on the continuum can be exercised, and the degree of centralization or decentralization is more a matter of managerial discretion and judgment than it is the computer causing either one of these two conditions to occur.

---

[9] Daniel Robey, "Computers and Organization Structure: A Review and Appraisal of Empirical Studies," paper presented at the national meeting of the Academy of Management, 1974, p. 19.

[10] Ibid., p. 15.

PREPARING FOR ORGANIZATIONAL CHANGE

Computers are only one of the many variables that affect organizations. One statement we can make with a great degree of certainty is that organizations are not static structures but on the contrary are continuously adapting to new technology. Organizational life is composed of dynamic relationships between people performing activities necessary to accomplish goals, and people, ideas, and technologies impinging on the organization in a multitude of ways.

Managers no longer debate the inevitability of change. In fact, their discussions of the present and the future center on the topic of planned change — how to bring about change in an orderly, systematic fashion. One topic which provides considerable food for thought is the computer — present and future uses, applications, implications for management, and impacts on organizations, people, and decision making. We have not discussed every conceivable impact of computers on organizations in this chapter; indeed the topic merits several books in itself. However, you now should have a better understanding of the role the computer plays in the organization and some of its effects. It is helpful to develop an expertise in programming and other technical skills, but from a managerial perspective it is more important to gain an appreciation of how the computer aids decision making and how it affects organizations. When you understand how it affects people and organizations, you should be able to begin to comprehend the monumental task of preparing for organizational change — for this is what the computer and computer technology inevitably bring.

ASSIGNMENTS

13-1. In what ways is there a similarity between the computer's impact on organizations and the telephone's impact on organizations? What differences are there?

13-2. Analyze the organization charts of several firms. Find out why the data processing department was placed where it was.

13-3. Why is the computer commonly located in the accounting departments of organizations? Discuss the merits of such an organizational location.

13-4. Which of the three alternative locations of the computer would probably be best for an insurance company? A university? A local city government?

13-5. What line-staff conflicts might result from locating the computer facility as a staff unit reporting to top management?

13-6. Are there any drawbacks to locating the computer as an independent department equal to the so-called "line" departments? Advantages?

13-7. How important is it that the manager of a computer installation of a corporation be in a major policymaking position?

13-8. How are span of control and the levels of management affected by the computer?

13-9. Evaluate the departmental impacts discussed in the chapter in terms of their likelihood of occurrence in a highly decentralized form of organization.

13-10. How important is the line versus staff authority issue in the determination of a computer's impact on an organization?

13-11. Discuss how functional authority can be used by managers of data processing departments. In what specific decisions might they want functional authority?

13-12. In what ways can it be said that the computer causes a kind of blurring of the traditional distinction between line and staff?

13-13. Is centralization or decentralization the most logical trend in organizations, as a consequence of computer availability? Discuss.

REFERENCES

Books

Gibson, James L., John M. Ivancevich, and James H. Donnelly, Jr. *Organizations: Structure, Processes, Behavior.* Dallas, Tex.: Business Publications, 1973.

Hodge, Billy J. and Herbert J. Johnson *Management and Organizational Behavior.* New York: John Wiley & Sons, 1970.

Kanter, Jerome *Management-Oriented Management Information Systems.* Englewood Cliffs, N.J.: Prentice-Hall, 1972.

Meyers, Charles A. (ed.) *The Impact of Computers on Management.* Cambridge, Mass.: M.I.T. Press, 1967.

Shultz, George P. and Thomas L. Whisler *Management Organization and the Computer.* Glencoe, Ill.: Free Press, 1960.

Stewart, Rosemary *How Computers Affect Management.* London: Macmillan & Co., 1971.

Whisler, Thomas L. *The Impact of Computers on Organizations.* New York: Frederick A. Praeger, 1970.

Whisler, Thomas L. *Information Technology and Organization Change.* Belmont, Calif.: Wadsworth Publishing Co., 1970.

Withington, Frederic G. *The Organization of the Data Processing Function.* New York: Wiley-Interscience, 1972.

Withington, **Frederic G.**   *The Use of Computers in Business Organizations.* Reading, Mass.: Addison-Wesley Publishing Co., 1971.

Articles

Gibson, **C. F.** and **R. L. Nolan**   "Managing the Four Stages of EDP Growth." *Harvard Business Review*, January–February 1974, pp. 76–88.

Gildersleeve, **Thomas R.**   "Organizing the Data Processing Function." *Datamation*, November 1974, pp. 46–50.

Klatzky, **S. R.** "Automation, Size, and the Locus of Decision Making: The Cascade Effect." *Journal of Business* vol. 43, no. 2 (April 1970), pp. 141–51.

Wagner, **L. G.**   "Computers, Decentralization, and Corporate Control." *California Management Review* vol. 9, no. 2 (Winter 1966).

Computers in the Nonbusiness World

Applications in Education. Health and Medical Applications, Applications in Government, Other Societal Applications

Computers and the Individual

Effects of Automation of Work Processes, The Issue of Privacy, Human Values and Individualism

Concluding Remarks

Assignments

References

Computers interface with society in a number of ways. There are numerous nonbusiness applications of computers which can be of benefit to society. The computer also affects the individual in a myriad of ways. The intent of this final chapter is to bring into focus some of the general societal applications, and issues of which you, as a student of business administration, should be aware.

14 Computers and Society

While students of business and management are most directly concerned with business applications and uses of the computer, the implications of computerization are much further reaching. The computer has numerous nonbusiness uses, and the effects of computerization have been felt in many aspects of society.

The individual born into today's society is immediately exposed to computerization; computers record births, monitor patient conditions, and regulate hospital stays. The college student who has not yet held a full-time job has been served or affected by the computer in a number of ways—college admission procedures, class registration, computer-scored examinations, library check-out procedures, football seating determinations, fee collections, medical records, and so on. In our technological society the computer touches everyone in numerous ways. One of the purposes of this chapter is to discuss some of these nonbusiness applications.

The role of the computer in the future will be increasingly important in the everyday life of the citizen. Already certain issues are taking shape as controversies which are likely to be subject to considerable debate. Though the computer as we know it is just over two decades old, a number of societal implications are coming into clear perspective.

One of these areas is the relationship between computers and work. Work is an integral aspect of life in our society because much social status derives from a person's working position. The most obvious issues in the social concern over the computer's impact on work are the implications of automation and computerization on work life. The automation issue will be examined briefly, with special consideration given to the computer's impact on employment.

One of the most sensitive issues emerging from computerization concerns privacy. With the proliferation of massive data banks emanating from both governmental and private sources, the question of the individual's right to privacy regarding certain personal data is becoming increasingly important. The information explosion taking place in our society, facilitated largely by computerized data banks, is causing substantial controversy. Indeed, the implications for individual rights of permitting federal and state governments and private business and associations to assemble in a central location facts about the citizenry are far reaching. There are other real or perceived impacts of information technology on the individual, such as dehumanization and power, and these will be briefly examined as legitimate areas of social concern.

In summary, this chapter will examine the following topics:

1. Computers in the nonbusiness world.
   a. Education applications.
   b. Health and medical applications.
   c. Government applications.
   d. Other societal applications.
2. Computers and the individual.
   a. The effects of automation.
   b. The issue of privacy.
   c. Human values and individualism.

COMPUTERS IN THE NONBUSINESS WORLD

The business applications of the computer that have been examined thus far have ranged from the traditional areas of accounting and finance to growing numbers of applications in banking and credit, manufacturing, and marketing. This treatment by no means exhausts the applications within the business environment, but it does suggest the pervasive nature of the computer revolution throughout the business community.

This computer revolution has left few areas of society untouched, including the many nonbusiness sectors. The various applications of the computer are far too numerous to mention here, but illustrations of some of the nonbusiness uses should give you an appreciation of the widespread nature of the computer's impact. Applications in education, medicine, and government will be discussed, among others.

Applications in Education

It has been estimated that in the near future education will become the largest industry in the United States. Along with this growth will come increases in the attendant bureaucracy and a surfeit of paper work and recordkeeping. The undergraduate student in a large university knows what it is like to be viewed as a number in a large system. As in business, educational institutions could not survive without the electronic capability for storing and processing records.

Educational research also would be seriously impeded without computers. Research and science prosper best when powerful analytical tools and large reservoirs of data are available—and the computer is at least a partial answer to both of these needs. Scientists and researchers need the computer's capabilities to advance the frontiers of knowledge.

In addition to administrative and research functions, the computer also can serve as an instrument for teaching. Computer Assisted Instruction (CAI), one of the exciting advances of recent years, permits the teacher to bring into the classroom a unique dimension of learning. Through keyboard consoles, students can "talk" to a computer by typing in responses to questions which have been asked via a computer display device or printout. Such approaches extend the instructor's capabilities in dealing with large numbers of students. Additionally, the student has the opportunity of working at his own pace, since he can interface with the programmed instructional materials whenever he chooses. CAI has demonstrated successes at the elementary, secondary, and university levels.

In the university business school environment the computer is assuming an increasingly influential role. Students are being expected to have the capability for conversing with the computer via terminals. This involves entering user-developed programs or using packaged programs which have already been written and are stored in the computer. In many management courses, students are given the chance to play business games—computer simulations of real-world business operations which permit the student to "make decisions" and then to see the consequences of these decisions after the inputs have been processed in accordance with the structure of the game.

It is logical that the computer should have an impact on teaching methodology, since it meshes nicely with concepts of individualized instruction and economies of scale, both of which are important in education today. In addition, the actual *content of education* at all levels has changed as a consequence of computer availability, and this can be expected to continue. A number of effects are likely: (1) changes in general education—that is, the knowledge to which students are introduced, (2) changes in specific areas of study, and (3) the introduction of different fields of study.

Changes in General Education. There is a need to educate the general population about computers—what they are, why we have them, what they do, and so on. It is conceivable that the day will come when basic instruction in computers is as common as teaching the fundamentals of reading, writing, and arithmetic. At an early age children could be taught the basics, without going into all of the intricacies of how and why computers work. An argument could be made that the computer should be taught to children the way we teach such topics as electricity as a source of power and airplanes as a mode of transportation without ever going into how and why electricity and airplanes work. It is likely that such a trend would take time, however, because many present teachers know very little about the computer.

Changes in Specific Areas of Study. Quite apart from the teaching of the computer in general education, changes in specific areas of study are also likely. In some fields the changes may be more dramatic than in others. Computers have had impacts on fields of study that the layman may know little about, such as music (e.g., music education, composition, sound generation, and acoustical research), historical research, classical literature, and the humanities. An entire journal, *Computers and the Humanities*, documents computer applications that might surprise you. The content and treatment of various areas of education have been impacted quite dramatically by the computer, and new ways of thinking are likely to continue to be generated in various disciplines by the computer's capabilities.

Changes in Fields of Study. New fields of study also are likely to be spawned by the computer. One of the most obvious is the field of computer science. Academic programs in computer science have been initiated at colleges and universities, and numerous vocational courses are offered for those who are interested in computer career positions such as computer operators, programmers, and keypunch operators. New fields of computer study have already spun off from computer applications in such areas as mathematics, physics, engineering, and architecture, and more will likely come in the future. Indeed, only the imagination bounds the new areas that may emerge as a direct consequence of computerization.

In sum, the computer has become an ever-present, necessary component in the field of education. In addition to having impacts on the administrative and research functions, it has become an exciting learning tool for students at all levels of the educational system.

Figure 14–1 illustrates a high school student interacting with a computer-based counseling information system by requesting career facts from a computerized library of vocational information.

Practically all students of business at colleges and universities in the United States today become acquainted with the computer in some way. This is necessary for two basic reasons. First, these students need to know more about the computer-oriented society in which they live; indeed, the computer is continually touching more areas of citizens' lives. Second, students must learn how to work

FIGURE 14–1
High School Student Interacting with a Computer-Based Counseling System

Courtesy of IBM

with computers and to understand how they work if they are to become productive members of management in today's complex business, educational, or governmental environments.

Futurists who speculate on the state of education in years to come seem to agree that the computer's role will continue to grow in scope and influence. Such expectations provide a rationale for the continuing development of computer education in the future.

Health and Medical Applications

The field of health and medicine has been somewhat slow in turning to computerization. Though numerous isolated applications of the computer in this field are appearing daily, by the mid-seventies the computer had been applied in only a small number of the *potential* areas. One of the major reasons is that physicians have been reluctant to permit impersonal situations like machine diagnosis of patients. This may be due to a generalized resistance to change, or it may be because medical practitioners are basically unsophisticated in their knowledge of computer usage. Cost is another factor. These conditions are rapidly changing, but the widespread employment of computers in health-related fields is contingent upon medical care experts coming to understand the computer and its potential in their field.

Applications in the field of health and medicine can be broadly divided into two major categories: clerical and bookkeeping applications, and patient-care-related applications.

Clerical and Bookkeeping Applications. These applications of the computer were, along with research, among the first to be developed in the field of medicine, primarily because of the rather routine nature of bookkeeping transactions. These applications include such tasks as keeping records of services to patients, updating patient accounts, billing, keeping inventory of supplies, and payroll preparation. These are simply some of the bread-and-butter applications of a typical business data processing system, and in medicine they are basically modifications of those that have been used in many other types of organizations. All hospitals and doctors' offices require functions that are common with business. With the need for medical facilities growing at an unprecedented pace, business applications capable of handling the growing volume of accounts are essential in this field.

A number of more advanced hospitals have extended the use of the computer to problems of scheduling and admissions. It is estimated that the lack of coordination in scheduling (beds, rooms, operating facilities, X-ray rooms, discharges) is one of the most wasteful aspects of hospital operations. The difficulties in using the computer for scheduling seem to emanate from the conflicting interests of various hospital power groups, which must be resolved by the development of some ground rules for the allocation and use of resources.[1] It is just a matter of time before hospitals and doctors' offices catch up with other organizations in regard to the administrative applications of computers.

Patient-Care-Related Applications. While resistance to change has inhibited the widespread application of computers to patient-related problems, evidence is accumulating that these barriers are being overcome. Medical applications of computers are still in the experimental stage, but many of the experiments are fascinating and have tremendous potential for improving patient care. Patient-related systems can be classified into four general areas: (1) diagnosis of patients, (2) patient-monitoring systems, (3) medical histories and recordkeeping, and (4) other services.

---

[1] G. Octo Barnett, J. H. Grossman, and R. A. Greenes, "The Computer's Role in Health Service Research," *The World of Computers*, ed. John Diebold, (New York: Random House, 1973), p. 243.

1. *Medical Diagnosis.* The use of computers for patient diagnosis by physicians can be documented by the growth in the market for computer-operated medical diagnostic equipment. It is estimated that this burgeoning market, which totaled $355 million in 1973, will grow to $485 million by 1977 and $755 million by 1982. Producers of this equipment expect a robust growth in business precisely because digital computers are available to analyze the readings generated by their equipment. In 1973 between 2 and 4 percent of a total $500 million worth of minicomputers went into the medical marketplace.[2]

"*HE INSISTS ON A SECOND OPINION.*"

©DATAMATION®

A number of illustrations of technological advancements in the diagnostic field suggest why growth has been widespread:

a. *Diagnosing heart disease.* Several powerful, probabilistic computer programs which employ a data base generated from 28,000

⎯⎯⎯⎯⎯⎯
    [2] "Computer Analysis and Innovations Spur Healthy Growth," *Computer Digest*, vol. 9, no. 5 (1974), p. 6.

patients have presented performance superior to that of a team of trained cardiologists in diagnosing heart disease from electro-cardiogram data. The advanced software correctly identified patient disorders in 88 percent of the cases examined, while the cardiologists' performance record was 64 percent accurate.[3]

b. *Organ profile system.* Automated blood analyzers used in conjunction with high-speed data communications have produced results for physicians in 90 seconds. This speed contrasts sharply with test results which at one time normally took hours to obtain. The computer system is based upon organ profiles which have been preprogrammed into a minicomputer. The computer has information which has been gathered from physicians in pathology, diagnostics, and internal medicine.[4]

c. *Simulated patient.* A simulated patient, SIM ONE, has been constructed by an engineering firm and is being used at the University of Southern California's School of Medicine. The simulated patient is a six-foot, plastic-skinned mannequin which has been used for anesthesiology training since 1968. Though SIM ONE does not talk (yet), it breathes, chokes, coughs, blinks, and regurgitates.

With the simulated patient, anesthesiology residents can develop skills in the delicate and potentially dangerous technique of endotracheal intubation before having to perform the technique on humans. Intubation is the process of inserting a semi-rigid tube down a patient's throat and upper chest for artificial lung ventilation. SIM ONE will respond to errors in procedure just as a real patient would — even to the point of "dying." In addition, SIM ONE can take on symptoms of a patient in shock — and unless the emergency room attendant follows the correct procedures, SIM ONE will "die." Conveniently, SIM ONE can be brought "back to life" with the flick of a switch. The use of artificial devices such as SIM ONE greatly aids the training of medical and paramedical personnel in developing diagnostic and treatment skills.[5]

2. **Patient-Monitoring Systems.** The development of computer systems for monitoring patients is another growth area in the medical field. Patient-monitoring systems exceeded $100 million in sales in 1972, a growth increase of 44 percent over the 1971 sales figure. The outlook is optimistic for systems which can monitor patients in

---

[3] "Small Computers Handle Complex Medical Program," *Computer Digest*, vol. 9, no. 4 (1974), p. 2.

[4] "Organ Profile System," *Computer Digest*, vol. 9, no. 3 (1974), p. 8.

[5] "Simulated Patient," *Computer Digest*, vol. 9, no. 4 (1974), p. 7.

hospitals as an extension of the physician's ability to watch over the patient's "vital signs" while under operating or recovery conditions.[6]

3. *Medical Histories and Recordkeeping.* The task of gathering medical histories and relevant personal data and keeping updated records or profiles on patients is another one which has been greatly facilitated by the computer. The initial responsibility is in gathering medical history information, and computers have been demonstrated to be effective in this task. A computer system at the University of Wisconsin–Madison Hospital collects case histories of patients in a fraction of the time it would take doctors to do this. The computer "talks" to the patient, never forgetting to ask a question, and stores all the answers in a neat, standardized form.

Computer interviews for data gathering purposes have been around for about a decade in one form or another. Initial models were used to gather history on general medical problems, allergies, and so on, but more extensive programs have since been designed to gather psychiatric histories. Some physicians, after having overcome initial resistance to machine intrusion in human communications, are pleased with this approach because the computer never gets bored or pressured by other duties.

The entire recordkeeping function in health care is being found amenable to automation, and this can mean a cost saving to the patient. A computer system which responds to telephoned inquiries can speed the flow of patient information between physician and laboratory. It has been shown that accelerating the transfer of patient test data to and from a laboratory can save a patient an extra day's hospital costs, or get him into surgery faster for a critical operation.

A centralized computer storage facility for patient medical histories could not help but improve health services. If all health facilities maintained patient medical histories in a centralized data bank rather than scattering each history among several doctor's offices, laboratories, and hospitals—possibly in different cities—the information function of health care could be greatly improved. Numerous central data bank systems are being experimented with along these lines.

4. *Other Medical and Health Services.* There are a multitude of other medical and health applications of the computer which have not been mentioned here. Two of these applications are illustrative of the computer's capabilities.

a. *Computer-aided pharmacists.* The Cleveland Metropolitan General Hospital has a computer which has been programmed to aid

---

[6] "Patient Monitoring Systems," *Computer Digest*, vol. 8, no. 3 (1973), p. 9.

pharmacists in spotting potential drug overdoses as they fill prescriptions. In addition, four hospital pharmacists with this system have the capacity to fill 400 prescriptions an hour, compared to approximately 80 per hour without the system. At the same time, the system identifies people whose past medical histories require special attention in the administering of drugs.[7]

b. *Audio response system for retail-medical billing.* A unique service is offered by a bank in Arizona to doctors, hospitals, and retail stores requiring over 100 patient or customer statements per month. On a daily basis, the customer of the bank's service simply calls at the end of the day and submits debit and credit information on the day's transactions. The users of this system are enthusiastic because it reduces their paper work, and all of their statements or invoices are mailed within 48 hours.[8]

As these examples illustrate, computer technology has already had an impact on the medical and health-related segments of our society. It is anticipated that advances such as these will increase as computer specialists and health-care experts develop a cooperative working relationship. This relationship will be necessary because most of the examples cited above require systems which are more than simple modifications of those already in existence in business, education, and government. There is some transferable technology, but many of the patient-related areas of application require unique systems. Some of these cannot even be readily transferred from one health center to another because of the unique characteristics of the centers. It is anticipated, however, that computer applications in the medical and allied fields will continue to be a growth segment of society for some time.

Applications in Government

Applications of the computer in government closely parallel its use in business, ranging from conventional data processing tasks to complex management information systems. The federal government is believed to be the single largest user of computers in the world— but that should come as no surprise to anyone even casually acquainted with our intricate tax system and complex administrative and service programs. The U.S. government uses thousands of computers of various sizes and types.

The data collection, analysis, and storage requirements of all gov-

---

[7] "Computer Aided Pharmacists," *Computer Digest*, vol. 8, no. 9 (1973), p. 5.

[8] "Unique Audio Response System," *Computer Digest*, vol. 8, no. 8 (1973), pp. 7–8.

FIGURE 14–2
Where the Government's Computers Are Installed

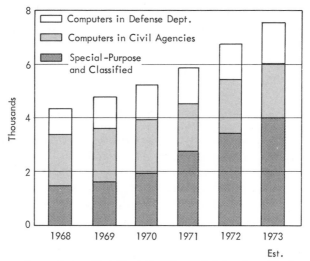

Source: *Business Week,* March 24, 1973, p. 18. Data from General Services
Administration and *Business Week.*

ernment agencies and departments easily qualifies the federal
government as the largest user and storer of data in the world. Almost
any department or agency of the federal government can be used as
an illustration: The Treasury Department issues thousands of checks
daily; the Labor Department provides complete and timely statistics
on U.S. employment; the Census Bureau performs numerous statistical analyses, analyzing data in practically every way known to man;
the Internal Revenue Service collects and files tax data for every
working citizen; and the Bureau of the Budget summarizes data in
thousands of tables and handles every figure comprising the federal
budget.

The data processing requirements of the Department of Defense,
the largest computer user within the federal government, are staggering. The problem of accounting for all the personnel and material
dispersed throughout the world for the Army, Navy, Marines, and
Air Force indicates the scope of the responsibility we are describing;
and this is only the clerical function. Military applications of the
computer get into such esoteric areas as missile-tracking facilities,
weapons systems, large-scale national defense mechanisms, and
worldwide control systems. Figure 14–2 indicates in which general
areas the government's computers are installed.

Computers in State Government.   It is obvious that the federal
government could not function effectively without the use of com-

puters, and the same is true of state governments, although they are miniscule in size compared to the federal bureaucracy. The states have many of the same needs as the federal government, though on a considerably smaller scale. State governments, due to their size among other reasons, have not experienced quite the success with computers as their federal counterpart has, but they are massive data processors, and state agencies are increasing their use of computers. In 1972 it was estimated by the National Association of State Information Systems that nearly 600 computers were installed in state government agencies (excluding higher education).[9]

The potential gains for state governments resulting from use of computers are much the same as those for the federal government—greater accuracy, reliability, speed, economy, and so forth. Studies in some states have revealed an exceedingly great lack of coordination among various state agencies; there has been a proliferation of computer equipment among state agencies, and numerous cases of duplicated effort have been noted. Recently several state heads have taken corrective measures, and there is evidence that some states are beginning to establish centralized control over their computer systems.

Some of the areas in which computers are currently being applied in state government include the following:

1. Administration and Finance
    a. Budgeting (appropriations accounting)
    b. Fiscal management reporting systems
    c. Investment
2. Resources and Development
    a. Economic and statistical data
    b. Regional planning
    c. Feasibility and impact studies
    d. Planning and development
3. Human Services
    a. Health service planning
    b. Medicaid programs
    c. Job-bank programs
    d. Workman's compensation
    e. Welfare management
4. Consumer Affairs
    a. Public utilities
    b. Measuring quality of services performed

---

[9] Alvin Kaltman, "Computers in State Governments," *Technology Review*, vol. 74, no. 4 (1972).

5. Public Safety
   a. Police telecommunications systems
   b. Vehicle registration and verification
   c. Laboratory analysis
6. Transportation and Construction
   a. Transportation planning
   b. Project management of construction projects
   c. Disbursement and control of building funds

It might be imagined that only large, wealthy states and cities can benefit from use of the computer in problem areas such as these, but that is not always the case. Little Rock, Arkansas, provides an example of how cities with a population of 200,000 and under can justify the use of exclusive police computers. That city's police department operates an on-line criminal information system, a remarkable accomplishment for municipalities of that size. The system provides automatic access in seconds to local, state, and national criminal data bases.

One of the unique characteristics of the Little Rock system is that it is a *dedicated* (i.e., devoted to a special purpose) law enforcement system, whereas most police departments share a larger, general-purpose municipal computer. The Little Rock system supports the police department in four major functional areas:

1. *Field requests.* Quick response is provided to officers checking on wanted persons, warrants, vehicles, and missing persons.
2. *Investigations.* Investigators can rapidly access and correlate facts that were previously available only in isolated and diverse sources. Data are available on known criminals and previous burglaries, for example.
3. *Recordkeeping.* The police are aided in maintaining a parking and traffic ticket system. This can be valuable because some states will not renew a person's driver's license or issue new plates until all parking and traffic tickets have been paid.
4. *Management controls.* The police are aided in tracing crime patterns. For example, a simulation model pretests the impact of contemplated changes in personnel assignments on departmental effectiveness.

Figure 14–3 illustrates how a dispatcher in the Chattanooga, Tennessee, police department receives, within seconds, computer-stored information on stolen vehicles which can then be relayed to a mobile unit. Like the Little Rock system, this system is linked to other centralized computers. In this case, the police system is linked to a central downtown computer which makes available information stored

FIGURE 14-3
Police Dispatcher Employing the Computer to Retrieve Information on Stolen Vehicles

Courtesy of IBM

in the computer in the state motor vehicle department in Nashville. The Nashville computer, in turn, is connected to the computer at the National Crime Information Center (NCIC) in Washington, D.C. The NCIC stores data on wanted persons, stolen vehicles and license plates, and other stolen property.

The existing and potential applications of computers in state and local governments are growing. This discussion has been far from comprehensive, but it is illustrative of the breadth and complexity of governmental operations that are likely candidates for computerization. It is anticipated that the area of government will become more computerized as time passes and as governmental leaders become more cognizant of the benefits that can be gained from applying resources in this vital area.

Other Societal Applications

Whole books have been written on the impact of computers on society. We have discussed how computers have affected education,

FIGURE 14-4
Reports of New Computer Applications

Driverless taxis controlled by minicomputers
Computers help prepare Christmas cards
Computers producing braille for nations' sightless
Computer talks to psychiatric patients
Computer bolsters apartment security
American Baseball League computerizes statistics
Computer converts rough sketches into complete drawings
Computer aids pharmacists
Forecasting earthquakes seen as new computer role
Computer responds verbally to hospital information requests
Computer aiding in city water distribution
Computer helps pick most beautiful girl in world
A computer aids in picking stage plays

medicine and health, and government, all dominant sectors of our society. It is difficult to imagine that there is an individual in our culture who has not been influenced in some way by computers.

New applications of the computer are appearing at such a rapid pace that it would be impossible to catalog them all, but those listed in Figure 14-4 are indicative of their widespread and pervasive nature. The applications listed suggest the scope of the kinds of activities that are amenable to computerization.

Unique applications such as those in Figure 14-4 appear with regularity, and it can be anticipated that the computer will touch the daily lives of people in areas that today are not even remotely connected or linked to computerization. The computer has become a tool for business, government, and education, and implications of usages that are international in scope are appearing. It is also anticipated that the computer will have a greater impact on the individual —the citizen, the consumer, the layman—and on human values and the quality of life. Future applications of computers will surely have implications for planning for the environment, scientific and cultural development, crime control, law enforcement, and other aspects of society.

COMPUTERS AND THE INDIVIDUAL

The first section of this chapter examined applications of the computer in areas unrelated to business, presenting numerous examples of how the computer has had a beneficial impact on the sectors of education, government, and medicine. There is a class of societal issues, however, which suggests possibly negative consequences of the use of the computer. These areas should not necessarily be considered detriments or drawbacks but problem areas which could lead to the judgment that the human costs of technological advances exceed their benefits. Most people in our society can readily see that in a cost-benefit analysis, the computer is contributing far more than it is taking away from society and the individual. Nevertheless, any technological advance brings certain changes, and those who are resistant to change are apt to impute negative consequences to them. This is true of computers, as it has been of most technological progress in our society at one time or another.

It is anticipated that people will develop means to ensure that computerization serves them, and not vice versa. However, certain issues have arisen that at first glance may suggest that computerization has gone too far and is having more detrimental effects than positive ones. Closer examination of these issues suggests that they are indeed areas of concern to society, but not of such great magnitude that progress should be inhibited because of the uncertainties associated with them. Three issues in particular stand out as societal problems in computer use: (1) the effects of automation, (2) the threats to individual privacy brought about by indiscriminate use of personal data, and (3) the potential for erosion of human values precipitated by computer-related dehumanization.

Effects of Automation of Work Processes

The effects of automation of work processes are of great concern to people; nothing seems as important as job-related matters, particularly those affecting the individual's economic security. When told of the possibility of automation, the first image that materializes in many minds is "I am going to be replaced by a machine!" The reaction is so natural that one can conjure up a scenario of humanlike robots being placed in an organization, followed immediately by the exit of a significant portion of the work force. Indeed this country experienced such an "automation scare" in the 1950s, when the concept of automatic machine-controlled work operations was introduced.

Objective examination of the experience of the past two decades indicates that such doomsday prophecies of unemployment attributable to automation have not been fulfilled. Nevertheless, there was considerable reason for the individual to become alarmed. Academic and other experts also suggested the end of the world of work as we knew it. For example, Norbert Wiener, in the 1954 revision of *The Human Use of Human Beings*, forecast that unemployment due to automation in the United States would overshadow the depression experience of the 1930s. This point of view found supporters and led to significant controversy.

The unemployment or displacement of workers which both proponents and opponents of automation were talking about is technological unemployment—that is, replacement of workers with automated, laborsaving machines. Experience has shown that the technological unemployment associated with initial automation was quite moderate and consisted mostly of short-term, transitional displacement of workers.

Most of the opponents of automation failed to see that many of their assumptions about the impact of automation were fallacious. For example, they argued from a rather static theory that there was only a certain amount of work to be done, and any laborsaving machinery was bound to reduce the number of workers who could be employed to do that work. Their assumption that there is just a fixed amount of work to be done proved to be more reminiscent of the depression days than the post–Korean War period in which most automation took place. The economic expansion of the 1950s and 1960s was not amenable to widespread technological unemployment.

Several observations can be made concerning the automation issue:

1. Though automation somewhat reduces direct labor for an unchanged level of output, it tends to create employment opportunities in other sectors.
2. New industries develop as a consequence of automation.
3. Over the long run, automation is likely to be accompanied by an increasing decline in working hours, and this will stimulate leisure-time industries and new occupations.
4. With a flexible, mobile work force, individuals temporarily displaced by automation should be able to find new jobs rather easily.
5. There will be a certain amount of short-term transitional unemployment associated with automation.
6. Generally, most fears about widespread unemployment resulting from automation or computerization are exaggerated.[10]

Wiener's estimation of widespread technological displacement of workers has proven to be an overstatement. Paul Einzig has suggested, in fact, that the "gravest danger arises not through an unduly high rate of automation but through an unduly slow rate of automation."[11]

> Those who are opposed to automation for fear of technological unemployment do not realize that if their policy were followed their country would be exposed to much more extensive and intractable nontechnological unemployment. Automation is bound to proceed sooner or

---

[10] Paul Einzig, "Must Automation Bring Unemployment?" in *The World of the Computer* ed. John Diebold (New York: Random House, 1973), pp. 335–44.
[11] Ibid., pp. 335–44.

later, whether we like it or not. Our choice does not rest between automation and full employment but between prompt automation with the possibility of moderate temporary unemployment and delayed automation with the certainty of grave perennial unemployment, until our progress has caught up with that of our competitors.[12]

Einzig's argument provides an interesting perspective on the automation issue. Our society has reaped the benefits of technological advances such as automation to an extent that it should be quite willing to continue to accept the temporary displacements which seem to accompany changes such as these. Undoubtedly, automation will become more prevalent as our society finds ways for machines to handle the drudgery once handled by humans, and in the process society is likely to perceive the long-range benefits as outweighing short-range inconveniences.

Substituting machine labor for physical labor promises to eliminate many of the undesirable, monotonous, routine tasks which employees today claim are at the root of job boredom and worker apathy. Management has a responsibility to ensure that in the process whereby machines take over manual labor, proper consideration is given to the man-machine interface. This is the main issue posed by automation, not the mass displacement of workers.

This problem is brought into clearer focus by consideration of what has come to be known as the *cybernation revolution,* a stage beyond simple automation. Automation in its earliest meaning referred to the performance of production processes by self-operating machines, whereas cybernation utilizes a combination of computer programs and the automated, self-regulating machine. Extensions of cybernation could mean the increasing intervention of computers into management-type work. Thus what we thought of as machine displacement of laborers might evolve into machine displacement of managers. As computers and their users become more and more sophisticated, the capability for simulating human thought processes such as managerial decision making becomes greater. However, we feel the security of managers is not in jeopardy. What is likely to occur is that the manager will be relieved of the tedious, routine aspects of his job. Those aspects that can be programmed will be taken over by computers, even to the extent of assuming control over what have been considered important management decisions.

With the responsibility for programmable-type decisions being assumed by the computer, modern managers should be able to focus their attentions on the multitude of human, social, and political issues that organizations face today. The positive outcome is that

---

[12] Ibid., pp. 343–44.

managers will have the time to direct their attention to problems they ought to be considering—those that are more ill-defined, unstructured, and heuristic in nature. The challenge to management will be to bring about this change in responsibilities while considering the individual worker and manager as a valuable resource in the man-machine relationship.

In sum, the major responsibility of organizations in regard to computer displacement of humans is to give people full consideration in job design as new man-machine relationships emerge. Most importantly, plans must be developed for converting to new systems which require different human roles than those assumed in the past. The human resource has a unique attribute in this regard; it is the only resource that cares how it is used in the production process. Considerable experience and research indicate that positive outcomes can be achieved and negative consequences avoided if such planning efforts are made for the human dimension. Though the issue will not be laid to rest by such encouraging statements, it is hoped that you will feel more optimistic about the employment situation that is likely to characterize a fully automated, computer-oriented society.

The Issue of Privacy

The trend toward large centralized data banks raises another critical social issue. This is the problem of ensuring individual privacy rights in a computer age which is characterized by the compilation of intimate personal data and their storage in centralized computer data banks which make information easily available.

The implications of permitting governments and businesses to assemble facts and information about citizens are indeed far reaching. The basic threat is to the individual's right to privacy regarding any information that pertains to his personal life. There is a serious hazard that considerable power could be placed in the hands of a few people who might control access to the information. Left uncontrolled, the data storage facility of the computer could conceivably create a Big Brother regime of the type anticipated in George Orwell's *1984*.

For the individual, one of the most serious drawbacks of computerized data banks is his inability to control what data are stored and made available, perhaps indiscriminately, by the system. In addition, such systems are usually not equipped to correct errors due to incorrect or biased sources or erroneous data entry. Consequently, massive amounts of data are stored in system data banks, and the individual has no means by which to see or challenge data that are entered incorrectly or perhaps incompletely. Figure 14–5 lists various federal government agencies that store data about individuals. The

FIGURE 14-5
Is Your Name in a Federal Computer?

More than 50 federal agencies, according to a survey by a Senate Judiciary Subcommittee on Constitutional Rights, have 858 separate data banks, containing more than a billion records on individuals. In these data banks, available at the touch of a button, are diverse bits of information on just about every American. Some examples—

Department of Health, Education and Welfare: 61 data banks, with 402 million records—including information on recipients of Social Security, medicare and welfare payments, among others.

Department of Commerce: 8 data banks, with 204 million records— including those on businessmen, recipients of loans.

Treasury Department: 46 data banks, containing 156 million records —dealing with taxpayers, individuals under scrutiny by the U.S. Secret Service, people with access to the White House, among others.

Justice Department: 19 data banks, with 139 million records—including fingerprint cards on file, details on individuals arrested on criminal charges, on people in "sensitive" Government jobs.

Veterans Administration: 29 data banks, with 73 million records— including files on veterans and dependents now getting benefits or those who received them in the past.

Pentagon: 497 banks, with 61 million records on service personnel, other persons investigated for employment, security or criminal reasons.

Department of Labor: 4 data banks, with 24 million records—many involving people in federally financed work and training programs.

Civil Service Commission: 13 data banks, with 19 million records— including data on people at work in the Government or who have applied for jobs.

Department of Housing and Urban Development: 27 banks, with 10 million records—including information on people who have bought homes with loans guaranteed by the Federal Housing Administration.

Department of Transportation: 18 data banks, with 6 million records —including files on Americans who have been denied drivers' licenses and those whose permits have been suspended or revoked.

Source: Reprinted with permission from *U.S. News & World Report*, July 1, 1974, p. 41.

scope of information that can be obtained from the 858 data banks represented by this list will no doubt be surprising to most of you.

In the final analysis, individual rights will have to be protected through public policy as expressed in law. Otherwise the individual will have no protection in the use of personal data and preventing unauthorized access to data files. Even when safeguards are employed, information systems are vulnerable to misuse. A case illustrating this point occurred several years ago in a large midwestern city. Three former employees of a large encyclopedia company copied computer tapes before they left the company's employment. The tapes, containing the names and addresses of two million of the firm's customers, were sold to mailing list brokers. In fact, one part of the list was sold to a competing firm in the encyclopedia industry!

In developing comprehensive data systems, care must be taken to create appropriate legislation which will safeguard the individual against abuse of centrally stored files. Even so, as the encyclopedia case illustrates, as long as human beings are a part of the system (and they certainly will be), the danger exists that individual rights can be violated.

Legislation which has been hailed as one of the world's first laws to end the invasion of privacy has been passed in Sweden, which has at least 500 government and 4,500 commercial data banks (defined as any computerized listing that identifies people)—membership rolls, payroll records, mailing services, and so on. Prior to the recent legislation, Sweden had laws which specified the public's "right to know" and thus permitted wide access to the data. The new legislation created a data inspection board to license commercial data banks, establish conditions of their operation, and provide advice on the operation of government data banks. The key points of the law, which suggest measures that may have to be taken elsewhere in the world, are as follows:

1. With the exception of government records, a data bank can exist only with the permission of the nine-man inspection board. The board will authorize how the data bank can be used and the particular methods it can employ.
2. Data banks are not permitted to catalog sensitive materials such as psychiatric treatment, criminal records, alcoholic problems, and so forth without demonstrated need to the inspection board.
3. Data banks cannot report religious or political affiliations.
4. Persons who are listed in a data bank are provided free printouts of their files. The inspection board may also instruct the operator of a data bank to notify everyone in it of his inclusion. Individuals can petition the board to require that corrections be made in their files, and they may file suit for damages if they are harmed due to misinformation.
5. A set of penalties for violations is provided which includes fines and jail terms.[13]

It is interesting to note that the Swedish computer industry itself lobbied for the data bank law because it feared the negative consequences if something were not done. Otherwise anticomputer senti-

---

[13] "Sweden Regulates Those Snooping Data Banks," *Business Week*, October 6, 1973, pp. 93–94.

FIGURE 14–6

IBM Reports

Four principles of privacy

For some time now, there has been a growing effort in this country to preserve the individual's right to privacy in the face of expanding requirements for information by business, government and other organizations.

In searching for appropriate guidelines, private and governmental groups have explored many avenues and considered many aspects of the privacy question.

As a company with a vital interest in information and information handling, IBM endorses in their basic purpose four principles of privacy which have emerged from various studies, and which appear to be the cornerstones of sound public policy on this sensitive issue.

1. Individuals should have access to information about themselves in record-keeping systems. And there should be some procedure for individuals to find out how this information is being used.

2. There should be some way for an individual to correct or amend an inaccurate record.

3. An individual should be able to prevent information from being improperly disclosed or used for other than authorized purposes without his or her consent, unless required by law.

4. The custodian of data files containing sensitive information should take reasonable precautions to be sure that the data are reliable and not misused.

Translating such broad principles into specific and uniform guidelines will, of course, not be easy. They must be thoughtfully interpreted in terms of the widely varying purposes of information systems generally.

In particular, the proper balance must be found between limiting access to information for the protection of privacy on one hand, and allowing freedom of information to fulfill the needs of society on the other.

But solutions must be found. And they will call for the patient understanding and best efforts of everyone concerned. In this search, IBM pledges its full and whole-hearted cooperation.

Courtesy of IBM

ments might develop which could have adverse effects on the growth of the industry.[14]

Several computer manufacturers in the United States have taken a

---

[14] Ibid., p. 94.

positive, socially responsive stance in regard to the issue of privacy. For example, IBM ran a message entitled "Four Principles of Privacy" in national magazines (see Figure 14–6). The advertisement gives public notice of the corporation's concern for the privacy issue and its view that the individual's right to privacy must be protected regardless of expanding requirements for information by business, government, and other organizations.

Lawmakers in the United States have also been giving increasing attention to the problem of privacy. One of the first significant laws passed was the Fair Credit Reporting Act of 1970, which was designed "to enable consumers to protect themselves against arbitrary, erroneous, and malicious credit information compiled and disseminated by consumer credit reporting agencies." Thus consumer credit reporting agencies such as the credit bureaus in most U.S. cities are required to reveal the contents of their files to those who are refused credit.[15]

The Privacy Act of 1974 was passed in the last days of the 93rd Congress.[16] While this law is the result of a compromise privacy bill, it does contain some significant provisions. A Privacy Protection Commission was established, though it has no enforcement power and a limited budget. This commission will investigate government and private data processing systems and make legislative recommendations on privacy to the Congress and the President. Other provisions of the Privacy Act of 1974 apply to all federal information systems, with certain exemptions for law enforcement, military, and civil service records. It allows individuals access to their files and permits them to obtain copies and to correct inaccuracies by mail. The legislation also requires federal agencies to enforce standards of accuracy, relevance, completeness, and timeliness in using or transferring information to other agencies, and agencies are prohibited from selling mailing lists. Federal, state, and local governments are no longer allowed to withhold a right, benefit, or privilege because of refusal to disclose a social security number.

While the Privacy Act of 1974 is a movement toward ensuring a measure of privacy in a computerized age, much still needs to be done. Legislation regulating the private sector is still needed and will undoubtedly be forthcoming.

In an era of increasing concern for individual rights, the potential that their privacy may be invaded through improper uses of data banks is becoming apparent to many people. Meanwhile, resistance to preventive legislative measures regulating business is likely to continue. The parallel trends of increased computer usage and height-

---

[15] "The Computer and Privacy," *Automatic Data Processing Newsletter*, March 20, 1972.

[16] Linda Flato, "Privacy Walks off with Easy Wins," *Computer Decisions*, January 1975, p. 10.

ened concern for individual rights are going to hit head on at some point, and the really tough questions that are being evaded now must be faced up to. These questions include such vital matters as: What are the relative rights of the data bank owner versus the individual? Is the philosophy held by many companies that data in their files are their private property valid? Who should have access to information and under what conditions? What rights do individuals have to correct or expunge data from their files in data banks?

Human Values and Individualism

Another area of concern which is emerging as a social problem is the perceived attack by the computer on the *individuality* of people. The issue of automation and invasion of privacy are closely related, because their consequences bear on the threats to individuality.

Individuality refers to personal identity—the condition of existing as a separate or unique person set apart from others. The threat of the computer in this respect is its inherent need to deal with people as numbers, or impersonal objects. The concept of individuality suggests that all persons are different, but the computer usually is not programmed to recognize these differences—especially differences in personality and humanity. Society is moving toward increasing recognition of individuality and individual rights and more toleration of different lifestyles. Evidence of this trend is the growing emphasis on individualized instruction in education, individual rights in law, individual differences in the workplace, and so on.

However, the computer, being a mass processor of records, is not completely equipped to deal with these individualistic characteristics and is thus widely accused of reducing the person to a cipher. In the popular view, the computer is dehumanizing. While it is true that the technology of computers requires a considerable depersonalization, this problem needs to be put in a proper perspective which accurately and fairly compares the long-run benefits to mankind of the computer with the short-term inconveniences or costs which inevitably accompany any technological change. Furthermore, it is only fair to suggest that much of what has been termed the impersonality of the computer to those who are affected by it is actually the impersonality of other persons and large systems of organizations that do not care to take the time necessary to deal with individuals as individuals. Thus the computer is simply guilty by association in some instances.

This cost-benefit perspective can be illustrated by several examples. The individual does not like the cold, impersonal efficiency of today's modern hospitals, with their machines, systems, automation, and so on. But the individual may not be aware that the mortality rate in these cold, impersonal buildings is far lower than in the personal, sympathetic hospitals of the 19th century. Today's students do not like mass herding through college and believe they are regarded as "only numbers" in a large, impersonal system of huge classes which requires computer printouts for class rolls and punched cards for payment and registration procedures. But can they surmise what conditions would exist if computers were not used? They would have to fill out separate forms for each course each quarter, wait for each applicant to be processed at registration, and anticipate delays due to time-consuming manual calculations of gradepoint averages and processing of grades. In addition to having to tolerate such inconveniences, many students might find that higher education would be so costly under these circumstances that they would not get a chance to acquire it.

People in our society have looked at automation with distrust, but if they thought out all of its potential consequences they would see that the only way to do away with all the dull, repetitive, routine, unrewarding jobs is to reduce them to machines so people will not have to do them. Then human beings will be able to concentrate on the really human tasks.

Putting into perspective the computer and its need to reduce the individual to a number requires reconciling the long-term, widespread gains derived from computerization with the short-term effects we are presently experiencing. There is also the task of educating the public as to how dependent we are on automation and computers and how these technological instruments are partially responsible for our high standards of living. Not being willing to put up with the short-term effects of computers is comparable to the mother who would not let her daughter receive free polio shots at school because she did not like needle pricks.

One other dimension of the individuality issue is the accusation that computer-based systems exhibit "power" over the individual. This is natural if the computer is perceived as a machine over which one has no control. Some feel that modern technology such as computers will somehow enslave humanity, making people the servant and machines the master. This issue could be debated, but Peter Drucker, the management expert, is able to dismiss it quite readily by relating the comment made to him by one of his students who was one of the early computer engineers: "I am being asked all the time whether I am not afraid of becoming the computer's servant. I do not understand the question. All I have to do is pull the plug."[17] This is perhaps an oversimplification because many organizations *are* too overly dependent on computers, but it does get at an important issue. Man created and developed the computer with his ingenuity, and

---

[17] Peter F. Drucker, *Management* (New York: Harper & Row, 1974), p. 225.

there is no reason to believe that the machine could somehow gain power over him. Misapplications and abuses of the computer by man are another problem, and safeguards must be developed to prevent them.

The real issue was perhaps captured by Margaret Mead, the anthropologist and social critic, who argued that the long-term benefits of automation (and computerization) far outweigh the short-term inconveniences. The problem is how to get through the transition period, and it is coping with change that poses the greatest challenge for mankind.[18] Many other technological advances have had similar effects on society—mass transportation, communication, production, and so forth—and man's position has usually been bettered because of his ingenuity and skills in mastering technology.

CONCLUDING REMARKS

Though it is only several decades since the first computer was commercially installed, computerization is affecting the life of every man, woman, and child in our society. The computer's capabilities have been applied to numerous nonbusiness as well as business spheres, and more applications are continually being developed. We may think we have seen a lot, but the progress which will take place in computers over the remainder of the 20th century is difficult to imagine. It has been estimated, for example, that by 1985 the costs of computer entry, storage, and access will fall below the cost of paper files, and the use of paper in the average office will decline dramatically. Such predictions indicate that organizations of the future will require some drastic adjustments in modes of operation.

It is inevitable that computers will grow in importance and come to touch our lives more frequently and in numerous ways. The challenge is to develop the best approaches by which man can maximize the positive and minimize the negative effects of computers on society. Trends in computer hardware and software are already moving in a direction which will make the computer more humane rather than making man less human. Audiovisual displays, English language programming, and "talking computers," are all evidence of this trend.

In the meantime, the issues of automation, privacy, individualism, and power are likely to continue to take on importance. It is hoped, and in fact anticipated, that they will become important not because they are neglected and thus create amplified social problems, but because man will find ways to capitalize on the inherent weaknesses

---

[18] Margaret Mead, "The Challenge of Automation to Education for Human Values," *The World of the Computer*, ed. John Diebold (New York: Random House, 1973), pp. 345–49.

of computer systems and thus provide a brighter technological future for society.

ASSIGNMENTS

14-1.   Do research of your own to reveal other nonbusiness applications of the computer. Extend your research to include projections of future applications up to the year 1985.

14-2.   What additional applications of the computer do you foresee for the field of education? At the university level? At the elementary and secondary school levels?

14-3.   Conduct a survey of the journal *Computers and the Humanities*. What is your appraisal of the computer applications discussed there?

14-4.   What additional applications do you foresee in the field of health and medicine? Do research on this topic.

14-5.   Discuss the relationship between automation and job satisfaction at the following levels — (a) the blue collar worker level, (b) the supervisory level, (c) the top-management level.

14-6.   Write a book review on *Databanks in a Free Society*, by Alan F. Westin and Michael A. Baker (Chicago: Quadrangle Books, 1974).

14-7.   What do you feel will be the relationship between the computer, automation, and leisure in the next five years?

14-8.   What exactly are the individual's rights to privacy? What boundaries would you place on the individual's rights in this regard?

14-9.   How might government ensure privacy rights in this era?

14-10. Your father has just learned that you are taking a course in Computers for Business and he rages that the computer is dehumanizing him and gaining power over him. Outline the argument you would give him against such accusations.

REFERENCES

Books

Avebury, Lord, Ron Coverson, John Humphries, and Brian Meek *Computers and the Year 2000*. Manchester, England: NCC Publications, 1972.

Diebold, John *The World of the Computer*. New York: Random House, 1973.

Drucker, Peter F. *Management*. New York: Harper & Row, 1974.

Ellul, Jacques *The Technological Society*. New York: Alfred A. Knopf, 1964.

Hoffman, L. J. *Security and Privacy in Computer Systems*. Los Angeles: Melville Publishing Co., 1973.

Martin, James and A. R. D. Norman *The Computerized Society*. Englewood Cliffs, N.J.: Prentice-Hall, 1970.

Mumford, Lewis *The Myth and the Machine: Technics and Human Development*. New York: Harcourt, Brace, & World, 1967.

Mumford, Lewis *The Myth and the Machine: The Pentagon of Power*. New York: Harcourt Brace Jovanovich, 1970.

Parkman, Ralph *The Cybernetic Society*. New York: Pergamon Press, 1972.

Rothman, Stanley and Charles Mosmann *Computers and Society*. Chicago: Science Research Associates, 1972.

Wiener, Norbert *The Human Use of Human Beings*. Boston: Houghton Mifflin Co., 1954.

Westin, Alan *Privacy and Freedom*. New York: Atheneum Publishers, 1967.

Westin, Alan, and Michael Baker *Databanks in a Free Society*. Chicago: Quadrangle Books, 1974.

Articles

Carroll, Archie B. "An Organizational Need: Forecasting and Planning for the Social Environment." *Managerial Planning*, May–June 1973, pp. 1–13; 20.

"Justice Department Has an 'Open Mind' on Ervin Bill for Federal Privacy Board." *Datamation*, March 1974, p. 118.

Kaysen, Carl "Data Banks and Dossiers." *The Public Interest*, no. 7 (Spring 1967) pp. 52–60.

Lauren, Roy "The Problems of Reliability, Privacy, and Security in Data Banks." In *Rethinking the Practice of Management*, ed. Diebold Group, Inc. (New York: Frederick A. Praeger, 1973).

Madnick, Stuart E. "The Future of Computers." *Technology Review*, July–August 1973, p. 35 ff.

Mead, Margaret "The Challenge of Automation to Education for Human Values." In *Automation, Education, and Human Values*, ed. W. W. Brickman and Stanley Lehrer. School and Society Books, 1966.

Appendixes

A
Glossary

B
The Binary Number System

C
The Punched Card and Keypunch Machine

D
St. Joseph's Hospital

Appendix
A

Glossary

A

Access Time The time interval between the instant at which data are called for from a storage device and the instant delivery begins.

Accumulator A register in which the result of an arithmetic or logic operation is formed.

Address An identification, as represented by a name, label, or number, for a register, location in storage, or any other data source or destination such as the location of a station in a communication network.

ADP Automatic data processing.

Algorithm A prescribed set of well-defined rules or processes for the solution of a problem in a finite number of steps, e.g., a full statement of an arithmetic procedure for evaluating sin x to a stated precision. Contrast with heuristic.

Alphanumeric Pertaining to a character set that contains letters, digits, and usually other characters such as punctuation marks. Synonymous with alphameric.

Analog Computer A computer in which analog representation of data is mainly used.

Arithmetic Unit The unit of a computing system that contains the circuits that perform arithmetic operations.

Array An arrangement of elements in one or more dimensions.

Assemble To prepare a machine language program from a symbolic language program by substituting absolute operation codes for symbolic operation codes and absolute or relocatable addresses for symbolic addresses.

Assembler A computer program that assembles.

Automatic Data Processing Data processing largely performed by automatic means.

Auxiliary Operation An offline operation performed by equipment not under control of the central processing unit.

Auxiliary Storage (1) A storage that supplements another storage. Contrast with main storage. (2) In flowcharting, an offline operation performed by equipment not under control of the central processing unit.

B

Batch Processing Pertaining to the technique of executing a set of computer programs such that each is completed before the next program of the set is started.

BCD Binary-coded decimal notation.

Benchmark Problem A problem used to evaluate the performance of hardware or software or both.

Binary (1) Pertaining to a characteristic or property involving a selection, choice, or condition in which there are two possibilities. (2) Pertaining to the number representation system with a radix of two.

Binary Code A code that makes use of exactly two distinct characters, usually 0 and 1.

Binary Digit In binary notation, either of the characters, 0 or 1.

Bistable Pertaining to a device capable of assuming either one of two stable states.

Bit A binary digit.

Block Diagram A diagram of a system, instrument, or computer in which the principal parts are represented by suitable associated geometrical figures to show both the basic functions and the functional relationships among the parts. Contrast with flowchart.

Boolean (1) Pertaining to the processes used in the algebra formulated by George Boole. (2) Pertaining to the operations of formal logic.

Branch A set of instructions that are executed between two successive decision instructions.

Buffer A routine or storage used to compensate for a difference in rate of flow of data, or time of occurrence of events, when transmitting data from one device to another.

Byte A sequence of adjacent binary digits operated upon as a unit and usually shorter than a computer word.

C

Calculator A data processor especially suitable for performing arithmetical operations which requires frequent intervention by a human operator.

Call To transfer control to a specified closed subroutine.

Card Hopper The portion of a card processing machine that holds the cards to be processed and makes them available to a card feed mechanism. Contrast with card stacker.

Card Stacker The portion of a card processing machine that receives processed cards. Contrast with card hopper.

Central Processing Unit A unit of a computer that includes the circuits controlling the interpretation and execution of instructions. Synonymous with main frame. Abbreviated CPU.

Character A letter, digit, or other symbol that is used as part of the organization, control, or representation of data. A character is often in the form of a spatial arrangement of adjacent or connected strokes.

Character String A string consisting solely of characters.

Closed Shop Pertaining to the operation of a computer facility in which most productive problem programming is performed by a group of programming specialists rather than the problem originators. The use of the computer itself may also be described as closed shop if full-time trained operators rather than user/programmers serve as the operators. Contrast with open shop.

COBOL (COmmon Business Oriented Language) A business data processing language.

Code In data processing, to represent data or a computer program in a symbolic form that can be accepted by a data processor.

Collate To combine items from two or more ordered sets into one set having a specified order not necessarily the same as any of the original sets. Contrast with merge.

Compile To prepare a machine language program from a computer program written in another programming language by making use of the overall logic structure of the program, or generating more than one machine instruction for each symbolic statement, or both, as well as performing the function of an assembler.

Compiler A program that compiles.

Computer A data processor that can perform substantial computation, including numerous arithmetic or logic operations, without intervention by a human operator during the run.

Computer Network A complex consisting of two or more interconnected computers.

Computer Program A series of instructions or statements, in a form acceptable to a computer, prepared in order to achieve a certain result.

Computer Word A sequence of bits or characters treated as a unit and capable of being stored in one computer location. Synonymous with machine word.

CPU Central processing unit.

Cybernetics That branch of learning which brings together theories and studies on communication and control in living organisms and machines.

D

Data A representation of facts, concepts, or instructions in a formalized manner suitable for communication, interpretation, or processing by humans or automatic means.

Data Bank A comprehensive collection of libraries of data. For example, one line of an invoice may form an item, a complete invoice may form a record, a complete set of such records may form a file, the collection of inventory control files may form a library, and the libraries used by an organization are known as its data bank.

Data Hierarchy A data structure consisting of sets and subsets such that every subset of a set is of lower rank than the data of the set.

Data Processing The execution of a systematic sequence of operations performed upon data. Synonymous with information processing.

Debug To detect, locate, and remove mistakes from a routine or malfunctions from a computer. Synonymous with troubleshoot.

Decimal (1) Pertaining to a characteristic or property involving a selection, choice, or condition in which there are ten possibilities. (2) Pertaining to the number representation system with a radix of ten.

Decision A determination of future action.

Decision Table A table of all contingencies that are to be considered in the description of a problem, together with the actions to be taken. Decision tables are sometimes used in place of flowcharts for problem description and documentation.

Deck A collection of punched cards. Synonymous with card deck.

Diagnostic Pertaining to the detection and isolation of a malfunction or mistake.

Digital Computer A computer in which discrete representation of data is mainly used.

Direct Access Pertaining to the process of obtaining data from, or placing data into, storage where the time required for such access is independent of the location of the data most recently obtained or placed in storage.

Document A medium and the data recorded on it for human use, e.g., a report sheet, a book.

Dump To copy the content of all or part of a storage, usually from an internal storage into an external storage.

E

EAM Electrical accounting machine.

Edit To modify the form or format of data, e.g., to insert or delete characters such as page numbers or decimal points.

EDP Electronic data processing.

Electronic Data Processing Data processing largely performed by electronic devices.

Emulate To imitate one system with another such that the imitating system accepts the same data, executes the same programs, and achieves the same results as the imitated system. Contrast with simulate.

Emulator A device or computer program that emulates.

F

Feedback Loop The components and processes involved in correcting or controlling a system by using part of the output as input.

Ferrite An iron compound frequently used in the construction of magnetic cores.

Field In a record, a specified area used for a particular category of data, e.g., a group of card columns used to represent a wage rate, a set of bit locations in a computer word used to express the address of the operand.

File A collection of related records treated as a unit. For example, one line of an invoice may form an item, a complete invoice may form a record, the complete set of such records may form a file, the collection of inventory control files may form a library, and the libraries used by an organization are known as its data bank.

File Maintenance The activity of keeping a file up to date by adding, changing, or deleting data.

Flowchart A graphical representation for the definition, analysis, or solution of a problem, in which symbols are used to represent operations, data flow, equipment, etc. Contrast with block diagram.

Format The arrangement of data.

FORTRAN (FORmula TRANslating system) A language primarily used to express computer programs by arithmetic formulas.

G

General-Purpose Computer A computer that is designed to handle a wide variety of problems.

H

Half-Word A contiguous sequence of bits or characters which comprises half a computer word and is capable of being addressed as a unit.

Hardware Physical equipment, as opposed to the computer program or method of use, e.g., mechanical, magnetic, electrical, or electronic devices. Contrast with software.

Header Card A card that contains information related to the data in cards that follow.

Heuristic Pertaining to exploratory methods of problem solving in which solutions are discovered by evaluation of the progress made toward the final result. Contrast with algorithm.

I

Initialize To set counters, switches, and addresses to zero or other starting values at the beginning of, or at prescribed points in, a computer routine.

Input Pertaining to a device, process, or channel involved in the insertion of data or states, or to the data or states involved.

Instruction A statement that specified an operation and the values or locations of its operands.

Internal Storage Addressable storage directly controlled by the central processing unit of a digital computer.

Interpreter A computer program that translates and executes each source language statement before translating and executing the next one.

I/O An abbreviation for input/output.

J

Job A specified group of tasks prescribed as a unit of work for a computer. By extension, a job usually includes all necessary computer programs, linkages, files, and instructions to the operating system.

Job Control Statement A statement in a job that is used in identifying the job or describing its requirements to the operating system.

K

Key One or more characters within an item of data that are used to identify it or control its use.

Keypunch A keyboard-actuated device that punches holes in a card to represent data.

L

Linear Programming In operations research, a procedure for locating the maximum or minimum of a linear function of variables that are subject to linear constraints.

Linkage In programming, coding that connects two separately coded routines.

Loop A sequence of instructions that is executed repeatedly until a terminal condition prevails.

M

Machine Instruction An instruction that a machine can recognize and execute.

Machine Language A language that is used directly by a machine.

Machine Readable Medium A medium that can convey data to a given sensing device. Synonymous with automated data medium.

Macro Instruction An instruction in a source language that is equivalent to a specified sequence of machine instructions.

Magnetic Card A card with a magnetic surface on which data can be stored by selective magnetization of portions of the flat surface.

Magnetic Disc A flat circular plate with a magnetic surface on which data can be stored by selective magnetization of portions of the flat surface.

Magnetic Drum A right circular cylinder with a magnetic surface on which data can be stored by selective magnetization of portions of the curved surface.

Magnetic Ink An ink that contains particles of a magnetic substance whose presence can be detected by magnetic sensors.

Magnetic Ink Character Recognition The machine recognition of characters printed with magnetic ink. Contrast with optical character recognition. Abbreviated MICR.

Magnetic Tape A tape with a magnetic surface on which data can be stored by selective polarization of portions of the surface.

Main Frame Same as central processing unit.

Main Storage The general-purpose storage of a computer. Usually, main storage can be accessed directly by the operating registers. Contrast with auxiliary storage.

Maintenance Any activity intended to eliminate faults or to keep hardware or programs in satisfactory working condition, including tests, measurements, replacements, adjustments, and repairs.

Management Information System An information system designed to aid in the performance of management functions. Abbreviated MIS.

Master File A file that is either relatively permanent or that is treated as an authority in a particular job.

Mathematical Programming In operations research, a procedure for locating the maximum or minimum of a function subject to constraints.

Medium The material, or configuration thereof, on which data are recorded, e.g., paper tape, cards, magnetic tape. Synonymous with data medium.

Merge To combine items from two or more similarly ordered sets into one set that is arranged in the same order. Contrast with collate.

MICR Magnetic ink character recognition.

MIS Management information system.

Modem (MOdulator-DEModulator) A device that modulates and demodulates signals transmitted over communication facilities.

Monitor Software or hardware that observes, supervises, controls, or verifies the operations of a system.

Monte Carlo Method A method of obtaining an approximate solution to a numerical problem by the use of random numbers.

Multiple Punching Punching more than one hole in the same column of a punched card by means of more than one keystroke.

Multiprocessing Pertaining to the simultaneous execution of two or more computer programs or sequences of instructions by a computer or computer network.

Multiprogramming Pertaining to the concurrent execution of two or more programs by a computer.

N

Nest To imbed subroutines or data in other subroutines or data at a different hierarchical level such that the different levels of routines or data can be executed or accessed recursively.

Numeric Pertaining to numerals or to representation by means of numerals. Synonymous with numerical.

O

Object Code Output from a compiler or assembler which is itself executable machine code or is suitable for processing to produce executable machine code.

OCR Optical character recognition.

Offline Pertaining to equipment or devices not under control of the central processing unit.

Offline Storage   Storage not under control of the central processing unit.

Online   Pertaining to equipment or devices under control of the central processing unit.

Online Storage   Storage under control of the central processing unit.

Open Shop   Pertaining to the operation of a computer facility in which most productive problem programming is performed by the problem originator rather than by a group of programming specialists. The use of the computer itself may also be described as open shop if the user/programmer also serves as the operator, rather than a full-time trained operator. Contrast with closed shop.

Operating System   Software which controls the execution of computer programs and which may provide scheduling, debugging, input/output control, accounting, compilation, storage assignment, data management, and related services.

Operations Research   The use of the scientific method to provide criteria for decisions concerning the actions of people, machines, and other resources in a system involving repeatable operations. Synonymous with operations analysis. Abbreviated OR.

Optical Character Recognition   The machine identification of printed characters through use of light-sensitive devices. Contrast with magnetic ink character recognition. Abbreviated OCR.

Optical Scanner   A device that optically scans printed or written data and generates their digital representations.

Output   Pertaining to a device, process, or channel involved in an output process, or to the data or states involved.

Overflow   That portion of the result of an operation that exceeds the capacity of the intended unit of storage.

Overlay   The technique of repeatedly using the same blocks of internal storage during different stages of a program. When one routine is no longer needed in storage, another routine can replace all or part of it.

P

Parallel Computer   (1) A computer having multiple arithmetic or logic units that are used to accomplish parallel operations or parallel processing. Contrast with serial computer. (2) Historically, a computer, some specified characteristic of which is parallel, e.g., a computer that manipulates all bits of a word in parallel.

Parity Bit   A check bit appended to an array of binary digits to make the sum of all the binary digits, including the check bit, always odd or always even.

Parity Check   A check that tests whether the number of ones (or zeros) in an array of binary digits is odd or even. Synonymous with odd-even check.

Pass   One cycle of processing a body of data.

Peripheral Equipment   In a data processing system, any unit of equipment, distinct from the central processing unit, which may provide the system with outside communication.

Predefined Process   A process that is identified only by name and that is defined elsewhere.

Problem Oriented Language   A programming language designed for the convenient expression of a given class of problems.

Procedure Oriented Language   A programming language designed for the convenient expression of procedures used in the solution of a wide class of problems.

Processor   (1) In hardware, a data processor. (2) In software, a computer program that includes the compiling, assembling, translating, and related functions for a specific programming language; COBOL processor, FORTRAN processor.

Program   A series of actions proposed in order to achieve a certain result.

Program Library   A collection of available computer programs and routines.

Programmer   A person mainly involved in designing, writing, and testing computer programs.

Programming Flowchart   A flowchart representing the sequence of operations in a program.

Programming Language   A language used to prepare computer programs.

Punch A perforation, as in a punched card or paper tape.

Punched Card (1) A card punched with a pattern of holes to represent data. (2) A card as in (1) before being punched.

Punched Tape A tape on which a pattern of holes or cuts is used to represent data.

R

Random Access (1) Same as direct access. (2) In COBOL, an access mode in which specific logical records are obtained from or placed into a mass storage file in a non-sequential manner.

Random Numbers A series of numbers obtained by chance.

Read To acquire or interpret data from a storage device, a data medium, or any other source.

Real Time (1) Pertaining to the actual time during which a physical process transpires. (2) Pertaining to the performance of a computation during the actual time that the related physical process transpires, in order that results of the computation can be used in guiding the physical process.

Record A collection of related items of data, treated as a unit, for example, one line of an invoice may form a record; a complete set of such records may form a file.

Register A device capable of storing a specified amount of data such as one word.

Rounding Error An error due to roundoff.

Roundoff To delete the least significant digit or digits of a numeral, and to adjust the part retained in accordance with some rule.

Routine An ordered set of instructions that may have some general or frequent use.

Run A single, continuous performance of a computer program or routine.

S

Serial Access Pertaining to the sequential or consecutive transmission of data to or from storage.

Serial Computer (1) A computer having a single arithmetic and logic unit. (2) A computer some specified characteristic of which is serial, e.g., a computer that manipulates all bits of a word serially. Contrast with parallel computer.

Sign Bit A binary digit occupying the sign position.

Simulate To represent certain features of the behavior of a physical or abstract system of the behavior of another system.

Simulation The representation of certain features of the behavior of a physical or abstract system by the behavior of another system, e.g., the representation of physical phenomena by means of operations performed by a computer or the representation of operations of a computer by those of another computer.

Software A set of computer programs, procedures, and possibly associated documentation concerned with the operation of a data processing system, e.g., compilers, library routines, manuals, circuit diagrams. Contrast with hardware.

Sort To segregate items into groups according to some definite rules.

Source Language The language from which a statement is translated.

Source Program A computer program written in a source language. Contrast with object program.

Storage Pertaining to a device into which data can be entered, in which they can be held, and from which they can be retrieved at a later time.

Syntax (1) The structure of expressions in a language. (2) The rules governing the structure of a language.

T

Table A collection of data in which each item is uniquely identified by a label, by its position relative to the other items, or by some other means.

Table Look-up A procedure for obtaining the function value corresponding to an argument from a table of function values.

Tape to Card Pertaining to equipment or methods that transmit data from either magnetic tape or punched tape to punched cards.

Telecommunications   Pertaining to the transmission of signals over long distances, such as by telegraph, radio, or television.

Time Sharing   Pertaining to the interleaved use of the time of a device.

Tracing Routine   A routine that provides a historical record of specified events in the execution of a program.

Transaction File   A file containing relatively transient data to be processed in combination with a master file. For example, in a payroll application, a transaction file indicating hours worked might be processed with a master file containing employee name and rate of pay. Synonymous with detail file.

Translate   To transform statements from one language to another without significantly changing the meaning.

Truncation Error   An error due to truncation. Contrast with rounding error.

Truth Table   A table that describes a logic function by listing all possible combinations of input values and indicating, for each combination, the true output values.

U

Underflow   Pertaining to the condition that arises when a machine computation yields a nonzero result smaller than the smallest nonzero quantity that the intended unit of storage is capable of storing. Contrast with overflow.

Unit   A device having a special function.

V

Variable   A quantity that can assume any of a given set of values.

W

Word   A character string or a bit string considered as an entity.

Word Length   A measure of the size of a word, usually specified in units such as characters or binary digits.

Write   To record data in a storage device or a data medium. The recording need not be permanent, such as the writing on a cathode-ray tube display device.

Appendix

B
The Binary Number System

The origins of the binary number system can be traced back over 5,000 years to China, but the first substantial work with binary was done by the German mathematician Gottfried Leibnitz (1646–1716). Of more recent interest, it was in 1946 that John von Neumann, originator of the stored-program concept, suggested that the binary number system be incorporated in computer designs.

There are several good reasons why the binary system should be used with computers:

1. To simplify the arithmetic/logic circuitry of the computer.
2. To provide a simple way of storing data and instructions.
3. To increase computer storage and processing reliability.

The binary number system is based on the number 2 rather than 10, as in the decimal system. Whereas in the decimal number system the number 436_{10} (the 10 identifies the number as being in decimal) can be viewed as

$$4 \times 10^2 + 3 \times 10^1 \times 6 \times 0^0$$

in binary a number such as 1101_2 refers to

$$1 \times 2^3 + 1 \times 2^2 + 0 \times 2^1 + 1 \times 2^0$$

BINARY TO DECIMAL CONVERSION

Converting a binary to a decimal number is not difficult. The important thing to remember in binary is that the place position of the digit represents a power of two (e.g., 2^0, 2^1, 2^2, 2^3, 2^4 . . .) as opposed to the tens, hundreds, thousands, etc. (e.g., a power of 10) in the decimal system. Consequently the decimal value of $0010\ 1011_2$ is as follows:

Binary number	0	0	1	0	1	0	1	1
Power of base	2^7	2^6	2^5	2^4	2^3	2^2	2^1	2^0
Or	128	64	32	16	8	4	2	1
Decimal equivalent	0 +	0 +	32 +	0 +	8 +	0 +	2 +	1
Or	43							

The digits in the binary number are simply multiplied by two raised to the appropriate positional power and then summed.

DECIMAL TO BINARY CONVERSION

Converting binary numbers to decimal can be performed through what is commonly referred to as the "remainder method." This method consists of dividing the decimal number by two and all successive answers by two until the process can continue no longer. The remainders generated form the binary equivalent.

For illustrative purposes let us use 250_{10} for an example:

			Remainder
1st Division	$2\overline{)250}$	125	0
2nd Division	$2\overline{)125}$	62	1
3rd Division	$2\overline{)\ 62}$	31	0
4th Division	$2\overline{)\ 31}$	15	1
5th Division	$2\overline{)\ 15}$	7	1
6th Division	$2\overline{)\ \ 7}$	3	1
7th Division	$2\overline{)\ \ 3}$	1	1
8th Division	$2\overline{)\ \ 1}$	0	1

The result is:

$$250_{10} = 1111\ 1010_2$$

The first binary digit (the 2^0's position) is the remainder from the first division, the second digit (the 2^1's position) is the remainder from the second division, and so on for the other digits.

To check our answer, let us convert back to decimal:

$$1111\ 1010_2 = 1 \times 2^7 + 1 \times 2^6 + 1 \times 2^5 + 1 \times 2^4 + 1 \times 2^3 + 0 \times 2^2$$
$$+ 1 \times 2^1 + 0 \times 2^0$$
$$= 128 + 64 + 32 + 16 + 8 + 0 + 2 + 0$$
$$= 250_{10}$$

BINARY ADDITION

In binary addition there are four rules to remember:

$$0 + 0 = 0$$
$$0 + 1 = 1$$
$$1 + 0 = 1$$
$$1 + 1 = 0 \text{ and a carry of } 1$$

Thus we may add 1110_2 and 1011_2 as follows:

carries: 111

1110_2	(14_{10})
$\underline{1011_2}$	$\underline{(11_{10})}$
11001	(25_{10})

In the 2^0's position, $0 + 1$ is 1, so we bring down 1 and move to the 2^1's position. There, $1 + 1$ is 10, so we bring down the 0 and carry 1 to the 2^2's position. There the 1 carried plus the 1 present gives 10, so another carry continues to the 2^3's position. Carrying the 1 to the 2^3's position, where $1 + 1 = 10$ is already present, gives 11, so we bring down the value of 1 and carry 1 to the 2^4's position. This 1 is then brought down, giving the final answer.

BINARY SUBTRACTION

Binary subtraction also has four simple arithmetic rules to be followed:

$1 - 1 = 0$
$1 - 0 = 1$
$0 - 1 = 1$ with a borrow from the next column of the minuend
$0 - 0 = 0$

Whenever a digit in the subtrahend is larger than a corresponding digit in the minuend, "borrowing" is necessary. A borrow will cause a 0 in the minuend to become a 1, and all succeeding 0's to be changed to 1 until a 1 can be changed to a 0. For example,

Minuend	1000_2	(8_{10})	10010_2	(18_{10})
Subtrahend	$\underline{-0001_2}$	$\underline{-(1_{10})}$	$\underline{1001_2}$	$\underline{-(9_{10})}$
	0111_2	(7_{10})	1001_2	(9_{10})

More could obviously be said about the binary number system. But managers seldom need to know much more than that there is a binary number system and most computers use a form of binary in their operations. The only skills required are knowledge of how to convert from one number system to another and how to perform the most basic arithmetic operations such as addition and subtraction.

ASSIGNMENTS

B-1. Convert the following binary numbers to decimal numbers:

    a. 1110_2

    b. $1110\ 1100_2$

    c. $0111\ 0001_2$

B-2. Convert the following decimal numbers to binary numbers:

    a. 326_{10}

    b. 18_{10}

    c. 37_{10}

B-3. Add the following numbers together in binary:

    a. $1110_2 + 0111_2$

    b. $101_2 + 18_{10}$

    c. $85_{10} + 14_{10}$ (convert to binary first)

B-4. Subtract the following numbers in binary:

    a. $1111_2 - 101_2$

    b. $1001_2 - 3_{10}$

    c. $15_{10} - 4_{10}$ (convert to binary first)

Appendix
C

The Punched Card and the Keypunch Machine

The most commonly used input medium is the punched card. Character-coded punched holes provide a means for communicating data and instructions to the computer. Typically, the holes are punched by a keypunch machine.

THE PUNCHED CARD

Many different varieties of punched cards exist. The most popular is the Hollerith punched card shown in Figure C–1. It can be seen that there are 80 columns available for storing characters. Each character is identified by a unique series of punched holes. There is seldom any need to know the coding scheme used.

Frequently, a group of columns is used for a specific purpose. For example, columns 30–38 on a card might be used for recording a

FIGURE C–1
Hollerith Punched Card

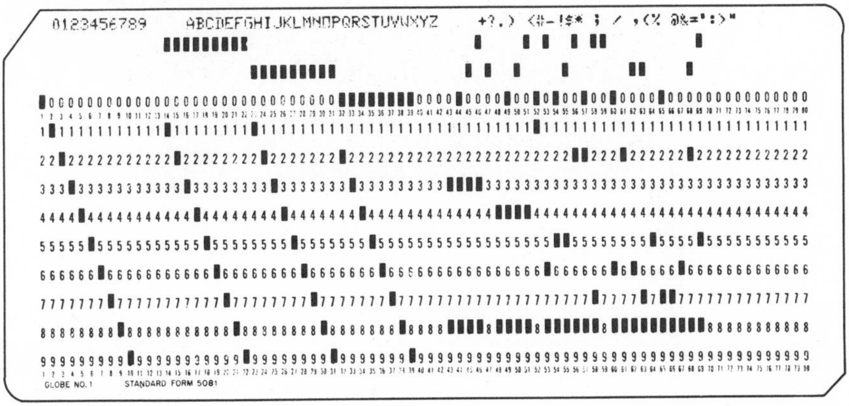

worker's social security number. When considered together, these columns are referred to as a *field*. Keypunching largely involves punching the desired data and instructions into the correct fields. Many punched cards are carefully designed to help avoid keypunching errors. Lines and words indicating the different fields are printed on the face of the card.

THE KEYPUNCH MACHINE

The most popular keypunch machine is the IBM 029 developed for use with the IBM System/360. This keypunch machine is shown in Figure C–2. Some of its most important components are indicated.

The first step in using the keypunch machine is to turn it on. The *main line switch* serves this purpose. The cards that are to be punched are placed in the *card hopper*. Next, attention is turned to the keyboard. The keyboard for the IBM 029 is shown in Figure C–3. Most

FIGURE C–2
IBM 029 Keypunch Machine

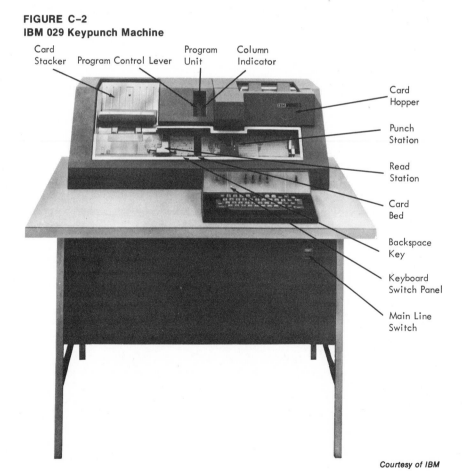

Card Stacker   Program Control Lever   Program Unit   Column Indicator

Card Hopper

Punch Station

Read Station

Card Bed

Backspace Key

Keyboard Switch Panel

Main Line Switch

Courtesy of IBM

FIGURE C–3
IBM 029 Keyboard

of the keys require no explanation because of their similarity to those on a typewriter keyboard. However, some of the more important *functional keys* warrant brief discussion. The functional keys largely direct the keypunch machine's operations.

NUMERIC   When pressed, the numeric key causes the numeric and special characters to be punched rather than the alphabetic characters.

FEED   Pressing this key results in a card being fed from the card hopper to the *card bed.*

REG   The register key is used to move a card into the *punch station* for punching or the *read station* for reading.

DUP   Pressing this key causes the contents of a card in the read station to be duplicated on a card in the punch station.

REL   Pressing the release key causes cards at the punch and read stations to be advanced.

MULT PCH   The multiple-punch key can be used to suppress column advancement so that more than one character can be punched in a single column.

The IBM 029 also has a number of *functional switches* that help control the keypunch machine's operations. These switches are on the *keyboard switch panel.* Figure C–4 shows these switches. The uses of the most important switches are as follows:

PRINT   When this switch is on, the character punched is also printed at the top of the card.

FIGURE C–4
IBM 029 Keyboard Switch Panel

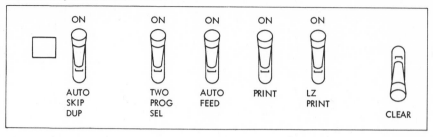

AUTO FEED   If this switch is on, all cards are automatically advanced, and a card is fed from the card hopper whenever the card being punched is released.

CLEAR   Pressing this switch causes all cards being proc-essed to be cleared to the *card stacker.*

Consider the actions of a typical user who is punching a program or data deck. The PRINT and AUTO FEED switches are placed in the ON position. The FEED key is pressed to feed a card from the card hopper to the card bed. Pressing the FEED key again causes the first card to be registered (moved to the punch station) and another card to be fed from the card hopper. The user then punches the de-sired characters on the card. If while punching the card there is some question as to which column is under the punch dies, the *column indicator* can be consulted. If there is a need to backspace to a previ-ous column, the *backspace key* can be pressed. Once the card has been punched, the REL key is pressed which releases the card. Because the AUTO FEED switch is ON, all of the cards are ad-vanced and another card is fed from the card hopper. Keypunching then continues. After the deck has been punched the CLEAR switch is pressed in order to clear all of the cards to the card stacker.

Not discussed in this appendix is the use of the *program control unit.* This unit is very useful when repetitive keypunching in specific fields must be performed; for example, skipping to a particular field on employee record cards to enter the number of hours worked. Given a situation like this, the IBM 029 manual should be consulted for instructions on how to use the program control unit. When this unit is not being used, the *program control lever* should be dis-engaged.

ASSIGNMENT

C-1.   Keypunch a card according to the following specifications. Start your entries in the leftmost column of each field (left *justified*).

Columns	*Contents*
1–20	LAST NAME, FIRST NAME MIDDLE INITIAL
21–24	BLANK
25–34	MAJOR
35–38	BLANK
39–46	TELEPHONE NUMBER(XXX–XXXX)
47–50	BLANK
51–70	ADDRESS
71–74	BLANK
75	0 if you prefer to work alone
	1 if you would like to work with someone in studying for the course

Appendix
D

St. Joseph's Hospital

$\mathbf{M}$r. Thomas Carter, a management consultant with Management Services Company, was discussing the current state of the development of a Hospital Information System (HIS) at St. Joseph's Hospital with Sister Mary Thomas, the hospital administrator. St. Joseph's Hospital is a voluntary, nonprofit general hospital operated by the Sisters of Hope and is accredited by the Joint Commission on Accreditation of Hospitals (JCAH). The hospital employs approximately 800 people and has a bed capacity of 350. The hospital offers an inpatient care program in the basic general services of medicine, surgery, obstetrics, pediatrics, psychiatry and intensive and coronary care. Outpatient care is also provided through an active and substantial emergency service, organized clinic service and a social service program. The hospital was originally opened in 1882 as a 30-bed complex. The present hospital complex consists of eight buildings, including the hospital proper, a laundry facility, a power plant, a computer center, living quarters for interns, residents, and student nurses and a nursing school. The hospital site covers $9\frac{1}{2}$ acres and is located one mile from the center of Benton, a city with a population of 135,000. The hospital's long-range plans include further expansion and modernization to meet the substantial increase in demand for additional hospital beds and related facilities, based on expected population growth as well as the changing technology.

Prior to 1950 the hospital purchased an NCR 3100 Bookkeeping Machine[1] for the purpose of recording pertinent financial data on ledger cards and to assist in the preparation of financial reports. In 1959 an NCR 390 Computer[2] was introduced to process data pertain-

---

[1] A particular model of a bookkeeping machine manufactured by National Cash Register Co. Not a computer; designed to post financial transactions to ledger cards.

[2] A small-model computer also manufactured by National Cash Register Co. Application of this computer was limited to financial transactions within the hospital.

ing to Accounts Receivable, Hospital Payroll and other General Ledger accounts. In March 1968, an IBM 360 Model 30[3] was installed at the direction of the Controller of the Order. Mr. Carter learned from the local IBM representative that his company had recommended a smaller model 360, based on a feasibility study performed by IBM. The decision was made to lease the Model 30, however, because it was thought to be more capable of handling a hospital information system than the smaller model.

Prior to the installation of this equipment, the data processing function was established as a separate hospital department reporting to the hospital controller (see Figure D–1). Mr. Alfred Massey, who had been employed as a computer programmer since January 1967, was promoted to manager of the department. Mr. Massey had completed one year of college in 1963 and had worked as both a programmer and a systems analyst for two and a half years before coming to the hospital. At the time Mr. Massey was promoted, a new programmer-analyst, Mr. John Fulton, was added to the staff. Mr. Fulton had completed one year of college in 1957, had four years' experience as a keypunch operator with both IBM and the U.S. Air Force and had also worked as a systems analyst for four and a half years before he was hired by the hospital. In January 1969, Mr. Fulton was promoted to Supervisor of Systems and Programming, and in October of the same year he was promoted to Assistant Department Manager.

When Sister Mary had first contacted Mr. Carter concerning the HIS, she expressed her concern over the development of this system and the progress that had been made to date. Prior to the meeting with Sister Mary, Mr. Carter did some research on Hospital Information Systems and found that this concept differed from the Management Information Systems normally associated with other types of businesses.

A total hospital system, he learned, went beyond the management information area to include information flow throughout the hospital in medical care services and patient accounting, as well as in management and control reporting. Carter believed that an effective management information system should be in operation before the total hospital information system could be introduced. A hospital information system could be envisioned as a master communication and

---

[3] A computer system consisting of a central processing unit (CPU), a printer, disk drives, and a card read-punch unit.

This case was prepared under the direction of the Director of the Case Writing Center, College of Business Administration, University of Notre Dame, by Lawrence Ryan and Patrick Brady. It is designed for class discussion rather than to illustrate effective or ineffective handling of an administrative situation. Distributed by the Intercollegiate Case Clearing House, Soldiers Field, Boston, Mass., 02163. All rights reserved to the contributors. Printed in the U.S.A.

FIGURE D–1
St. Joseph's Hospital: Organization Chart, Data Processing Department

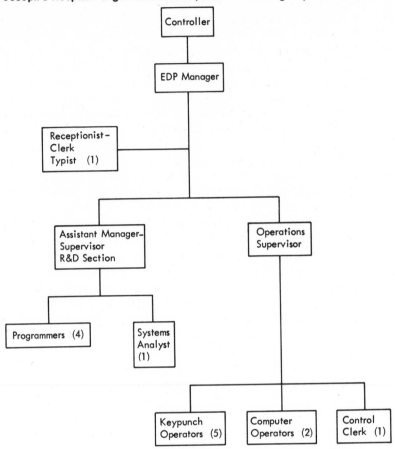

monitoring system with a broad data base of retrievable information. The system requires a computer which is linked to a network of terminal devices in key locations throughout the hospital for transmission of input and output data. These strategically located terminals are connected to the central computer through a network switching device. Data are transmitted to or received from the computer through each of these terminals. A total HIS operates on-line or on real-time so that the computer can be called on for data processing tasks, if required, at all information terminals at the same time. Carter believed that any HIS system would be "as unique as the hospital that implements it."

Generally patient information begins with the initial hospital contact and is maintained and updated during the entire time that the patient receives treatment at the hospital. Pertinent patient information is immediately processed through a terminal to the computer for the purpose of updating the patient's record, scheduling treatment, medication and any laboratory and X-ray service that might be required. The system also maintains a record of the charges for all services performed and medication received so that a bill can be prepared at the time the patient is discharged.

During their meeting Sister Mary stated that the basic objective of the Hospital Information System was to improve the quality of patient care as well as to stabilize the cost of this care at the lowest possible level. She also stated that a fully established hospital information system can achieve this objective by:

1. Minimizing the length of time a patient stays in a hospital, thus conserving physical facilities and reducing cost.
2. Maximizing hospital revenue by instituting control of the patient at the point of origin.
3. Conserving physicians' and other health care professionals' time through prompt scheduling, reporting of findings and compliance with directives.
4. Maximizing the return on expense dollars through the development of systems for personnel scheduling, inventory control and financial forecasting, reporting and planning.
5. Allowing physicians to predict potential results of alternative decisions through simulation.

Sister Mary added that in developing this type of system, two major factors should be considered. The first is cost. "This is an extremely expensive system to install and operate. It is anticipated that the direct data processing expenses for this fiscal year will increase by approximately $35,000 over last year with an additional increase of $61,000 being budgeted for in the coming fiscal year. The budgeted figure represents a 50 percent increase over last year's cost." The second major factor arises from the difficulties of planning and designing a system as large and complicated as the Hospital Information System. "In this area," she said, "there is a general lack of experience in both data processing technique as well as development of an HIS by the members of top management at the hospital." She went on to explain that the present management team virtually inherited the present computer facilities, since none of the team participated in the decision to convert to the IBM 360 Model 30. In fact the decision to adopt this machine had been made by the previous administration. The original rationale behind this decision was the development of the Hospital Information System.

At the completion of their discussion, Sister Mary charged Mr. Carter with the following tasks:

1. Review the events leading up to the current time concerning the development of an HIS.
2. Observe the data processing operation and evaluate its contribution toward achieving objectives.
3. Recommend a course of action for management to follow to see that this objective is attained.

Mr. Carter had known Sister Mary for just a few months. He knew that while this was her first assignment as a hospital administrator, she had worked as an assistant administrator in a hospital in California for two years prior to coming to St. Joseph's Hospital. She held a BS in Medical Records and a Master's Degree in Hospital Administration, and had held the position of Medical Records Librarian for five years prior to obtaining her Master's Degree. She was a member of the American College of Hospital Administrators and served on the Board of Directors of two medical associations.

Mr. Carter began by discussing the department's operations with Mr. Massey and learned that a Hospital Data Processing Committee had been established in early 1969 at the request of the Hospital Controller in order to share the responsibility for the direction of the data processing function. Mr. Massey produced copies of the minutes of all meetings held to date. The minutes revealed that the Committee consisted of the two Assistant Hospital Administrators, the Director of Purchasing, the Director of Personnel, the Director of Nursing Service, the Data Processing Manager, and the Controller, who served as chairman. The Committee had not met regularly during the past year nor were its functions clearly defined. The function of the Committee was limited to the review of requests for personnel and equipment and to making recommendations on such requests to the Administrator. Based on discussions with some of the Committee members it appeared that proposals for the development of new systems were presented to the Committee, generally in the form of a sketchy listing of titles, along with the Data Processing Manager's appraisal of when the work could be accomplished.

Systems design for the new computer began nine months before its installation with the Inpatient Billing and Discharged Inpatient Billing systems. The Inpatient Billing System was implemented one year later, and the Discharged Inpatient Billing System was implemented approximately 17 months later. Both systems were partially redesigned after they had been in use less than one year. Design of an Outpatient Billing System had begun approximately one year ago, but it had not yet been completed. Mr. Massey explained that work on this system had been temporarily terminated because of the changes that had to be made to the existing Discharged Inpatient Billing System. He estimated that the Outpatient Billing System would be ready for implementation in another month. The only other existing system was the Payroll System, which took 15 months to complete. "At the present time the General Ledger System is being developed," Mr. Massey stated, "as well as a Personnel Reporting System for staffing requirements." He estimated that both of these systems would be operational within the next six months.

For a period of two weeks, Mr. Carter remained in the Data Processing Department to observe the operation and evaluate its contribution toward achieving hospital objectives. In reviewing the backgrounds of the employees of the department, he found that none of the personnel had any significant formal education beyond high school, and their experience for the most part was very limited. No one in the department had any prior supervisory experience. Mr. Carter observed that Mr. Massey seemed to spend as much time on systems development and maintenance as he did on managing the department. He also devoted nearly 25 percent of his time to supervising the operations section of the department, which involved the supervision of the keypunch and computer operators.

Mr. Fulton spent approximately 75 percent of his time working as a systems analyst, and the one systems analyst in the department spent nearly 90 percent of his time in the systems design area. Mr. Massey stated that because of the workload, it was necessary for Mr. Fulton to perform the duties of a systems analyst. A review of the job description for the department manager and the systems personnel showed contradiction in responsibilities, and it appeared to Mr. Carter that the education and experience requirements included in the job description were, for the most part, based on the qualifications of the person presently holding the position rather than on the position itself. For the most part the job descriptions were vague, and there was a significant overlap of duties in each job description. Mr. Carter learned that while a job description for the assistant manager had been written, it was eliminated because it was felt that the responsibilities of the assistant manager were virtually the same as those of the manager. While many employees expressed a lack of job satisfaction, the employee turnover rate within the department was very low. Most of the department employees interviewed were satisfied with the working environment as well as the salaries they were receiving. The main complaint seemed to stem from the fact that there was a lack of formal scheduling of personnel activities toward the accomplishment of well-defined plans for the department. Most of the staff felt technically qualified to perform their duties and felt that job satisfaction and productivity could be improved with better management. Several employees were not certain as to the proper channels of authority and communications within the department. One employee stated that since Mr. Massey had developed the

Patient Accounting and General Ledger Systems, the personnel working on these systems looked to him for direction, but since Mr. Fulton developed the Payroll System, all direction on this system came from him. In addition several employees complained that operator instructions were generally either inadequate or out of date and that operation schedules were not prepared or posted.

The Data Processing Department also rendered services to other organizations, both related to and independent of St. Joseph's Hospital. The services to the related organizations were for jobs that utilized the hospital Payroll and General Ledger Systems. Services to independent organizations were limited to the sale of computer time, using programs designed and maintained by the independent organizations. The rendering of these services did not limit any processing time for the hospital and generated an average income of $800 per month. Mr. Carter observed, however, that charges for the services for the related organizations were 12 percent lower than those charged by other reputable service bureaus in the area.

Carter decided to interview the Hospital Controller to learn more about top management's attitudes concerning the situation. The Controller stated that a cohesive long-range plan for the development of a Hospital Information System had never been prepared by top management, and she felt that specific management activities in this area should include:

1. Establishment of both long-range and short-range objectives.
2. Allocation of resources commensurate with approved plans.
3. Organization and recruitment of an appropriate staff.
4. Periodic review and updating of accomplishments, objectives and plans.

"These activities have not been accomplished at this hospital," she stated, "and management involvement with the data processing functions has generally been restricted to this office." The members of the management team had recently been assigned to their present positions, and their participation on the Data Processing Committee was passive because they were not sufficiently informed to carry out a more meaningful role. "I feel that one of the major problems within the Data Processing Department is the lack of a broad vision of the scope of their activity," she said. "This could be the result of either this lack of awareness of the overall needs of the various departments or the lack of ability to perceive the implications of such systems on the users. I think that the basis for this problem is the fact that the data processing personnel are technically oriented individuals, and they are most comfortable doing technical jobs." She stated that some departments are really unaware of what data processing can really contribute to their needs. "In certain instances, departments that are receiving computer services are still maintaining a duplicate set of records manually to assure that they have the accurate data when needed." The Controller went on to say that while the data processing staff had adequate technical training, they had little ability in verbalizing concepts, communicating with department heads and management, and developing and presenting plans and objectives.

Interviews with other department heads within the hospital indicated a lack of confidence in the Data Processing Department attributed to a lack of education and involvement on the part of the users, a lack of communication ability and effort on the part of the data processing staff, and a lack of involvement and review by hospital management. One member of top management expressed doubt that an effective Hospital Information System could ever be implemented because of the increased expense of additional hardware and the general lack of experience and knowledge of Hospital Information Systems on the part of the hospital staff.

After completing his last interview, Mr. Carter returned to his office to organize and evaluate the data he had gathered. He had hardly begun his work when he received a call from Sister Mary. She stated that she had just received some interesting and possibly pertinent information from the Martin Automation Company, and she wanted Mr. Carter to evaluate this information and include recommendations concerning their activity in his report. The Martin Automation Company, a division of McDonnell Douglas Corporation, is a professional client-oriented service organization which has its headquarters in St. Louis, with six other offices located throughout the country. MAC was established in 1960 to provide commercial automation services to clients in all types of industries. It offers the following service capabilities: consulting, systems analysis and design, programming and processing. The current computer services operations consist of 51 computer systems, including an IBM 360 Model 85, and approximately 1,500 terminals.

On March 1, 1970, MAC acquired a hospital-shared data processing service in Peoria, Illinois which is the core of its National Multi-Hospital Data Processing Service. This service is the result of over 10 years of EDP application development in a multi-hospital environment. Personnel staffing this service are highly experienced in data processing systems development. The company employs accounting-oriented data control personnel and prices its data control services separately from processing charges. The reason for this approach is to allow users to eliminate program coordinators from their hospital staff.

At the present time MAC has the following automated patient care systems installed and fully operational in three hospitals comprising 1,200 beds:

1. *Admitting*—including pre-admission control, bed availability control, recommended room list, transfer-discharge control, daily bed census reports, and other statistical reports.
2. *Radiology*—including remote ordering of service, scheduling control, final consultation reports, patient charging and consolidated summaries.
3. *Laboratory*—including remote ordering tests, scheduling control, specimen-collection schedules, test reporting and patient charging.

Other systems under development include:

1. Pharmacy.
2. Central Supply.
3. Nutritional Services.
4. Other Ancillary Services.

In addition MAC offers a fully operational Hospital Financial Control System (HFC) which consists of the following subsystems:

1. Patient Billing.
2. Accounts Receivable.
3. Payroll and Personnel Profile.
4. Accounts Payable.
5. Financial Statements, Reports, and Budget Information.

Sister Mary was quite enthusiastic about the services offered by MAC and felt that this might represent the best course of action for St. Joseph's. While the cost of this service was roughly equivalent to the present cost of leasing the IBM equipment, she envisioned a significant reduction in payroll expenses which would result from the reduction of personnel in the Data Processing Department, since as a minimum there would no longer be a requirement for the two managers, the programmers or the systems analyst with the department.

Mr. Carter stated that he would prepare a preliminary report covering his findings and evaluations and would also include an initial evaluation of the Martin Automation Company proposal based on the information available at that time. He estimated that his report would be ready in two days.

ASSIGNMENTS

Answer the following discussion questions concerning the St. Joseph's Hospital case. Draw upon the material in Chapters 10, 11, 12 and 13 in developing your answers.

D-1. Evaluate the manner in which the hospital came to acquire the IBM System 360/30. What sequence of steps should have been followed?

D-2. Discuss the qualifications of the personnel in the data processing department. Do you feel that they are capable of developing an HIS?

D-3. Comment upon the internal organization of the data processing department. How does the department fit into the entire organizational structure?

D-4. Evaluate top management's actual and ideal role in managing the data processing department.

D-5. Referring to the Information System Evolution Matrix of Figure 10–4, where in the matrix does St. Joseph's currently fit?

D-6. In addition to those problems already discussed, what others exist?

D-7. Prepare a recommended program of action for St. Joseph's, much like the one Mr. Carter has been asked to develop. Include in your analysis comments about buying services from the Martin Automation Company.

Index

A

Abacus, 51
Access, 95–97
  direct (random), 95–96
  indexed sequential, 95–97
  sequential, 95–96
Access time, 97
Accounting applications, 29–30
Accounts payable, 199–200
Accounts receivable, 199
Accumulator, 121
Acoustic coupler, 134
Action-document program, 202
Address, 82–83
Airlines industry applications, 44–45
Algorithm, 113–15
Analog computer, 5–6
Analog model, 226–27
Analytic mode, 229
Argument, 186
Arithmetic/logic unit, 19–21, 76–77
Arithmetic/logic unit circuitry, 87
Array, 126
Atanasoff, John Vincent, 62–63
Authority, 335–36
  functional, 336
  line, 335
  staff, 335
Automation, 362–65

B

Babbage's analytical engine, 55
Babbage's difference engine, 55
Banking applications, 31–34
BASIC, 14–15, 130–57
  arithmetic operators, 138
  branching, 145–46
  character string, 152
  characters, 136–37
  computations, 137–39

BASIC—*Cont.*
  constants, 137
  DEF statement, 154–55
  DIM statement, 151–53
  END statement, 144
  executable statement, 135–36
  FOR-TO-STEP and NEXT statements, 146–48
  functions, 154–55
  GO TO statement, 145–46
  GOSUB statement, 155
  IF-THEN statements, 145–46
  input, 140–41
  INPUT statement, 141
  LET statement, 139–40
  library functions, 154
  line numbers, 136
  literal data, 143
  looping, 146–48
  nested loops, 148
  non-executable statement, 135–36
  output, 141–42
  PRINT statement, 141–42
  READ and DATA statements, 140
  relational operators, 139
  REM statement, 144
  RESTORE statement, 141
  STOP statement, 144
  string variable, 152
  strings, 152–54
  subroutines, 155
  subscripted variables, 151–52
  substitution activity, 139
  systems commands, 144, 148–49
  variables, 137–38
Basic data processing systems, 260–70
Batch processing, 15, 132–33
Binary digit (bit), 78–80
Binary number system, 385–87
Boole, George, 87

Boolean algebra, 87
Buffer, 99
Byte, 81–82

C

Canned programs, 134, 230–32
Central processing unit, 18–21, 76–77
Centralization–decentralization, 337–40
Change, 293
    resistance to, 294
Coding, 12
Compiler, 159
Computer, 4–5
    advantages of, 4
    disadvantages of, 4–5
Computer-assisted decision making, 113,
    195, 225–47
Computer execution, 21–24
Computer generations, 67–71
Computer leasing, 291
Computer program, 6
Computer purchasing, 291
Computer renting, 291
Computer search for optimality, 240–43
Computer simulation, 315
Computer system selection, 289–93
Control unit, 21, 76–77
Counter, 119
Credit applications, 31–34
Current wire, 78
Customer billing, 198
Cybernation revolution, 364

D

Data, 6–7, 266
    external, 258
    internal, 257–58
    objective, 258
    subjective, 258
Data base (bank), 259
Data base management system, 263, 267
Data cell, 94, 97–98
Data element, 9, 258
Data hierarchy, 258–60
Debugging, 16
Decentralization–centralization, 337–40
Decision maker, 266
Decision making, 338–39
Decision models, 225–26
Decision-support orientation, 265–66
Decision-support systems, 266–68, 270
Departmentation, 333–35
Descriptive model, 228–29
Deterministic model, 229
Diagnostic, 16
Digital computer, 6
Documentation, 16–17

E

EBCDIC, 81–82
Eckert, J. Presper, Jr., 61–63

Edit program, 201
Education, computer applications in,
    348–51
EDVAC computer, 63
EFTS, 34–36
Electronic data processing, 6
Electronic Funds Transfer Systems
    (EFTS), 34–36
End-of-file card, 120
ENIAC computer, 61
Equity Funding scandal, 30

F

Facilities management, 293
Fair Credit Reporting Act of 1970, 369
Feasibility study, 283–89
    nature of, 284–85
    need for a study, 283–84
    steps of, 286–89
Ferrite core, 78–80, 103
Field, 142, 161, 389–90
File, 9, 258–59
Finance applications, 29–30
First generation computers, 67–68, 71
Formal information systems, 256–57
FORTRAN, 14–15, 158–91
    A format, 183–85
    actual argument, 186
    arithmetic assignment statement,
        164–68
    arithmetic operators, 186
    arithmetic statement function, 186–87
    branching, 174–76
    CALL statement, 188
    comment card, 161–62
    constants, 165
    CONTINUE statement, 177–78
    decimal, 165
    DIMENSION statement, 182
    DO loop, 177–78
    dummy argument, 186
    END statement, 173–74
    executable statement, 163
    F format, 169–73
    FORTRAN function, 187–88
    function defining statement, 186
    GO TO statements, 174
    I format, 169–73
    identification field, 162
    IF statements, 174–76
    input/output statements, 168–73,
        183–85
    integer, 165
    job control cards, 160
    library functions, 185–86
    literal data, 172
    looping, 176–78
    nested loops, 177–78
    non-executable statement, 163
    READ-FORMAT statements, 168–71,
        183–85

FORTRAN—*Cont.*
  RETURN statement, 187–89
  simple variables, 181
  statement number, 162
  STOP statement, 173–74
  subprograms, 185–89
  subroutine, 188–89
  subroutine statement, 189
  subscripted variables, 181–83
  WRITE-FORMAT statements, 171–73,
    183–85
Fourth generation computers, 69–71

G–H

Government applications, 356–60
Hardware, 7–8, 17–21
Header card, 120
Health and medical applications, 351–56
Heat generation applications, 47–48
Heuristics, 244
Hierarchical information structure,
  264–65
High-level language, 13
Hollerith's punched card machine, 58
Hospital administration applications,
  45–46
Hotel-motel industry applications, 46–
  47

I

Iconic model, 226–27
ILLIAC IV computer, 64–65
Individualism, 370–72
Informal information systems, 256
Information, 6–7
Information systems, 255–72
Information systems evolution, 268–71
Information systems evolution matrix, 268
Inhibit wire, 78
Initializing a variable, 120
Input unit, 18
Instructions, 84–87
Integrated data base, 263–64
Integrated data processing systems, 260,
  270
Intelligent terminals, 338
Inventory analysis, 232–40
  carrying costs, 233
  classical method, 232–36
  modern method, 232–33, 236–40
  ordering costs, 233
  stockout costs, 233
Inventory control, 197–98

J–L

Jacquard loom, 54
Keypunch card, 161, 389–90
Keypunch machine, 389–92
Language translator, 13
Last-record check, 120–21
Leavitt, Harold, 310, 331–32

Leibnitz calculator, 54
Logic error, 16

M

Machine language, 12, 14, 84–85
Machine-readable, 18
Macro instruction, 13
Magnetic disk, 94–95, 97–98
Magnetic drum, 94, 97–98
Magnetic tape, 90–92
Management control, 264
Management exception report, 198
Management information system respon-
  sibilities, 271–72
Management information systems,
  261–66, 270
Management science models, 225–26
Managerial levels and computer impact,
  306–19
  lower management, 306–8
  middle management, 308–13
  top management, 313–16
Manufacturing applications, 36–40
MARK I computer, 60
Marketing applications, 40–43
Mathematical model, 227
  characteristics, 227
Mathematical programming, 231–32
  constraints, 231–32
  objective function, 231–32
  simplex method, 231–32
Mauchly, John W., 61–63
Microcomputer, 66
Minicomputer, 38–40, 65–66
Models, 226–27, 266
Monte Carlo method, 236–40
Multiprogramming, 100

N–O

Numeric mode, 229
Object program, 13
On-line, 38
Operating system, 23, 98, 101
Operation code, 84
Operational control, 264
Operational models, 267
Optimization model, 228
Organization of data processing function,
  328–29
Organizational location of computers,
  324–28
Organizational structure, 323–24
Output unit, 21

P

Packaged programs, 134, 230–32
Paper tape, 92–94
Pascal's calculator, 53
Payroll, 202–11
  check program, 208–9
  edit program, 206–7

Payroll—*Cont.*
  inputs, 206
  journal program, 209
  master file, 204
  periodic reports, 209
  register program, 207–8
Physical model, 226–27
Planning, 317
Planning for computers, 278–83
Primary storage unit, 18–19
Privacy, 365–70
Privacy Act of 1974, 369
Probabilistic model, 229
Procedure-oriented languages, 13–14
Program flowchart, 10–12, 107, 113–24, 126–29
  branching decision, 117–18
  loops, 118–24
  single-pass execution, 115–17
  subscripted variables, 126–29
  symbols, 114–15
Programming error, 16
Programming statements, 15
Punched cards, 89–90

R

Real-time, 38, 132–33
Record, 9, 258
Reference file, 201
Register program, 201–2
Registers, 85–87
Routine data processing applications, 28, 133, 195–96
Routine data processing programs, 200–2

S

St. Joseph's Hospital case, 394–402
Sales order processing, 197
SCERT, 290
Scheduled reports, 260
Second generation computers, 68, 71
Secondary storage, 21, 89–98
Sense wire, 78
Sequence checking, 214–15
Service bureaus, 292
Simulating managerial thought, 243–47
Simulation, 236, 240
Slotnick, Daniel L., 64
Software, 7–17
Sorting, 212–14
Source program, 13

Span of control, 329–30
Statement number, 162
Steering committee, 271
Stock brokerage application, 45
Storage, 76–77
  external, 76–77
  internal, 76–77
  off-line, 76–77
  on-line, 76–77
  unit, 76–77
Strategic models, 267
Strategic planning, 265
Subtotals, 217–19
Summary program, 202
Symbolic language, 14
Symbolic model, 226–27
Symbolic programming language, 12
System, 227
Systems analysis and design, 107–10
Systems design and programming, 296–97
Systems flowchart, 9–10, 107, 110–13
  illustrations, 112–13
  symbols, 110–11
Systems thinking, 227

T

Table lookup, 215, 217
Tactical models, 267
Terminals, 131–34
Third generation computers, 69, 71
Time-sharing, 14, 134
Trailer card, 120
Transaction file, 201
Travel bureau applications, 45
Tree diagram, 245–46
Turnaround, 100

U–W

UNIVAC I computer, 63–64
Update program, 201
Variable, 116, 137–38, 165
  accumulator, 121
  counter, 119
  name, 12, 116
  single, 126
  subscripted, 126–29
Verbal model, 227
von Neumann, John, 63
Whisler, Thomas L., 310, 312, 331–32
Word, 83–84

*This book has been set in 10 point and 9 point
Caledonia, leaded 2 points. Chapter numbers
are set in 60 point Goudy and chapter titles
are set in 24 point Helvetica. The size of the
type page is 27 x 46½ picas.*